John Stevenson was educated at Worcester College and Nuffield College, Oxford. Since 1976 he has been Lecturer in Modern History at Sheffield University, having previously taught history at Oriel College, Oxford, for five years. His publications include *Popular Protest and Public Order* (edited with Roland Quinault) and *Social Conditions in Britain between the Wars*.

Chris Cook has been editor of *Pears Cyclopaedia* since 1976, having previously been head of a research unit at the London School of Economics. He was educated at St Catherine's College, Cambridge (where he took a 1st Class Honours degree in History) and Nuffield College, Cambridge (where he completed a doctorate on modern British politics). His other major books include *Post-War Britain: A Political History* and *The Age of Alignment*. His definitive five-volume *Sources in British Political History* (described in *The Times Literary Supplement* as 'a towering work of scholarship') has established him as the leading authority on contemporary British archives.

Also by John Stevenson and Chris Cook

The Longman Atlas of British History, 1700–1970: A
  Visual Guide to British Politics and Society
British Historical Facts, 1760–1830

Also by John Stevenson

Popular Protest and Public Order (*Ed. with Roland
  Quinault*)
Social Conditions in Britain between the Wars (*Ed.*)
London in the Age of Reform (*Ed.*)

Also by Chris Cook

The Age of Alignment: Electoral Politics in Britain,
  1922–1929
A Short History of the Liberal Party, 1900–1976
By-Elections in British Politics (*Ed. with John Ramsden*)
Sources in British Political History, 1900–1951 (*with
  Philip Jones et al.*)
European Political Facts, 1848–1918 (*with John Paxton*)
The Decade of Disillusion (*Ed. with David McKie*)
British Historical Facts, 1830–1900 (*with Brendan Keith*)
Crisis and Controversy: Essays in Honour of A. J. P.
  Taylor (*Ed. with Alan Sked*)
The Politics of Reappraisal, 1918–1939 (*Ed. with Gillian
  Peele*)
European Political Facts, 1918–1973 (*with John Paxton*)

The Slump

John Stevenson and Chris Cook

QUARTET BOOKS
LONDON   MELBOURNE   NEW YORK

Published by Quartet Books Limited 1979
A member of the Namara Group
27 Goodge Street, London W1P 1FD

First published by Jonathan Cape Limited,
London, 1977

ISBN 0 7043 3280 9

Printed in Great Britain by The Anchor Press Ltd
and bound by Wm Brendon & Son Ltd
both of Tiptree, Essex

*To our parents
who lived through the worst
years of the Slump*

Contents

Illustrations

Preface and Acknowledgments

Work first began on this book when both authors were research students at Nuffield College, Oxford. A very deep debt is due to the Warden and Fellows of the College for providing conditions so admirably suited to research. The Library of Nuffield College, with its superb holdings of material on this period, greatly facilitated our research.

In any work of this sort, one is indebted to those colleagues and friends who have provided help and advice. We would particularly like to thank Judith Green, Tony Hearn, Philip Jones, Jackie Johns, Ross McKibbin, Alice Prochaska, John Ramsden, John Rowett, Josephine Sinclair, Tom Stannage, David Steel, Jeffrey Weeks and Judith Woods. A particular debt is due to Irene Wagner, the Librarian of the Labour Party, for facilitating access to the records of the party. Hywel Francis, of the South Wales Miners' Library, provided much help and assistance. Miss Enid Lakeman, of the Electoral Reform Society, generously loaned material which provided the basis for some sections of this book. The Librarian of the Marx Memorial Library was very helpful in providing access to the Library's collection of material on the National Unemployed Workers' Movement. We are grateful to the South Wales Miners' Library and the University of Swansea for permission to quote from the Eddie Jones and Claude Stamfield manuscripts.

Finally, a special debt is due to two people. Paul Addison read the whole of the manuscript and provided many valuable suggestions. David Machin, whose enthusiasm from the very outset of this project has spurred the writing of this book, has been the model of a long-suffering publisher.

The typing of the manuscript was done with unfailing energy and kindness by Eileen Pattison and Jean Stone, and Deborah Shepherd did the copy-editing.

J.S. and C.C.

I

Myth and Reality: Britain in the 1930s

Of all periods in recent British history, the thirties have had the worst press. Although the decade can now only be remembered by the middle-aged and the elderly, it retains the all-pervasive image of the 'wasted years' and the 'low dishonest decade'. Even for those who did not live through them, the 1930s are haunted by the spectres of mass unemployment, hunger marches, appeasement, and the rise of fascism at home and abroad.

Mass unemployment, more than anything else, gave the inter-war period its image of the 'long weekend'. For almost twenty years there were never fewer than a million people out of work in Great Britain, representing a tenth of the insured working population. But the level and intensity of the depression varied during these years. In the 1920s, heavy unemployment reflected the special problems of the 'ailing giants', the staple export industries of coalmining, textiles, iron and steel, and shipbuilding, which had been the basis of the country's prosperity in the years before the First World War. Their dislocation as a result of foreign competition and the contraction of world trade led to depression and unemployment in the old industrial areas. By 1929, the depression was a major political issue. The General Election of that year was fought primarily on domestic policy and resulted in a Labour Government under Ramsay MacDonald, pledged to conquer unemployment and restore the nation's prosperity.

It was not to be. Almost as soon as it came into office in June 1929, the new government began to be affected by the international crisis which has been called the 'Great Slump'. The promise of recovery in the depressed industries, and of a reduction of unemployment, was swept aside by the consequences of the Wall Street crash of October 1929. The speculative boom in American stocks and shares collapsed with disastrous effects upon confidence and world trade. Business activity declined in the European economies which had been sustained by American loans and credits; primary products fell in price and reduced their producers' ability to buy manufactured goods from the industrial nations. Investment and trade declined. The reviving economies of Europe and the booming American markets were plunged into a deep and generalised depression. The immediate consequence was a rise of world-wide unemployment. By the middle of 1930 there were estimated to be over 11 million unemployed in 33 countries, double the figure before the onset of the slump. Britain was no exception. The country's exports were almost halved in value between 1929 and 1931. The industries which had been depressed in the 1920s now had to face an economic blizzard of unprecedented severity, but the slump also affected almost every branch of business activity. Instead of falling, the unemployment figures continued to rise; by July 1930 there were over 2 million people out of work.

In May 1931, the failure of the Vienna Bank, the Credit Anstalt, sparked off a crisis of confidence in Germany and a run on the Reichsbank. When the ripples of the European banking crisis spread to Britain, the Labour Government was already in dire straits. The need to restore financial confidence had forced it to consider economy measures which were bound to create conflict within the Cabinet. The publication of the May Report on National Expenditure in August 1931, revealing a large deficit and recommending major economies and new taxes, precipitated a financial crisis and a run on the reserves. Unable to agree upon a programme of economy measures, the Labour Government resigned. Ramsay MacDonald and a small group of Labour M.P.s joined the Conservatives to form a 'National' Government on 24 August.

The new government's tenure was confirmed two months later in a General Election which gave it a crushing majority of 497 seats and reduced the Labour Party to 52 seats in the House of Commons. It did not, however, end the economic crisis. Within a month of its formation the National Government was forced to abandon the Gold Standard. But the worst effects of the international slump were still to be felt. Unemployment continued to rise through the winter of 1931–2, reaching a peak in the third quarter of 1932 when there were almost 3 million people out of work in Great Britain. The government's response was to implement economy measures, including cuts in unemployment benefit and the introduction of the means test. Financial orthodoxy and economic conservatism became the dominant features of its strategy to cope with the slump. For the next nine years, National and Conservative Governments presided over the consequences of the Great Crash. Although a measure of economic recovery began to be felt as early as 1933, when unemployment began to fall, there were still over 2 million people out of work in 1935. It was not until the first year of the Second World War that unemployment fell below a million.

Thus from 1929 until the outbreak of war, successive governments struggled to deal with the impact of world-wide depression. These years, the years of the slump, have been harshly judged. A. J. P. Taylor has written:

> The nineteen-thirties have been called the black years, the devil's decade. Its popular image can be expressed in two phrases: mass unemployment and 'appeasement'. No set of political leaders have been judged so contemptuously since the days of Lord North.

But Taylor continues:

> Yet, at the same time, most English people were enjoying a richer life than any previously known in the history of the world: longer holidays, shorter hours, higher real wages. They had motor cars, cinemas, radio sets, electrical appliances. The two sides of life did not join up.[1]

However accurate this view, it has had little influence upon the popular mythology of the 1930s. By the outbreak of the Second World War, the decade had already been condemned by self-confessed critics as a period of missed opportunities and wasted time; a judgment which the disasters of the early years of the war seemed only to vindicate. In a sense the intervention of the Second World War served to perpetuate the more depressing image of the thirties, partly at least because the politics of the immediate post-war era were fought on the record of the pre-war years. As late as 1951 the Labour Party campaigned with the election slogan of 'Ask your Dad!' an illustration of the way in which the emotive image of the 'hungry thirties' had become part of the repertoire of political cliché. The popular view of the 1930s as a period of unrelieved failure was undoubtedly hardened and reinforced in the years after the war; a view which became sharpened against the background of full employment and affluence in the 1950s and 1960s. Even today the ghost of the thirties stalks political platforms and the media as a symbol of economic disaster, social deprivation and political discontent.

But the very pervasiveness of the image of the 'hungry thirties' has done much to distort our view of the period and its more constructive and substantial achievements. A concentration upon unemployment and social distress does not represent an accurate portrayal of the decade. Even during the 1930s social investigators, such as Seebohm Rowntree, and organisations, such as the Pilgrim Trust, sought to obtain a balanced account of social conditions. So too did writers such as George Orwell and J. B. Priestley, to name but two. Moreover, historians of the period were soon to revise the popular mythology. C. L. Mowat gave a measured judgment on the National Government when he wrote:

> Its responses were not bold. It retreated before aggression; it rearmed but at first too slowly. In fact it was not unsuccessful in its economic policies but fatally narrow in its political conduct. Failure in the latter sphere darkened its reputation in the former; in retrospect it has been blamed for all the misfortunes of the time, partly because its opponents rose to power by reiterating their version of its history and its period.[2]

In recent years, other writers have examined the responses of the second Labour Government to the slump. Robert Skidelsky has shown the attitudes which shaped its inability to provide a solution to mass unemployment. In addition, more attention has focused upon the advances made in the economic and social sphere. A. J. P. Taylor put the point in a nutshell when he asked of the decade, 'which was more significant for the future – over a million unemployed or over a million private cars?'[3]

It would, of course, be fatuous to suggest that the 1930s were not for many thousands of people a time of great hardship and personal suffering. But beside the picture of the unemployed must be put the other side of the case. There were never less than three-quarters of the population in work during the 1930s and for most of the period considerably more. Alongside the pictures of the dole queues and hunger marches must also be placed those of another Britain, of new industries, prosperous suburbs and a rising standard of living. Any attempt to do justice to the condition of Britain in the thirties must give full weight to what J. B. Priestley described in 1934 as the England of arterial and by-pass roads, filling stations and factories that look like exhibition buildings, of giant cinemas and dance-halls and cafés, bungalows with tiny garages, cocktail bars, Woolworths, motor coaches, wireless, hiking, factory girls looking like actresses, greyhound racing and dirt tracks, swimming pools, and everything given away for cigarette coupons.[4]

For those in work, the 1930s were a period of rising living standards and new levels of consumption, upon which a considerable degree of industrial growth was based. This was the paradox which lay at the heart of Britain in the thirties, where new levels of prosperity contrasted with the intractable problems of mass unemployment and the depressed areas. Mowat claimed that it was the depressed areas which 'tarnished the picture of recovery and were the basis for the myth of the "hungry thirties" '.[5] The concentration of Britain's staple industries created conditions in which whole areas were in industrial decay as a result of the depression in world trade. But the problem of the unemployed and the distressed areas was only a part of the total picture of Britain in the thirties. Economic historians have long recognised that as well as being a period of prolonged depression in the old staple industries, these years can also be seen as the time when a new industrial structure was being established which provided the real basis for the export boom and the rising prosperity of the second half of the twentieth century.[6] The picture of depression was not evenly spread, but was concentrated in the old industrial areas. Unemployment rates in 1932 varied for the different regions of the country between 36 per cent in Wales and only 13 per cent in London and the south-east. By the mid-1930s the disparity was even more striking, with unemployment rates in some towns in the depressed areas revealing tragic stories of the decay and impoverishment of whole communities; places such as Brynmawr, Dowlais, Jarrow, Gateshead, Greenock and Motherwell had almost three-quarters of the insured population out of work in 1934, while other parts of the country were experiencing almost boom conditions.

With a majority of the population in work, even in the worst years of the depression, most people in Britain were better off by 1939 than they had been ten years earlier. This was less because of substantial improvements in wages, though there were some, than because of the fall in the cost of living by almost a third during the inter-war period; a fall which the 1930s experienced as much as the 1920s and which especially affected the price of food and manu-

B

factured goods. The result was a quite perceptible improvement in the standard of comfort witnessed by many people, especially the middle classes. Though people in government service saw their wages cut in the trough of the depression from 1931 to 1934, they also benefited from the fall in prices and a greater disposable income because of smaller families. For many salaried people affluence began not in the 1950s but in the thirties, when it became possible for an average salaried person to buy his own house, usually on a mortgage, run a car, and begin to afford a range of consumer durables and household goods hitherto considered quite out of reach.

Some of the older myths on the economy and the standard of living had their parallel in the political arena. MacDonald's decision to form a National Government and his 'betrayal' of the Labour Party have both heavily coloured existing interpretations of the politics of the thirties. Thus we tend to see the 1931 election disaster for Labour as a consequence of MacDonald's betrayal. Yet the electoral unpopularity of the second Labour Government was clearly in evidence in the by-elections of 1929 to 1931. Labour would undoubtedly have lost any General Election in the early 1930s whether or not MacDonald had deserted the party.

Nor was 1931 the total electoral disaster for Labour that some historians suggest. Labour secured more votes in 1931 than in any previous election except 1929. Labour even secured in 1931 a higher percentage share of votes cast than in December 1923 – the election which first brought Labour to power. The difference in 1931 was that Labour's opponents were *united*, not that Labour had lost its basic core of working-class support. The events of 1931 did not break the Labour Party. Its recovery after 1931, in local elections and by-elections, was rapid and impressive, but not as great as is sometimes argued. There still exists a myth concerning the Labour Party that, if a General Election had been held in 1939 or 1940, somehow Attlee would have led Labour to an electoral victory. There is simply no evidence to support this view. Certainly it cannot be interpreted from by-elections or municipal elections. The mood of public opinion only changed during the course of the war.

Indeed, there is a curious paradox in British politics. For just as Hitler aided Britain's economic recovery (by spurring rearmament) so Hitler's wars paved the road to Labour's 1945 election victory. The Jarrow marchers may have shocked the conscience of the nation, but it was the events of Dunkirk and after that turned the tide of public opinion to Labour.

Perhaps understandably, the Labour Party has attracted more interest from historians during this period than either the Liberal or Conservative Parties. There is no available published study of the Liberals from 1929 to 1945. The Conservative Party is almost as badly served. Electoral politics have been almost as poorly covered. There is no published study of the 1931 election. The 1935 election has been equally neglected in published works. This book attempts to cover some of these themes, though it is not a political history of the 1930s.

Rather this book attempts not merely to question the social and political myths of the 'devil's decade' but to pose other questions. How prosperous was the England of the new industries? How depressed were the depressed areas? What, if anything, did the hunger marches achieve? Why were both the communists and fascists confined to the sidelines of British politics? Why did the electors vote as they did? Why was there no revolution in Britain? And what has been the real legacy of the slump?

Not everyone will accept the answers to these questions given in this book. History is a controversial subject. And recent history is more controversial than most. The passions of the thirties are still very much alive even though more than a generation has gone by since the Jarrow marchers began their long trek to London. The slump has left an indelible mark on British history. It is now time to begin to assess its real significance from the distance of a generation.

II

The Dawn of Affluence

The popular image of the 1930s is that of the decade blighted by economic depression—the years of mass unemployment, dole queues, the means test and the hunger marches. Indeed, this is an image securely based upon reality for the many thousands of families who suffered from the miseries of mass unemployment. But there was another face to the thirties. As well as being the years of the slump, they also saw a remarkable degree of economic and social advance, with new industries, economic growth, prosperous suburbs and a rising standard of living for those in work.

For some years, economic historians have been revising the traditional view of the thirties as a period of unrelieved economic disaster. This revision has focused upon the growth achieved in the British economy during the 1930s, especially in the years following the trough of the depression in 1931–2.[1] From the middle of 1933 the economy began to revive on an upswing which was partially checked in 1937, but continued with rearmament in 1938–9. Revival was at first concentrated in a range of so-called 'new' industries, primarily producing consumer goods, such as motor vehicles, processed foods, electrical appliances and building. This period of growth has been seen by some historians as one in which the British economy made a decisive movement in the direction of a higher growth rate and the utilisation of new techniques, laying the foundations for post-war economic expansion and affluence.[2] Thus Peter Mathias has contrasted the depressed state of the old staple industries of coal, cotton, iron and steel, and shipbuilding with the underlying buoyancy of other sectors:

> ... the inter-war years could be seen also as the time when a new industrial structure was being established which provided the real basis for the export booms and the rising prosperity of the second half of the twentieth century. So much depends upon

whether the spot-light is turned upon Jarrow or Slough; on Merthyr Tydfil or on Oxford; on Greenock and Birkenhead or on Coventry, Weston-super-Mare and the environs of London.[3]

D. H. Aldcroft has compared favourably the economic performance of the years between 1929 and 1939, with the record of the British economy before 1914. He has argued that the case for the thirties as a period of rapid economic growth is so clear-cut that it would be profitable if scholars in future devoted more attention to the factors underlying this growth pattern, rather than in discussing the economic disasters which characterised the period.[4] Even those who have sought to question the more exaggerated claims for the thirties as a period of rapid economic growth have conceded that the annual growth rate for the decade averaged between 2·3 and 3·3 per cent, depending upon the indices of production taken. The result was a substantial rise in national income and national income per head during the thirties.[5]

In spite of the intervention of the worst years of the depression from 1929 to 1932, the 1930s overall saw a continuation of the growth achieved by the economy in the 1920s. The mid-1930s, indeed, saw what has been called 'the largest and most sustained period of growth in the whole of the inter-war period'.[6] By 1937, unemployment had fallen from its peak of almost 3 million in 1932–3 to $1\frac{1}{2}$ million. Between 1932 and 1937, there had been a rise in domestic output by a quarter; industrial output had risen by almost half; and domestic investment had risen by the same amount. Although there is evidence that the economy was beginning to enter a downturn in the middle of 1937, with a perceptible check to growth and a renewed rise in unemployment, it was a short-lived decline of only 1 or 2 per cent in production, during which real incomes and consumption continued to rise. By 1939 the economy was moving upwards again, reinforced by large-scale rearmament and the revival it brought to the heavy industries. Overall, the inter-war period witnessed a growth in industrial production of 61 per cent and a rise in income per head of about a third, of which the 1930s had provided a major share.[7]

The economic record of the 'devil's decade' was therefore a paradoxical one. While the old staples declined to the lowest level of activity in the aftermath of the Great Crash and the financial crisis of 1931, the 'new' industries forged ahead at an unprecedented rate. In several sectors, the British economy enjoyed the almost boom conditions of expansion experienced by the American economy in the years before the Great Crash. Among the most striking of these new industries was electricity supply. In 1926 a Central Electricity Board was set up with monopoly powers over the production of electricity. The Board rationalised the large number of small, inefficient power stations and built a new generation of super-stations connected by a national grid of high-voltage transmission lines. By 1933 the grid was virtually complete, giving Britain one of the most advanced systems of electricity supply in the world.

As a result consumption of electricity rose fourfold between 1925 and 1939. Whereas in 1920 only one house in seventeen had been wired up for electricity, by 1930 the figure was one house in three, and by 1939 it was two houses in three. In the late 1930s, new consumers were being added at a rate of 700,000–800,000 per year. The growth of electricity supply enabled industries to move away from the old centres of production, based on the coalfields, to 'greenfield' sites in areas hitherto little affected by industry. The light industries of the south-east, especially the London area, owed a great deal to the geographical dispersal made possible by electricity. Industries, particularly consumer industries, were able to site themselves near to the largest markets. In the home, electricity brought not only a more efficient form of lighting, but by the end of the 1930s, the first wave of electrically-powered domestic appliances, such as mains radio, vacuum cleaners, cookers, gramophones and electric irons. The impact of electricity's growth upon the economy was seen in the doubling of employment in the industry from 156,000 in 1924 to over 325,000 by 1938. With an investment requirement of about £29 million for the National Grid and a large and growing source of employment, the industry played a vital part in the development of the economy during the decade.[8]

Among the most important of the other growth sectors of the economy in the 1930s was the motor-vehicle industry. Using the mass production methods of assembly-lines and large modern factories, the number of motor vehicles produced each year rose from 95,000 in 1923 to over 500,000 in 1937. Production became rationalised in about a score of firms by 1939, dominated by Morris Motors, based on Oxford, Ford's, the British branch of the American concern, based on Dagenham in Essex, and Austin at Longbridge. Austin had produced the first mass-market car in the Austin Seven in 1921, but was soon followed by Morris and Ford. These three firms accounted for two-thirds of car production by 1939. Mass production led to a fall in prices, so that by 1935–6 a typical small family car could be bought for half what it would have cost ten years earlier. The location of the industry was strikingly different from that of the old heavy industries, being primarily concentrated in the Midlands and the London area, especially in Coventry, Birmingham, Luton, Oxford and Dagenham. Closely related to the development of the motor industry was growth of aircraft production, relying in large part upon the same skills as the motor vehicle industry. Rearmament from the mid-1930s ensured a steady flow of orders, while the continued growth of civil aviation also provided a ready market. By the outbreak of the war, cities such as Coventry and Bristol were major centres of aircraft production. Underlying the growth in motor vehicles, aircraft manufacture and consumer durables was the expansion of the engineering industry, providing the skills and tools for increasingly complex activities. By 1937 the engineering industry had increased its output by 50 per cent in a decade.[9]

Another sector of the economy to show major development was the chemical industry. Rationalisation produced giant combines, such as Imperial Chemical Industries (I.C.I.) and Courtauld. The latter played an important part in the development in Britain of the artificial fibre industry, mainly based on rayon. By 1939 the industry employed 100,000 people in factories all over Britain, including some in depressed areas, such as the North Wales coast. I.C.I. produced a wide range of products, including artificial dyes, pharmaceutical goods, explosives and fertiliser.[10] An important part in the revival of the British economy was also played by the construction and building industry. Though there were no major advances in productivity, there was a surge in demand for both private and public building. As a result, the industry grew at almost double the average rate for the economy as a whole during the inter-war period, but its fastest expansion occurred during the domestic house-building boom of the middle and late thirties. The industry employed directly almost three-quarters of a million men, with at least another quarter of a million involved indirectly.[11] In addition, the industry had an important multiplier effect, having repercussions upon the host of industries involved in producing materials and fittings. Demand was stimulated for bricks, woodwork, glass, cement, and a variety of other products such as paint, plumbing and electrical apparatus.

By the mid-1930s there were also signs of recovery in the heavy industries which had been hardest hit by the depression. Steel production, which had fallen to 5·2 million tons in 1932, rose to 7 million tons in 1933, and went through a prolonged expansion to

The Slump

reach 13 million tons by 1937. The main sources of expansion were the new steel plants set up to make use of the low-grade ironstone ores of Lincolnshire and Northamptonshire. A completely new integrated steelworks was constructed from 1932 around the village of Corby in Northamptonshire by Stewart and Lloyds. A new plant was built at Ebbw Vale by Richard Thomas and Company and opened in 1938. In North Wales, the following year saw the opening of John Summers's steel sheet-making plant at Shotton. In several other centres, such as Workington, Consett, Sheffield and Lancashire, new capacity was opened. By 1934 production had passed the level reached in 1929 and Britain's share of world output began to rise. The industry was aided by a $33\frac{1}{3}$ per cent tariff introduced in 1932 and the formation in 1934 of the British Iron and Steel Federation (B.I.S.F.) to co-ordinate the industry and to aid rationalisation.[12]

Shipbuilding showed a less spectacular recovery. Of all industries it had probably been hardest hit in the depression with a precipitate decline in tonnage completed during the worst phase of the slump, from 1·4 million tons in 1930 to 133,000 in 1933. Under a ruthless policy of reducing shipbuilding capacity a private company, National Shipbuilders' Security, bought up and dismantled 137 berths with a capacity of close to one million tons, including Palmers' yard at Jarrow. Its activities were followed by the British Shipping (Assistance) Act of 1935 which granted a subsidy to tramp shipping and encouraged the scrapping of surplus shipping capacity. Although the tonnage of ships launched failed to reach the levels of the years before the Great Crash, output steadily revived from the trough of 1932–3, reaching 920,800 tons in 1937.[13]

In the coal industry, recovery was also less spectacular, but a degree of stabilisation was achieved after the worst years of the slump. Production revived from its most depressed levels of 1932–3, though it still remained 7 per cent lower than the figure for 1929, and 16 per cent below that of 1913. The British coal industry failed to recapture its large export markets of the years before the First World War and continued to face increasing competition from gas and electricity. None the less, significant improvements in productivity were registered, especially in the large modern pits sunk in Yorkshire, Nottinghamshire and Scotland. By 1939 61 per cent of coal was cut by machinery and output per man had risen by over a third between 1924 and 1938. Although the industry remained a fiercely competitive one, a degree of government intervention became normal during the thirties. Part II of the Coal Mines Act of 1930 set production quotas for each district and determined a minimum price. Further attempts at reorganisation were resisted by the coal-owners, but in 1938 the government nationalised the royalties of the mining companies and handed over the task of reorganising the industry to the Coal Commission. By 1942 the nationalisation of royalties had been completed at a cost of £66·5 million.[14]

The textile industries also achieved a measure of stabilisation after a painful period of transition, in which production capacity was drastically reduced. The cotton industry entered the worst phase of the depression after 1929 with approximately the same amount of capacity as in 1913 to compete with strong foreign competitors for a much reduced market. Spindle capacity was reduced by a fifth between 1929 and 1935 under voluntary schemes. From 1936 the government acted to reduce it still further. By 1939 spinning capacity had been reduced to 39 million spindles compared with 56 million in 1929, and weaving capacity was cut by a third over the same period. The industry remained affected by excess capacity, outdated machinery and inefficient organisation, but, like coal, it had achieved a measure of stabilisation by the mid-1930s.[15] Woollen textiles were less badly affected by the depression. Unlike cotton, wool had never relied so heavily upon its export markets. As a result it suffered less from the decline of Britain's exports and benefited from the rise in domestic demand in the mid-1930s. Though employment contracted during the period, the industry was producing a higher output in 1939 than in 1930.[16]

Thus even the 'ailing giants' showed a measure of revival by the middle and late thirties, most marked in steel and shipbuilding, with stabilisation in the case of coal and textiles. But above all, it was growth in the new industries which provided the basis for a revival of the British economy in the mid-1930s. Unlike the old staples, they were more dependent upon the home market. It was this range of industries which produced the most dynamic elements in the economy in the middle and late thirties. It was, however, a revival which was highly localised: the new industries were freed from dependence upon the coalfields by electricity and the development of motor transport. The London area provided the largest market in the country for a wide range of light industrial and consumer goods. The results were seen in the booming industrial suburbs to the north and west of London, where new factories lined the main arterial roads, such as the Great West Road and Western Avenue. A large number of these factories produced components for the new industries, as well as

consumer goods. Between 1932 and 1937, four-fifths of the new
factories in Britain were sited in Greater London, including two-
thirds of new employment.[17]

But though the London area and the Midlands took the lion's
share of renewed economic activity, some of the depressed areas
also began to participate in recovery based upon expanding industrial estates and new factories. For example, the Ebbw Vale
steelworks brought some mitigation to the massive unemployment
of South Wales. At Merthyr Tydfil, the late thirties saw a branch of
Imperial Chemical Industries and an engineering works established.[18]
New trading estates also provided some alleviation of the unemployment problem in the depressed areas. In North Wales, the decline
of the coal and slate industries was to some extent offset by Courtauld's building a number of rayon factories in Flintshire and the
construction of the Shotton steelworks on reclaimed land in the Dee
estuary. In the north-east, the decline of traditional sectors such as
coalmining and shipbuilding was compensated for by the growth of
the chemical industry at Billingham on Teesside. In the north-west,
the decline of coalmining and cotton continued to pose acute problems for the communities which had depended upon them for a
livelihood, but revival was beginning to take place on new industrial
estates, such as Trafford Park near Manchester, which attracted a
wide range of new industries and employed almost 50,000 people by
1939.[19]

Many important changes in the organisation and pattern of
economic activity also took place in the inter-war period. The
rationalisation of smaller companies into huge combines was one
of the most striking features of business development during the
period. Out of the mergers of the 1920s and 1930s emerged industrial
giants like I.C.I., E.M.I., Unilever, Courtaulds and Royal Dutch
Shell. Several of these large firms were involved in trading in different
countries, but in many cases the impetus to rationalisation came
from the rise of mass consumer markets, new forms of distribution
through motor transport, and the economic advantages given by
size and concentration. Significantly, a large number of the giant
concerns were involved in the new industries, such as Nestlé's in food
processing and Dunlop in tyre making. On the retailing and marketing side, the growth of monopolistic enterprises was matched by the
development of trade associations, varying in importance and purpose, but showing the same characteristics of defensive growth seen
in the mergers of manufacturing industry. Trade associations and

cartels generally concerned themselves with price fixing and control, sometimes arranging quotas for internal and overseas markets.[20] At the manufacturing level, factories tended to be larger, employing more men. In 1935, it was found that over half the insured population worked in factories employing 500 men or over. Many of the new factories constructed in the 1930s were large-scale enterprises, employing thousands rather than hundreds of workers. Ford, for example, employed 7,000 people at its Dagenham factory by 1932 and several of the firms developing sites on the fringes of London built on a similar scale, such as the Hoover factory opened at Perivale in 1933.[21]

As mass production methods began to be used for the manufacture of consumer goods, important developments occurred in patterns of trading and marketing. Goods were now more usually packaged and priced by the manufacturer, rather than by the shopkeeper. Motor transport allowed direct delivery to multiple branches and the first mail order schemes were introduced. Under the impact of this 'retailing revolution', almost a thousand chain stores were built in the inter-war period, showing virtually no decline with the depression. Marks and Spencer, for example, one of the most successful of the clothing retailers, opened 129 stores from 1931 to 1935 and extended 60 more. Turnover in the company rose from £2,493,000 in 1929 to £23,448,000 by 1939 and the company had opened or extended 258 stores.[22] By the outbreak of the Second World War, Marks and Spencer, Lipton's, Sainsbury's and Woolworth's had become household names in almost every medium-sized town, bringing with them a wider range of foodstuffs, clothing and household goods than had been available at the traditional corner shop and retailer.[23] Many of these developments were stimulated by the progress of advertising, as mass production for a consumer market and the development of new outlets in newspapers and cinemas created a wider range of opportunities for sales promotion. By 1938 it was estimated that over £100 million was being spent on advertising of all kinds, mainly through newspapers.[24] The growth of the press and of advertising proceeded in an almost symbiotic relationship, each reciprocating the other. Even during the worst years of the depression, national and local newspapers bombarded the public with advertisements for clothing, cosmetics, cigarettes, foodstuffs and household goods of every description. Sales gimmicks of every kind played a large part in promoting brand names into household words, with free gifts, sales, and special offers such as Woolworth's famous boast of 'nothing over sixpence'. For many items credit facilities were becoming more readily available. By 1938 two-thirds of all larger purchases were made using hire-purchase agreements, bringing a wide range of household goods, such as furniture, within the reach of sections of the community who could not in the past have afforded them.[25] Though none of these developments originated in the 1930s, the decade saw considerable advances in almost every sphere, in several cases faster than in the 1920s.

The growth of consumer industries and of different patterns of marketing and retailing led to important developments in the location and structure of the labour force. The service industries, such as distribution, transport and administration, showed rapid growth throughout the inter-war period, continuing to rise even through the worst years of the slump. The distributive trades showed the greatest increase, from 1,661,000 workers in 1920–2 to 2,436,000 in 1937–8. Job opportunities were expanding for shop-workers, clerical staff, transport employees and the professional and managerial salariat. The growth of white-collar employment was registered in a census of employment which found an increase in administrative staff from 11·8 per cent in 1924 to 15·1 per cent in 1935. Many of these posts were taken up by women, especially in the clerical field, adding substantially to the numbers of women in employment. The overall effect was to increase the proportion of the workforce involved in the service sector. The heavy industries suffered a net loss of workers during the 1930s, while the service sector witnessed a rise which was to continue after the Second World War. Even before the economic expansion of the post-1945 period, the pattern of employment which is traditionally associated with affluence – the transference of workers from producing goods to providing services – was being developed in the middle and late 1930s at a faster rate than at any other point in the inter-war period.[26]

The background to many of these developments is the aspect of the thirties which is most easily forgotten amid the prevailing image of the 'hungry thirties', namely the overall rise in living standards enjoyed by the great majority of the population who were able to remain in employment during the decade. The inter-war period as a whole witnessed an increase in national income per head by a third between 1920 and 1939, reflecting the effects of increased output and a relatively static population.[27] Only part of this increase was distributed in wages and salaries, but the overall tendency in the twenties had been for wage levels to rise. After the onset of the worst years of the slump, the situation became rather complex. Naturally those out of work were unable to receive any benefit from wage movements, while for those in work the years between 1929 and 1934 saw an adverse trend of wage cuts, reduced working hours and intermittent employment. Wage cuts were heaviest in the staple industries, such as cotton and heavy engineering, ranging up to 20 per cent in some cases. The government gave a lead to private industry by reducing the wages of its own employees, with cuts ranging from 6 per cent for civil servants to 11 per cent for teachers. After 1934, these were relaxed, and wage rates in general began to move upwards again. By the end of the decade the general trend for average wage rates had more or less balanced the adverse effects of the worst phase of the depression. Average wage rates remained either a little above, or a little below, what they had been in 1929, with few major changes.[28]

Averages, of course, concealed a mass of variations between different industries and regions. The average industrial weekly wage remained at just under £3 throughout the 1930s, but this could vary between nearer £2 in depressed industries such as coalmining, to £4 for skilled workers in more prosperous trades. Even within a particular industry, take-home pay varied with region, seasonal factors, and cyclical movements in the economy. Coal miners, within the same coalfield, were dependent upon the demand for their particular type of coal, which dictated the number of shifts they would be able to work.[29] Many trades were still organised on a casual basis, of which the most important were dock workers, whose earnings fluctuated widely. Even in the more modern industries, such as motor vehicles, seasonal factors were an important influence upon real earnings as demand for cars was subject to regular seasonal fluctuations. Skilled workers and salaried staff tended to be less affected by these factors and after the reductions of the period 1931–4, their wage rates held up and even improved. Above all, more were in full-time employment, so that they were in a good position to improve their standard of living. Thus for those who remained in work, wages held up well under the impact of the slump and were often higher than they had been at the outbreak of the First World War. The onset of the slump had not eroded to any more than a marginal extent the advances made in wage rates during the war years and the 1920s.[30]

But trends in wage rates alone were not sufficient to create improved living standards even for those in regular employment. The main reason was the fall in prices which occurred after 1920 and continued until 1933–4. Between 1920 and 1939 the cost of living index fell by a third, with one of the most dramatic declines occurring in the early 1930s. Set against the movement of wages, the reduction in prices generated a rise in real incomes. By 1938, average real wages were a third higher than they had been in 1913 and the thirties alone saw a rise of the order of 15 per cent for those in regular employment. Again this is an average figure, but it represented a significant experience of improved living conditions for most middle-class families, largely unaffected by unemployment, and for a large section of the working classes. The impact of the reduction in prices was seen most clearly in cheaper food and manufactured items, such as household goods, furniture, clothing and processed foods. As a recent economic historian has commented: 'Expenditure patterns and budgetary surveys suggest that many families enjoyed a considerable improvement in their standard of living during this period.'[31] Another has seen in the inter-war period, including the 1930s,

> an appreciable rise in the standards of comfort and welfare of working-class families, particularly those in which the wage earners were in regular employment. This conclusion is supported by the remarkable increase in small savings, including working-class savings, showing some margin of income over bare subsistence.[32]

Also the trend to smaller families which began to be evident in the twenties and became more pronounced in the 1930s meant that there was a higher proportion of income per head available in each family. The result was a greater income left over after the purchase of food and rent for consumption. The typical family of the Ministry of Labour's budgetary inquiries in 1937–8 had more than double the real income of a family in 1913–14. As it had to be spent on only four-fifths as many persons, income per head had risen by about two-thirds over the period.[33] Similarly, whereas a working-class family in 1914 had typically spent about 60 per cent of its income on food and a further 16 per cent on rent, by 1937–8 these figures had fallen to 35 per cent and 9 per cent respectively.[34] This greater degree of disposable income was spent in different ways depending upon family habits and circumstances. A large portion went upon extra food; food consumption rose by about a third in the thirties and there was more money available to spend on a greater variety of fresh and processed foods. Expenditure on luxuries, services and entertainment also showed substantial increases, while the most prosperous workers were able to consider buying their own houses. Savings showed a large increase, especially in building societies whose share and deposit accounts rose from £82 million to £717 million between 1920 and 1938.[35] For the middle classes, increased spending power brought the first real taste of affluence with better houses, motor cars, consumer durables and foreign holidays. The consumer expenditure which fuelled the housing boom, the new light industries, the service sector, and many other aspects of the constructive side of the 1930s was the result of a general rise in living standards which created for many families an improved quality of life.

One of the most important preconditions for the improvement in general living standards was a reduced rate of population growth during the thirties. The total population rose from 43·74 million in 1920 to 47·49 million in 1938, a very slow rate compared with the years before the First World War. The rate of natural increase was small because of a major fall in the birth rate from an average of 96 per thousand women of marriageable age in 1914 to 62 per thousand by 1938. The reduction was fairly even throughout the inter-war period, though the lowest point was reached in 1933. The trend towards fewer children meant that average family size fell from 4·2 persons in 1929 to 3·2 in 1939.[36] Though some contemporaries saw these changes as being the result of the depression, it is now clear that they reflected a complex set of developments which had been taking place since before 1914. Greater contraceptive knowledge and greater freedom for women contributed to the trend. New ideas about the desirability of smaller families which were becoming fashionable among the middle classes, as well as the growing career opportunities for women in manual and office work, also had their effect. However alarmed some writers might have been that deaths would soon exceed births, the threat proved less serious than feared, but during the thirties the changed pattern of family size and expenditure had important repercussions upon living standards.[37]

The 1930s also saw advances in health. In spite of set-backs in the depressed areas, the decade after 1929 saw a continuation of the progress which had been made in public health since the First World War. By 1939 Britain was a healthier nation on average than it had been ten years earlier, in spite of many problems which still required attention. The general picture was shown by the improved chances of survival. Life expectancy had increased from forty-five years in

1900 to sixty years by 1932, mainly as a result of the conquest of infectious diseases. Though death rates concealed many variations between classes and regions, the overall trend was downwards even during the thirties. Thus the standardised death rate for England and Wales was 13·5 per 1000 persons in 1911–14, 9·7 in 1931–4, and 9·3 by 1937.[38] Infant mortality had also shown a dramatic fall. Deaths of children under one year per 1000 live births fell from 80 in 1920 to 60 in 1930, and 56 by 1940.[39]

A clear indication of the improvement of general health standards was shown in the classification of men called up for military service in the Second World War. When the Ministry of Labour and National Service reported on the results of their examinations it was found that under a third of the men who had passed through their hands had been unfit for military service, whereas in the First World War the percentage was nearer to two-thirds, using the same terminology and classification. Even allowing for any changes in interpretation by the doctors concerned, the improvement was dramatic. Evidence of this improvement could be seen in the level of mortality for some of the major diseases such as tuberculosis, typhoid and influenza.[40]

Infant mortality also showed that the threat from some of the major diseases was considerably reduced by the thirties, most noticeably in the declining death rate from scarlet fever, diphtheria, whooping cough and measles.[41] These improvements were attributed by Carr-Saunders and Caradog Jones in the 1937 edition of *A Survey of the Social Structure of England and Wales* to 'improvements in housing, sanitation, hygiene, and medical skill'.[42] *The New Survey of London Life and Labour* attributed the progress found in the standard of public health in London since the end of the nineteenth century to five main developments: the rehousing of the population in healthier conditions, better maternity care, the medical inspection of school-children, the introduction of old age pensions, and steps to deal with venereal disease. It concluded that:

> there has been vast improvement in the health of the London population during the last thirty years. The gains accruing from advance in material prosperity, from greater cleanliness, from improved drainage, scavenging, and medical, surgical and nursing services, have far outweighed any added risks ... [43]

An important aspect of generally improved health was the better diet which higher average disposable incomes and cheaper food prices made possible. Compared with the period before 1914, there was significantly higher average consumption of the more nutritious foods. It was calculated that average annual consumption per head had risen between 1909–13 and 1934 by 88 per cent for fruit; 64 per cent for vegetables; 50 per cent for butter and margarine; and 46 per cent for eggs.[44] On the other hand, consumption of bread and potatoes had fallen, producing a considerably improved diet for the average family. Thus even those most critical of existing health and nutritional standards were forced to admit that conditions in the thirties were an improvement on what had gone before. John Boyd Orr, whose study *Food, Health and Income* came out in 1936, was highly critical of the standard of nutrition which was still current. Having drawn attention to the deficiencies which still existed in the dietary standards of many sections of the population, he concluded his examination by saying that, 'Bad as the picture is, however, it is better than the picture of pre-war days. Since then, the national dietary has improved ... Accompanying that improvement in diet, there has been a corresponding improvement in national health.'[45]

Improved housing conditions were one of the major advances made in the thirties. Although large areas of appalling slums remained in the major conurbations, there were remarkable advances in the field of housing in spite of an often unfavourable economic climate. The inter-war period saw the completion of over 4 million houses, $2\frac{1}{2}$ million for private sale, and the rest for rent by local authorities. The bulk of this housing boom came in the 1930s when nearly 3 million houses were built, mainly for private sale. Within twenty years, the housing situation was transformed from a position where there were 610,000 fewer houses than families, as in 1918, to one in 1938 where there was a theoretical surplus of over 500,000 houses.[46] Slum clearance had been a preoccupation of enlightened local authorities and politicians for decades, but it was only during the 1930s that it got under way to a significant extent. The record of the 1920s had been disappointing, with only 11,000 slum houses cleared and 17,000 people rehoused by 1930. The slum-clearance acts of 1930 and 1933 began to have their effect by the mid-1930s, however, for local authorities were given subsidies and charged with producing five-year rehousing plans. Between 1932 and 1939 local authorities rehoused about four-fifths of slum dwellers.[47]

Much of the new housing was built on extensive estates on the fringes of the main towns and cities. At Kirkby near Liverpool,

C

Solihull and Longbridge outside Birmingham, and Becontree outside London, for example, large new council estates were created which were almost miniature towns in themselves. For many housing experts they represented the great hope for a better future through the provision of a physical environment which was a vast improvement upon conditions in the slums. In the most imaginative developments where the 'garden city' concept pioneered at Letchworth before 1914 was copied, the result was often attractive, with tree-lined avenues, extensive open spaces, and adequate community facilities. Among the best examples were Welwyn Garden City, founded in 1920 and rapidly expanded in the thirties, and Wythen-shawe, outside Manchester. The latter was founded by the efforts of one of the great housing pioneers of the inter-war period, Sir Ernest Simon, and planned as a garden suburb to house 100,000 people. By 1939, 7,000 houses had been built.[48] Even the most utilitarian estates offered a far higher standard of comfort than had been possible for many families in the past. Basic amenities such as adequate space, light and ventilation, the provision of bathrooms and inside toilets, and well-built houses which avoided the depressing battle with damp and vermin so common in the slums were among the most tangible gains. Seebohm Rowntree, having criticised some of the defects of the new council housing in York, turned to a comparison with slum housing:

> Compare the Council housing estates with these houses, and any criticism of them appears ungracious! Instead of being forty or fifty to the acre, on no Council estate does the number of houses per acre exceed thirteen, on some it is as low as ten; the average is twelve. The chief roadways are of ample, some indeed of excessive width, and there are grass verges about nine feet wide, often with trees planted in them, between the roadway and the footpath. Every house has a front and back garden usually of from 200 to 300 square yards. In summer they are ablaze with colour. It is indeed amazing how soon families, most of whom had never had a garden before, turn the rough land surrounding their new houses into beautiful gardens.[49]

Elsewhere, local authorities were beginning to experiment with high-rise flats, often modelled upon similar developments in Central Europe. At Leeds, the municipality pioneered the construction of large blocks of flats in the Quarry Hill scheme near the centre of the cito, where 2,000 slum houses were demolished and 938 new flat dwellings built at cost of £1½ million. There was a lively debate about the relative advantages of flats as opposed to houses, generally decided in favour of the latter. Often they formed part of ambitious schemes of town planning, as in Liverpool, where the new estates were grouped in a semi-circle round the outer limits of the city, on a system of new arterial roads, radiating out from the city centre. Sir Ernest Simon looked forward to a large-scale reconstruction of the southern half of the city of Manchester:

> In Manchester practically all the houses in the slum belt, numbering about 80,000 will have to be demolished and replaced by modern houses or flats, before the city's housing can be regarded as satisfactory. This means that there will be a splendid opportunity for replanning the central area on the best modern lines, and for making a comprehensive plan for Manchester's whole future development; it is most important that this opportunity should be utilised to the full, so that all the congestion and ill-health and waste caused by the lack of any planning when the slum belt was first built may be prevented in the future.[50]

With these ideals went the hope that a decent physical environment would abolish 'not only the slum house, but also the slum tenant'. Whatever the shortcomings of the new housing developments, there had been greater progress by the end of the 1930s in providing an adequate solution to the housing conditions of the working class than in any previous decade.

But slum clearance was only the minor part of the housing picture in the thirties, for the most dramatic developments took place in private house-building. Over 2 million houses were built for private sale during the decade. Houses were relatively cheap; a typical 'semi' could be bought for as little as £450, about twice the annual salary for an average professional man. Mortgages were available on very easy terms, with an average interest rate of around 4½ per cent and repayments which came well within the range of most of the middle classes and a significant portion of the better-off working classes. Deposits on new houses could be as low as £25, particularly towards the end of the decade when the number of house completions topped 350,000 and gave the market a more competitive edge. In a fairly typical example of the situation in the late 1930s a London company offered houses for £800 on payment of a £25 deposit, with all legal expenses paid by the builder. Speculative development could produce jerry-building and the uglier features of 'bungaloid growth', but its obverse side was probably the most favourable period for house purchase in the twentieth century. Builders and estate agents wooed potential customers with visits to new developments in the suburbs and attractive rates of interest. The favoured style was the smallish, uniform semi-detached houses, usually tiled rather than covered with more expensive slate, lighter and airier than Edwardian houses, with larger gardens and more room for garages, garden sheds and greenhouses. They were nearly all wired up for electricity, and except for a minority built with some acknowledgment of changes in architectural style since the nineteenth century, they were constructed on traditional lines and decorated with pebbledash, leaded panes and mock-Tudor timbering.[51]

The evidence of this housing boom could be seen in the new suburbs which sprang up outside the existing urban areas and the ribbon development which lined the main arterial roads. In the south-east, the growth of 'semi-detached London' into hitherto unspoilt rural areas created new suburban estates in north and west Middlesex and in parts of Surrey and Essex. The south-east absorbed about 60 per cent of the total population increase in the country during the inter-war period and by 1939 Greater London had a population close to 9 million. About a fifth of the population of Great Britain now lived within a radius of 15 miles from Charing Cross. Over a million people moved into the London area from other parts of Britain and the Midlands also registered a net inflow of people, mainly as a result of the increasing employment opportunities offered by the newer industries being set up there. But even in the depressed areas, new estates of private housing were built up.

The improvements in living standards, diet and health, and in the general quality of housing were only part of the social developments which came in the inter-war period and during the 1930s too. One of the most significant was the motoring revolution. In 1920, there were about half a million motor vehicles of all kinds in Britain; by 1930 the figure was $1\frac{1}{2}$ million; and by 1939 had reached over 3 million, 2 million of which were private cars. The production of motor vehicles not only created a new industry, but substantially altered the way of life of large sections of the population. Cars, vans, buses, lorries and coaches provided an infinitely more flexible means of transporting people about the country than had hitherto been available. The retailing revolution was heavily dependent upon the ubiquity of motor transport to ease distribution. The horse-drawn delivery cart was entering a permanent decline and the introduction of tractors into agriculture was already sounding the death-knell of the use of horses for farm work, with over 55,000 tractors at work by 1939. For public transport, a Royal Commission in 1931 had recommended the elimination of trams and their replacement by motor buses. The number of trams was reduced by half in the 1930s, while in a major city such as Birmingham, bus passengers rose from 43 million to 225 million a year. For holidays and excursions, the charabanc began to be an effective rival to the railways.[52]

But it was private motoring which brought the greatest social effects. Mass production methods enabled cars to be manufactured at ever-cheaper prices. A basic family car could be bought for about £100 in 1931, and was thus within the reach of a wider range of people. With the growth of private and public motoring went the ancillary services of car parks, garages and traffic controls. New arterial roads, such as the North Circular and Western Avenue in London, were an attempt to cope with the beginnings of the traffic problem. The Sunday afternoon drive and the Bank Holiday traffic jam were already familiar aspects of social life by the end of the 1930s. The motor car also opened up rural areas such as Cornwall and North Wales to the car-borne tourist. Road accidents reached an unprecedented peak, higher in the late 1930s than in the early 1970s. For many, the cheaper alternative to a car was the motor-cycle, of which there were half a million by 1931. The internal combustion engine was to have a far more pervasive influence upon twentieth-century Britain than even the coming of the railways. In the Britain of the 1930s, private and public motor vehicles were already having a widespread social impact.[53]

Equally one of the most important features of the thirties was the growing availability of holidays for people of all classes. The most significant development was the spread of paid holidays. In 1931 only 1½ million people were entitled to paid holidays, whereas by 1939 the figure was over 11 million. This meant for many working people the first opportunity for an extensive holiday away from home. The British holiday resorts reached a peak of popularity with a host of new hotels, boarding houses, entertainments, and amenities. Twenty million people visited the seaside annually by the late 1930s, 15 million on extended holidays. The most popular, Blackpool, had over 7 million overnight visitors in 1937, half a million visitors over the August Bank Holiday alone, brought by 50,000 motor vehicles and 70 trains. To capitalise upon the holiday boom, the first all-in holiday camps were built. Billy Butlin opened his first camp at Skegness in 1937 and by the outbreak of the war holiday camps had accommodation for half a million people.[54] For the car-owner, camping and caravan holidays were becoming increasingly common. Holiday caravans were transformed from lumbering structures based upon gipsy caravans to the more streamlined versions which were beginning to litter the coastline with caravan parks. Cycling also became a popular pastime in the thirties, not just as a means of getting to and from work, but also as a way of getting out into the countryside. Cycles could be bought for about £5 or a few shillings a week on hire purchase. Cycling clubs grew up in many towns and villages, providing one of the most popular forms of recreation, organised by national bodies such as the Cyclists' Touring Club and the National Cyclists' Union.

Cycling was only one aspect of the popular craze in the thirties for outdoor recreation, seen in the passion for hiking and rambling. The Youth Hostel Association, founded in 1930, had some 400 hostels by 1939 used by over a million people. With a membership of over 100,000, the Y.H.A. and organisations like the Ramblers' Association catered for a new spirit of enjoyment in fresh air, healthy exertion and company. Special ramblers' excursions were run by the railways; there were mass hikes, mystery hikes, and even a popular song called 'I'm happy when I'm hiking'. This enthusiasm for the outdoors was part of a general movement for physical culture which affected much of Europe during the inter-war period and was reflected in Britain by the keep-fit craze, which spilled over into cycling, hiking and rambling, physical training and naturism. The Women's League of Health and Beauty, founded in 1930, had 166,000 members by 1939. So impressed was the government with the new cult that a team of British observers went to Germany to examine the 'Strength through Joy' movement. It reported enthusiastically, though condemning the over-disciplined character of the German movement; its recommendations were incorporated into a Physical Fitness Bill which was debated in parliament in the same week as a Festival of Youth took place in Wembley Stadium. *The Times* described how 'the young people were clad as for the day and, in their flimsy array, they marched forth to greet the sun and to gambol in its radiance!' Some thirty organisations were represented, and were praised for 'that disciplined vigour of the body which is the first security for the facing of moral and spiritual problems with the sane intelligence of free people'.[55]

In other spheres, the 1930s offered a wider range of entertainment than any previous decade. Though some commentators may have looked to a world in which the lower classes would no longer gamble, drink or spend a significant part of their leisure hours at the cinema or the dance hall, these were exactly the ways in which an increasing portion of the population chose to spend their time and money. It has been claimed that the generation which grew up between the wars had a wider range of entertainment open to it than any in previous history. The cinema was in its heyday with the development of 'talkies' and colour. By 1939 the cinema was easily the most important form of mass entertainment with 20 million tickets being sold and 3 new cinemas being opened each week. By 1939 there were nearly 5,000 cinemas, many of them rebuilt supercinemas, with plusher seating, carpets, Wurlitzer organs and exotic decor. A survey in Liverpool revealed that 40 per cent of the population visited cinemas once a week, while 25 per cent went twice or more.[56] Admission cost only a few pence and provided probably the cheapest form of mass entertainment available in most towns and cities. Music hall and variety theatre continued to flourish in many towns, but fought a steadily losing battle against the growth of cinemas. The major competitor with the cinema was the dance hall. Dancing had become one of the most popular forms of mass entertainment during the twenties and continued to cater for a broad age-group.

Many sports went through a boom period in the thirties as the combination of mass unemployment and a taste of affluence swelled the ranks of spectators and participants. Traditional sports continued to attract large crowds. Cricket and football in particular were firmly established as large crowd-pullers. Cricket retained a certain snobbish cachet, test-matches being accorded a status reserved in the 1960s and 1970s for association football, still primarily a proletarian game without the veneer of glamour it was to acquire in the television age. Boxing, too, remained a lower-class sport, with an immense following in a decade which had no shortage of 'hungry fighters'. The inter-war period has been called the 'brutal hey-day of boxing', with the abuses of the boxing booths which the Boxing Board of Control only began to tackle after 1934. The popularity of sport during the thirties was shown by the continued growth of two creations of the previous decade, greyhound racing and speedway. Significantly, both catered for an urban, largely working-class audience. The first dog-track had been opened at Belle Vue in Manchester in 1926 and by 1939 tracks had been opened in most important towns. Much of the sport's success lay in the fresh outlet it offered for betting. In 1936, gambling was estimated by *The Economist* to be Britain's second biggest industry, involving a turnover of £200 million a year. The football pools, a creation of the 1930s, became firmly established as a national habit. By 1938, over 10 million people sent in a coupon during the football season, making a combined stake of over £40 million. Though it was disapproved of by most social commentators, gambling was one of the most thriving popular pastimes in the 1930s.[57]

Apart from these developments in popular recreation and leisure, there were also advances in the social services. Although the picture of the social services has been blighted by the image of the 'means test' and the dole, there was a degree of progress in spite of the depression and enforced economy. By the end of the 1930s, Britain was spending an extra £100 million on the social services compared with the end of the First World War and health insurance was extended to cover 20 million wage-earners by 1938. The Poor Law was transformed by the ending of the Poor Law Unions and their Guardians in 1930. Their work was transferred to a smaller number of Public Assistance Committees. As we have seen, housing acts also provided the legislative and financial framework in which rehousing programmes could be undertaken. In the field of health, the Midwives Act of 1936 required local authorities to provide trained personnel. Both the B.M.A. and independent inquiries suggested the need for a unified health service with greatly extended insurance provisions. It was a period of what has been called 'steady and purposive advance' in the social services, slow in comparison with the war years, but which helped to lay the foundations for them. Policy had been evolved in a pragmatic way rather than with any broad strategy in mind, but it none the less represented a significant advance in an adverse economic climate. By 1939, it was recognised that Britain had a more comprehensive set of welfare services than almost any other country.[58]

Much of this advance depended upon the development of a climate of opinion in which social problems were recognised and a sense of urgency about their solution generated. The range of social surveys and inquiries which emerged during the 1930s was remarkable. The intellectual thrust of many of these social inquiries was towards a more scientific appraisal of contemporary society. In doing so, the social investigators highlighted the main areas in which problems such as poverty, ill-health and poor housing could be alleviated. Malcolm Muggeridge commented wryly on the trend towards social investigation: 'From the London School of Economics and other places went annually many earnest persons, male and female, to plant their tents in depressed areas, housing estates, malnutrition belts.'[59] The 'many earnest persons', however, produced a wide-ranging analysis of the condition of Britain and added a new dimension to the debate on social issues. Rarely in so short a space of time had so many aspects of British social life been examined. This spirit of inquiry was paralleled in 1936 in the founding of Mass Observation by the social anthropologist Tom Harrisson, the poet Charles Madge and the film director Humphrey Jennings. It recorded details of everyday life in Britain and attitudes to national events, such as Armistice Day and the Coronation, employing techniques which were put to use during the Second World War to test civilian morale. There was even a monthly magazine called *Fact*, which examined social, economic and political issues of the day. This new documentation conditioned a whole generation of social thought. The more committed literature did much to turn issues such as unemployment and social problems such as housing and ill-health into political questions, by educating a new generation of public opinion about the many problems which remained unaffected by the general improvements in living conditions.

The conclusions of the social investigators of the 1930s were to have profound consequences for post-war Britain. They highlighted the need for greater State intervention, more rational planning of the social services, and the ending of mass unemployment. These inquiries played a vital part in the emergence of what has been called 'a consensus on social responsibility' in the years leading up to the Second World War. Many of the recommendations on social policy underlying the Welfare State were derived from the investigations and social thought of the thirties. Articulated through the social literature and given form in reports from professional bodies and groups such as P.E.P. (Political and Economic Planning), they were already finding limited acceptance in government circles in the years before the war.[60] The State was already spending more, intervening more positively and taking on greater responsibilities, but as yet it had not formulated a comprehensive policy. None the less, many of the views of the social investigators were to find realisation in the Beveridge Report of 1942 and the Butler Education Act of 1944.

That it took the People's War to turn these ideas into reality, should not obscure the achievement of the thirties in laying the foundations for the Welfare State. In general the 1930s had seen a marked improvement in the standard of living and the quality of life for those in work. Advances measured in terms of wages and prices were only one aspect of the progress made.

In addition, there were increased opportunities for travel, greater leisure time and more opportunities for spending it. Most important of all, Britain was on average better paid, better fed, better clothed and housed, and healthier than it had been in 1918. Thus the economic and social climate for political extremism during the inter-war period was much less favourable than has often been depicted. Indeed, after 1933 when Britain moved out of the trough of the depression, British society began to display some of the characteristics of affluence which are more commonly associated with the 1950s and 1960s. Unemployment was falling, industrial production was rising, especially in the new industries, and consumer spending was reaching new levels. With these developments went patterns of consumption and recreation which gave little scope for political extremism to flourish except in the ranks of those who failed to share in the growth of the economy.

III

The Hungry Thirties

Although the 1930s can be seen in a much more favourable light by an examination of the statistics of economic performance and an analysis of average social trends, there remained a substantial section of the population which existed in conditions of chronic poverty, poor housing and ill-health. Even before unemployment became a major preoccupation of social investigators, there was already a considerable literature dealing with social questions. The 1920s had seen the beginning of the *Social Survey of Merseyside* and *The New Survey of London Life and Labour*. Regional studies such as H. A. Mess's *Industrial Tyneside* were the forerunners of many of the investigations of industrial areas which were to follow in the next decade. Sir Ernest Simon had also started the detailed evaluation of the housing situation and its remedies. There was therefore a social literature and the concern which went with it even before the worst phase of the depression. The tendency towards social investigation which some saw as a purely thirties phenomenon was, in fact, well under way in the twenties. Though some studies were concerned with unemployment, a whole range of social problems came under the microscope. In the main unemployment was seen as an aspect of other issues and only singled out in the middle and late thirties as the most pressing social problem facing the nation. In the meantime, the mainstream of academic social investigation continued and gathered momentum. Studies of poverty, housing, diet, health and many other issues were produced, providing a wide-ranging analysis of British society in the years before 1939.

The picture which emerged from these inquiries was hardly conducive to complacency or self-satisfaction. In spite of advances in average living standards and in material comfort during the inter-war period, they showed that poverty survived among a significant section of the working population. One of the primary objectives which the social investigators set themselves was to define 'poverty', recognised by all serious writers as a subjective and relative term. Advances in knowledge about nutrition, however, allowed the investigators to apply more objective standards of poverty and human needs than ever before. In 1933 the British Medical Association estimated that an average man required 3,400 calories a day to maintain health and that this would cost 5*s*. 11*d*. per week to provide. This was the expenditure required 'if health and working capacity are to be maintained'.[1] The standard allowed only for bare subsistence, taking no account of special needs, such as particularly heavy work. Seebohm Rowntree, who had experience from before the First World War in constructing 'poverty lines', claimed that in the thirties a family of five required an expenditure of 43*s*. 6*d*. exclusive of rent. Although higher than the standard he had adopted in his first survey of York in 1899, he defended it as a level of expenditure which erred on the side of stringency rather than extravagance. To live on such a standard demanded constant watchfulness and a high degree of skill on the part of the housewife. Just over three shillings was allowed for all luxuries, such as beer and tobacco, all travelling to and from work, all savings for holidays—indeed almost every item of expenditure not absolutely required to maintain the family in physical health. Rowntree declared it a 'minimum sum on which physical efficiency could be maintained ... a standard of bare *subsistence* rather than *living*'. To make the point as clear as possible he described life under the conditions imposed by his poverty line:

A family living upon the scale allowed for in this estimate must never spend a penny on railway fare or omnibus. They must never go into the country unless they walk. They must never purchase a halfpenny newspaper or spend a penny to buy a ticket for a popular concert. They must write no letters to absent children, for they cannot afford to pay the postage. They must never contribute anything to their church or chapel, or give any help to a neighbour which costs them money. They cannot save, nor can they join sick clubs or trade unions, because they cannot pay the necessary subscriptions. The children must have no pocket money for dolls, marbles or sweets. The father must smoke no tobacco, and must drink no beer. The mother must never buy any pretty clothes for herself or for her children, the character of the family wardrobe, as for the family diet, being governed by the regulation 'Nothing must be bought but that which is absolutely necessary for the maintenance of physical health, and what is bought must be of the plainest and most economical description.' Should a child fall ill, it must be attended by the parish doctor; should it die, it must be buried by the parish. Finally, the wage-earner must never be absent from his work for a single day.[2]

In 1935–6 Rowntree undertook an extensive survey of living standards in York, which repeated his study of 1899. Then he had found 43 per cent of the working class in poverty, 15·5 per cent in what he defined as 'primary poverty' with an income insufficient to provide the basic physical requirements of food and rent. The others so disposed of their income that they were left with insufficient income for the necessities of life. On the same standard as he had used in 1899, he found only 6·8 per cent in primary poverty in York in 1935–6. He had increased his minimum standard by the thirties, however, and by this standard 31·1 per cent of the working-class population, or 18 per cent of the total population, were found to be in poverty, half of them in primary poverty.[3] Similarly, *The New Survey of London Life and Labour*, published in 1934, compared the situation found by Booth in late Victorian London with that of the late 1920s. It found that poverty had been reduced by about two-thirds. In the 'Eastern Survey Area', which approximately covered the East End of London, it showed that the number of those in poverty had fallen from 700,000–800,000 people to around a quarter of a million, approximately 12 per cent of the total population of the area.[4] Herbert Tout demonstrated that even by the end of the 1930s, in a relatively prosperous town such as Bristol, where average living standards were more than twice as high as minimum needs, 10·7 per cent of families fell below the poverty line. This figure owed relatively little to the effects of unemployment, because even if full-time work had been available, three-quarters of the families would still have been in poverty.[5]

Rowntree's house-to-house surveys in York revealed the plight of many of the families suffering from the effects of primary poverty. In *Poverty and Progress* he laconically reported the conditions of life found in the poorer districts of the town:

1 bedroom and kitchen. Rent 9s. Woman aged 31, and 6 children aged 12, 10½, 8, 3½, 2½ and 7 months. Woman is separated from

her husband who is a labourer and allows her 21*s.* a week. She also receives 10*s.* from the Public Assistance Committee. Four of the children get free dinners at school. The woman has been separated from her husband for eight months, but he now visits the house and would be willing to live with his wife again if there was room. The house has been condemned and they are hoping to obtain a better one. The house is in a yard with nine others. There is no water laid on in the house, and ten families have to share two water taps and two grates in the yard. The w.c.s are about fifty yards from the houses.

2 bedrooms, living-room and scullery. Rent 4*s.* 6*d.* House scheduled for demolition. Man aged 38, wife 39, and 6 children aged 14, 12, 8, 6, 3 and 6 months. Man is off work, ill. He has had a lot of illness – fourteen weeks at one stretch. He is getting 18*s.* National Health Benefit, and 12*s.* from a sick club. The daughter, aged 14, works in a factory and earns 11*s.* The woman is £3 in arrears with rent, and is trying to pay this off at 2*s.* 6*d.* a week. She is having a terrible struggle.[6]

He also gave examples of families in 'secondary' poverty where income was in theory sufficient to meet basic needs, but was not spent in such a way as to afford them:

2 bedrooms, parlour, kitchen, and scullery. Rent 8*s.* Man aged 32, wife 29, and 7 children aged 9, 8, 7, 6, 4, 2, and 2 weeks. The man is a warehouse clerk and earns 74*s.* 10*d.* Two of the children get milk at school, for which they pay $\frac{1}{2}d.$ a day. The woman said she would let the others get milk at school if she could afford it. She looks very weak.

2 bedrooms, parlour, kitchen and scullery. Rent 8*s.* 6*d.* Man aged 37, wife 39, and 2 children aged 8 and 5. The man is a fitter and earns 55*s.* a week. The house is poorly furnished. They are paying off a heavy doctor's bill.[7]

Rowntree, like other social investigators, was alarmed to find such a high level of poverty, particularly when it was clear that there had been an advance in average standards. In particular, he noted that the results he had found could not be blamed exclusively upon the effects of the economic depression, for the worst of the depression was over by the mid-1930s and York was relatively prosperous. It was plain that the causes of poverty familiar to the pre-1914 investigators, such as old age, chronic sickness, low pay and large families, remained potent influences upon living standards in the thirties. *The New Survey of London Life and Labour* found that one of the principal causes of poverty was old age, accounting for a third of all families in poverty in the East End of London. Among the other major causes were illness of the chief wage-earner, large families and low wages.[8] Seebohm Rowntree was able to compare his findings in the mid-1930s to those of his 1899 survey. As had been the case then, poverty was often still the result of old age and inadequate wages, though unemployment was another important cause.[9] In Bristol, Tout also found that low wages, old age and unemployment accounted for almost 70 per cent of those in poverty. Tout recognised that individual circumstances crucially affected whether a family fell below the poverty line. An unemployed worker with a small family could, in theory at least, have enough income to meet basic needs, but an unemployed man with a large family of three or more would be unable to do so. Similarly, in the case of old people, Tout found that if they could not find anywhere to live rent free and had only their old age pension on which to live, they would automatically fall below the poverty line.[10] This finding was confirmed in a survey of Oxford which showed that the elderly made up the predominant claimants for public assistance.[11]

One of the most striking conclusions of the social investigators was that the proportion of children in poverty was much greater than the proportion of families in poverty. Large numbers of children were found to be in families which were below the poverty line. Tout discovered that it was children under fifteen who were the most likely age-group to suffer from poverty; he estimated that one working-class child in five in Bristol came from a home where income was insufficient to provide a minimum standard and that nine out of ten families with four or more children were below the level of sufficiency.[12] Rowntree summed up the problem of child poverty in York:

> We would be labouring under a delusion if we got into our heads the idea that only 31·1 per cent of the working class population suffer from poverty. We see that 52·5 per cent of the children under one year of age, 49·7 per cent of those over one

and under five, and 39·3 per cent of those over five and under fifteen are living below the minimum.[13]

The tangible effects of child poverty could be seen in many of the poorer areas, where children were clearly ill-clothed and undernourished. Frank Cousins reported an incident during the thirties in a transport café on the Great North Road, when he encountered a young couple with a child who were walking from South Shields to London in search of work. He reported:

> They came into the café and sat down, and they fetched a baby's feeding bottle out, and it had water in it. They fed the baby with water, and then lifted the kiddy's dress up — it was a small baby — and it had a newspaper nappy on. They took this off, and wiped the baby's bottom with it and then they picked up another newspaper and put that on for a fresh nappy.[14]

The other major group to suffer from poverty was the elderly. The introduction of old age pensions in 1908 had gone a long way to relieving the worst aspects of poverty in old age, but there remained a considerable number of old people who found it impossible to maintain a standard of living which met the minimum requirements of the social investigators. Thus while the *New Survey of London* was able to conclude that the number of old people receiving poor relief in the capital had been reduced to a quarter of the number at the end of the nineteenth century, they also found that any person of sixty-five or over living alone with no resources other than the pension would fall below the poverty line. Their investigators found that half of the old people of pensionable age living alone in the East End of London were in need of poor relief. Elderly couples usually managed to survive because of the economies they could make in fuel and light.[15] In York, Rowntree came across many examples of elderly people in poverty. Among others, he cited:

> One combined room. Rent 5s. Man aged 74, wife 70. Both receive an old age pension of 10s. and have no other source of income. The man says that though they have sons and daughters living in York, they have never been visited by them since he ceased working. He thinks this is because they are afraid they will have to assist them. Though they could do with a little poor relief, they refuse to apply to the Public Assistance Committee. They say that if their family will not voluntarily help them, they

will force them to do so by applying for relief. The wife used to do a little charing, but is now unable to go out.[16]

Moreover, the social investigators discovered that the problem of the elderly was likely to increase because of the effects of better medical care upon life expectancy. The problems created by an ageing population were already becoming evident.

Besides children and the elderly, the other groups to suffer hardship most persistently were the sick, the widowed, the low-paid and the unemployed. The latter group, however, made up the largest group of poor in only one study. The problems of the chronically sick and the families which lost their male wage-earner had changed little since the years before the First World War. Prolonged illness in a working-class family, especially a large family, meant a bitter struggle against poverty. Fenner Brockway quoted an example of a steel-worker in Sheffield who had poisoned his hands and was incapable of working. His family received a total income of 27s. 6d. with which to feed six children. Brockway commented that 'The woman is heroically trying to keep the house clean and healthy, but her task is impossible.'[17] Many widows found themselves caught in a trap so that if they earned more than a small amount, they forfeited their widow's pension. Frequently this condemned them to eking out a poverty-stricken existence on the pension or accepting low-paid, menial work. In Oxford it was recorded that widows were the most common claimants of poor relief after the elderly.[18]

That large numbers of low-paid workers fell below the poverty line had been recognised by social investigators before 1914. Rowntree found that low pay remained an almost intractable cause of poverty and was likely to remain so while wages were paid which fell below the minimum standard needed to maintain families of any size in reasonable health. He found that there was little to distinguish low-paid from hundreds of thousands of others in terms of skill and ability. Many were employed in occupations with a tradition of low wage-rates, so that even full-time working made it difficult to support a family. A large number of unskilled trades fell below what Rowntree considered as a minimum wage and he picked out the building trades, transport, and municipal and government employment as examples. Agricultural labourers were also poorly paid, with average wages which fell several shillings below Rowntree's specially adjusted poverty line for those working on the land.[19] Average earnings for many workers were below the minimum

D

standard because of short-time working resulting from the depression or a tradition of casual employment in the industry.

Thus many coal miners, cotton workers and ship-yard employees found themselves dependent upon the number of days or shifts they could work. Average wages in the coalmining industry fell below Rowntree's poverty line for most of the 1930s (see Table 3.1).

TABLE 3.1   AVERAGE WEEKLY CASH EARNINGS OF MINE WORKERS (SHILLINGS)[20]

1930	1932	1934	1936	1938
43/9	42/1	44/6	50/6	55/11

These averages concealed great regional variations, with considerably higher wages in some areas. But a combination of low rates and short-time working brought many coalmining families in less favoured areas such as South Wales, Scotland and the north-east close to, if not below, subsistence level. Instances were quoted in the House of Commons in 1931 of families with only 30*s*. a week to provide food, rent and clothing.[21] Fenner Brockway interviewed a cotton worker in Lancashire who, although both he and his wife worked, was unable to bring the family income up to a sufficient level to keep themselves and their three children adequately fed.[22] Even in the relatively prosperous sectors, such as the motor-vehicle industry, seasonal lay-offs and short-time working could push many families below the poverty line.

Women workers were paid on average only about two-thirds of male wage-rates, with the result that single or widowed women were also likely to fall below the standard of minimum needs set out by Rowntree and others. Large numbers of women in shop and office work had some of the lowest rates of pay given to any group of workers, while even as skilled workers doing the same work as men as in the textile trades, they fell below the poverty line.[23]

The problems of poverty and ill-health were closely interrelated. A persistent refrain of the social investigators in the thirties was that the survival of poverty condemned a significant portion of the population to ill-health. The various poverty lines drawn up by the social investigators were usually based upon a level of income which was necessary to maintain adequate health. Thus Rowntree wrote that any worker on his 'human needs' standard who indulged in expenditure beyond that required for his barest physical needs, did so only at the cost of his own physical efficiency and that of his family.[24] These standards were based upon what was known about the food requirements of average individuals and by the 1930s dietary knowledge was sufficiently advanced for a relatively accurate assessment to be made of the average requirements of vitamins, proteins and calories. Equipped with these objective measures of human needs, much greater attention was paid to the role of diet and nutrition in determining health. Studies of the diet of the poor revealed only too clearly that in many cases income determined diet, which in turn affected standards of health. Thus while the general health of the population in the 1930s was gradually improving, attention focused upon the areas of ill-health which remained and especially those which were associated with poverty. Undoubtedly, one of the most influential studies of the thirties was John Boyd Orr's *Food, Health and Income*, published in 1936. Using an American standard of nutritional needs, he examined the diets of over 1,000 families, divided into six income groups. He found that the lowest income group, composed of $4\frac{1}{2}$ million people when translated on to the national scale, enjoyed a diet which was inadequate in all respects. The next group of about 5 million people had a diet which was inadequate in vitamins, calories and essential minerals. Only groups five and six, representing a third of the population, enjoyed a diet which met Orr's stringent requirements. His findings showed that a tenth of the population, including a fifth of all children, were chronically ill-nourished, while a half of the population suffered from some sort of deficiency.[25]

Orr's work was strongly criticised on the grounds that he had applied too severe a standard and taken too small a sample, none the less his findings corroborated evidence gathered from other sources. An investigation in Newcastle-upon-Tyne, published in 1933, showed that at least a third of school-children from the poorer districts of the city were unhealthy or physically unfit. The results were matched with a sample of children from professional families. The comparison showed that poorer children suffered from eight times as much pneumonia, ten times as much bronchitis, and five times as much rickets.[26] A survey by Dr G. C. M. M'Gonigle in Stockton-on-Tees found that the death rate among the poorest section of the population, spending only 3s. a head on food, was twice that of the most affluent, who spent 6s. a head on food. He drew the conclusion that almost 37 per cent of all children examined showed some deviation from the normal at the time of examination and that these conditions were largely the result of poor diet and bad housing. Moreover, the situation was not confined to a few blackspots such as Tyneside. Dr M'Gonigle reported the results of a survey carried out by the school medical staffs in a number of education authorities in 1933, which found that 11·1 children in every 1,000 were suffering from malnutrition of a sufficient degree to require treatment, while a similar number required observation.[27]

The findings of John Boyd Orr and other investigators suggested that a high degree of poor nutrition and ill-health was built into the lives of the poor, especially poor children, irrespective of the effects of unemployment. The Coles summed up the most pertinent features of the situation by comparing the diet of a family of five earning the average industrial wage of £150 per year with a middle-class family earning £500–£600 per year:

> *Per head* the richer family will consume on the average 12 per cent less bread and flour and 16 per cent less potatoes than the poorer. On the other hand, it will eat nearly 36 per cent more meat, more than twice as much fish and 68 per cent more eggs; 56 per cent more butter, 38 per cent more cheese, and much more than twice as much fresh milk ... It will use nearly 20 per cent more sugar, jam and similar products, but only about half the quantity of margarine and about the same amount of tea. Finally, the richer family will eat about two-and-a-half times as much fruit as the poorer and about three times the quantity of vegetables apart from potatoes ... We have here a sharp contrast in standards of diet, not between the richest and poorest groups in the population, but between reasonably typical working-class and middle-class families of a certain size.[28]

The differences in dietary standards uncovered by the investigators were reflected in the mortality statistics for the different classes. Although there had been considerable improvement in the general level of mortality, life expectancy was still determined by social class.[29] Death rates were much higher in the poorer regions, particularly those affected by high levels of unemployment. Thus death rates were higher in Scotland, Wales and the north of England than in the south of England. Standardised death rates in England and Wales averaged 113 per 1,000 in 1937, which varied from Oxford with 80 and Cambridge at 73 to the Rhondda at 134 and Wigan at 138. Within London, the more prosperous suburbs had relatively low rates, such as Harrow at 73 and Ealing at 78, compared with the poor inner areas, such as Stepney with a death rate of 115 or Finsbury which reached 128.[30]

There was considerable concern about the infant mortality rate in the 1930s. The years since the turn of the century had shown major advances, mainly through the control of infectious diseases. None the less, epidemics of diphtheria and whooping cough still killed thousands of children each year. For Great Britain as a whole, however, the infant mortality rate had fallen from 142 per 1,000 live births in 1900–2 to 68 in 1931. By 1937 it had fallen still further to 58 per thousand.[31] Though official reports tended to regard this improvement as satisfactory, bringing the level of infant mortality near to the irreducible minimum, the social investigators found clear evidence that the infant mortality rate was still higher than in countries with a lower per capita income than Great Britain. Whereas the infant mortality rate for England and Wales averaged 57 per 1,000 live births in 1935 – the lowest figure for the 1930s – the rate in New Zealand was 32, in Australia 40, and in Sweden 47. Even in comparable environmental conditions, international comparisons did not show British experience in a very favourable light.[32] R. M. Titmuss quoted the example of Chicago, which had reduced its infant mortality rate from 74 to 38 between 1925 and 1937. In the same period, Liverpool's rate fell from 99 to 82. Within Great Britain, there were marked variations between town and country, and between different areas. Thus the south-east had an infant mortality rate of 47 in 1935, compared with 68 in the north, 63 in Wales, and 76·8 in Scotland. The rate for Greater London was 51, while that for Jarrow was 114.[33] C. E. McNally carried out a survey of the infant mortality rate in a number of towns in the period from 1928 to 1933, which found that mortality varied considerably between prosperous and poorer communities.[34]

Infant mortality was found to vary even within towns. In 1931, the rates of death from bronchitis and pneumonia for children under two years of age was 1·46 per 1,000 in Bethnal Green and 1·40 in Shoreditch, compared with 0·68 in Hampstead and 0·64 in Lewisham. Similarly, McNally found that the infant mortality rate in the poorest wards of Middlesbrough was 101 in 1932–3, compared with an average for the whole town of 87·7. The Medical Officer of Health for Birmingham in 1933 divided the city into three rings – the central wards, the middle areas, and the outer suburbs – which corresponded roughly to social strata, the poorest population living in the central, slum districts. The results are given in Table 3.2.[35]

TABLE 3.2 INFANT MORTALITY RATES IN BIRMINGHAM, 1933

	Total infantile mortality rate	Children aged 4 weeks to 1 year
Central Wards	81	50·3
Middle Ring	66	33·2
Outer Ring	59	27·6

Similar results were found by Allen Hutt in his comparison of the poorest and most prosperous wards in Manchester and Liverpool.[36] Titmuss made the obvious inference from these figures, that 'healthiness depends upon economic position'. He claimed that the figures showed that social inequalities, as measured by infant deaths, were as high as before the First World War. Eight poor children in every 1,000 died as against three of the rich, a statistic which Titmuss blamed upon differences in family income, diet, housing and medical care.[37] Nor were these isolated findings. Seebohm Rowntree had found a familiar pattern in York: the infant mortality rate was twice as high for people below the poverty line as it was for those above it. This showed, Rowntree concluded, 'how far we have to go before we establish a standard of health for the workers which could be regarded with any degree of satisfaction'.[38] The Registrar-General's *Statistical Review* very much confirmed the picture revealed by the social investigators.[39]

Just as infant mortality was regarded as a clear indication of the continued effects of poverty and social inequality, so the maternal mortality rate was also regarded with considerable concern. With some justice, for whereas there had at least been a fall in infant mortality, there was no comparable improvement in maternal mortality, which had showed little progress since 1900. Indeed, after 1925 the maternal mortality rate began to rise and reached its worst point in 1934 with 4·6 deaths per 1,000 live births in England and Wales. By 1937, however, considerable improvements had taken place, when the rate reached the lowest point ever recorded.[40] There was much debate about the reasons for the obstinate refusal of the maternal mortality rate to yield the same dramatic improvements as the infant mortality rate. Great Britain seemed to be lagging far behind much of the Continent and parts of the Empire in the quality of maternal care. A committee of the Ministry of Health which investigated the problem in 1929 concluded that half the deaths could be avoided by better ante-natal care, better training of mid-wives, improved obstetrics and antiseptic methods.[41] The Coles concluded that the rate of maternal mortality was largely governed by the adequacy of local maternity services. Although they considered a large proportion of the causes of maternal mortality could be prevented, they complained that many smaller local authorities had taken no positive steps to reduce the rate, nor had there been adequate pressure from central government.[42]

Allen Hutt compared the maternal mortality rate in depressed Lancashire with conditions during the 1920s and earlier. In Preston, he found that the period 1926–30 had an average rate of 6·32 compared with 4·51 in the period 1911–15. He wrote:

It is a staggering and infuriating reflection upon the development of capitalist society, with its boasted science and culture, in Lancashire, that the young married weaver (let us say) who leaves the mill today to be confined runs a greater risk of an agonising death in childbirth than her mother, or even her grand-mother did.[43]

The Coles added their weight to the chorus of disapproval:

It is nothing less than a scandal that amid the general improvement of mortality rates, this glaring exception has been allowed to continue ... In no respect is the contrast between rich and poor more glaring than in the degree of care and attention bestowed on the expectant and nursing mother; and in no sphere of social policy could a relatively small public expenditure in improving the service be relied on to produce larger immediate results.[44]

The dramatic improvement in the mid-1930s, however, came with economic revival. In 1936, the Midwives' Act required local authorities to provide trained personnel, while the number of ante-natal clinics in England and Wales had risen to 1,795 by 1938. A limited start was also made for the provision of cheap or free milk to expectant mothers who attended Welfare Centres. But it was not until the war that all expectant mothers were given free milk, orange juice, cod-liver oil and vitamin tablets.[45]

Great passion was generated by the issue of how much mal-nutrition existed in Britain during the 1930s. It became the focal point of a highly political debate in which the protagonists were the official spokesmen of the Ministries of Health and Education and the more avowedly left-wing writers. With the benefit of hindsight, it is clear that one of the major difficulties was the absence of reliable criteria with which to judge the extent of malnutrition and the difficulties of obtaining uniform standards. Local Medical Officers of Health could become inured to a level of poor nutrition which led them to adopt a different standard from outside investigators. D. M. Goodfellow revealed that a nationwide inquiry into malnutrition in 1937 came up with the conclusion that a prosperous suburb of London had higher levels of malnutrition than some of the poorer areas of Tyneside. Goodfellow suggested that local Medical Officers 'tend to take the general standard of their own district as "normal"'.[46] Similarly, Dr G. C. M. M'Gonigle found that the standards of assessment used in different parts of the country were at variance. He showed that in London, different proportions of children were recorded as suffering from actual or suspected malnutrition from those given free school meals, for which the qualification was supposed to be evidence of malnourishment. Examination by specialists for evidence of poor nutrition tended to reveal much higher levels of 'abnormality' than routine school examinations. Dr M'Gonigle showed that in 1932–3 special surveys in a number of areas had led to nearly 40,000 children being accorded school meals by their local authorities because they were suffering from malnutrition.[47]

None the less, the build-up of evidence over the 1930s was that a significant proportion of people was suffering from an inadequate diet and that the incidence of diseases which could be related to poor nutrition was highest among the poorer income groups. Even if John Boyd Orr had applied a high standard, his findings could not be dismissed when they were matched with the findings of other inquiries. The government itself gave tacit acknowledgment of the problem in the subsidised milk scheme for school-children in 1934 and the provision of free school meals by some local authorities. Innumerable local officials in the depressed areas were convinced that malnutrition was endemic. Increases in the incidence of rickets, tuberculosis, dental decay, and lowered resistance to epidemic disease were the usual symptoms recorded. While the precise extent of the problem could not be resolved finally because of the difficulties of measurement, the thirties saw confirmation that a problem existed. An enormous gap lay between the 4 per cent of children taking free school meals in 1938–9 and the 28·2 per cent of children whom Rowntree estimated were in families where income was below the level of human needs. Given the standards of measurement available for the period, it is impossible to reconcile these figures. Significantly, however, much legislation after 1939 was designed to extend the income, diet and health of poorer families and their children.[48]

A number of serious diseases were also found to be related to poverty. John Boyd Orr argued that the effects of poor diet could be seen in the incidence of rickets, dental decay and anaemia. Admitting that data was incomplete and that there were difficulties of diagnosis involved, he claimed none the less that 'minor degrees of rickets are still prevalent and probably more prevalent in the poorer classes'.[49] In Co. Durham, Dr G. C. M. M'Gonigle claimed that as many as 83 per cent of a sample of 2,676 children could be classified as suffering from rickets, while only 6 per cent were entirely free from the disease. Although Dr M'Gonigle's standard was unusually high – official figures, for example, recorded an incidence of under 2 per cent – there was corroborative evidence from a special examination of London school-children in 1931 in which 87·5 per cent were found to be suffering from the disease. According to this survey, the percentage of children who were free from the disease ranged from 22 per cent in the better class of school to under 9 per cent in the poorer schools.[50] John Boyd Orr found striking evidence that the incidence of anaemia was much higher among the poor than among the rich. He quoted the results of an investigation which compared poor children of pre-school age with a group of better-off children of the same age. Of the former, almost a quarter were found to be 'definitely anaemic', and of the latter group, none. Boyd Orr concluded his study by saying that rickets, dental decay and anaemia were 'fairly widespread' in the lower income groups and were caused by inadequate nutrition, in part at least the result of poverty.[51]

Probably the most feared disease of the inter-war period was tuberculosis. In fact, T.B. was on the decline. The death rate for the disease in England and Wales had fallen from 1,066 per million of the population in 1922–4 to 687 by 1937.[52] Progress, however, had been unequally distributed. As a disease which was encouraged by bad housing and inadequate diet, its incidence remained highest among the poor. The Registrar-General's *Statistical Review* found that the mortality rate varied according to social class, the upper and middle classes having only half the rate of the unskilled workers.[53] The death rate was heaviest in the blackspots of poverty, such as South Wales and the north-east. For the years 1931–5 it was found that the death rate for women aged 15 to 35 was more than twice as high in Gateshead, South Shields and Merthyr than in the rest of the country. While the death rate had fallen by about 9 per cent in the more prosperous areas of Great Britain between 1925 and 1932, it had fallen by only 5 per cent in the depressed areas.[54] In Tyneside, where rates of T.B. were particularly high, improvement had lagged behind the rest of the country. At the end of the thirties, D. M. Goodfellow compared the rates of T.B. in the area with those in England and Wales as a whole. He found that the gap between Tyneside and the rest of the country was widening rather than narrowing.[55] A special investigation of Jarrow by Dr Bradbury highlighted the problems of overcrowding and poor diet as principal factors in the incidence of the disease. As a result, many commentators were beginning to regard further improvement in the poorer areas as an economic rather than a medical problem.[56] Thus C. E. McNally wrote that prevention of the disease was impossible unless improved housing and dietary conditions could be assured; cures would remain ineffective in the long term, unless patients returned from a sanitorium to a better environment than the one they had left.[57]

The medical services available in the 1930s also drew criticism. Provision for the sick consisted of a patchwork of State intervention, voluntary contribution, private enterprise and philanthropy. The poorest could obtain free hospital treatment, but the financial implications of prolonged illness for the families of the lower income groups often discouraged early treatment. Manual workers who fell ill were usually covered by State sickness insurance which entitled them to a payment of 15s. a week. As there was no allowance for dependents, many families also paid contributions to private insurance schemes and sickness clubs. A long illness or a large family forced people to appeal to the Public Assistance Committee, whose rates of assistance were near to subsistence level. State insurance enabled those in employment to seek free advice from a doctor, but again this did not extend to dependents, who had to be covered by private arrangements. A wide range of ancillary services were only available through the payment of fees. Preventive dentistry was virtually unknown in the poorer income groups and opticians' fees were beyond the reach of many families too. The supply of maternity services was also on a voluntary basis and maternity homes were generally only available to those who could afford fees. As a result, relatively few births took place in maternity homes and hospitals, a factor which helped to contribute to the high rate of maternal mortality. The health services tended to reflect differences of income, class and region, often leaving the most needy inadequately served.[58]

Although the thirties witnessed important advances in public and private housing, poor housing remained one of the most pressing social issues of the decade. The principal problems derived from a net shortage of houses at the beginning of the decade which was being exacerbated by a trend towards a larger number of separate family units. Housebuilding had lagged behind demand for decades, in spite of local and central government attempts to remedy the situation. The main result was overcrowding, compounded by the poor condition of much of the older housing stock, producing problems of disease, damp and vermin. In 1935 it was estimated that approximately 12 per cent of the population lived at a density of more than two persons per room, in what was officially regarded as overcrowded conditions. Inner London had one of the worst problems: a survey in 1933 revealed that almost half a million people in the capital were living in overcrowded conditions. Almost half the families in Islington, Finsbury and Shoreditch were living at a level of three or more families per house, in houses which usually consisted of four or five small rooms. In Finsbury 60 per cent of families were living in one or two rooms; Stepney had over 50,000 people living two or more to a room, while 16,000 lived three or more to a room. One four-roomed house in Shoreditch was found in a survey to contain thirteen occupants. Two of the rooms were taken by couples without children, while the other two were occupied by families. One consisted of a woman, a boy of sixteen and a girl of four who shared a small bed. The other family consisted of six people, including three small children. The room was described as 'terribly verminous, dilapidated, and damp; it is often smelly, and the roof leaks over the bed, though it has recently been mended'.[59]

Outside London, almost every large town or city had its areas of old, overcrowded housing. The six most overcrowded boroughs in England and Wales were in the north-east. In Co. Durham 20 per cent of the population, a quarter of a million people, lived in overcrowded conditions. Liverpool had some of the worst slums in the country. Some 89,000 people lived at a density of two or more to a room, while 20,000 people lived three or more to a room. The central wards of St Anne's and Exchange had the worst housing. In St Anne's 42 per cent of families lived more than four families to a house. The *Social Survey of Merseyside* commented:

Many of the larger houses in St Anne's ward go back to the
late eighteenth century, when they were the dwellings of prosperous merchants. Now they make slums even more deplorable
than the back-to-back cottage, each room sub-let to a separate
family, dilapidated and comfortless, lacking sanitary con-
veniences and even taps and sinks, nearly every family dependent
for its cooking and heating of water on an incredibly unsuitable
fire-grate.[60]

In 1932 there were still a hundred families in Liverpool living in
cellars of the type condemned by Engels in the middle of the nineteenth century. Over a thousand houses remained in eighteenth-
century courts which, though structurally unsound and in 'serious
danger of collapse', coud not be evacuated because of a shortage
of alternative accommodation for the inhabitants.[61] The other
major conurbations had their share of people living in overcrowded
conditions: 68,000 in Birmingham, 49,000 in Manchester, 41,000 in
Sheffield, and 28,000 in Leeds. Scotland suffered from severe overcrowding more than England and Wales. In Glasgow 200,000 people
lived more than three to a room, many of them in the tenement
blocks of the dockside areas.[62]

The classic slum was well defined by the thirties. Sir Ernest Simon
quoted the dictionary definition of the slum as 'a fully populated
neighbourhood where the houses and conditions of life are of a
squalid and wretched character'.[63] Over half a million houses in the
major conurbations were condemned as unfit for human habitation.
Many of these were back-to-backs which had been due for clearance
before the First World War. Birmingham alone had 40,000 back-to-
backs, built at a very high density with outside toilets and water
supply. Areas of squalid housing, rotting with damp and infested
with vermin, sprawled over the whole country. In South Wales,
Allen Hutt quoted the Medical Officer of Health in Swansea who
condemned all the pre-1914 housing in the town as 'unsatisfactory
in one respect or another ... the prevailing defects are decrepitude,
dis-repair, lack of damp-proof courses, smallness of rooms, low
bedrooms, small windows, narrow staircases, and lack of amenities'.
Hutt gave an example of a family in Dowlais living in a house which
had been unrepaired for fourteen years. The windows failed to shut
tight and the house was damp. The lavatory was 30 yards away and
two families shared a water-tap in the yard.[64]

In Manchester, Sir Ernest Simon described conditions he had

found in one house in the slum district of Angel Meadow:

> No. 4, F Street. The general appearance and condition of this house inside are very miserable. It is a dark house and the plaster on the passage walls, in particular, was in a bad condition. There is no sink or tap in the house; they are in the small yard, consequently in frosty weather the family is without water. In this house live a man and wife, and seven children, ranging from 15 to 1, and a large, if varying, number of rats.[65]

Commenting upon the area as a whole, he wrote:

> Throughout the areas covered by the surveys, dampness, leaking roofs, peeling plaster, and general dilapidation were so common as to be almost the rule; the same can be said regarding infestation with bugs, which is a normal feature of slum houses and which is practically impossible to deal with in a house which has been infested for years.[66]

Descriptions such as these were not an exception in the social investigations of the thirties. Little special pleading was required to show that housing in many urban areas was grossly inadequate. The countryside fared little better. Over 4,000 parishes in England and Wales lacked a piped water supply and over 100,000 cottages were condemned as unfit dwellings.[67]

Sir Ernest Simon drew up his own order of priorities for dealing with the slum problem, suggesting the need to 'Get the children out of the slums.'[68] In London two investigators argued that: 'Old people can well be left in the slums longer than those with young families ... They have lived in worse conditions and will take no great harm from spending the last of their days there.' On the other hand, they claimed, 'All the clinics in the world will not undo the evil wrought by keeping a child for a few seasons in a slum.'[69] Several writers saw rehousing as only part of the solution. A number were concerned that the new council houses had higher rents than the slum properties and this could lead to a decline in living standards. Among some of the poorer families in London, it was found that a lower proportion of money was spent on food as a result of the need to find higher rents. Alternatively, the poorer inhabitants drifted back to the slum areas. The Coles argued that:

> Even if a million homes are built in the next few years, that will not prevent overcrowding unless the poorer families are able to

support a higher standard of life. Moreover, even if the poor were forcibly prevented from huddling too closely together, without their income being raised, the consequence would be mainly to aggravate the evils of malnutrition — to shift the incidence of poverty from housing to the food budget, and thereby probably make matters even worse than before.

The Coles also argued that the new housing often made greater demands upon the poorer households because of the cost of travel to and from work, the need to 'keep up appearances', and the absence of the old sense of communities. With considerable prescience, the Coles foresaw the problems of creating bleak, utilitarian estates on the fringes of the great conurbations, ill-served by community facilities, shops and local transport.[70] By the outbreak of the Second World War, opinion was still sharply divided between writers such as Sir Ernest Simon and Seebohm Rowntree who, while not blind to the faults of the new estates, regarded them as a major step forward not only in curing the evils of ill-housing, but also in turning the slum tenant into a decent citizen, and commentators like the Coles who saw slum clearance as an attack upon the symptoms rather than the causes of poverty.[71]

Apart from unemployment, the issues of poverty, ill-health and bad housing dominated social concern in the inter-war period. Although all three could be related to unemployment, they were problems which pre-existed unemployment and were usually aggravated by unemployment rather than caused by it. The social investigators demonstrated clearly that a considerable portion of the population was condemned to live in poverty, ill-health and poor housing, whatever the passing movements of the trade cycle or the short-term policies of the government. One of the major reasons for conducting social investigations in the thirties was the attempt to discover how far Great Britain had progressed towards the elimination of poverty, malnutrition and other social evils. In almost every case, similar conclusions were reached by the more objective commentators. They showed that the average level of living standards, health and housing had improved. The major concern was whether progress had been sufficiently rapid and whether with existing policies and techniques the current residue of problems would be reduced in the foreseeable future. Thus the Coles were in no doubt when concluding *The Condition of Britain* that they had found 'incontestable proof of the continued existence of "two nations" '. On the other hand, they were forced to admit that 'the main body of the working classes is absolutely a good deal better off today in terms of material goods ...' As far as poverty was concerned, they applied a relative standard:

> Doubtless poverty used to be worse than it is now, for the majority of the people. But poverty has to be judged by a relative rather than an absolute standard. A people is poor whenever it is poorer than it needs to be, in view of the national capacity for the production of wealth. By that standard, Britain today is poorer than China. It is wasting far more resources which it possesses all the ability to use.[72]

While alone the Coles' arguments might have been regarded as special pleading—they were avowedly political writers—their comments were supported by other social investigators. Thus the *New Survey of London* recorded that the percentage of people in poverty in the early 1930s was only a third of that found in Charles Booth's surveys. Though this was an 'immense reduction', the authors of the *Survey* argued that the reduction of poverty was 'hardly as great' as might have been expected from the rate of average improvement. Thus they concluded:

> It is quite satisfactory from the Street Survey that the level of poverty in East London is now only about one-third as high as in Charles Booth's time. It is much less satisfactory to learn that in spite of this shrinkage there are still more than a quarter of a million persons living below the poverty line. When we consider how very low and bare is the minimum standard of subsistence which marks the Booth poverty line, it is impossible to rest content with a condition of things under which one in ten of all the human beings in the Eastern Survey area are living below this level.[73]

Seebohm Rowntree was in a particularly strong position to put the state of the nation in perspective with the benefit of his two surveys of York, separated by almost forty years. Thus he wrote in 1941:

> The economic condition of the workers is better by 30 per cent than in 1899, though working hours are shorter. Housing is immeasurably better, health is better, education is better. Cheap means of transport, the provision of public libraries and cheap books, the wireless, the cinema and other places of entertain-

ment, have placed within the reach of everyone forms of recreation unknown, and some of them unthought of, forty years ago. It is gratifying that so much progress has been achieved, but if instead of looking backward we look forward, then we see how far the standard of living of many workers falls short of any standard which could be regarded, even for the time being, as satisfactory. Great though the progress mau. during the last forty years has been, there is no cause for satisfacu.n in the fact that in a country so rich as England, over 30 per cent of the workers in a typical provincial city should have incomes so small that it is beyond their means to live even at the stringently economical level adopted as a minimum in this survey, nor in the fact that almost half the children of working-class parents spend the first five years of their lives in poverty and that almost a third of them live below the poverty line for ten years or more.[74]

Similarly, in the field of public health, the findings of the social investigators were that there had been a broad general improvement in health which had continued into the 1930s. There were areas where improvement had not taken place, such as maternal mortality, and areas where the onset of the worst years of the depression had slowed down the rate of progress, as in the fields of infant mortality and tuberculosis. None the less, even these were beginning to show improvement in the years immediately before the war. Poverty, poor nutrition and bad health had been shown to be closely related factors. Even John Boyd Orr, who had produced some of the most damning evidence that the poorer income groups had a diet which was inadequate to maintain health, was moved to conclude that conditions were much better than they had ever been before. Thus he wrote in the conclusion of *Food, Health and Income*, 'Bad as the picture is, however, it is better than any picture which could have been drawn in the past — much brighter than the picture of pre-war days.'[75] As with the writers on poverty, the real complaint was that further improvements lay within reach. An improved level of public health depended upon a better diet, which in turn demanded higher incomes.

During the 1930s the issues of poverty, ill-health and bad housing were highly politicised. Many writers were critical of the complacency which they felt was representative of the government in the face of serious social problems. In retrospect, however, it is plain that the truth lay somewhere between the claims of the major protagonists, so far as generalisation is possible. The official line on poverty and ill-health could often be regarded as complacent, but central government was almost entirely dependent upon the reports of local officials. One of the points which these debates made plain was the difficulty of obtaining objective criteria for poverty, malnutrition, overcrowding, and so on. As a result, a great deal of time and energy was spent by the serious social writers in establishing the standards by which they judged social conditions. Although some of the more polemical writers could be disregarded, because they took too small a sample, mistook short-term fluctuations for general trends, or based their generalisations upon rather impressionistic evidence, the findings of men of the calibre of Seebohm Rowntree, Herbert Tout, John Boyd Orr and the other more academic investigators could hardly be regarded in the same way. The concern to establish scientific criteria by which to study social conditions was a major part of their work and their findings were based upon a statistical appreciation of specific groups or areas. Rowntree, for example, based his information about York upon a detailed house-to-house survey of 16,362 families.[76] The conclusions of these investigators could not easily be disregarded. Naturally, there were errors and difficulties of interpretation, but the conclusions of the inquiries of the 1930s pointed clearly to the survival of major social problems.

E

IV

The Problem of Unemployment

From the collapse of the post-war boom in 1921 until the first year of the Second World War, Great Britain suffered unemployment on an unprecedented scale, with never less than a million people out of work. Depression during the 1920s gave way to the slump which followed the Wall Street crash of 1929. Britain's worst years were experienced in the aftermath of the financial and political crisis of August 1931. From 1931 until 1935, the number of unemployed never fell below 2 million people and in the winter of 1932–3 reached its highest point at just under 3 million. Moreover, as the official figures were based upon insured workers, they excluded categories such as the self-employed, agricultural workers, and married women who did not sign on for the dole. As a result the total of unemployed was almost certainly higher than official figures suggested.[1]

The problem of unemployment derived in large part from the structural problems of Britain's major export industries. Before 1914, coalmining, textiles, iron and steel, and shipbuilding had provided almost three-quarters of the country's exports, accounted for half of national production, and employed a quarter of the working population. After the First World War, however, these industries suffered severe dislocation and contraction, bringing with them the hardships of mass unemployment. The war resulted in the loss of markets to industrial rivals such as Japan and the United States, reducing demand for British goods. A declining level of world trade, an over-valued currency, as well as weaknesses in finance, management and labour relations, contributed to depression in the industries which had once assured Great Britain dominance.[2] Production in the staple industries was in decline by the early 1920s. Exports of cotton textiles in 1922 were less than half the 1913 figure; coal production in 1921 was 40 million tons below the 1913 figure and exports were only a third of the pre-war level. In the iron and steel industry, there was serious over-capacity for post-war conditions; by 1925 Britain was using only about half of her iron- and steel-making capacity. Shipbuilding never recaptured the prosperity of the years before 1914. Apart from a boom year in 1920, when shipping stocks were built up after the destruction of the war, the industry consistently fell below the level of tonnage launched in the years before the First World War. In 1921, shipping launched totalled only 1·1 million tons compared with 1·93 million tons in 1913. Even in the more prosperous years at the end of the twenties, the industry was building only three-quarters of the average tonnage completed in 1911–13.[3]

Employment figures showed the crisis in the heavy industries during the 1920s. By 1929 the number of coal miners had fallen by a fifth from pre-war totals. The number employed in shipbuilding fell by a similar proportion and this pattern was repeated in textiles and the iron and steel industry. The traditional centres of heavy industry were already marked by large-scale unemployment even before the world crisis of 1929–31. By 1929, a quarter of all coal miners were unemployed and a similar percentage of iron- and steel-workers. Almost one cotton worker in two was out of a job and almost one in three in the shipbuilding industry.[4] How concentrated the unemployment problem was in particular industries can be seen from the Pilgrim Trust's estimate that of a total of 53,000 men who had been out of work for more than a year in 1929, 38,000 were coal miners. They concluded that long-term unemployment was 'mainly a localised abnormality of coalmining districts dependent on mines abandoned or permanently closed'.[5] Thus a pattern was emerging clearly during the 1920s of 'depressed areas' based upon the regions where heavy industry was situated. By 1929, the level of unemployment was two or three times higher in the old industrial areas than in London and the Midlands, where new industries had already begun to develop.

It was Britain's once-powerful export industries which were hardest hit by the worst of the depression from 1929. Steel production fell from 9·6 million tons in 1929 to 5·2 million tons in 1931. The shipbuilding industry, which had managed to complete at least a million tons of shipping each year in the 1920s, launched only 133,000 tons in 1933. Coal output fell, from 257 million tons in 1929 to 207 million tons in 1933. Cotton exports were reduced by more than half between 1929 and 1931, while by 1930 total output had fallen to under half the figure for 1912–13.[6] Virtually no industry was left untouched by the depression in the early 1930s, which at the peak left a quarter of the insured population out of work. None the less, the worst effects of the slump were felt in the industries which had already been struggling during the 1920s and they retained a high level of unemployment when the economy as a whole entered a more prosperous phase after 1933. Thus the percentage of unemployed in the 'ailing giants' was consistently above the average level for industry as a whole.[7]

Unemployment in the 1920s was a regional problem, affecting most acutely the areas dependent upon the declining export industries. Although all regions were affected in the trough of the depression, by the middle and late 1930s unemployment had reverted to the pattern of the previous decade. This was recognised in 1934 by the creation of the Special Areas which were to receive government assistance. The areas were South Wales, Tyneside, West Cumberland and industrial Scotland. These did not necessarily define the worst affected areas of the country. Northern Ireland, for example, had the highest percentage of unemployment in the United Kingdom, but was considered to be beyond the scope of legislation at Westminster. Other areas had too varied a pattern of employment to give the whole region 'special' status and were left to fend for themselves. There was a striking disparity between the unemployment rates of the more prosperous southern half of England and the regions of the west and the north.[8] Out of 1,717,000 registered unemployed in July 1936, over two-thirds were to be found in Scotland, Wales, Northern Ireland and northern England. The northern districts alone accounted for almost three-quarters of a million and Scotland over a quarter of a million, many of them long-term unemployed.[9]

Within the depressed areas, there were wide variations of experience, depending upon the industrial complexion of the area and changing circumstances. In South Wales, for example, some areas had very high unemployment rates. In 1934, 74 per cent of male workers were unemployed in Brynmawr, 73 per cent in Dowlais and 62 per cent in Merthyr. Conditions, however, were less severe in the coastal towns of South Wales and the eastern half of the coalfield suffered more than the anthracite and tinplate districts of the west: the coal industry accounted for 45·6 per cent of insured workers in 1929 and 37·1 per cent in 1935 when the worst of the depression was over. It also provided the highest percentage of unemployed. Unemployment among coal miners reached 42·4 per cent in 1932 and was still 34·4 per cent in 1935. In 1932 85,600 miners were out of work in South Wales and in 1935 the figure still stood at 55,105. The western valleys of Neath, Swansea and Amman maintained a higher level of employment than the rest of the region, although even here the lowest level of unemployment was 22 per cent in 1931. By 1935, some areas of the coalfield had the relatively low level of 13–15 per cent unemployment. The worst affected areas were the mining towns of the inland valleys, such as Merthyr, Rhondda and Aberdare. These three valleys accounted for over half the total of unemployed between 1931 and 1935 in South Wales. In the Merthyr and Rhondda valleys, unemployment was actually higher among coal miners in 1935 than in 1931. In 1935 45·6 per cent of miners in Rhondda and 51·5 per cent in Merthyr were out of work.[10]

But while there were great variations even in the most depressed areas, the greatest disparity existed between the relatively prosperous towns of southern England and the depressed areas (see Table 4.1).

TABLE 4.1   PERCENTAGE OF INSURED WORKERS UNEMPLOYED IN
VARIOUS TOWNS IN 1934[11]

Jarrow	67·8	Coventry	5·1
Maryport	57·0	Oxford	5·1
Merthyr	61·9	Luton	7·7
Motherwell	37·4	St Albans	3·9

Thus whereas Glasgow had a total of 89,600 unemployed in 1936, Birmingham, a city of comparable size, had only 21,000. Similarly, Brighton had only 3,000 unemployed compared with Oldham's 15,000. As the thirties wore on, the contrast between the reviving industries of the southern half of England and the depressed areas tended to grow. Though the absolute level of unemployment fell in many of the depressed areas, the gap between them and the more prosperous regions tended to widen. The Pilgrim Trust investigators studied six communities: Rhondda Urban District, Crook in Co. Durham, Blackburn, Leicester, Deptford and Liverpool. In Deptford they found only 7 per cent of the industrial population unemployed, while in the Rhondda Urban District the figure was 35 per cent. They concluded that there were two major differences between the depressed areas and the more prosperous regions; not only were the numbers of unemployed greater, but there were more long-unemployed. In towns of the same size in 1936, the number of long-term unemployed was seventy times greater in the depressed areas than in the more prosperous.[12]

Unemployment had a variety of meanings. It included those temporarily stopped from work because of seasonal fluctuations in trade or the casual nature of their work. In the 1930s unemployment took on a new aspect with the growth of long unemployment, usually defined as more than twelve months continuously out of work. The number of long-unemployed rose throughout the depression, from 5 per cent of the total in 1929, representing 53,000 unemployed, to 10 per cent in 1932, representing 300,000 unemployed. Long unemployment reached its highest absolute total in July 1933, when there were almost half a million men who had not worked in the past twelve months, out of a total of $2\frac{1}{2}$ million unemployed. The number of long-unemployed, however, failed to fall as rapidly as the overall total of unemployed after 1933. The proportion of long-unemployed to the total was as high in 1935–6 as it had been in 1932–3.[13] Indeed, by 1937, the proportion was actually rising. As revival spread through British industry in the middle and late 1930s, long-unemployment and short-term unemployment tended to predominate. The latter reflected a return to normal conditions in which there was a large amount of casual and part-time working. The survival of long unemployment, on the other hand, reflected the creation of a new phenomenon, a seemingly intractable problem of men who had been out of work for twelve months or more, and might never work again.

The Pilgrim Trust found that the long-unemployed were concentrated disproportionately in the most depressed areas. In Deptford, they found that 62 per cent of those out of work in 1932 had found a job by 1936. In Liverpool the figure was 29 per cent, and in Rhondda U.D. 23 per cent. Thus they concluded, 'As the queues [of unemployed] become longer, at the same time their composition changes.'[14] The regional figures showed a similar tendency for the depressed areas to suffer disproportionately from long unemployment.[15] Given the regional distribution of the long-unemployed, it was hardly surprising that they predominated in the depressed export industries upon which these regions depended for their livelihood. Their numbers were greatest in coalmining, shipbuilding, the iron and steel industry, and cotton textiles. Also high on the list of long unemployment were pottery workers and seamen. The Pilgrim Trust investigators found 52,000 men in 1936 who had been out of work for over five years and 205,000 who had been out of work for two or more. In Crook Town they found that nearly three-quarters of the unemployed had been out of work for over five years.[16]

Earlier studies of unemployment had shown that youths and older men were particularly susceptible to unemployment. The problem for younger men was that they were often employed at low wages until the age of 18 or 21 and then thrown out of work when they would have to be paid the full rate. This was especially true of industries such as coalmining and textiles, where cost-cutting had become necessary for survival. Both in South Wales and in Lancashire, innumerable examples were found of this process. In the textile districts of Lancashire and Yorkshire, there was a keen demand for young boys and girls, who were dismissed when they had worked for three or four years. A report on Lancashire commented, 'It is a striking and deplorable fact that very large numbers of children continue to enter the cotton industry in areas in which that industry is overcrowded.'[17] John Gollan, writing on the problem of juvenile unemployment, commented that: 'The chief characteristic of juvenile unemployment is its concentration in the depressed areas, the staple industries of which ... can no longer offer progressive employment, and which, when recruiting new labour, do so rather to decrease labour costs than to increase production.'[18] The tendency for school-leavers to enter dead-end occupations with little prospect of employment after the age of 21 was also recorded by the Save the Children Fund. 'All reports', they claimed, 'refer to the very large amount of "blind alley" juvenile occupation and of the tendency of the juvenile population to drift into such employments.'[19] The Carnegie Trust reported that the annual fraction of time spent unemployed increased with each year up to the age of 24, when almost two-thirds of the year was spent out of work. They found that the year of maximum employment was 15 in Glasgow and Cardiff, and 16 in Liverpool.[20]

In some areas there was virtually no work at all for school-leavers. The position was particularly bleak in the areas with a limited range of depressed industries, offering few enough openings for experienced men, still less the inexperienced boy from school. A study of South Wales in 1934 found that 30 per cent of boys and 40 per cent of girls were unemployed four months after leaving school. In the worst district, Ebbw Vale, the figure for boys was 56·6 per cent. Fenner Brockway reported that in Merthyr and Dowlais in

1931, 697 fresh applications had been received at the Labour Exchange from school-leavers. Twelve months later, only 143 were found jobs, 88 locally and 55 elsewhere.[21] In Lancashire, Jewkes and Winterbottom found in 1932 that 22 per cent of boys and 18 per cent of girls were out of work three months after leaving school. By 1936, the revival of industry had begun to affect the overall total of young people out of work.[22] The Coles recorded that the younger age group had benefited more than the older unemployed. The age group between 18 and 24 now had the lowest proportion of unemployed for their share of the labour force.[23]

The older age groups were worst affected by unemployment. The Coles found that the percentage of unemployment rose consistently with age, with those in the 55–65 age group suffering most. Although they made up only 12 per cent of the male labour force in 1936, they accounted for 18·4 per cent of the unemployed. In addition, it was the older unemployed who found it hardest to obtain work in the revival of the middle and late 1930s. The result was that an increasing percentage of the unemployed were older men – the dole queue grew older as it grew shorter. Thus by 1936 over a third of the unemployed were between 45 and 65. Many of these men had worked in the heavy industries, but were prevented by family responsibilities from moving to new areas to find work. The effect was to create the problem of long-unemployed, older workers, who had virtually no chance of ever working again. By the mid-1930s, more than a tenth of unemployed workers aged 60–4 had been out of work for more than a year, compared with only 3 per cent among the 25–34 age group. Over two-thirds of all long-unemployed workers were aged between 45 and 65, although they made up only a third of the unemployed as a whole. Even in the more prosperous areas, it was found that the older men had a much greater chance of being unemployed.[24]

Faced with a problem of these dimensions, government policy operated on two different levels. On the one hand, there was the budgetary, or financial policy through which the government hoped to restore business confidence, revive trade and reduce the level of unemployment. Beyond this, and largely dictated by it, were the various ameliorative policies which government offered to the unemployed. These included policies for public works, the transference of workers and special assistance, as well as unemployment relief and welfare work. The two levels were obviously closely connected. The Labour Government of 1929–31 was forced to resign when the financial and budgetary policy imposed upon it by the business community came into conflict with its commitment to a comparatively high level of unemployment relief. The National Government, on the other hand, subordinated itself to a long-term policy of restoring business confidence by strictly orthodox budgetary and financial measures. These dictated its attitude to the second tier of unemployment policy. Priority was given to the need for economy, balanced budgets, and cautious financial policy. Schemes for assistance to the depressed areas and the system of unemployment relief were subject to the constraints of this strategy.

The response of the Labour Government to the world economic crisis has been frequently discussed.[25] The weakness of a minority government, inexperienced in matters of international finance, was revealed when the financial crisis came to a head in 1931. More fundamentally, there were also serious ideological difficulties for a socialist party operating in a capitalist system; policies of nationalisation and massive public works were prohibited by the need to secure international approval by reducing the budgetary deficit. Thus Robert Skidelsky has argued that the Labour Government of 1929–31 lacked a coherent policy and was faced in 1931 with a conflict between its ideological preferences and the economic realities of the situation in which it operated.[26] The Labour Government was forced to resign when the demands for a deflationary policy, through heavy cuts in government expenditure including substantial cuts in unemployment relief, divided the Cabinet. Recent work has suggested that this division was made insoluble by the pressure of the unions upon the parliamentary Labour Party for a maintenance of relief levels.[27]

The rump of the Labour administration led by Ramsay Mac-Donald joined with the Conservatives to establish the National Government on 24 August. It almost immediately introduced emergency measures to raise extra taxation and make economies on the lines recommended by the May Committee. In September the National Government was forced to abandon the Gold Standard and devalue the pound. Almost from that point, during the period of the National and Conservative administrations, economic orthodoxy dictated the attitude of the government towards unemployment. The main objectives of government were to balance budgets and restore business confidence, a view which was shared by the great majority of economists and Treasury advisers. High expenditure by government was regarded as a wasteful use of resources and the concept of heavy borrowing and deficit financing appeared wildly unorthodox. This policy of economy and balanced budgets essentially ruled out any major initiatives to cure mass unemployment. Keynesian ideas still lay outside the view of most politicians, although Lloyd George and Mosley were prepared to implement policies along these lines. Such views, however, found little favour with the economic experts or with the leaders of the National Government. Nor were clear lessons available in international experience during the thirties. The two economies which seemed to have waged the most successful war on mass unemployment were totalitarian regimes, Germany and the Soviet Union. Other countries which tried new policies, such as the New Deal in America, were not conspicuously successful in reducing the level of unemployment faster than Great Britain.[28] Thus in the absence of an alternative which seemed acceptable for Britain, the government stuck to its course of deflation, economy and a balanced budget. Fatalism and 'making the best of things' were attitudes which affected the government as much as the unemployed, forcing Chamberlain to announce in his budget speech of 1933 that Britain was likely to suffer from heavy unemployment for another ten years.[29]

The National Government has been the whipping-boy of successive writers, who have judged its failures in terms of post-war prosperity and reference, often misleading, to the experience of other countries. Britain's unemployment problem, particularly in the depressed areas, was a result of structural weaknesses, as much as of the downturn in world trade. The solution would have required large-scale changes in the pattern of industrial and social investment. The years of rearmament and war postponed a solution of these difficulties, which were to remain a feature of post-war Britain. It is a harsh judgment which condemns the National Government for failing to alter the regional imbalance of unemployment at a time of worldwide recession, when the problem still remains after thirty-five years of affluence. In addition, the international economic structure within which the government operated was very rudimentary and offered far less room to manœuvre than existed after 1945. The State played a less active role in the economy, its budgets were relatively small and its instruments of intervention were fewer. There was no tradition in peace-time of a British government interfering with the operation of industry at large. None the less, the 1930s did see some movement in the direction of rationalisation and short-term planning. Middle opinion moved steadily towards the need for a degree of reorganisation in British industry as part of an attempt to slim down capacity in the old staples. Although this had benefits in terms of efficiency and profitability, it reduced rather than created employment.[30]

The implications of this highly conservative policy were seen most clearly in the National Government's attitude to public works. The Labour Government had spent almost £77 million on public works through grants to the Unemployment Grants Committee. It has been calculated that a maximum of 60,000 men worked on these schemes in 1931 and taken with unassisted local authority schemes they provided work for no more than 130,900 people at their peak. The government, however, wound up its grants for public works in 1931–2 and most local authorities were forced to economise on relief expenditure during the worst years of the slump.[31] The reasoning behind the government's policy of curtailing public works at the trough of the depression was revealed in Cabinet discussions in 1932. A memorandum on unemployment submitted to the Cabinet emphasised the 'grave danger to the stability and prosperity of the country', but committed itself only to pursuing voluntary schemes which involved 'little capital cost to the nation'. The Cabinet proceedings recorded the opinion that:

> most of those who had been in office during the last five years were agreed that, whatever the past attractions of a public works policy, its application had been in many cases ill considered and its disadvantages now far outweighed such advantages as it might once have possessed.

They continued, 'Experience has taught us that they (relief works do less good in the direct provision of work than harm in the in) direct increase of unemployment by depleting the resources of the country which are needed for industrial restoration.' An allotment scheme undertaken with the help of the Society of Friends, physical education for men and training in domestic service for women were seen as the only positive measures that could be taken. It was suggested that voluntary agencies should concentrate upon teaching the unemployed clothing repairs, handicrafts, gardening and other useful occupations.[32]

The one initiative of the National Government concerning the unemployed was the Special Areas (Development and Improvement) Act, 1934. It was increasingly apparent that the problem of the older industrial areas would not be solved by a mere upturn in world trade. In 1932 industrial surveys were made by universities of some of the most depressed areas and published by the Board of Trade. They concluded that the collapse of export markets and the exhaustion of local resources were such that there was little hope of revival in staple industries on a sufficient scale to employ the resident labour force. No action was taken for two years. But in 1934 the government was under increasing pressure to do something about the problems of the worst affected areas. As a result the government appointed four special investigators to examine conditions in Scotland, west Cumberland, Durham and Tyneside, and South Wales. Their reports confirmed the picture shown by the Board of Trade studies. In spite of the revival which was beginning to be felt in the south-east and the Midlands, these areas were still suffering from massive unemployment. Some areas of South Wales were described by Sir Wyndham Portal as 'derelict'; while Sir Arthur Rose calculated that the depressed areas of Scotland had a permanent 'surplus' of 64,000 men.[33]

The Depressed Areas Bill was introduced into parliament in November 1934. It proposed two full-time, unpaid Commissioners for the areas, one to take charge of those in England and Wales and the other to supervise Scotland. A grant of £2 million was initially allocated to them for their work. Their powers, like their finances, were strictly limited; they could not supplement state unemployment benefits, add to grants from other departments, or aid firms working for profit. From the outset, these provisions were attacked. Lloyd George commented:

> The age of miracles is past. You cannot feed the multitude with two Commissioners and five sub-Commissioners. The new Commissioners are being sent on their apostolic mission, not without purse and scrip, but pretty nearly that – just with a little bit of cash to deal with a problem costing £100,000,000 a year.[34]

Aneurin Bevan described the measure as 'an idle and empty farce', while the Lord Mayor of Newcastle described it as 'a mere flea-bite and a sop'. Nor was opposition confined to Labour and Liberal supporters. Harold Macmillan also criticised the bill for its cautious approach. Nevertheless, the Act received the Royal assent on 24 December, though its name was modified from the Depressed Areas Act to the Special Areas Act in the House of Lords. According to the *Manchester Guardian's* political correspondent, opinion in the government was divided between those who saw it as a 'flexible and unconventional' response to the depressed areas, while others saw it as 'a good and inexpensive way of evading the question'.[35]

Under the Act as it was implemented from 1934, grants were given to local authorities and to voluntary agencies, such as the National Council of Social Service, to initiate improvement schemes for water supply and sanitation, hospital building and other amenities. Assistance was also to be given to land resettlement schemes. Though help was given to some larger projects, such as the location of a new steel works in Ebbw Vale, there remained a widespread feeling that the funds and powers of the Commissioners were inadequate for the purpose. By 1938, the Commissioners had actually spent about £8·5 million, but only 121 new firms had been set up, creating 14,900 jobs. When he resigned as Commissioner in November 1936, Sir Malcolm Stewart admitted that 'no appreciable reduction of the number of unemployed has been effected'.[36] Eventually the government did extend the powers of the Commissioners by the Special Areas (Amendment) Act, 1937, to allow them to remit rates, rent and taxes for firms settling in the Special Areas. Trading estates were set up with all facilities laid on and in which firms could lease premises. Those at Treforest in South Wales, Team Valley near Gateshead, and North Hillington near Glasgow provided work for over 5,000 people by the outbreak of the war. None the less, fewer than 50,000 new jobs were created under the Special Areas legislation. Many areas, such as Lancashire, were left outside the scope of the legislation and the policy had more of an air of expediency than of a well-considered and whole-hearted attempt to solve the problems of the depressed areas.[37]

The second Labour Government inherited an industrial transfer programme inaugurated by the Ministry of Labour in 1928. The scheme aimed to give financial assistance for the transfer of people from the depressed areas to more prosperous regions. Training centres were established to give the adult unemployed new skills and there were also separate Juvenile Instruction Centres. Between 1929 and 1938, the centres handled over 70,000 men of whom 63,000 found work. Another 100,000 were covered by centres in the depressed areas which were intended to restore morale and fitness to the long-unemployed. It has been calculated that a third of the latter received employment by 1938. Between 1928 and 1937 190,000 people were assisted to transfer to other areas, of whom over a quarter eventually returned to their home area.[38] Transference was a natural corollary of the National Government's policy, easing the flow of labour from areas where it was not required to the regions where industry was more buoyant. The policy was adopted by the Commissioners for the Special Areas. Sir Malcolm Stewart wrote:

> Transference of individuals and families out of the Special Areas must in my view be regarded as one of the essential measures of relief. My policy is, therefore, aimed at making clear the desirability of encouraging the younger persons to take every opportunity of obtaining employment outside the areas.[39]

In the six years 1927–33, almost 20,000 juveniles under the age of 18 were transferred from the depressed areas. Almost the same number were transferred in the three years 1934–6, reaching a peak in 1936 when 16,000 juveniles were involved. The effects of transference can, however, be exaggerated. Even at its peak it was overtaken by the much larger volume of voluntary migration. In addition, it was most difficult to operate when it was most needed, in the early 1930s; the Cabinet recorded in 1932 that the difficulty in obtaining jobs even in prosperous areas was forcing it to consider closing all Transfer Instruction Centres.[40] The areas from which the transfers were drawn also felt that they were being drained of their youngest and most active workers by the scheme.[41]

In the absence of a more active policy to combat unemployment, the major impact of government upon the unemployed was through the provision and administration of unemployment relief. The policies of government in the area of relief have left a legacy of bitterness, mainly centred around the means test and its application to the unemployed. There are widespread memories of parsimony, petty humiliation and callousness in the administration of unemployment relief during the 1930s. Certainly, there were many examples of all these things, as government attempted to grapple with a problem of quite new dimensions. Up to the late 1920s it was believed that the problem of unemployment would be reduced in the not too distant future. By the early 1930s, however, the Labour and then the National Government had to deal with an unemployment problem which grew rather than declined, which had serious repercussions upon the financial stability of the country, and which demanded permanent rather than *ad hoc* solutions.

In many respects Britain had a generous system of unemployment insurance by the late 1920s. Although not lavish, it provided in return for contributions by employers and employees, payments of 17s. for a man and 26s. for a married couple in the event of unemployment. The number of workers covered by the Unemployment Insurance scheme rose from 11 million in 1920 to 15·4 million in 1938. Groups such as agricultural workers, domestic servants and the self-employed were not included. In their case, unemployment was to be met through the local Poor Law Authority. Relief was administered by Public Assistance Committees and partly funded by the rates. The main body of workers, however, were covered under the Unemployment Insurance scheme, the fund of which was supposed to be self-supporting. Unfortunately the scheme had been based upon an estimated unemployment of 4 per cent and had to be funded by the Treasury when unemployment in the twenties was persistently higher. By 1928 the fund was in debt to the tune of £25 million. Many of the unemployed had been out of work for so long that they had exhausted their right to statutory benefits under the scheme and had to be supported by *ad hoc* payments, called 'transitional benefits', whose cost was also borne by the Treasury. Between 120,000 and 140,000 unemployed, excluding dependants, were outside the insurance scheme altogether and were looked after by the Poor Law. Thus by the early 1930s, virtually three separate schemes of unemployment relief were operating for different categories of the unemployed. Apart from the administrative confusion, however, there was the more serious question of the cost.[42]

In fact, the cost of unemployment benefit to the government had risen from £51 million in 1929 to £125 million in 1931 and was causing serious disquiet in financial circles. If anything, the Labour Government had loosened the purse-strings further by the Unemployment Act of 1930 which allowed people with a minimum of contributions to claim benefit and abolished the clause demanding that benefit should be paid only to those 'genuinely seeking work'. Even so, half a million people were receiving the transitional benefits paid for by the Treasury, having exhausted their entitlement to benefits under the insurance scheme. The government's expenditure on unemployment benefit became the centre of the battle to restore confidence in the economy. The May Committee Report, published on 1 August, 1931, recommended drastic economies to reduce the budget deficit. Cuts in government expenditure totalling £96 million were suggested, of which £66 million would be saved on unemployment relief. As a result, the issue of economies in unemployment relief brought about the Cabinet crisis which led to the formation of the National Government.[43]

The fall of the Labour Government and the formation of the

National Government led to a reappraisal of the level and entitlement to relief. Employees' contributions were raised to 30*d.* a week and unemployment benefits reduced by approximately 10 per cent. The regulations governing entitlement to benefit were tightened, and many married women were cut off from benefit by the Anomalies Act. It has been estimated that this measure alone disallowed 134,000 married women from benefit by the end of 1931. The most emotive part of this package, however, was the means test. The period for which unemployment benefit could be drawn as of right was limited to 26 weeks. After this period those requiring relief had to apply for 'transitional payments'. Although they were to be paid through the Employment Exchange, the claimants had first to undergo a household 'means test' carried out by the local Public Assistance Committee, the successors to the Poor Law Guardians. The Committee then notified the Employment Exchange of the circumstances of the claimant and assessed what rate of relief they should receive. Any form of income, including pensions and contributions from sons and daughters, was to be taken into account in determining household circumstances. Savings and even household possessions could also be taken into account. The maximum payment which an adult male could receive was 15*s.* 3*d.* and the aim of the P.A.C. scrutiny was to economise on the level of relief by a strict assessment of need and available means.[44]

The outcry against the means test is a very well-attested feature of the thirties. Even today, people still regard it as one of the most hated aspects of the social services between the wars and one of the most emotive symbols of administrative meanness. In part, this was because many of the people being means-tested had been brought up to believe that unemployment benefit was a right, earned through their weekly contributions. The Public Assistance Committees were still associated with the Poor Law and the Board of Guardians, and in many cases they were the same personnel. Thus many respectable and skilled workmen found themselves under the scrutiny of public officials for the first time in their lives. The means test also often involved an intrusion into the homes of the unemployed, and the officials, more used to dealing with the 'residuum', were often insensitive. Not all were, by any means, but there were sufficient instances of prying and harshness to create a formidable catalogue of complaints. Too often, as G. D. H. Cole suggested, unemployment benefit was being dispensed not as of right, but as an act of charity or 'prevention of nuisance'. He wrote:

It is therefore — for charity begins at home — to be strictly limited to the smallest sum that will keep the unemployed from dying or becoming unduly troublesome; and their relations as far as possible to be made to bear the cost of maintaining them in order to save the pockets of the taxpayers. Behind this system is still the notion that unemployment is somehow the fault of the unemployed, from which they are to be deterred if possible; and an attempt is made to persuade their relations to help in deterring them, because they will be made to contribute to their support.[45]

By January 1932, almost a million unemployed were registering for transitional benefit and coming within the scope of the means test. Resources had to be disclosed at the threat of legal sanction. Large numbers of people were cut off from unemployment benefit under the means test and many others found their relief reduced. In Lancashire, it has been claimed that only 16 per cent were awarded the full transitional benefit, while a third were disallowed altogether. The T.U.C. compiled a dossier of cases of acute hardship caused by the operation of the means test, including cases of young people and pensioners forced to move out of their family home because their earnings or pensions had led to a reduction in the unemployment relief of the householder. Certainly, within a year 180,000 people were removed from receipt of unemployment benefit under the Unemployment Insurance scheme through the operation of the means test.[46] Over the country as a whole, half of those applying for transitional benefit had received less than the maximum payments. In the first year of operation £24 million were saved, but at a cost in suffering and ill-feeling which found some expression in the hunger marches and demonstrations of 1931–2. G. K. Chesterton expressed his own feelings in characteristic style: 'It is inhuman, it is horrible ... People who are already clinging with their teeth and fingernails to the edge of the chasm are to be formally and legally kicked into the chasm.'[47]

A number of Public Assistance Committees in Labour-controlled authorities opposed the operation of the new regulations. In some of them, they had recourse to allowing the maximum benefit in almost every case. At this point they were warned by the Ministry of Labour against 'illegal' payments. Among those warned were Durham County, Glamorgan County, Rotherham and Barnsley. To break this revolt by local P.A.C.s, the ministry suspended

F

Rotherham P.A.C. and later Durham County. In each case the local officials were replaced by commissioners from London with orders to operate the regulations in the spirit intended. These examples put recalcitrant Public Assistance Committees in a cruel dilemma. Either they could follow their principles and allow the ministry's commissioners to 'do its own dirty work', as Middlesbrough P.A.C. put it, or they could put the ministry's regulations into operation and attempt to mitigate them in practice. Most areas submitted. In West Ham the Public Assistance Committee put out a public statement: 'We were threatened with supercession, and in face of that threat we prefer to keep our poor under our own care and do what we can for them rather than hand them over to an arbitrary Commissioner from whom they could expect little humanity.' Similarly in Birkenhead, the *Birkenhead News* expressed the commonly held view that any attempt to mitigate the operation of the means test would simply lead to a take-over from London. From the point of view of Whitehall it proved an effective way of containing the protests of the unemployed by allowing the most unpleasant work to be done by local bodies.[48]

Reform of this system was attempted. In 1930 the Holman Gregory Commission on Unemployment Insurance was set up to look into the administration of relief to the jobless. Its report in 1932 confirmed the view within government circles that the administration of relief required drastic reorganisation and rationalisation. Part I of the Unemployment Act of 1934 put the Unemployment Insurance scheme on a sounder footing with the Unemployment Insurance Statutory Committee to act as a supervisory body. In addition, the economy cuts in benefit were restored and provisions made to bring agricultural and 'black-coated' workers within the scope of unemployment insurance. Part II of the Act set up the Unemployment Assistance Board which was to take responsibility for all insured workers who had exhausted benefit by being out of work for more than 156 days. Thus the responsibility for transitional benefits was to be taken out of the hands of the local authorities and the P.A.C.s. A national administration with its own scale of relief payments was to provide more settled and centrally funded benefits for the unemployed. In addition, the U.A.B. was to take over the able-bodied unemployed at present supported by the Poor Law. The Poor Law authorities would then be left to cater for their original concern, the sick and the aged. The scheme also had the benefit of taking the unemployment issue out of politics, by setting up the U.A.B. as an independent body which could recommend alterations in the scale of relief or contributions without submitting them for parliamentary approval. When details of the scheme were published, however, there was an outcry because relief scales were often lower than those operated by the local authorities. As a result, a Standstill Act was introduced which operated for two years and allowed the unemployed whichever form of benefit was the higher, either that of the U.A.B. or the Public Assistance Committee. Eventually in 1937–8 the scheme was implemented without undue fuss. A means test was retained, but the regulations governing it were relaxed somewhat, taking some of the edge off its operation. A greater degree of discretion was allowed to local officials, and though not always exercised imaginatively, was generally an improvement on what had gone before.[49]

For all its failings, the U.A.B. did begin to grapple with the need to provide adequate maintenance for the unemployed. It did not tackle underlying problems of poverty, nor could it hope to deal with unemployment as such. It was a policy of alleviation rather than of reconstruction. None the less, the principle of less eligibility was destroyed once and for all and the rigours of the Poor Law were mitigated. The means test undoubtedly caused much bitterness and hardship, but the provision of unemployment benefit, as with other social services, was probably more comprehensive in Britain by 1939 than in any other country which operated a democratic system.

Apart from the dole, the government was not prepared itself to take on primary responsibility for the welfare of the unemployed. The Cabinet proceedings for 1932 recorded the decision that:

> It is our considered view that neither local authorities nor the Central Government should assume direct responsibility for welfare work for the unemployed, and that it can more appropriately and effectively be undertaken by private agencies with limited financial assistance in appropriate cases from National Funds.[50]

The National Council for Social Service was to be invited to act as the main agent of the government in providing welfare work of this kind. The National Council was launched by a speech of the Prince of Wales at the Albert Hall in January 1932. With the aid of government grants it co-ordinated the various voluntary schemes and activities in the areas of heavy unemployment. Not a great deal of money was involved; the total sum expended by 1938 came to around £250,000. In all, something in the region of 150,000–200,000 men were involved at various times and there were at the peak around a thousand centres. The T.U.C. was suspicious of the Social Service Movement, describing it as an attempt 'to shelve responsibility for the welfare of the unemployed', but permitted local branches to co-operate. More radical voices saw it as a deliberate attempt to allay discontent among the unemployed.[51] The communist Allen Hutt lumped together the efforts of 'the churches, the Quakers, the "Social Service" ladies and gentlemen and other charity mongers' as attempts to demoralise the unemployed.[52]

There was, perhaps, some justification for this view. The timing of the inauguration of the movement did come just after the first wave of demonstrations and disturbances in the autumn of 1931. However, the movement was not well enough funded to suggest that the government saw it as a major barrier to revolution. The government believed that voluntary welfare reached only a fraction of the unemployed and regarded it more as a cheap palliative for a minority of those out of work rather than a mass programme. The numbers involved were too small to have a really significant impact. If anything, its major influence came after the worst of the slump was over, providing some outlet for the unemployed in the most heavily depressed regions. Its effectiveness varied from region to region. The amateur drama group which J. B. Priestley found on Tyneside was in marked contrast to the more useful tasks undertaken in some of the South Wales valleys. It brought together the host of well-meaning local efforts to do something, however small, to cope with the problem. By providing something to do, it may well have taken the edge off militancy for a minority, but at best it was a philanthropic scheme, with no wholesale programme of retraining or education in mind.

The policies of both the Labour and National Governments in the face of the world depression were essentially cautious, placing their emphasis upon financial and economic orthodoxy. The emergent doctrines of Keynes or the more moderate doctrines of the 'middle way' found few influential supporters in government during the thirties. Financial and budgetary conservatism dominated the response of the Labour Government to Mosley's proposals in 1930, but their social commitments made it impossible for the majority of the Cabinet and the party to accept the demands for economy on the part of the financial community. In turn, the National Government saw its task in terms of restoring confidence by pursuing traditional deflationary policies, which dictated its response to the depressed areas and to the unemployed in general. Thus the initiatives of the National Government were few in the direction of economic policy, and the Special Areas Act and transference schemes were carried with little conviction and slenderer means. Unemployment relief represented what one historian has called 'a tangled mass of opportunistic legislation' and it does not seem an unfair description for a system which had developed as a series of *ad hoc* expedients to deal with a rapidly changing situation. Even when rationalisation was attempted, it was bungled, and only very painfully adapted to the new conditions of relatively large, long-term unemployment. On the other hand, it was a difficult period and it took a war to transform the experiences and lessons of the thirties into a new attitude towards unemployment relief and the social services in general. The tragedy was that so much unnecessary suffering was added to the experience of the unemployed by the way in which unemployment relief was administered, providing a generation of people from the depressed areas with bitter memories of the means test. Essentially the National Government could offer no constructive alternatives; it awaited the processes of natural recovery. Until that occurred and transformed even the depressed areas into thriving centres once again, it could offer only palliatives.

V

The Impact of Unemployment

Unemployment was not a new problem: there had been cyclical and seasonal unemployment in the years before 1914, usually associated with low-paid, casual work. It was traditionally regarded as one of the causes of poverty rather than a problem in its own right. W. H. Beveridge's *Unemployment: A Problem of Industry*, published in 1909, saw it primarily as a problem of the 'residue' – those least fitted for normal employment because of physical, mental or moral inadequacy.[1] Even after 1918, it was only slowly recognised as a social question with its own characteristics and effects. For much of the 1920s, commentators were mainly concerned with the industrial conditions which created unemployment. *The Third Winter of Unemployment*, published in 1922, looked at the areas where declining demand for British exports had created a problem of over-capacity and surplus labour.[2] In the same way, R. C. Davison's study of the unemployed, published in 1929, examined the economic dimensions of unemployment, with relatively little regard for its social effects.[3] The government's interest was also largely confined to its purely economic implications.[4]

It was only after 1929 and the onset of the depression on an unprecedented scale that unemployment began to be studied seriously. The pioneer study was by the American, E. W. Bakke, who examined the condition and attitudes of the unemployed in Greenwich in 1931.[5] Although it marked the most comprehensive attempt to understand the impact of mass unemployment, its major failing was that Greenwich was not very typical of the most depressed areas. More comprehensive was the Pilgrim Trust's *Men Without Work*, published in 1938, which examined the scale and effects of long-term unemployment based on a sample of a thousand unemployed drawn from six communities. It was a voluntary initiative, but was organised on scientific lines with a specialist team of investigators. A record of each case was kept, with details of employment record, family circumstances, attitude and intelligence.[6] Equally thorough was the Carnegie Trust's investigation, *Disinherited Youth*, which examined the effects of unemployment upon young people in South Wales.[7] There were many other academic studies which used the statistical techniques which were becoming common in the social sciences in general.[8] In addition, however, the problem of unemployment gave rise to a wave of more popular studies. There were the semi-documentary accounts, such as Fenner Brockway's *Hungry England* and George Orwell's *The Road to Wigan Pier*. By the end of the thirties there was a considerable 'dole literature' which included novels, memoirs, and accounts of particular areas or themes.[9] It was this literature more than anything else which helped to shape the popular image of unemployment as the principal social evil of the thirties. Much of this literature was clearly political in its intentions, such as Allen Hutt's *The Condition of the Working Class*.[10] With the formation of the Left Book Club in 1936 by Victor Gollancz, a new market in serious social writing was opened up, in which studies of unemployment featured prominently. Books such as Gollan's *Youth in British Industry*, M. Cohen's *I Was One of the Unemployed*, and Wal Hannington's *The Distressed Areas* brought the problem of unemployment to a wider audience.[11] By the end of the 1930s, unemployment was clearly seen as one of the major issues of the day and considerable concern was expressed about its impact upon social conditions in the depressed areas.

But amid this plethora of comment upon the issue of unemployment it is still difficult to form a clear view of the impact of the problem in the context of social conditions which prevailed at the time. Several writers expressed the view that the Left exaggerated the sufferings of the unemployed in order to make a case for the reconstruction of British politics and society. Thus Arthur Bryant wrote of his reading of *The Road to Wigan Pier* in the preface to G. A. Tomlinson's book *Coal Miner*:

> I have recently been reading a very interesting example of the kind of publication to which Mr Tomlinson's book is so refreshing a contrast. It is called *The Road to Wigan Pier* and was, I believe, one of the choices of the 'Left Book Club'. It was written by a young literary man of refined tastes who at some apparent inconvenience to himself had 'roughed it' for a few weeks at Wigan and Sheffield. The impression left by the

first part of his book is that Wigan and Sheffield are Hell ... but though Wigan and Sheffield may perhaps genuinely seem Hell to a super-sensitive novelist paying them a casual visit, they do not seem Hell to the vast majority of people who live there. That is just the difference between propaganda and reality.[12]

Thus, even for contemporaries, the picture was by no means clear. The true impact of unemployment upon social conditions was often obscured by the more emotive and committed writings on the subject.

What then were the major effects of unemployment? The most obvious effect was upon family income. During the worst years of the depression, from 1931 to 1935, a man with a wife and three children received a maximum of 29*s*. 3*d*. per week. From 1931, anyone unemployed for more than six months underwent a means test in which any other source of household income, including savings and effects, could be counted and deducted. In 1936, the rates were raised to a level of 36*s*. for the same size of family. Although the level of benefit was lower than the average industrial wage, it was also higher than earnings in a number of industries. In South Wales it was found that a third of single men and almost a half of married men were receiving more in unemployment allowances than they were in their last job.[13] A great deal depended upon the fortunes of families in dealing with the officials responsible for unemployment benefit and a host of factors such as the ability of housewives to cope on a restricted budget, family size and expenditure. As the Carnegie Trust noted, the economic consequences of unemployment were first felt in the sphere of home life; 'The family income is immediately affected and reduced, for the housewife this entails an immediate adjustment of expenditure; some things must be "cut out" if debt is to be avoided.'[14] Single men were also forced to budget carefully if they were to make their unemployment allowance serve them. Again, a great deal depended upon individual circumstance. Young men living on their own — often necessary if the family's total allowance was not to be reduced — were especially hard pressed. Max Cohen wrote: 'During my period of unemployment I had learnt the meaning of the word hunger. I knew what it was to have to count my pennies carefully and to spend them with hesitation and misgiving. I knew the dull finality of having no money at all.'[15]

The social investigations of the period saw unemployment as a potent cause of poverty. In the East End, the *New Survey of London* found that 35 per cent of families were in poverty as a result of unemployment, the greatest single cause of poverty. In 1936 Rowntree found that unemployment accounted for 44·53 per cent of poverty in York, compared with only 2·31 per cent in his first survey in 1899. York, however, was not one of the worst-hit towns in the depression. He concluded that unemployment relief was inadequate: 'The relief at present is not sufficient to raise the recipients above the minimum.'[16] In Bristol Herbert Tout found that unemployment was the single most important cause of families falling below his minimum standard. A third of families were below this poverty line, 'because benefit and relief scales are below the survey scale of "needs" '.[17] The Pilgrim Trust investigators came to broadly similar conclusions. 'Our impressions were', they wrote, 'that the economic level at which families were living in many homes visited was such as to cause nervous anxiety and in some cases physical deterioration.' Three out of every ten households of the long-term unemployed were described as below the poverty line. Half of these were considerably worse off, living at a level of bare subsistence or below.[18]

The experience of unemployed families differed widely in relation to their circumstances. The source of unemployment relief could condition whether a family was living above or below the poverty line because some types of relief were more generous than others. By the late thirties it was found that almost four-fifths of those dependent upon the Unemployment Assistance Board were in poverty, compared with only two-fifths of those on local relief scales.[19] Local conditions could also make significant differences to the living standards of the unemployed. In Lancashire, for example, there was a strong tradition of female labour in the cotton factories, so that many families had a higher proportion of wage-earners than was usual elsewhere. Thus it was common to find at least one wage-earner in families in the textile districts and consequently less dependence upon unemployment relief. The availability of cheap fuel in the coalfields, whether scavenged or pilfered from tips and beaches, also made an important difference to family income. In South Wales, it was so common that the Pilgrim Trust investigators altered their poverty line to take the availability of cheap fuel into account.[20] Such regional differences accounted in part for variations in the incidence of poverty among the unemployed. It was found that Liverpool, and more surprisingly Leicester, a relatively prosperous city in some respects, had the highest rates of poverty among the unemployed of the six communities they studied in depth. A more general factor which determined living standards was family size. Large families were generally associated with poverty, and they were found to be a major cause of poverty among the unemployed too. Of 97 unemployed families in Liverpool with two or more children under 14, 83 were found to be below the poverty line.[21]

Many families were in poverty mainly as a result of unemployment and some of those maintained by the State were given a level of benefit which was insufficient to meet the relatively stringent poverty lines of investigators such as Tout and Rowntree. The Pilgrim Trust came to the same conclusion. Unfortunately for the unemployed, many of these reports only emerged at the end of the 1930s or in the early part of the war, so that their findings came too late to provoke major changes in the level of unemployment relief. Yet many of these investigations also revealed that unemployment in itself was not the sole cause of poverty. Many of the unemployed would have been below the poverty line even if they had been in work. Some were better off with a regular income from unemployment relief than they would have had from casual employment. In addition, the much-hated means test was found to be of relatively little importance as a cause of poverty and much more emphasis was placed upon local and individual circumstances. None the less, a sufficient amount of impartial evidence proved conclusively that even when the worst years of the depression were over, a large section of the unemployed was forced to live in poverty.[22]

Poverty usually had the inescapable consequences of poor diet and ill-health. A number of writers took up this issue: Fenner Brockway produced examples of families who were existing far below the poverty line outlined by Rowntree. He quoted a correspondent from Yorkshire who after two years out of work was existing on 29s. 3d. for himself, his wife and three children. After paying for rent, fuel, and unavoidable deductions, the family had only 9s. 7d. to spend on food for five people. The father blamed the diet for recurrent illness in the youngest child. After examining the budgets of some unemployed families, Brockway wrote: 'If I am asked how these unemployed people make up the deficit in the minimum diet required for a normal family after the relief allowance has run out my answer is: I do not know.'[23] Confirmation of the threat to the health of the unemployed was given by John Boyd Orr at the Chadwick Lecture in 1934: 'So far as the evidence goes,' he said, 'it suggests that people living at the economic level of the dole are living near or below the threshold of adequate nutrition.'[24] An inquiry into the household expenditure of some unemployed families in Newcastle found that 'The unemployed families were found to be living on a diet below the standard considered necessary to maintain health and working capacity.'[25]

As a result there was a highly charged debate involving politicians, doctors and social investigators about the issue of malnutrition among the unemployed. In 1931, Sir George Newman, Chief Medical Officer of the Board of Education, claimed that the depression 'does not appear to have exerted, as yet, any measurable ill-effect upon the child population'. In 1933, the Minister of Health made a still broader claim, when he told the House of Commons that 'there is at present no available medical evidence of any increase in physical impairment, sickness or mortality as a result of the economic depression or unemployment'.[26] Within a few years, however, a number of writers were blaming unemployment for the variation in mortality and morbidity rates between the depressed areas and the more prosperous parts of the country.

There was some evidence that unemployment was having an effect upon mortality rates in the depressed areas. In Stockton-on-Tees Dr M'Gonigle compared the death rates for employed and unemployed living in the same area in the period 1931–4. He found that there was a significant difference in the standardised death rate. This result, however, was based upon a relatively small sample and not all commentators were prepared to accept its validity.[27] Concern, however, continued to be expressed about the effect of unemployment upon mortality rates, and in particular upon infant and maternal mortality. The difficulty here was to isolate the effects of unemployment from those of poverty in general. For example, the Chief Medical Officer of the Ministry of Health published figures in 1934 which showed that the depressed areas had an overall death rate which was only a little above the average, but an infant mortality rate which was significantly higher than that of the country as a whole. The report, however, went on to say that this imbalance had existed before the depression and could not be related directly to unemployment.[28] Similarly, a report compiled in Sunderland and Co. Durham in 1934 to investigate the same problem concluded that it could find 'little evidence of any increase in disease and none of increased mortality'.[29]

In fact, death rates were a very indirect means of measuring social hardship in the depressed areas, being subject to a wide range of factors, many of which owed little to unemployment. Writers who seized upon the local or temporary movement in death rates as evidence of a relationship between unemployment and ill-health were often proved mistaken when all the evidence was available. Rates of infant and maternal mortality also showed patterns which defied simple correlation with unemployment. Infant and maternal mortality had always been concentrated in the poorer industrial areas of the country and it was virtually impossible to assess the relative impact of unemployment given the range of factors which could operate. Thus it proved nothing about the effects of unemployment to point to a higher infant mortality rate in Gateshead than in Brighton, for example, or to compare unfavourably the maternal mortality rates of Jarrow with those of Bedford. Moreover, anomalies abounded when crude comparisons were made. Merthyr Tydfil, a heavily depressed area, had one of the lowest rates of maternal mortality, while the Isle of Wight, hardly a depressed area, had one of the highest.[30] The rate of maternal mortality depended heavily upon a range of intervening factors, such as housing, income, family size, general health, and the quality of local health services. Again, no simple correlation fitted the general pattern of maternal mortality in the country as a whole. There was evidence, however, that the link between maternal mortality and unemployment was stronger than that with infant or general mortality. An investigation by Dr Singer, quoted by the Pilgrim Trust, suggested that the effects of malnutrition, nervous illness and the reduction of medical services accounted for over 3,000 deaths a year among women in childbirth.[31]

Similarly the effects of unemployment upon general health standards were hotly debated during the decade. Even official reports admitted that the unemployed lived near to or below the poverty line and were therefore likely to suffer some deficiencies of diet. It was precisely this factor which was most commonly seized upon by social commentators. There was ample evidence that the depressed areas had higher rates of most diseases; the question was whether unemployment had widened the gap. The most that official writers would concede was that it had retarded the rate of improvement. This view received some confirmation from the inquiries of the Pilgrim Trust who claimed that the effects of unemployment on diphtheria and other childhood diseases were traceable to only a slight degree.[32] There was considerable concern, however, that the progress which had been made in the prevention and treatment of tuberculosis would be halted and even reversed by unemployment. A number of writers also suggested that the gap between the depressed areas and the rest of the country was widening as a result of the effects of unemployment.[33] This seemed confirmed in the case of the north-east, where progress in reducing the incidence of T.B. was halted for a number of years during the depression. But while it was tempting to relate the very high rate of the disease in Jarrow, for example, to the incidence of unemployment, such correlations were extremely treacherous. Jarrow and Tyneside in general had always had a high rate of T.B., even in periods of full employment. The study undertaken by Dr Bradbury in 1933 revealed that 'unemployment is not specially associated with the disease in Jarrow' and blamed poverty, bad housing and topography. These conditions proved more intractable in industrial areas, making it less easy to register improvements than in other places. Hence the gap tended to widen between the poorer and the more prosperous areas of the country even without the effects of unemployment.[34]

Greater attention was being paid to the psychological problems of the unemployed by the late thirties. The Pilgrim Trust found that many of the long-unemployed they encountered suffered from symptoms of 'nerves' and depression. They quoted an investigation carried out in Glasgow by Dr Halliday which showed that the incidence of 'psycho-neurotic' illnesses increased with the duration of unemployment. He found that approximately a third of the unemployed people suffering from sickness had no organic illness. The percentage rose to 42 per cent among those who had been out of work for six to twelve months. He wrote of his figures:

> They suggest that after falling out of work there is a short period of release (a holiday freedom): gradually anxiety and depression set in with loss of mental equilibrium; finally after several years, adaptation takes place to a new and debased level of life, lacking hope as well as fear of the future.

He gave a number of examples of men who had 'gone to pieces' under the pressure of unemployment, among them the following:

> Man, single, aged 40. In normal health until unemployed. After four years' unemployment complained of choking and pains in the head, but specialist reported no lesion. Later developed alleged throat trouble, but again specialist found no physical signs. Finally, had severe stomach pains for which there was no organic explanation. Only psychological explanation adequate.[35]

Another study of mental illness concluded that 'Unemployment is often the immediate cause of a severe psychic illness.' Unemployment was blamed for undermining the character of the affected individual, destroying the socialising influences of training, altering attitudes to life, and developing neurosis in individuals, many of whom had they remained in employment 'would not have developed a declared illness of so serious a nature, nor so soon in their lives'.[36] Recounting his experience of unemployment, M. Cohen wrote:

What is astonishing is not that there are some unemployed men and women who are nervous wrecks and psychopathic cases (the medical statistics on this question would surprise many people), but that there are not many more. It is, however, not the least crime of the present social system that there are today, at this very moment, thousands upon thousands of people who are suffering what can literally be described as excruciating mental tortures. They suffer in this way not because they are congenitally more neurotic than the average, but solely and simply because anarchic forces have uprooted them, and undermined their social, economic, and therefore psychological stability.[37]

The extent to which the unemployed were driven to the most desperate of courses, suicide, was touched upon by a number of writers and officials. The causes of suicide are complex and difficult to reduce to a single factor such as unemployment, however strong the circumstantial evidence might be. Accurate analysis of suicide figures at all times is bedevilled by variations in the definition of suicide used by coroners and police.[38] None the less investigations such as those of the Pilgrim Trust revealed many cases of depression which had some, at least, of their origins in unemployment.[39] Although it is impossible to know how many unemployed people who committed suicide would have done so if they had been in work, there was evidence to suggest that unemployment was sometimes a precipitating factor. According to Home Office figures in 1932, two unemployed men committed suicide every day.[40] In Birkenhead during the crisis in the shipbuilding industry in 1932, there were several reports of unemployed men committing suicide, in some of which unemployment seemed to have played an appreciable role. In April, a 56-year-old man was reported to have gassed himself the evening after being told he was no longer wanted at work. When another unemployed man committed suicide in October, the coroner blamed it upon depression caused by unemployment and illness.[41] Fenner

Brockway compiled a dossier of newspaper reports of suicide among the unemployed from different parts of the country. He quoted one example in which the coroner blamed an adverse means test decision for the death of an unemployed man in Birmingham.[42] So serious did concern become that the Minister of Health was asked in 1934 to account for a 60 per cent rise in the number of suicides among young men under 25 in the ten years 1921–31.[43] Although no conclusive answer was possible about the relationship between unemployment and suicide, it made a sufficiently strong impression on contemporaries to be regarded as a significant factor in a rising suicide rate.

Many investigators found that the worst sufferers from unemployment were not the unemployed themselves but their families: the Pilgrim Trust wrote that 'Beyond the man in the queue we should always be aware of those two or three at home whom he has to support.' They calculated that the 250,000 long-term unemployed were responsible for 170,000 wives and 270,000 young children. A survey of unemployed households with three or four children concluded that 'almost invariably there was definite want, either of food or clothing, or more probably of household equipment'. The ability of housewives to maintain standards made some difference, but could not fully provide an adequate living for the family as a whole.[44] An S.C.M. publication came to a similar conclusion, 'that the average unemployed family must in any case be somewhat undernourished'.[45] Although the Carnegie Trust found examples of energetic attempts to keep up standards of cleanliness and respectability, they also found cases where the prolongation of unemployment was dragging down living standards. They commented on homes where women 'had lost all pride in personal appearance and appearance of the home'.[46] But in many homes it was the wives who bore the brunt of the reduction in living standards. Women were found to be sacrificing their own health and well-being in order to maintain their husbands and children. The Pilgrim Trust's investigators found that in some cases women were 'literally starving themselves in order to feed and clothe the children reasonably well' and that the wife was suffering from ill-health in a third of the families they visited, while the children were affected in only a quarter. On the other hand, they found that the number of homes in which special care was being taken of the children was three times that of those where there was evidence of neglect. Many writers felt that it was this situation which accounted for the high rate of maternal mortality in the depressed areas.

Run-down, ill-nourished and anxious women were naturally more likely to succumb to the difficulties of childbirth.[47]

The psychological response to unemployment varied enormously. Inevitably, personal and environmental characteristics had a major influence upon how people reacted. Hilda Jennings wrote about Brynmawr, a South Wales mining village which suffered from heavy unemployment throughout the thirties:

> One man will approach the Exchange with impatience and bitterness at his dependence and impotence to help himself; one in a mood to find cause of complaint and irritation with the officials; one with growing apathy and with no conscious feeling except when his pay is threatened; one, again, with each visit, feels a need for a change in the economic and social system; his political conscience aflame, and he will fumble in his mind for an alternative, or shout the current formula at the next 'unemployment' or 'party' meeting, according to his mental outlook and capacity.[48]

Reactions to unemployment also altered over time. Early feelings of shock and numbness were often replaced by a 'holiday' feeling. Others felt a sense of immediate injury with anger and fear for the future. Initial reactions were usually followed by periods of calm and creative attempts to seek work. Long-term reactions included hopelessness, apathy, fatalism, and often a bitter sense of humiliation. Again, there was no completely typical set of reactions, but a variety of responses which could affect individuals in different ways and at different times.[49]

Some groups of workmen seemed to be particularly badly affected by unemployment. The Coles argued that the effects of the depression were felt most keenly among the skilled workmen. Pauperism, they maintained, had now spread to the 'homes of respectable people', the skilled artisans who had once been the aristocracy of their communities. It was they who frequently registered the greatest sense of bitterness and humiliation. As the Coles commented:

> The abnormal extent of the present unemployment has affected the well-paid, skilled and regularly employed artisan and tradesman; even the lower grades of the salaried class are faced with unemployment. On these classes the strain of unemployment is greater and the public relief much less effective. The insurance allowance represents a much greater fall from their accustomed standard of living; they are much more reluctant to

seek Poor Relief to supplement insurance benefit ... and in case of exceptional family need, the relief works instituted are usually unsuitable for them and the worry of enforced idleness is more oppressive. There is abundant evidence of mental strain and suffering in this class.[50]

In Stockton-on-Tees, J. B. Priestley found 'a large number of citizens, excellent skilled workmen, who have been unemployed not merely this year and last year but for seven or eight years, who might as well be crossbow-men or armourers, it seems, for all the demand there is for their services'.[51] Several witnesses referred to the pride in their work which characterised the skilled workmen, who now, without it, often experienced an obsessive feeling of uselessness. Those whose lives had been centred on work tended to suffer from a sense of isolation and loneliness. A. M. Cameron echoed these impressions of the loss of confidence and self-respect among the skilled unemployed:

He is ashamed of his lapse from higher standards, but the shame only depresses him the more. He wanders about with no end in view, more and more alone, chewing the cud of all the insults, and slighting remarks he may have addressed to him, a ghost among living men, inhabiting a no-man's-land, without hope, without purpose, without human contact.[52]

Often it was the older men who suffered the most, knowing that loss of work was likely to be permanent. A shoemaker from Leicester, who had worked thirty-seven years for the same firm, admitted, 'When I saw the new manager going through and saying: "The whole of this side of this room, this room, and this room is to be stopped", I knew it would be uphill work to get something.'[53] It was of men such as this that the Pilgrim Trust wrote:

Anyone who has visited a number of these older men, and knows the hopelessness of men faced with an empty future— whom neither education nor work has ever given an opportunity to learn how to spend leisure—knows the urgency of their case. Five years in a man's life is a long time; and if at the end of five years' uncertainty there is only (as there is now) the certainty of a pension at a yet smaller rate, it is a fate that can scarcely be tolerated. The ordinary working man is not very easily moved, and the sight of some of these older men, broken down and unable to speak for the moment as they looked ahead into the future, is not one that will be soon forgotten.[54]

G

The fate of the young unemployed also worried several investigators. One commented:

> At a time when it has become obvious that the most radical readjustments in the direction of our economy are necessary, we subject the necessary agents by which this can be brought about—the next generation—to just the influences which will sap their confidence, dissipate their enthusiasm and endanger their industrial skill and knowledge.[55]

The Carnegie Trust found that after an initial holiday feeling, depression and irritability were common reactions amongst the young. They claimed that the experience of unemployment was leaving a permanent mark:

> Lacking the stability of age and experience they are emotionally more liable to become drifters. For many, self-confidence is shattered and this, in itself, becomes a barrier to further employment. Personal worth tends to be assessed at a lower level and, in contrast to the ambitions and day-dreams of their earlier days, they go forward to maturing manhood with more limited ideas as to the worth of their contribution to life and work. Their decreased sociability, their irritability and sometimes open violence, are common manifestations of heightened emotional instability due to unemployment. The higher their ideals and ambitions, the more seriously does prolonged unemployment tend to depress them. As an escape from this conflict, some are apt to become fatalists and adopt as a protective measure the 'don't care a damn' attitude.

The most ambitious suffered the most distress, they concluded, fighting to maintain self-respect by a variety of means: 'they have no function in society. They are the unwanted hangers-on of a community in the life of which they are unable to play their full part.'[56]

Similarly, investigators were alarmed when a third of young men in Liverpool had to be classed as 'work-shy'. The fear that the young would be permanently affected was widely expressed in almost all the depressed areas. Long-term unemployment did have its effects upon the will to work and it was the younger men who were found to be most vulnerable.[57]

The fear that demoralisation might lead to crime and social conflict was put forward by several commentators with experience of conditions in the depressed areas. As one wrote: 'Enforced idleness leads ultimately to demoralisation, to loss of pride in one's own person and appearance, to envy of those better placed in society, and envy leads to hatred as hatred leads in the last resort to social conflict.'[58] This was expressed most publicly in concern that unemployment would lead to an increase in crime. In fact, no direct correlation was found between unemployment and adult crime.[59] Juvenile crime, however, showed an apparent increase from 200 indictable offences per 100,000 population in 1929, to 568 per 100,000 in 1936. Articles began to appear in newspapers with titles such as 'Young Bandits' and 'The Deadly Dole: From Idleness to Crime'.[60] In 1932 the Chief Constable of Birkenhead accounted for an increase in larcenies by reference to unemployment:

> In very many cases it is fairly conclusive that the incidence of unemployment has been primarily responsible for crime, and it is becoming more and more apparent that the industrial conditions are having a most disastrous effect upon the character of the youth and young men of the borough who find it impossible to obtain employment.[61]

A number of prison governors were quoted by investigators as saying that they believed unemployment to be the source of the problem. The Governor of Durham Prison claimed: 'The country is raising a population of unemployables, loafers and thieves.'[62]

Support for these impressions came from a comprehensive study of crime in England and Wales by H. Mannheim. Assessing a number of influences upon crime rates, he found that there was a link between juvenile crime and unemployment. He admitted, however, that the correlation between the two was far from simple. Some towns recorded increases in crime among unemployed youth while others did not.[63] The Home Office also conducted a number of inquiries into the problem and concluded that juvenile crime 'appears to be part of a general problem, that is it seems to be connected with general social and economic factors ... '.[64] Thus, by the end of the 1930s it was recognised that unemployment was only one of a number of contributory factors leading to juvenile crime.

The Pilgrim Trust identified three broad attitudes among the unemployed: those who were still work-orientated and thought only in terms of obtaining a job; those who were beginning to think in terms of unemployment and only continued to look for work out of force of habit; and finally, those who had adjusted to a position of unemployment and could scarcely conceive of another form of existence.[65] They documented some of the pressures which conditioned these reactions. The initial shock of losing work, especially to those who had taken pride in their work, often resulted in an anxiety about obtaining work again. Here they found that reactions varied between workers of different skill. It was usually the skilled men who felt their respectability and independence most threatened by unemployment. Many men felt lost when they were cut off from the familiar community of work. Often the effect of prolonged unemployment was apathy and fatalism, expressed as a lack of 'spirit' or 'heart'. The investigators were especially disconcerted to find examples of younger men who were more ready to accept unemployment than the older generation. A life-time of work had conditioned the older men to such a degree that they could not adjust to a situation of unemployment, though they frequently had the most unfavourable chance of obtaining a new job.[66] Unemployment also had less obvious effects upon the mental attitudes of those thrown out of work, not all of which were necessarily bad. For some at least, unemployment meant an opportunity to educate themselves, to take up new activities, and even to change direction in their lives. It led others to view with a more critical eye the conditions in which they had been working and frequently produced in mining districts a determination not to allow the next generation to work underground. The Pilgrim Trust acknowledged the grim reality that often the only course open was to accustom the older men to a state of permanent unemployment. They noted that in some cases the long-unemployed older men were even beginning to enjoy their forced leisure. They quoted an observer in the Rhondda who claimed that 'the older men were probably now as happy as or happier than they had ever been'.[67]

One of the most obvious reactions to unemployment was the attempt to find new work. Many of the unemployed made almost heroic efforts to find a new job, and reports frequently told of men walking or cycling miles in order to obtain a position. Often this meant endless queues at factory gates or fruitless interviews in competition with scores or even hundreds of other men. None the less, unemployed men continued to look for work for months or even years, refusing to accept that the position might be hopeless, at least in the area in which they lived. Examples were cited of old men with virtually no chance of ever working again who 'yet make it a practice to stand every morning at six o'clock at the works gates in the hope that perhaps they may catch the foreman's eye'.[68] Instances were also quoted of young men who went out daily in search of work and had cycled all over Lancashire and Yorkshire in pursuit of a job. For some, the only hope of work lay in moving from the depressed areas. Often, this meant a move without a promise of a job, frequently to a strange locality. This could involve a different kind of anguish. A woman in Co. Durham recorded her feelings about the imminent departure of her husband to find work in southern England: 'Every week that there's an extra shilling I've bought a little extra cocoa or sugar or something to help me over the time he goes ... But he's in a sweat about going, for he's heard that the people are not friendly.'[69]

For many of the unemployed, the overriding reaction was a form of fatalism. Partly, this was derived from a sense of powerlessness in the face of a world-wide crisis. The sense of national emergency generated after 1931 reinforced the concept of the depression as a natural catastrophe for which there was no obvious solution or scapegoat. W. G. Runciman suggested that because whole communities tended to suffer in common, there was relatively little resentment or ill-feeling among the unemployed. They tended to measure their status and position in relation to a relatively small frame of reference. This suggests that their perceptions of unemployment were conditioned by the experience of those about them. If they too were suffering from unemployment, then there was little sense of what Runciman calls 'relative deprivation'.[70] Thus the Pilgrim Trust investigators found in Co. Durham that the most common reaction of the unemployed was a 'sturdy refusal to give up'.[71] J. B. Priestley encountered a similar response when he toured the Lancashire cotton towns in 1932, remarking on one middle-aged couple who were both out of work: 'Both of them, good independent folk, insisted that they didn't want to ask for anything. Lots worse off than them. They all say that.'[72] Orwell recorded the tendency he found in Wigan for people 'to sit it out', living normal lives in reduced circumstances: 'They have neither turned revolutionary nor lost their self-respect; merely they have kept their tempers and settled down to make the best of things on a fish-and-chip standard.'[73]

Moreover, life could be filled with a round of cheap diversions. The cinema was obviously very popular for all classes and half the unemployed in Cardiff managed to find sufficient money to make a weekly visit. Others filled the day with odd-jobs about the house, while others rose late 'because there's nothing else to do'.[74] Orwell expressed the sense of 'making do' when he wrote that people out of work turned to cheap luxuries:

> When you are unemployed, which is to say when you are underfed, harassed, bored and miserable, you don't *want* to eat dull, wholesome food. You want something a little bit 'tasty'. There is always some cheaply pleasant thing to tempt you. Let's have three pennorth of chips! Run out and buy us a twopenny ice-cream! Put the kettle on and we'll all have a nice cup of tea! *That* is how your mind works when you are at the P.A.C. level.[75]

In the last resort there was always a visit to the Labour Exchange to talk to other people out of work. People passed hours simply standing and talking, or merely watching the goings-on in the street. It was the crowds of men and boys hanging about on the streets which frequently shocked visitors to the depressed areas. J. B. Priestley recorded his impressions at Jarrow: 'Wherever we went there were men hanging about, not scores of them but hundreds and thousands of them.'[76] E. W. Bakke found that in Greenwich the unemployed regarded the cinema as the most exciting event of the week, but the streets themselves were the most common focus for passing time. 'It would be difficult', he wrote, 'to find any leisure-time institution which compares, in numbers involved, with the streets.'[77]

Popular indignation was frequently excited by stories of people marrying on the dole – the infamous 'dole brides' – and of great expenditure on gambling and drink by the unemployed. There was a pervasive myth that the betting shops and public houses had done well out of the depression. Clearly there was an element of exaggeration in these allegations, but there was some truth in all of them. Several writers, including Orwell, pointed out that the unemployed attempted to lead as normal a life as possible on the dole and this often involved marriage and the continuation of customary recreations at a reduced level.[78] The statistics on marriage are not easy to interpret. The percentage of married people in the population as a whole had been rising since the beginning of the century, and the figure for 1931 showed a continued rise in spite of the depression. There was evidence, however, of a fall in the number of marriages among the younger sections of the population.[79] Bakke had noticed that in Greenwich there was a tendency for the unemployed to postpone marriage until conditions improved. In some of the more depressed areas, however, young couples were marrying on the dole, as there was little prospect of improved conditions in the near future and it seemed fruitless to postpone marriage any longer. In addition, the structure of the dole encouraged marriage, providing two could live as cheaply as one and there were not too many children.[80] Thus the Carnegie Trust found that about a third of the unemployed between 18 and 25 in Liverpool and Glasgow had married on the dole. It was not irrelevant to the issue of marriage on the dole that the percentage of illegitimate births was rising during the worst years of the depression, perhaps influenced by the difficulties of affording marriage.[81]

Fears that the unemployed were turning to drink were not borne out by experience. The total and *per capita* consumption of alcohol was declining throughout the inter-war period. By 1929 the amount of beer consumed compared with 1900 had fallen by half and that of spirits by three-quarters. The main reasons were increasing prices and the rise of other forms of leisure. Combined with the decreasing strength of beer, this led to a decline in offences related to drunkenness. In York, Rowntree found that the number of prosecutions had fallen from 52·6 per 10,000 inhabitants in 1900–9 to 12·3 in 1930–7. He commented that 'one may pass through working-class streets every evening for weeks and not see a drunken person'.[82] The onset of depression had little impact upon these long-term changes. H. Mannheim argued that drunkenness was a crime of affluence rather than slump.[83] This was backed up by evidence from the depressed areas that there was no increase in drunken offences. The pub did not figure prominently in the recreations mentioned by the unemployed and Bakke noted that in Greenwich the unemployed tended to drink less than normal because it was too expensive.[84] Thus, while there were certainly isolated examples of unemployment turning people to drink, it was not a feature which was sufficiently common to be regarded as a major problem. Nor did the depression lead to an increase in the consumption of alcohol in general: the consumption of beer continued to decline during the depression and there is no evidence to suggest that it rose in the depressed areas or among the unemployed.

There was, however, more truth in the allegation that unemployment had not halted the passion for gambling which many social investigators lamented. Britain experienced a widespread gambling boom in the thirties, partly stimulated by the growth of new outlets, such as the football pools, greyhound racing, and the technically illegal Irish Sweepstake. Almost all commentators were agreed that gambling was a firmly entrenched part of working-class life by the

time of the depression and that there was a tendency for the unemployed to keep up the habit in spite of their reduced circumstances.
Rowntree said that it was regarded as Public Enemy Number 1 by
police, magistrates and social workers. He calculated that each
household spent between £20 and £40 a year on betting, commenting,
'There is no doubt that among a vast number of people, football
pools have become an obsession and actually constitute the chief
interest of their lives.'[85] Bakke found that gambling was kept up
more than drinking among the unemployed, but they placed smaller
bets.[86] The Pilgrim Trust also commented upon the 'all-pervading
atmosphere of football pools, greyhounds and horses' which they
found among the Liverpool unemployed. 'The extent to which the
interests and indeed the whole lives of so many of the Liverpool
unemployed centre round the pools must be seen to be believed,'
they wrote.[87] Betting provided some excitement and diversion from
the boredom of unemployment and it was hardly surprising that
many refused to give up what pleasure they could still obtain by
placing small bets on the pools, dogs or horses.

Unemployment had many different effects, in most cases extremely difficult to distinguish from the operation of other factors.
Both at the time and subsequently, unemployment was blamed for
a host of social problems, many of which would have existed even
in conditions of full or almost full employment. Poverty, ill-health
and bad housing, for example, were endemic features of life in the
inter-war period for a substantial section of the population. Unemployment often exacerbated these problems but it can rarely be
regarded as either the sole or the major cause of them. A classic
instance of the bogus correlation between unemployment and social
conditions was cited earlier in the case of the incidence of tuberculosis
in Jarrow; the disease was in fact found to be related less to unemployment than to more general social conditions. The repetition of
this example is important because it illustrates much that was
wrong with the more impressionistic reporting in the depressed
areas at the time and the less excusable features of later writing.
The more serious-minded social investigators were only too well
aware of the difficulty of assessing the relative role of unemployment as a factor in the social conditions in the depressed areas. By
the end of the 1930s, unemployment had become a synonym for
the 'condition of England question'. A number of writers self-
consciously used the issue of unemployment as the spearhead of a
general attack upon social conditions and the political system which

allowed them to arise. In this climate the impact of unemployment became blurred by the desire to proselytise about the condition of the depressed areas, with little regard for the niceties of the precise role of unemployment in bringing them about.

Clearly, unemployment did have ill-effects upon substantial sections of the population. In many cases it slowed down improvements which had been taking place during the first decades of the century and in some cases reversed the trend altogether. On the other hand, there was little hard evidence that the depression had brought the depressed areas to the brink of social collapse. Even where a link could be established between unemployment and a social problem such as juvenile crime, there were usually many other factors at work too. It is important to remember Orwell's comment that, although he had seen every kind of privation in Wigan and Barnsley, 'I probably saw much less *conscious* [sic] misery than I should have seen ten years ago.' He recorded with great perception the way in which the unemployed had 'settled down ... without going spiritually to pieces'.[88] Thus it does no justice to the thousands of families who endured unemployment to exaggerate their sufferings. These were real enough and were recorded faithfully by many conscientious investigators.

While it would be impossible to deny that unemployment brought misery and suffering to many thousands of people, with all the bitterness and humiliations that poverty and powerlessness could create, it is plausible to argue that unemployment was often only an added burden to existing social deprivation. This and the characteristic fatalism of the unemployed help to explain the absence of greater social reaction to mass unemployment. Poverty and ill-health were almost certainly made worse in some areas by unemployment, but there was a striking degree of normality. Crime and suicide rates showed little clear evidence of social breakdown, nor did the behaviour of the unemployed suggest that major changes were taking place in the patterns of working-class life. But social reactions were not the only ones feared as a consequence of mass unemployment. The slump also brought on a political crisis which to many people appeared as alarming as the prospects of social dislocation and suffering. How would the unemployed and the electorate as a whole react to the onset of depression and unemployment on an unprecedented scale, both in terms of voting patterns and support for extremist movements? It is to these reactions that we must now turn.

VI
Labour and the Working Class: The General Election of 1931

The political repercussions of the slump were first felt by the second Labour Government, which had taken office under Ramsay MacDonald after the 1929 General Election. For two years after 1929, the government had struggled ineffectually to reduce unemployment and to restore business confidence in the face of a worsening economic climate. The financial and political crisis of August 1931 led to the resignation of the Labour Government and the formation of the National Government under Ramsay MacDonald. The General Election which followed was the first test of the changed political climate and the mood of public opinion after the collapse of the Labour Government. It produced, as was seen earlier, a massive landslide for the National Government. This defeat in the October 1931 election is still very much part of the mythology of the Labour movement. For Labour supporters, 1931 was the election when the party went down to cataclysmic and catastrophic defeat, betrayed by MacDonald and deserted by its working-class supporters. For them, 1931, like 1924, was a Red Scare election, a trick contest. It was an election of savings bank alarms and scurrilous National Government propaganda.

The reason for this mistaken mythology is not difficult to find. For both historians and activists at the time, Labour's defeat in the 1931 election and MacDonald's 'betrayal' are inseparable. It is worth approaching 1931 from a different angle. If there had been no split in the party, no rushed election in 1931, what would Labour's electoral chances have been?

The answer to that question can be given with some certainty: a Labour reverse was almost inevitable. Long before the crisis of

1931, public disillusion with the Labour Government was growing. One recent historian has written of the second Labour Government:

> Few governments have entered office with higher hopes and wider goodwill, few have fallen less lamented by friends as well as foes. It entered office just as the illness of the British economy, chronic since the war, took a desperate turn, brought on by the widening world depression. Labour, by desperate remedies, might have saved the day. Instead, it followed the half measures of its predecessors. When these failed, it forfeited the nation's confidence and opened the gate once more for the Conservatives. It was weakened from within, by resignations, and by criticism from the Left. It fell a victim of its own shortcomings as much as of some strange political manœuvres.[1]

Mowat's devastating criticism of the MacDonald administration can be seen echoed at the time in a growing series of by-election reverses for Labour.

One of the first by-elections after the 1929 General Election, Fulham West on 6 May, 1930, showed a 3·4 per cent swing to the Conservatives. Shortly afterwards, however, in by-elections in Nottingham Central and Glasgow Shettleston, the swing against the government averaged 9 per cent. Despite a creditable result for the government in Norfolk North on 9 July, 1930, the by-elections in the late autumn of 1930 showed a persistent and strong anti-government swing.

To some extent, however, Labour's unpopularity in these contests was overshadowed by the various Empire Crusade candidates fighting against Baldwin's party line. At Bromley, on 2 September, 1930, an Empire Crusade candidate secured 24 per cent of the poll; at Paddington South on 30 October, 1930, an Empire Crusader won the seat against Conservative and Labour opposition by 941 votes.

These divisions in the Conservative ranks, which came to a head in the famous by-election in the St George's division of Westminster, were of little consolation to the Liberals, whose by-election performance proved no less dreary than the party's parliamentary performance. In the first contests fought by Liberals after the 1929 General Election, the Liberal vote was uniformly down, with particularly poor results at Twickenham (August 1929), Nottingham Central (May 1930) and Bromley (September 1930). Although the party did well at Shipley (November 1930) and Whitechapel (December 1930), in three-cornered contests the Liberal vote had slipped substantially. The shift in public opinion was also to be seen in the 1930 local government contests. The elections of November 1930 provided the first check for eight years to Labour's municipal advance. In line with the parliamentary by-election performance of the party, the check was substantial. As the *Yorkshire Post* commented, the Conservative gains were sufficiently emphatic to indicate a direct swing of the political pendulum. Labour gained only 27 seats, losing 92. This net loss of 65 seats was sufficient for Labour to lose control of Leeds, Hull, Swansea, Barnsley and Blackburn – in this latter borough, 10 of the 11 Conservative candidates swept the board. The Conservatives enjoyed a net gain of 69 in the large boroughs, while the Liberals, despite this anti-Labour swing, still suffered a net loss of 8 seats. Neville Chamberlain, Chairman of the Conservative Party, saw in the results 'A striking example of Labour's complete failure to cope with the distress under which the country is now suffering'.

Such a statement was a little ingenuous. The results were partly a natural swing back from 1927, partly a protest at the government, but perhaps as much as anything due to a renewal and extension of Conservative–Liberal municipal pacts.[2] None the less, however, these municipal elections were confirmation that Labour's electoral peak of 1929 now lay far behind.

During 1931, increasingly high swings against Labour developed. The absence of a Liberal candidate in the by-election at Liverpool East Toxteth (5 February, 1931) produced a somewhat freak 14·9 per cent swing to the Conservatives. In by-elections in East Woolwich and Ashton-under-Lyne in April, the anti-Labour swing was 6·5 per cent and 8·3 per cent respectively. As 1931 progressed, even higher swings were recorded – 9·6 per cent in St Rollox (7 May) – and by the time the crisis was at its height swings of 13·9 per cent were recorded in Gateshead (8 June) and 11·1 per cent in the Wavertree division of Liverpool (23 June). Curiously, during the lifetime of the second Labour Government, Labour had lost only 3 seats – at Fulham West, Shipley and Ashton-under-Lyne – but far more significant in terms of any future General Election had been the Liberal collapse. In every contested by-election (except for Scarborough, where no Labour candidate stood) the Liberal share of the poll had fallen, in many cases disastrously.

This, however, was of little comfort for the Labour Party. For the lessons of the by-elections were clear. Long before MacDonald 'betrayed' the Labour Party, the electorate had already given clear indications of its disenchantment with the shortcomings of the government.

There was a second, and perhaps even more fundamental, reason why the Labour Party faced a General Election with much to fear from the voters. The reason lay in the circumstances of the 1929 election. In that year, though emerging for the first time as the largest single party, Labour did not fare nearly as well as some historians would have us believe.

In the euphoria of Labour's success in May 1929, a variety of features of the party's victory had been obscured. Though the party had, for the first time in its history, become the largest single party, a large proportion of its victories had been won with the slenderest of margins. In addition, the chance workings of the electoral system had actually benefited Labour. With fewer votes than the Conservatives, Labour had actually won more seats. As a result, with many seats won by narrow margins, even a small decline in Labour's popularity at any subsequent election was likely to produce widespread losses. Labour had a further source of concern. Many of these Labour victories had been achieved in three-cornered fights on a minority vote. No less than 41 per cent of Labour-held seats in 1929 had been won on a minority vote, compared to 21·9 per cent in 1924. The 1929 figure was the highest in the party's history.

Underlying all these factors, however, was the crucial problem of the Liberal vote and seats. If, as Liberals themselves were privately admitting, 1929 had been a battle lost, the chances of Liberals retaining either the seats or votes achieved in 1929 were fairly remote. But, as Labour realists accepted, the only immediate beneficiary of a Liberal collapse could be the Conservative Party. Of the 59 seats won by Liberals in 1929, 40 had been gained on a minority vote. In the great majority of these seats, Conservatives were the main challengers. Any small movement of Liberal votes to Conservative would thus produce a large number of Conservative gains. Ironically, even on a movement of Liberal votes to Labour, though possibly giving Labour victory in such Liberal-held industrial seats as Middlesbrough or Wolverhampton, or in London seats such as Bethnal Green and Lambeth, the most likely consequence of Liberal votes shifting to Labour in the rural areas would be to *increase* the likelihood of a Conservative victory—the old process of alignment that had happened in 1924.

Thus, the 1929 General Election, though a marked step forward for Labour, had hardly been the secure victory that on the surface it appeared. It was difficult to see where Labour could easily advance: it was very easy to see its flank dangerously exposed to either a Conservative revival or a Liberal collapse. History, with an unkind twist, presented the Labour Government with both in the period from 1929 to 1931, as the by-elections examined earlier revealed.

These were the fundamental, background factors that faced Labour in any General Election. The advent of the National Government added two more disastrous factors in the equation. Labour was now a divided party (even if divided in unequal parts). Even more vital, the opposition parties were likely to present a united front for the next election.

Here was the cardinal fact that decided, not merely the 1931 election, but the electoral politics of the following decade. The once-great Liberal Party had become, in reality if not in name, an adjunct of the Conservative Party.

This is not to say that the Liberals entered the National Government wanting this. Rather, once the Liberals entered the Coalition, they were ensnared in a trap from which there was no escape. No party fought more bitterly against the 1931 election than the Liberals under Samuel. But they had no effective way of preventing an election. MacDonald himself, with only the support of a tiny breakaway Labour group, could provide no barrier. To add to the Liberal dilemma, those Liberals following Simon, who were much closer to the Conservatives, were secure in the knowledge that they would not face Conservative opposition. Hence they were not slow to discomfort Samuel by agreeing with the Conservative clamour for an election.

Samuel and the Independent Liberals were hopelessly ensnared. On the evening of 5 October, the Cabinet decided on an appeal to the country. On 6 October, MacDonald formally saw the King. Polling day was fixed for 27 October. Despite their opposition to an election, neither Samuel nor Reading resigned from the government. Meanwhile Lloyd George fumed at the decision and two of his family resigned junior posts.

In many ways, the circumstances of the dissolution had already foreshadowed the way the contest would go. The nominations completed this scenario. Not surprisingly, Labour entered the nominations with considerable handicaps. Finance was one factor making the selection of candidates, especially in the remoter rural seats, very difficult. The most embarrassing situations were in those constituencies, such as Kilmarnock or Bassetlaw, where the sitting M.P. was a

National Labour supporter. Thus in MacDonald's own constituency of Seaham, the local Labour Party voted by a majority of only one vote to disown their leader. With the constituency party split down the middle, there was virtually no time to elect new officers or ward organisers. Even more of a handicap from Labour's point of view was the fact that all the party literature and publicity had to be totally rewritten after MacDonald's defection in the minimum of time.

These were severe handicaps for Labour. It is testimony to the party's will to fight on that it was still able to field some 516 candidates. The Liberals, by way of contrast, presented an abject sight; the party entered the election in the most hopeless position in which it had yet found itself.

With Lloyd George hostile to the election, no money was forthcoming from his Fund. In consequence, only a mere 118 candidates were fielded by the Samuelites, leaving many of the promising seats fought in 1929 uncontested. Money, however, was not the only factor. Few Liberals in 1931 evinced much fighting spirit. The will to win had vanished. For, in everything but name, the Liberals fought the election as prisoners of a Conservative-dominated Coalition.

Though the Liberals fought 1931 as allies of the National Government, the relationship between Liberals (at least the Samuelites) and Conservatives was not always harmonious. Thus, although Samuel himself was supported by Baldwin, no less than 5 Liberal ministers were opposed by Conservatives, whereas all 30 Conservative ministers were unopposed by Liberals. No less than 81 clashes took place between Samuelite Liberals and Conservatives.

By way of contrast, the Simon Liberals enjoyed a much happier position. Not only, by and large, were their constituencies more safely Liberal, but by agreeing to support the government's tariff proposals, they enjoyed far more Conservative goodwill. No less than 35 of the 54 Conservative candidates withdrawn in 1931 were removed from the lists to support Liberal Nationals. Only one straight fight occurred between a Conservative and a Liberal National, whereas 26 occurred between Conservatives and Samuelite Liberals, and only 4 constituencies saw a clash of Simonite and Conservative candidates. Thus, although the Simonite Liberals fielded only 41 candidates, their electoral prospects were immeasurably brighter. Their likely success, however, lay not in their own strength but in their good relations with the Conservatives, whose restraint in bringing candidates against them was the vital factor.

Their position, as effective prisoners of the Conservatives, was also shared by the rump of National Labour M.P.s who followed MacDonald. Even more than the Liberal Nationals, they had no real grassroots strength or organisation of their own. Consequently, they were dependent on the Conservatives not fielding candidates against them, and Stonehaven, the Chairman of the Conservative Party Organisation, put in strenuous efforts to prevent Conservatives taking the field. None the less, MacDonald was bitter that he was not doing enough (an unjustified charge), while clashes occurred in several constituencies. In the event, 20 National Labour candidates were fielded, dotted fairly evenly throughout the country.

Out of this variety of cross-currents, at the close of nominations the totals of party candidates provided some important evidence of relative strength and morale. Labour eventually was able to field a total of some 516 candidates, including 25 unendorsed candidatures. This figure represented a fall of 53 from the 569 candidates fielded in 1929. In all, however, Labour could not be too unhappy in the circumstances of 1931 — it was still putting up slightly more candidates than in 1924, and a far greater total than the 427 fielded in 1923 when it had gone on to form its first administration. Six Labour M.P.s were returned unopposed in 1931, whereas none had enjoyed this luxury in 1929.

It was the Liberals who showed the greatest reduction in candidates in 1931. In 1929, the party had brought forward a massive 513 candidates, fighting a host of seats that had rarely been contested in the decade after 1918. In 1931, the total number of Liberal candidates was a mere 118 — easily the smallest total fielded by the Liberals in the inter-war period and a dramatic indication of how far the disintegration of the party had progressed. The Liberal Nationals put up 41 candidates and enjoyed 7 unopposed returns. Of the other minor parties, the communists fielded 26 candidates and Mosley's New Party 22 standard-bearers.

The significance of these figures cannot be emphasised too strongly. The greatly reduced field of Liberal candidates, together with Conservative support for Liberal Nationals and National Labour, meant that Labour's opponents were more united than at any previous election. This was reflected in a massive reduction in three-cornered contests and a correspondingly large number of straight fights. These figures are clearly demonstrated in Table 6.1.

In over 400 constituencies, Labour candidates found themselves faced with a single opponent. Only 99 Labour candidates faced

TABLE 6.1   TYPES OF CONTESTED ELECTION, 1918–31

	straight fights	three-cornered contests	more than 3 candidates
1918	311	211	47
1922	293	212	23
1923	280	254	1
1924	318	223	5
1929	98	447	26
1931	409	99	14

both Conservative *and* Liberal opponents, compared to 447 in 1929. At no previous election in the inter-war period had there been so many straight fights or so few three-cornered contests.

This coming-together of Labour's opponents greatly diminished Labour's electoral prospects. These prospects received their final body-blow as the election campaign developed. From the start, the way in which the battle-lines were drawn successfully precluded the possibility of a clear-cut campaign for and against the Conservatives, and covered over the threatened split in the government ranks over the issue of Protection. The call to unity, MacDonald's key appeal, was echoed again and again by Baldwin and Samuel. MacDonald's own personal position was exploited as much as possible in the campaign, though whether he really carried the Labour vote with him is highly debatable.

In many ways, the main struggle of the election was between the official Labour Party and the ex-Labour ministers of the National Government, each side attacking the other for betrayal and desertion in the hour of crisis. Snowden in particular attacked his erstwhile Labour colleagues as 'the party that ran away', while Labour's personal hatred was most concentrated on MacDonald and to a lesser extent on Thomas and Snowden.

Both at the time and later, there was much discussion that the electorate was panicked into voting for the Coalition in 1931.[3] The Post Office Savings Bank scare was the tactic most frequently cited. According to Mowat, the stratagem was to frighten savers into the belief that their hard-earned savings would be squandered by a Labour government to pay for the dole.[4] Henderson attacked the statement (originally made by Runciman and taken up by Snowden) as 'simply an attempt to alarm the electors at the eleventh hour'.

H

The extent to which this alarmist attempt worked is debatable, but it was certainly true that some of the largest increases in turn-out came from the north-east. In retrospect, party activists placed much blame on this cause. Yet analysis of the votes hardly supports this theory. Runciman in fact made this particular speech in South Shields, a town on the south side of the mouth of the river Tyne. However, the drop in Labour support in South Shields itself was well below the average for the country as a whole, as well as below the average for the north-east.

The whole assumption of a panic election has rightly been disputed. Bassett, for example, cites a comment from the *Manchester Guardian* of 29 October to the effect that 'it has been a remarkably quiet election' and though there were some reports of rowdyism these were very much isolated incidents.

Probably far more important than any scare or panic was the inadequacy of the Liberal campaign. In 1929, the Liberals had polled over 5·3 million votes. Now, with only 118 candidates, many hundreds of thousands of previous Liberal voters had no candidate of their own. How would they vote? And what would happen in the constituencies with Liberal candidates? Everything would depend on the nature of the Liberal campaign.

The Liberals had entered the election campaign with few illusions about the likely result. As Ramsay Muir admitted, the dice were loaded against the party. On every side, the prospects were bleak. The Liberals had simply no independent policy to put forward — except support for National candidates who were in most cases Protectionist. Meanwhile, the fact that the Liberals supported the National Government and were represented in it had not stopped Conservatives attacking sitting Liberals.

With Lloyd George opposed to Samuel's policy, and urging Liberals to vote Labour in the absence of Liberal candidates, the hapless Liberal Party entered the election attempting to travel in three directions simultaneously. The Simonites had adopted a semi-Conservative position, the Samuelite official party offered a non-Conservative, anti-Labour stance, and Lloyd George attempted to revive a Liberal-Labour alliance.

In the circumstances of 1931, a victory for the National Government was probably inevitable. In the event, the Conservatives were returned with no less than 471 seats. Labour secured a mere 52 seats, the Liberal Nationals returned 35, the Samuelite Liberals 33 and the Lloyd George family group numbered 4. There were 12

National Labour members. The full results are displayed in Table 6.2.

In terms of gains and losses, Labour could hardly have fared more disastrously. Labour had lost no less than 215 seats, with not a solitary gain to compensate for this disaster. The Conservatives, with 202 gains and not a single loss, had captured no less than 182 Labour seats. Liberal Nationals had captured another 10 Labour seats, while Liberals had taken 14. Though the New Party had fared

TABLE 6.2   RESULTS OF THE 1931 GENERAL ELECTION

party	total votes	% of total
National Government:		
Conservative	11,905,925	55·0
National	72,820	0·3
National Liberal	809,302	3·7
Liberal	1,403,102	6·5
National Labour	341,370	1·6
Total Govt vote	14,532,519	67·1
Opposition:		
Labour	6,649,630	30·7
Independent Liberal (L.G.)	106,106	0·5
New Party (Mosley)	36,377	0·2
Communist	74,824	0·3
Irish Nationalist	123,053	0·6
Others	133,864	0·6
Total Opp. vote	7,123,854	32·9
Total vote cast	21,656,373	100·0

disastrously, and National Labour not much better, for Labour there was hardly any comfort.

For the Labour leadership, the results were even worse: the parliamentary Labour Party had been almost completely annihilated, and its leading figures had suffered worst than most. Arthur Henderson, Foreign Secretary under MacDonald and Leader of the Party after the defection, went down to defeat in Burnley. No fewer than 12 other former Cabinet ministers were defeated, and 21 former junior ministers. The list of casualties included Clynes, Dalton, Greenwood, Johnston and Morrison, leaving only Lansbury of the former Labour Cabinet holding his seat. Two other junior ministers, Attlee and Cripps, also survived – Attlee by 551 votes in his East End stronghold of Limehouse, and Cripps by 429 votes in Bristol East. Thus not only had some 215 Labour M.P.s gone crashing down to defeat, but the most experienced and able of the party's leadership was either out of parliament or had defected with MacDonald.

Even the most seemingly secure of the party's strongholds had been lost: five seats in Durham alone had gone, including such working-class bastions as Blaydon, Houghton and even Jarrow. Five more seats went in Glasgow, including Springburn and Camlachie. In industrial Scotland, the Labour strongholds of Lanarkshire virtually all fell. Of the big cities, Labour was totally without representation in such towns as Birmingham, Salford, Cardiff, Wolverhampton and Plymouth. Almost incredibly, no less than 30 constituencies with a Labour majority of over 10,000 in 1929 had fallen in 1931, while some 96 Conservatives, 7 Liberal Nationals and 2 National Labour enjoyed majorities over 20,000. Not a single Labour or Liberal candidate enjoyed such support.

Not all parts of the country, however, were equally disastrous for Labour. As we shall examine later, many of the mining areas – especially South Wales, west Lancashire and west Yorkshire – remained unshaken in their loyalty to Labour and the party still retained much of its strength in the slum areas of the East End of London and in Glasgow. These, however, were small consolations as Labour viewed the triumphant Coalition forces.

However, not all partners in the Coalition had achieved the same degree of electoral success. For the real prizes had been captured by the Conservatives. As Kinnear has written of the Conservative triumph, the Conservatives had secured nearly everything in 1931, and had sufficient M.P.s from England alone to govern with an overwhelming majority.[5] The Conservatives took no less than 182 seats from Labour, including a massive tally from virtually every major town and industrial area. The Conservatives also took 9 Liberal seats, 6 from Independent and 4 apiece from the New Party and from National Labour.[6]

Virtually the only areas not to return Conservatives in the 1931 landslide were Wales (where Labour remained entrenched in the mining valleys) and the East End of London (where the Coalition successes were mainly secured by Liberal or Liberal National candidates).

The National Labour Party emerged from the election in a rather peculiar position. As a party, National Labour hardly existed. But its leading figures enjoyed personal success. Thus MacDonald himself was returned for Seaham with a 5,951 majority. Jimmy Thomas romped home in the double-member constituency of Derby with a majority over 27,000. Malcolm MacDonald was returned at Bassetlaw, a Nottingham mining seat. Outside these constituencies, however, the National Labour Party they represented had shown itself to be a pathetic force: at best a party of chiefs rather than Indians. With 20 candidates, it had polled a mere 341,370 votes – only 1·6 per cent of all votes cast. Though returning 13-strong to Westminster (with 3 gains and 2 losses), outside a very few seats it had proved to possess no real voting appeal.

Rather like the Lloyd George Liberals after the 1918 Coalition, the party clearly lacked both a constituency base and any real electoral support. Of the party's 13 elected M.P.s, only 5 would probably have still been elected if Conservative candidates had been in the field.[7] The other eight constituencies – seats such as Kilmarnock, Nottingham South and Cardiff Central – were all highly likely to have returned Conservatives if these had not let National Labour candidates enjoy straight fights.

Like their Conservative allies, but unlike National Labour, the Liberal Nationals had good reason to be pleased with the outcome of the election. Of the 41 Liberal National candidates, 35 had been elected. In all, the party had polled over 809,000 votes. The Liberal Nationals had gained a variety of normally secure Labour strongholds, both in London, the north-east and in Scotland.[8]

As a result of the 1931 election, the Samuelite Liberals numbered 33, and there were in addition the four Independent Liberals, all members of Lloyd George's family group. In all, therefore, the combined Liberal ranks numbered 72 and, on the surface, the Liberals had increased their representation by 13. This, however, was an increase in numbers without real substance. Its seats gained were won from Labour in the absence of Conservatives, whereas in 1929 its seats had been won by its own merit.

Only 10 of the 72 elected Liberals had been faced with Conservative opponents, 6 of these in Wales or Scotland. The Liberals held 46 of the seats won in 1929, losing 13 (all to Conservatives) and taking 26 – again all from Labour. Thus, in Durham, Liberals captured such normally solid Labour seats as Consett and Bishop Auckland in the absence of Conservative candidates. At least in 1931, however, the Liberal leadership survived. But although Samuel retained his seat at Darwen with a 4,000 majority, Donald Maclean only narrowly held North Cornwall. Two Liberal ministers, Milner Gray in Mid-Bedfordshire and E. D. Simon in Penryn, were both defeated.

It was in terms of votes cast, however, that the Liberal reverse was most noticeable. Compared to 1929, the combined Liberal vote had fallen by over 3 million, the Labour vote by only 1½ million. From virtually every side, the Liberals had lost ground. In the 51 seats contested in 1929 and 1931 by all three parties, the Liberal vote slumped. Only where no Conservative candidate was in the field were Liberals able to benefit from the swing to the National Government. Once again, as the party looked at the debris of the 1931 battle, the old truth again became apparent. Without Lloyd George, the Liberal Party did indeed seem doomed.

Lloyd George played relatively little part in the electoral landslide of 1931. But at the other political extreme, one politician had attempted to play a dramatic role. For, in 1931, Mosley had led his followers in the New Party into battle. From whichever side Mosley looked at the results, the figures revealed a total humiliation. The party had fielded 24 candidates; all but two of these went down to the ignominy of a lost deposit, the highest proportion of any party.[9]

The New Party had placed its highest hopes in 1931 on the sitting M.P.s who chose to fight the election, but they fared disastrously. In Galloway, a rural constituency in south-west Scotland, the New Party candidate, Dudgeon, who had represented the constituency as a Liberal, secured only 3 per cent of the vote. In the industrial West Renfrewshire division, Robert Forgan, the sitting Labour member, secured only 4 per cent of the vote as a New Party candidate.

In Merthyr Tydfil, a New Party candidate did well to take 30 per cent of the vote in a straight fight with Labour, but by far the best result for the party was, predictably, in Stoke. Here Sir Oswald Mosley contested the seat his wife had represented for Labour. Although finishing in third place, Mosley secured 24 per cent of the votes cast. The Conservatives captured the seat from Labour.[10] No less than 17 candidates polled a derisory 2½ per cent of the poll or less. In all, the 22 candidates of the New Party had polled 36,777 votes. Skidelsky has called the formation of the New Party in February 1931 as 'surely the most bizarre episode in modern British politics'. The electoral venture in 1931 certainly bears out this statement.

For Labour supporters, the humiliation of the New Party was

little comfort to their own party's disaster. But how disastrous, in fact, was Labour's performance? A closer analysis of Labour in 1931, looking beyond the statistics of seats gained and lost and examining *votes cast*, shows the result rather differently.

The first fact that cannot be too strongly emphasised is that the figures in Table 6.3 show Labour polled more votes in 1931 than in any previous election except for 1929.

TABLE 6.3   THE LABOUR VOTE: 1922–31

	votes cast	*% of all votes cast*
1922	4,237,349	29·7
1923	4,439,780	30·7
1924	5,489,070	33·3
1929	8,370,417	37·1
1931	6,649,630	30·8

Even the average vote obtained by Labour candidates in 1931 was higher than in 1918 or even 1922. The simple reason why Labour had lost 4 out of every 5 seats it was defending was that its opponents were united. Linked to this was the collapse of the Liberal vote. This Liberal collapse, not desertions from the Labour faithful, was the key factor.

No doubt Labour lost some votes to the National Government candidates, but what really hurt was the solid Liberal support for those candidates. It appears that few Liberal voters in 1931 heeded Lloyd George's advice to vote Labour where there was no Liberal candidate. As a result, Labour had to depend on the seats where it could count on a clear majority of the voters. Hence, the great difference in 1931 was not the collapse of the Labour vote, which in some areas held remarkably well; it was the joining forces of the Liberal and Conservative ranks.

In explaining many facets of political behaviour in the thirties, this fact is of cardinal importance. For in many of its industrial heartlands, the Labour vote did not collapse in 1931. One such example can be seen in South Wales. In the mining areas of Glamorgan Labour's vote, far from collapsing, actually increased. In every constituency in the county, Labour's vote was up from its 1929 level.[11]

It says little for MacDonald's appeal to working-class Labour voters that in the constituency he had once represented, Aberavon, the Labour vote increased. Other Labour seats were equally rock-solid in 1931. Thus in Neath, Labour had never before polled such a high percentage of votes cast, a feat equalled in the Pontypridd division.

Labour's support in the mining seats of Monmouthshire was equally impressive. The absolute Labour vote was up by 6½ per cent in Pontypool, and by 23 per cent in Monmouth, helped in this case by the withdrawal of a Liberal. Elsewhere in Monmouthshire, Labour was unopposed in Abertillery, Bedwellty and Ebbw Vale, a luxury the party had not enjoyed in 1929. In the Carmarthenshire mining seat of Llanelli the Labour vote was also up, by 19·6 per cent over 1929. As far as the valleys of South Wales were concerned, 1931 was one of the best-ever electoral performances by the Labour Party.

Perhaps the most interesting display of the solidarity of the Labour vote can be seen, not in South Wales, but in Durham and the north-east, the very area where MacDonald's personal influence might be expected to be strongest. Labour's solidarity in Durham was remarkable.[12] Thus, in such seats as Barnard Castle, Bishop Auckland or Sedgefield the Labour vote had either stayed virtually the same as in 1929 or even increased. Apart from MacDonald's own constituency at Seaham, where his personal following is the only explanation for the collapse in the Labour vote, it was ironic that Labour's next worst result was none other than Jarrow, the very symbol of the depression in the north-east.

It was not only Durham which demonstrated the solidity of the Labour vote in 1931. Elsewhere in the north-east, Labour's support in its working-class strongholds held remarkably well. The figures show an extraordinary Labour resilience, most noticeably in the large coastal towns such as South Shields and Stockton-on-Tees. The two most noticeable exceptions to this rule, Newcastle and Gateshead, are significant. Both were towns where Liberals had retained considerable strength during the 1920s. In addition, the Newcastle Central constituency had a large proportion of middle-class voters and a strong business vote which may well explain Labour's relatively weaker performance. Tynemouth, also a poor result, was a town in which N.U.W.M. influence was strong and communist sympathies may have weakened the Labour cause. Overall, however, Labour's vote in the north-east held well.

Just as Seaham was unrepresentative of the north-east, so also was Derby far from representative of other railway towns. Here Jimmy Thomas, the N.U.R. leader and one of the best-known figures who had followed MacDonald, achieved a good result. But his influence failed to extend to other railway towns. Thus, Swindon and Carlisle actually saw increased Labour votes in 1931, while two more, Crewe and York, had only a slight decline. The heavy fall in the Labour vote at Derby (in a town of heavier unemployment than the other railway centres) is undoubtedly attributable to Thomas's personal following and the subsequent divisions in the local party. But Thomas, despite his N.U.R. background, seems to have carried few railway workers with him elsewhere in the country.

An important corollary of Labour's relative success in working-class strongholds was the fact that Labour was also doing well in areas of the greatest unemployment. The depressed areas had always been solidly Labour. The vital fact of 1931 is that they remained so.

TABLE 6.4   AREAS OF HIGHEST UNEMPLOYMENT: 1932[13]

Borough	% unemployed	% of 1929 Lab. vote retained in 1931
Sunderland	36·6	93·4
South Shields	35·9	108·3
Merthyr Tydfil	35·8	108·5
West Hartlepool	34.7	130·8
Middlesbrough East	27·7	98·9
Middlesbrough West	27·7	97·8
Newcastle East	26·9	83·8
Newcastle West	26·9	80·2
Rhondda East	25·9	116·2
Rhondda West	25·9	99·1

In the twelve borough constituencies with the highest levels of unemployment, the Labour vote was 95 per cent of its total in 1929 (see Table 6.4).[14] In four seats, its absolute vote had risen, in four more it was over 90 per cent of its 1929 level.

These figures are interesting evidence of the extent to which MacDonald carried the working-class vote with him. One view of MacDonald's influence has been clearly stated by Bassett:

The clearest indications of Labour support for the Government came from the many Labour strongholds won by non-Labour

National Government candidates. These included well over thirty constituencies in which Labour had had a majority of over ten thousand in 1929 ... No Conservative or Liberal, merely as such, could have won any of these seats: they were won because of the extensive Labour support for MacDonald and his associates; a fact which conditioned the political situation in the subsequent years.[15]

This certainly seemed to be confirmed in the results of MacDonald himself at Seaham, Thomas at Derby, and Malcolm MacDonald at Bassetlaw. Contemporary Labour figures tended to spread this belief. Hugh Dalton explained the Labour débâcle in 1931 by declaring that 'the contagion of Seaham spread like a plague through Durham and Northumberland'.[16]

To some extent, such mining seats as Bishop Auckland, Dalton's own constituency, seemed to add further support to this view. For the mining seats of the north-east fell to the National Government, while similar seats in South Wales (where no major Labour figure defected) were retained by Labour.

Clearly, the support for the MacDonald thesis lies very much in the evidence of Durham and Northumberland, one of the areas where Bassett argued there was a major defection of solid working-class support from Labour.

As was seen earlier, however, this observation is simply not true. In seats such as Bishop Auckland and Sedgefield, the Labour vote did *not* collapse. Only in Seaham itself is there any clear evidence of working-class support deserting the party. Here the Labour vote dropped by 23 per cent, a sharp contrast to the other mining seats. And Seaham was a special case. As one recent study of the north-east has observed:

In the unusual circumstances of 1931, the organisation of the Seaham Labour Party, normally remarkably efficient, was in a state of collapse; the haste with which MacDonald's replacement as official Labour candidate had to be chosen precluded any successful attempt at regaining the confidence of the electorate. In this atmosphere of confusion and uncertainty many people preferred to remain with the familiar figure in whom they had reposed so much faith in the past.[17]

With the exception of Seaham, the Labour seats lost in the north-east were not due to a collapse in the Labour vote. Rather, many of the

National Government victories in this area can be accounted for largely in terms of a combination of increased turn-out and of former Liberal votes going to the Conservatives in the several cases where there had been a Liberal candidate with a substantial proportion of the vote in 1929 and no candidate in 1931.

In 1929 the Liberals had been fairly strong in Durham and Northumberland, perhaps because of the large numbers of Non-conformists (Presbyterians in Northumberland, and mainly Primitive Methodists in Durham). In 1931, this vote went almost entirely Conservative. Clearly, a major factor in Labour's ability to hold a seat in 1931 was not the loyalty of the working class. Rather, it was the proportion of middle class. This is most clearly demonstrated in Labour's mining strongholds. Labour, even in 1931, retained three-quarters of these mining seats where fewer than 10 per cent of the population was middle class. But Labour could hold only one in five of the mining seats where over 10 per cent was middle class.

Labour's share of the total vote was invariably worst in towns where the middle-class vote was largest. In none of the major provincial cities in 1931 did Labour obtain over 50 per cent of the votes cast. However, Labour's *relatively* best results were in the working-class towns, such as Stoke, Sheffield and Hull, and the worst in more middle-class areas such as Portsmouth, Nottingham and Edinburgh. Birmingham, as ever, was an exception to this rule – a working-class town with a very poor Labour performance.

Labour's poor poll was a reflection, not so much of the desertion of its own supporters, as of the massive middle-class vote for the National Government. Nowhere was this middle-class flight to the Conservatives more obviously at work than in London and the Home Counties. In a variety of London suburbs, the Conservative vote rocketed. It was up by 78·7 per cent in Wood Green, 81·2 per cent at Finchley, 78·2 per cent in East Lewisham and 79·1 per cent in Hornsey. Yet this was in no way accompanied by a collapse in the Labour vote; indeed, in two of the seats just mentioned, Hornsey and Finchley, Labour's absolute vote rose.

The same pattern was true of the outer suburbs. The flight to the safety of the Conservative Party was not accompanied by a collapse in Labour's support. Table 6.5 sets out the figures for a variety of the commuter suburbs.

In these boroughs, the average Tory poll had rocketed by 99 per cent, yet the Labour vote was down by only 7 per cent. Similar results can be found in the strongly middle-class seats elsewhere in the

TABLE 6.5 VOTING IN THE COMMUTER OUTER SUBURBS: 1931

	% increase Con. vote	% decrease Lab. vote
Harrow	113·9	9·2
Wimbledon	81·0	2·6
Twickenham	166·3	3·1
Kingston	71·7	14·5
Bromley	85·0	8·3

country: seats such as Wallasey, where the Tory vote surged 87·2 per cent upwards, or seaside resorts such as Southend, with a 68·7 per cent Conservative increase. In all, taking the 14 most middle-class constituencies throughout the country in which comparable figures can be obtained, the Conservative vote rose by over two-thirds (67·9 per cent). But almost 9 out of 10 Labour votes remained stable compared to 1929.

When all these statistics are analysed, the reasons for Labour's electoral defeat become clearer. The middle-class flight to the National Government, the Liberal collapse and the united front facing Labour were far more vital in Labour's defeat than the desertion of the working-class vote – a desertion which was scarcely measurable in the depressed areas.

In addition, a wide variety of causes, some temporary, some more fundamental, contributed to and accentuated Labour's defeat. Labour's press support in 1931, for example, was almost non-existent. Apart from the party's own *Daily Herald*, sympathetic press coverage was restricted to the *Manchester Guardian* and *Reynolds News* – neither having the mass circulation of the Beaverbrook and Rothermere press.

This was a long-term weakness for Labour. Short-term factors in 1931, such as the Post Office Savings Bank scare and the general fear of renewed financial chaos if Labour was returned, may have swelled the middle-class flight to the National Government. As we have seen, there is little evidence that these issues carried much weight with traditional Labour voters. In terms of organisation, Labour was obviously at a disadvantage in 1931. The party split meant that the party's election literature had to be rewritten; many candidates had to be adopted at the last moment, sometimes in seats where the sitting Labour M.P. had defected. Not least, the party had to fight the election with nearly £20,000 less money available than in 1929.

Labour's own inquest on the election, presented to the N.E.C. on 10 November, 1931, by Arthur Henderson, tended to concentrate almost hysterically on the fact that people regarded the Labour Party as men who had 'run away' from the crisis. Henderson also placed much of the blame on the election broadcasts of such people as Snowden. In the aftermath of 1931, such sentiments were understandable. It was only with Labour's rapid recovery at local level after 1931 that it became apparent even to the party hierarchy that Labour's basic support and vitality had not been destroyed in 1931.

VII
Politics and the People, 1931–5

In the General Election of October 1931, the Labour Party had suffered a bitter defeat. Before Labour could embark on the road to recovery, a further humiliation was suffered by the party; for the municipal elections of November 1931 produced a disaster of commensurate proportions to the General Election. After the General Election, the Labour Party no doubt anticipated a major setback. The results easily fulfilled their worst expectations. In the 80 largest boroughs, only 149 of the 709 Labour candidates were successful. Labour gained a mere 5 seats for the loss of 206. The statistical details of the massacre can be seen in Table 7.1.

TABLE 7.1 MUNICIPAL ELECTIONS: NOVEMBER 1931

party	candidates	successful	gains	losses
Con.	465	350	149	5
Lib.	154	107	26	5
Lab.	709	149	5	206
Comm.	50	–	–	–
Ind.	258	154	46	10
	1,636	760	226	226

Even worse than these national figures were the performances in individual boroughs. Not a single Labour candidate was elected in Birmingham, Bradford, Birkenhead, Stockport or Middlesbrough. Only one was returned in Salford and Cardiff. Only 2 of the 31 Labour candidates in Liverpool secured election, 2 of the 12 both in Swindon and Derby, and a mere 3 out of 14 in Coventry. Only Leeds, Sheffield and Manchester (each electing 7 Labour councillors) escaped the worst of the holocaust.

To some extent, the Labour losses were exaggerated by the combination of Conservatives and Liberals. But no excuse could entirely hide the scale of the disaster. In several aspects, however, the municipal elections had followed the pattern of the General Election. In general, the Labour vote had not collapsed; instead, Liberals and Conservatives seemed to have polled their full vote. After the electoral disasters, it was some comfort for Labour to know that its vote had not totally gone. But this was only relatively small consolation.

For the disaster of the municipal elections, following in the wake of the General Election, left the party facing a long and hard road to recovery. It was a path made more difficult by financial weakness at headquarters, where the party faced a deficit in 1932 of some £7,000.[1] To help reduce this deficit, all the staff at Transport House were asked to accept a 5 per cent cut in their salaries, and a variety of other economies were introduced.[2] The most harmful result of these economies, however, was to reduce hard-pressed constituency parties to really desperate measures. Constituency parties eager to engage agents to help rebuild at local level found finance unforthcoming and appointments could not be made. Lack of finance at constituency level made the purchase of party literature almost impossible, which in turn worsened the party's plight at national level.

The most serious consequence of parlous finances, however, was that most closely related to the party's recovery: the inability to field candidates at by-elections. In no less than 5 by-elections during 1932, in such constituencies as Eastbourne, Henley, North Cornwall, St Marylebone and Richmond, no Labour candidates were brought forward.[3] None of these seats was remotely good territory for Labour, but finance was the main reason for Labour's inability to fight. At the same N.E.C. meeting that this was reported, the N.E.C. stated that it felt 'more and more importance should be attached to by-elections'. Thus the curious paradox of Labour's financial weakness was the important decision to establish a central By-Election Insurance Fund, whereby needy constituencies faced with by-elections could be subsidised from the fund for as much as £375. The By-Election Insurance Fund came into operation on 1 January, 1933.

By the late autumn of 1932, the party's organisation and morale had begun to make a noticeable recovery. Labour's new 'A Million New Members and Power' campaign had made much headway, both in terms of publicity and in concrete terms with new members.

By the end of the year Shepherd, the National Agent, was able to inform the N.E.C. that membership had increased by 100,000 with especially good increases in London, the North and the Midlands.[4]

At the same time, there were gradual signs of Labour's electoral recovery. This could be detected in the first parliamentary by-elections since the General Election, held on 9 February, 1932. Both were in rock-solid Conservative strongholds – at South Croydon, and New Forest and Christchurch. On very low turn-out, in straight fights, Labour achieved a swing of 12·8 per cent in Croydon but a mere 1·3 per cent in the New Forest. Neither were contests from which any significant conclusions could be drawn. No Labour candidate contested the Henley by-election of 25 February. A more important contest occurred in Dunbartonshire on 17 March, when Labour achieved a swing of 9·6 per cent. Labour's first by-election victory occurred on 21 April, 1932, when Wakefield was recaptured from the Conservatives, by the narrow margin of 344 votes, on a swing of 8·1 per cent.[5] After a strong Labour poll in the by-election in Montrose Burghs (on 28 June, 1932), Labour went on to gain a second by-election victory at Wednesbury, on 26 July, 1932. Only two further by-elections occurred during 1932, at Twickenham and Cardiganshire. However, the 17·8 per cent swing recorded to Labour in the straight fight at Twickenham was the largest swing-back to Labour yet evidenced. It was a portent of another major area of Labour revival – the municipal elections of November 1932.

The results of 1931 had been a nightmare for Labour. A mere 12 months later, however, a reversal of Labour's fortunes at municipal level had very suddenly occurred. The number of Labour candidates fielded, and their success in comparison with 1931, can be seen in Table 7.2.

TABLE 7.2　RELATIVE SUCCESS OF LABOUR CANDIDATES IN MUNICIPAL ELECTIONS: 1931–2

1931	candi-dates	elected	1932	candi-dates	elected
Con.	465	350	Con.	490	218
Lib.	154	107	Lib.	174	87
Lab.	709	149	Lab.	836	458
Ind.	308	154	Ind.	329	106

Labour won 458 seats (52·7 per cent of the sample) in 1932, one of its highest success rates to date. Although, compared with 1929, Labour only gained a net tally of 15 seats, this was a gain over one of its previous best years. The size of the Labour recovery compared to 1931 was remarkable.[6]

The exact extent of Labour's recovery in 1932, in terms of swing since 1931, is difficult to determine precisely. However, an analysis of comparable contests shows a strong pro-Labour swing. Some of these large swings (of 14 per cent in such towns as Salford and Gateshead) undoubtedly reflected the return of Labour supporters who had abstained in 1931. In many towns, turn-out rose in 1932 to nearer the levels achieved in 1929–30. Thus in Leicester, turn-out had dropped from 44 per cent in 1930 to 33·9 per cent in 1931. But in 1932 it recovered to 38·7 per cent.

The return of the Labour faithful and the recovery of Labour confidence and morale at this local level, especially in areas where the issues of unemployment and the means test were most explosive, undoubtedly explain the subsequent failure of the communist and N.U.W.M. challenges. Only a year after the débâcle of 1931, Labour was again a party to be reckoned with in municipal politics. Any chance of a vacuum for extremist parties to exploit had gone.

In the wake of these highly successful municipal contests, Labour's record in parliamentary by-elections also improved as 1933 began. During 1933, Labour regained a variety of seats lost to the Conservatives, including the industrial Rotherham seat and a spectacular win in East Fulham. It was not merely in terms of seats gained, however, that Labour was doing well. It was achieving very large and consistent swings in its favour. Although the 29·1 per cent swing in East Fulham was exceptional, Labour's good performance in such middle-class areas as Hitchin and Ashford was perhaps even more cause for optimism than the huge swings in such working-class seats as Rotherham. Party organisers noted that Labour seemed to be polling the full Labour vote, and this itself seemed to confirm that the party's membership and similar propaganda campaigns were being effective. Labour organisers rather neglected to note that the almost invariable collapse in the Liberal vote might not be a feature that would occur so easily in a General Election.

All this, however, lay in the future. In the medium term, Labour's recovery, already marked in 1932, reached new heights in the local elections of 1933. In municipal terms, 1933 was one of the best years the party ever enjoyed. In the urban district council

I

elections, Labour appeared to have regained, and probably sur-
passed, its previous high-water mark. Sweeping Labour gains in the
November elections brought Labour to power in such towns as
Sheffield, Norwich, Leeds, Bootle, Swansea and Barnsley – adding to
the 15 boroughs controlled prior to November 1933. In 7 boroughs
in 1933 Labour gained a council majority for the first time. In 4
others (Barrow, Lincoln, Newport, Oldham), Labour moved up to a
position of equal strength to the combined forces of its opponents
while in such cities as Canterbury the party won its first-ever seats.

With 181 gains and only 5 losses, with 444 of its 880 candidates
successful, and with Labour winning control of a variety of boroughs
for the first time, the party had achieved a goal that would have
seemed impossible in the wake of MacDonald's actions two years
earlier. Neither Conservatives nor Liberals had any crumbs of
comfort from 1933 – the Conservatives gained 6 seats, losing 112;
the Liberals picked up 5 for the loss of 33.

Labour's continuing, and at times dramatic, by-election recovery
carried on during 1934. In a trio of by-elections in February 1934,
Labour achieved swings of 18·5 per cent in Cambridge, 14·9 per cent
in Lowestoft and 8·7 per cent in Portsmouth North. The late spring
of 1934 saw Labour recapture two seats in the London area, both on
very high swings: North Hammersmith (17·8 per cent swing to
Labour) on 24 April and the Upton division of West Ham (16·7 per
cent swing) in mid-May. Equally large swings were obtained in such
safe Conservative territories as Twickenham and Weston-super-
Mare during the summer. Labour received a further fillip in the run-
up to the November municipal elections with two by-election
victories in late October. The North Lambeth constituency was
easily won on 23 October. Two days later, the railway town of
Swindon was captured on a 9·3 per cent swing.

Labour's exceptionally good by-election results in the London
area were matched at municipal level by the party's triumph in
the London County Council elections. For the first time in its
history, Labour captured control of the largest local government
unit in the country – and captured it with a vengeance (Table 7.3).
No doubt unemployment, rents and other domestic issues accounted
for Labour's victory, but that victory came on a remarkably low
poll. Even in London, apathy remained a very noticeable phenomenon. Meanwhile, outside London, the provincial municipal contests in November 1934 provided Labour with its third successive
year of widespread gains. Labour, attacking the seats lost in the

TABLE 7.3   LABOUR STRENGTH ON THE LONDON COUNTY COUNCIL:
1925–34

	Labour	*M.R.*	*Progressives*
1925	35	83	6
1928	42	77	5
1931	35	83	6
1934	69	55	–

débâcle of 1931, secured 203 gains for a loss of only 8. Conservatives and Independents suffered a net loss of 165, the Liberals a net loss of 30. Heavy Labour gains in Derby, Stoke and Hull gave Labour control of councils lost in 1931. Five Labour gains won Labour control of Burnley for the first time. Elsewhere in Lancashire, one of Labour's best areas, the party won Oldham and secured a tie of councillors in Birkenhead. Persistent Liberal losses to Labour were the order of the day.

The optimism engendered by these excellent municipal results was reinforced in the Putney by-election of 28 November. In an extremely safe Conservative seat (where the Conservatives had taken over 81 per cent of the vote in 1931) a massive swing of 26·9 per cent almost gave Labour victory. Party organisers were convinced that the unemployment question was largely responsible for this good result.

Although Labour's capture of the Wavertree division of Liverpool was a freak result (with the Conservative vote split and Randolph Churchill picking up 23·9 per cent as an Independent Conservative), the party's good result in Lambeth Norwood (14 March, 1935) seemed confirmation that the tide was still flowing strongly in Labour's direction.

The Norwood by-election, however, was followed by a trio of by-elections in Scotland in the early summer of 1935. The Perth result, complicated by the absence of a Liberal candidate, was not easy to analyse. But in both Edinburgh West and Aberdeen South, Labour's vote was considerably below the level achieved in 1929. Organisers in Scotland such as Arthur Woodburn, the Secretary of the Scottish Labour Party, were clearly alarmed that the national tide was not flowing for Labour north of the Border. To some extent, the by-election in West Toxteth on 15 July, 1935, restored Labour morale. The party captured the seat on an 18·9 per cent swing from Conservative in a straight fight.

After West Toxteth, only one more by-election was to take place before the General Election. In the rural Scottish Dumfriesshire seat, the Liberal Nationals comfortably held off the Labour challenge in a seat not remotely winnable for Labour.

By the autumn of 1935, Labour could seem to be reasonably confident that the electoral trough of 1931 had long since been left far behind. In parliamentary by-elections, Labour had captured no less than 10 seats from the government. A variety of urban seats had been regained for the party. In municipal elections, the party had recovered so fast from the débâcle of 1931 that it reached targets in 1933 and again in 1934 that it had not reached in the best years of 1926 to 1929. Boroughs that had never before been controlled by Labour, such as Burnley and Greenock, were won by the party. The reasons for the optimism of both Labour agents and the party leadership were understandable.

But was this really so? Or were there features of Labour's revival, both in by-elections and municipal elections, that were more worrying? Certainly, one aspect of Labour's revival, overlooked at the time, was its patchiness. The Labour recovery at the grassroots was far from nationwide. There were certain exceptions which were of far more than local importance. The most important example was in the west Midlands.

In local as in national politics, throughout the 1930s Birmingham's political behaviour was out of line with the rest of the country. Thus, while there was a swing to the Conservatives in 1930 and 1931, and a reaction to Labour in 1932 (when Labour secured 13 seats and polled 10,000 more votes than the Conservatives), later in the 1930s Labour totally failed to make any electoral headway. With only a representation of 27 in a council of 140 in 1938, Labour was weaker in Birmingham on the eve of the Second World War than it had been even in the 1920s.[7] Also in the west Midlands, the party entered a very bad phase in Wolverhampton during the 1930s. The explanation lay partly in the split in the local Labour Party.[8]

These regional variations in Labour's electoral recovery were one disturbing element. A further, and far more fundamental factor which deeply affected the electoral politics of the 1930s lay in the continued disintegration of the Liberal Party.

The General Election of 1931, as we have seen, was an utter disaster for the Liberals. The declining importance of the party in parliament, Samuel's decision to leave the National Government and the growing rift with the Simonite Liberal Nationals were all the consequences of the 1931 verdict. In electoral terms, the continued decline of the party in the constituencies was to be seen both in municipal elections and in by-elections. Both were to play an important part in the electoral realignments of the 1930s. The two trends that had dominated municipal Liberal politics in the decade after 1918 continued in the years from 1929 to 1935: a slow but persistent fall in the number of candidates brought forward and an equally uninterrupted and persistent net loss of seats each November.[9]

The proportion of Liberal candidates, which had stood at 18 per cent in 1922, had fallen to 12½ per cent by 1929. By 1931, the total had fallen below 10 per cent. By 1935 it was down to 7·9 per cent. The Liberals, in local as well as national politics, were becoming of increasing irrelevance. The reduction in the number of Liberal municipal candidates, in itself a symptom of the malaise afflicting the party, was mirrored in the net loss of seats suffered each November. In every year apart from the anti-Labour landslide of 1931, Liberals suffered a net loss of seats.[10] Perhaps a better indication than this was to be found in the *share* of seats won by Liberals each November. In 1931, one in seven council seats was won by a Liberal; by 1935 this was down to one in ten.

These overall figures of gains and losses to a certain extent disguised a significant change in the type of seats won by Liberals during the 1930s. During this period Liberals lost steadily and persistently to Labour in a variety of Midland and northern industrial districts, while themselves picking up isolated gains from the Conservatives in a few seaside and middle-class resorts. Thus, in 1934 the Liberals lost their last remaining seats on Wigan Council to Labour, and suffered heavy losses in Lancashire and the Midlands.[11] At the same time, they picked up occasional Conservative seats in Bath and Bournemouth.

Throughout the 1930s the temptation of hard-pressed Liberal councillors to join forces with the Conservatives in an anti-Socialist 'municipal alliance' continued to increase. Each November, it was possible to detect another borough where the anti-Socialist forces had joined ranks. Thus, in 1932, it was the turn of Plymouth. Conservatives and Liberals united for the first time, 8 Labour seats were gained, and only 4 out of 18 Labour candidates emerged successful. In 1934, the Liberals and Conservatives in Doncaster (where some form of co-operation had existed for a long time) were now combined in a 'Progressive Non-Party Group'. Similarly at

Ipswich, a 'People's Party' was brought about by a merger of Conservatives and Liberals.

In the late 1920s earlier anti-Socialist pacts had often provoked division and dissent within the Liberal ranks, especially from the more radical Young Liberals. During the 1930s no such revolts occurred. Indeed, one of the most consistent features of municipal Liberalism in the 1930s was the absolute lack of any attempt to provide an Independent Liberal challenge.

Thus, in Hull, no Independent Liberal ever challenged the united force of the Hull Municipal Alliance; in Coventry, no challenge came forward against the Progressives; in Bristol, even with the municipal 'General Election' of 1936, not a single Liberal ever ventured to do battle with the Citizens' Party. These examples can be multiplied many times. The phenomenon was as true in Reading as in Rotherham, in Newcastle as in Plymouth. Any attempt at an Independent Liberal challenge in these towns was conspicuous only by its absence.

It was symbolic of the new era of two-party politics that Liberalism should finally also have surrendered its independence in the spiritual home of radicalism and Free Trade — Manchester. In 1931, Liberals and Conservatives entered into a pact at municipal level which marked the end of the road for the party.

This dreary record of the Liberal Party at municipal level was reflected in the by-election record of the party. In a series of depressing results, a few individual disasters seemed to stand out. Thus, in 1933 in a humiliating by-election at Manchester Rusholme on 21 November, the party polled a mere 9 per cent, compared to 33 per cent in 1931. Even the Liberal move into opposition, far from restoring the fortunes of the party, only served to make them worse. The by-elections of 1934 were even more dispiriting than in 1933. On 8 February, the Liberals polled a mere 7 per cent at Cambridge, a seat where they had picked up 25 per cent of the votes in 1931. Only 5 of the 12 by-elections between April and December 1934 were fought by the party, with disastrous results in Weston-super-Mare, Rushcliffe and North Lambeth.

A very poor by-election record, further defections from the party and a collapse in the constituencies together constituted the record of the party from 1931 to 1935. But where had the Liberal vote gone? Here was one of the crucial questions of the 1930s. For whichever party could secure the 5 million votes captured by the Liberals in 1929 would surely achieve the necessary electoral basis to win a General Election.

In 1931, as we have seen, the overwhelming bulk of the Liberal vote clearly went to the National Government. After 1931 the picture is more complex. Certainly, in some municipal elections, especially in urban areas of previous Liberal strength, the old Liberal vote went to Labour. In a variety of other areas where Labour had previously been very weak, in local elections the Liberal vote went over. Yet equally in other towns the Liberal vote, following the lead of Liberal councillors and local associations, went Conservative.

If at municipal level the picture is complex, so also is the by-election record. As was noted earlier, Labour never really secured gains in *middle-class* seats from 1931 to 1935. Although a few good results in suburban seats such as Norwood suggested that the Liberal vote was going Labour, it cannot be too strongly emphasised that these were by-elections. The fate of the government was not at stake. Whether Liberals would risk voting Labour at a General Election was a very different point. Here, indeed, may be found the most important single factor in the electoral politics of the 1930s. As John Ramsden has written of the by-elections of this period:

> ... on the one hand, Labour was winning back support which it had lost in 1931, and which it would now expect to retain; on the other hand, the National Government was generating protest votes which would disappear as soon as its survival was in doubt.[12]

In the circumstances of the 1935 election, with Labour emphasising its Socialist policies, with its leadership weak in comparison to the National Government and with increasing prosperity in many areas of the country, much of the Liberal vote either stayed Conservative or stayed at home. The middle ground of British politics was lost by Labour.

The middle ground was to hold the key to victory in the 1935 election. But in the aftermath of 1931, extremism seemed to pose the most dangerous threat to existing electoral patterns. For in 1931, with unemployment still rising and with official Labour shown only too clearly to have failed, there seemed to be all the classical ingredients for extremism to flourish: a political vacuum and a leaderless working class.

This in fact was not to happen. Neither the communists (see Ch. viii) nor the fascists (see Ch. xi) ever really emerged from the political fringe. A few localised extremist groups surfaced briefly in local politics (most noticeably the sectarian Scottish Protestant League which fought local elections in Glasgow). In general the fate of the more militant extremist breakaway group was fairly rapid oblivion. A further example can be found in the Nationalists. In Scotland a few Scottish National Party candidates were put up, but with mixed results. Of the four S.N.P. candidates, two lost their deposits (in Montrose Burghs, on 28 June, 1932, and in East Fife, 2 February, 1933). The party's two best results were Dunbartonshire (17 March, 1934), where the party achieved 13·4 per cent of the poll, and Kilmarnock, where although bottom in a four-cornered contest the S.N.P. picked up 16·9 per cent of votes cast. None had thus achieved even one in five of the votes cast.

Another such example was the Independent Labour Party, which broke away from Labour in August 1932. Its electoral record was soon to prove calamitous. The 1933 municipal elections, in which numerous I.L.P. candidates came forward, were an electoral disaster. Except in the very special case of Glasgow, where I.L.P. achieved 11 per cent of all votes cast in the city, and to a much lesser extent Bradford, the spiritual home of the I.L.P., the party went down to a resounding and crushing defeat.

A good example was to be found in the Manor ward of Sheffield, a seat the I.L.P. valiantly attempted to defend against a Labour, communist and Progressive challenge. Labour easily won the seat, the I.L.P. finishing in fourth place with a mere 8·4 per cent of the poll. In most cases, except for the occasional sitting councillor able to defend his seat successfully, the I.L.P. challenge in the large towns of the Midlands was both weak in terms of candidates fielded and weaker still in terms of votes polled. Only a solitary I.L.P. candidate came forward in Birmingham, Coventry and Northampton. Their average vote was 5 per cent. In Nottingham, 3 I.L.P. candidates averaged 156 votes apiece, again very near to 5 per cent of votes cast. These results in the Midlands were very much in line with the northern industrial towns. Thus, in Barnsley the 3 I.L.P. candidates between them amassed a mere 102 votes, an average poll of 2 per cent in each contested ward. In nearby Wakefield, the lone I.L.P. candidate achieved 4 per cent in the Eastmoor ward. As with the communists, apart from a few candidates who enjoyed straight fights with Labour in such areas of the Socialist heartland as West Ham or Merthyr, the 1933 municipal elections offered little hope to the I.L.P. Even in Scotland, though the I.L.P. did well in such smaller burghs as Cowdenbeath or Coatbridge, its impact was relatively slight.

A year later, in the municipal elections of November 1934, very little had changed. In a very few strongholds (such as the East Bowling ward in Bradford and in parts of Merthyr), retiring I.L.P. councillors fought off challenges to their position. But they were the exception to the rule. In such boroughs as Derby and Sunderland, retiring I.L.P. councillors went down to defeat, usually by large margins. Very few I.L.P. candidates came forward at the elections, and none at all in such towns as Birmingham, Northampton or Nottingham where they had fielded candidates the previous year. In such towns as Derby and Sheffield where an occasional I.L.P. standard-bearer was to be found, it was rare for a party candidate to obtain more than 2–3 per cent of the votes cast.

The parliamentary by-election record of the I.L.P. was equally dispiriting. Thus, in 1933 an I.L.P. candidate challenged Labour in Kilmarnock (2 November), picking up 20·9 per cent of the vote. In the only two by-elections contested by the I.L.P. in 1934, however, the party fared disastrously. Fighting the Upton division of West Ham in May 1934, Fenner Brockway polled a mere 748 votes, only 3·5 per cent of the votes cast. When Campbell Stephen fought the Merthyr by-election a month later, he polled less than 10 per cent of the votes cast, just slightly more than Wal Hannington obtained for the communists.

It is a remarkable comment on the stability of British politics that, even when the slump was at its worst, the electoral and political scene remained remarkably quiescent. No extremist candidate of the Left ever won a by-election. No other protest party – be it I.L.P. or S.N.P. – came remotely near a by-election victory. No Liberal ever won a by-election in the 1930s. No fascist candidate even contested a parliamentary by-election. Perhaps the most remarkable aspect of electoral behaviour after 1931 was not political volatility, but rather a general apathy. Thus, turn-out in contested by-elections dropped by no less than 12 per cent compared to 1931. At the same time, in local elections turn-out was regularly low, dropping at times to little more than a third of those eligible to vote. Nowhere was this more evident than in London, where the working-class strongholds remained apathetic despite strong Labour organisation. Partly, perhaps, this may be explained in economic and ideological terms, but it is none the less a remarkable phenomenon. It is tempting to see this low turn-out and lack of interest as the result of the psychological effects of prolonged unemployment. Unfortunately, there is no correlation between low turn-out and high unemployment. This is particularly noticeable in Oxford, a town scarcely touched by unemployment in the 1930s but where the predominant feature of municipal politics was apathy. Thus in 1931, only one ward was contested for the Council; at the General Election a Conservative was returned unopposed. In 1932, there was still only one contest, while in 1933 'traditional apathy was more marked than ever'.[13]

It would be wrong, however, to judge the political temperature merely at the ballot box. Both communists and fascists appealed for their supporters to take to the streets. It is time to examine the response to that call.

VIII

The Communist Party

In 1929, on the eve of the depression, the Communist Party of Great Britain had 3,000–4,000 members, half of them concentrated in the mining areas of South Wales and Scotland. The party had just undergone a process of 'Stalinisation' in which control of its operations in Britain was vested in a narrow clique who, in turn, were responsible to Moscow. Following the Moscow line, the party embarked upon a 'class against class' policy in which it severed connections with sympathetic left-wing organisations such as the I.L.P. and liquidated or 'Bolshevised' organisations containing both communist and non-communist members. The effect was to drive many people from the party and into the ranks of other organisations. By November 1930 the British Communist Party was effectively cut off from official contact with the Labour Party, the T.U.C. and the I.L.P., while its membership had dwindled to just over 2,500 members, virtually extinguishing the party's influence beyond a hard core of activists. It was in this condition that the Communist Party found itself as the economic and political crisis of the Labour Government came to a head in 1931.

The fall of the Labour Government in August 1931, followed by the triumphant return of the Coalition Government, seemed to mark a watershed in British politics. The Labour Party, or so it appeared, lay leaderless and broken; a divided party routed at the polls. With unemployment still rising, with official Labour shown only too clearly to have failed, there seemed to be all the basic ingredients for the Communist Party to flourish.

It was a situation looked on by the Communist Party hierarchy with some optimism. For in the immediate aftermath of the collapse of the Labour Government, membership of the party grew impressively. By the General Election of November 1931, party membership had doubled. In addition, the 'Invergordon Mutiny' attracted much public attention to the party—publicity that the communists were only too willing to make the most of. As Henry Pelling has written of the Invergordon demonstrations:

> ... although [they] were not initiated by Communists and were entirely the produce of harsh and inequitable cuts in their pay, it suited the government to claim that Communist propaganda had been a major cause, and it suited the Communists to claim the credit thus offered to them. The principal leaders of the disturbances were discharged from the Navy shortly afterwards, and two or three of them, who had been made much of at Communist demonstrations, later joined the party.[1]

Though the party had these encouraging signs, its great obstacle lay in its past electoral record. Even in the 1929 election, when the country generally had swung to the left, the communists had made virtually no impact at the polls. Although the party had fielded 25 candidates, they had polled in all only 50,634 votes, an average of only 2,025 per candidate. Nine of the 25 candidates had polled so abysmally as to collect under 2 per cent of the votes cast in the constituencies—the lowest vote being the 242 (0·6 per cent) collected by S. Usmani fighting Darwen. No less than 21 of the 25 communists had polled less than 8 per cent of votes cast. The only 4 exceptions are set out in Table 8.1.

TABLE 8.1 HIGHEST POLLS BY COMMUNIST CANDIDATES: 1929

candidate	constituency	% comm. poll
W. Gallacher	Fife West	20·5
A. Geddes	Greenock	20·4
A. Horner	Rhondda East	15·2
S. Saklatvala	Battersea North	19·2

Even these results were far from comforting. Saklatvala had been beaten in Battersea, the party's best hope. In all, the party's total vote in 1929 was less than in 1924 and in the 4 comparable contests had also shown an absolute decline.[2]

Although in 1929 the communists had a nuisance value for Labour (robbing Labour of two seats—Greenock and Bethnal Green South-West), in none of Labour's heartlands were they a real threat. Wales and Scotland were slightly more favourable soil for the communists, as Table 8.2 shows, but even here their electoral appeal had been negligible.

TABLE 8.2   AVERAGE VOTE OBTAINED BY COMMUNIST CANDIDATES

	no. of candidates	average % vote obtained
England	12	3·5
Wales	3	5·5
Scotland	10	6·8
U.K. (total)	25	5·1

If the 1929 election was a disappointment, the communists also failed to benefit from Labour's growing unpopularity in the by-elections of the second Labour Government. The first communist to contest a by-election (at Leeds South-East on 1 August, 1929) polled only 512 votes, a mere 4 per cent of the votes cast. An almost identical percentage was obtained in Kilmarnock on 27 November, 1929, and at Sheffield Brightside on 2 June, 1930, the latter a particularly disappointing result for one of the most solidly working-class areas of the whole country. Perhaps the most galling result was in the Shettleston by-election of June 1930. In Wheatley's old constituency, the party fielded a very strong candidate in Saklatvala, the former communist M.P. for Battersea North. Even in this Clydeside seat in the heart of industrial Scotland the communists could poll only 1,459 votes, a mere 5·8 per cent of votes cast. In the Shipley by-election, on 6 November, 1930, the communists again fielded a strong candidate in Willie Gallacher, the man who was later to become the party's M.P. in West Fife. In Shipley, however, Gallacher's efforts were in vain. He polled only 701 votes (1·7 per cent), while the Conservatives snatched the seat from Labour by 1,665 votes.

The only other by-elections contested by the communists were on more favourable soil. The first was in the Whitechapel and St George's constituency in the heart of Stepney. In this safe Labour seat, the communists fielded Harry Pollitt. After a spirited campaign, Pollitt finished with a creditable 2,106 votes, over 9 per cent of the total vote.

By far the best result, at least in percentage terms, occurred in the Ogmore contest on 19 May, 1931. A rock-solid Labour mining seat, Ogmore had been held for the party since 1918 by the veteran Labour Cabinet Minister, Vernon Hartshorn. It was his death that occasioned the by-election. In 1929, the communists fought the seat, taking mere 3·8 per cent in a four-cornered fight. In the by-election (with the same candidate, Campbell, whose name had been a *cause célèbre* in 1924), the communists enjoyed a straight fight with Labour. In these circumstances, Campbell polled 5,219 votes, over 21 per cent of the total. This, however, seems to have been mostly an anti-Labour protest vote, for in the 1931 General Election the communist vote plummeted to 3,099, only 8 per cent of the votes cast and another lost deposit.

However, the useful poll that Pollitt had obtained, together with the Ogmore result, were hopeful pointers that the party might at last be gaining some real support from a bitterly disillusioned industrial working class. The collapse of the second Labour Government and the 'betrayal' of the Labour leadership also encouraged the party to field 26 candidates in the 1931 election. The party's hopes were highest in London and in the mining areas, most particularly in South Wales and Scotland.

In fact the General Election proved a catastrophe for the party. Not a single communist M.P. was elected, while 21 of the party's 26 candidates lost their deposits. The more closely the party's results are examined, the more disastrous they appear. The worst individual result occurred in the Duddeston division of Birmingham, where the party managed a mere 327 votes. Only in a very few cases could communists poll respectable totals.[3] In only 7 seats had communists obtained over 10 per cent of votes cast. Their 26 candidates had, in all, polled only 75,000 votes. In only the two solid mining seats of Rhondda East and Fife West had the party obtained over one in five of the votes cast. In Rhondda East, Arthur Horner, the miner's leader, captured over 10,000 votes, but this was in a straight fight against Labour. In a sense, the party's best result was in Fife West, where although the Communist Willie Gallacher finished in third position, his percentage share of votes cast was up from 20·5 per cent to 22·1 per cent. The communist vote also rose noticeably in Aberdeen North (up from 5·8 per cent to 11·2 per cent) and Bethnal Green South-West (up from 7·7 per cent to 17·4 per cent). But these were very much the exceptions to the rule. Most communist candidates were treated to derisory polls; 7 failed to poll even 1,000 votes. If the unemployed in Seaham were disgusted by MacDonald's behaviour, they were hardly enchanted by the C.P., for out of the 52,682 votes cast in Seaham, the communist managed 677. As Pelling notes, in only 8 seats could communists poll even one-fifth of their Labour rivals' number of votes.

But this was not to say that communist candidates did not have a very real nuisance value. In 5 seats, communists took sufficient Labour votes to let Conservatives or National candidates in on a split vote.[4] These seats included the Attercliffe division of Sheffield, Bothwell and West Fife in Scotland and Whitechapel in London's East End. The communists in 1931 had achieved little in the election. But whether blinded by ideology or simply indulging in wishful thinking, some of the party's spokesmen began making statements that appeared more than usually optimistic. One such was Palme Dutt. Writing in the *Daily Worker* immediately after the election, Dutt declared, 'The workers have lost confidence in the Labour Party, and seek elsewhere ... The Labour movement, the old Labour movement, is dying. The workers' movement, the independent workers' movement, is rising.'[5] Not surprisingly, even within the communist ranks such absurd claims tended to be ridiculed.[6] Indeed, even though the party's membership had risen, it was still pathetically small. At 6,000 it looked ludicrous alongside the major parties and the recent increase in membership, especially among the unemployed, brought little real value. As Pelling has written, the new recruits added little to the party, for being mostly unemployed they could not pay their dues and would soon drift away as the miners had done after 1926.[7]

However poorly the communists had fared in 1931, they did not despair of electoral battles in the years of the depression. A variety of communist candidates were brought forward in the more promising industrial constituencies, as shown in Table 8.3.

TABLE 8.3   COMMUNIST CANDIDATES AT BY-ELECTIONS: 1931–5

	constituency	candidate	vote	% comm.
17 March, 1932	Dunbarton-shire	H. McIntyre	2,870	7·5
28 March, 1933	Rhondda East	A. L. Horner	11,228	33·8
1 Sept., 1933	Clay Cross	H. Pollitt	3,434	10·8
7 Nov., 1933	Skipton	J. Rushton	704	1·7
24 April, 1934	Hammersmith North	E. F. Bramley	614	2·4
5 June, 1934	Merthyr Tydfil	W. Hannington	3,409	9·5

In five of these six contests, the party had polled disastrously. In Skipton and North Hammersmith, the party had polled less than 1,000 votes or 2½ per cent of the poll in each seat. Even the N.U.W.M. hero, Wal Hannington, picked up only 9·5 per cent of the vote in the mining stronghold of Merthyr. In Clay Cross, a safe Derbyshire mining seat even in 1931, the electors returned Arthur Henderson safely to Westminster, leaving Harry Pollitt with a lost deposit and much loss of face. The only comforting by-election was in East Rhondda, as luck would have it the party's best seat in the whole country. In 1931, this had been by far their best result—the only constituency in the country in which they had polled over 30 per cent of votes cast. Indeed, with the exception of West Fife, it was the only constituency where a communist had polled over 20 per cent of the total vote.

The Rhondda was synonymous with depression: a working-class stronghold where poverty and unemployment were at their starkest. The communists could have hoped for no better seat to fight and their vote was impressive. But the Rhondda was an isolated phenomenon. It was a combination of chance and personality that was to have no parallel for the communists except in West Fife in 1935.

The party also fought strongly during these years at municipal level. Each November many of the large industrial centres were attacked by communists, either standing overtly as communists or shielding themselves as N.U.W.M. candidates. The fate of these communist electoral challenges at the local level during the years of the slump has not yet received serious investigation. It is an unfortunate omission, for there is much to be gleaned of the nature and strength of communist support at the grassroots from these municipal contests. In general these local elections confirm the weakness of the communist appeal at parliamentary level. To state that no council in England was ever controlled by communists in the 1930s, or indeed that in no council were communists ever the second largest party, is to imply that communists may have had *some* degree of electoral strength in the major towns. Such is not the case.

This is best observed by examining the local elections in the year when communists were probably more active than they had ever been in municipal contests: 1933. Both in the urban district council elections in April and the borough elections in November, communists were nominated to fight industrial wards in a variety of working-class centres. Communists made particularly vigorous efforts in parts of London, especially Dagenham and Tottenham, and in such northern towns as Shipley and Normanton. The results were utterly disastrous. Six communist candidates in Dagenham polled less than 1,000 votes between them.[8]

In Tottenham, the communist candidate polled less than 6 per cent in his ward, while the N.U.W.M. candidate managed 9·9 per cent. As the *Tottenham Herald* commented, on a 16 per cent poll, it was an insipid finish to an insipid election. So downhearted was the Left that neither 'The Red Flag' nor the 'Internationale' was heard after the declaration.[9] Even these disastrous London results were better than the results in the north.[10] In all, they hardly augured well for the November municipal elections.

One of the largest challenges put foward by the communists took shape for the November elections, but it was a challenge remarkable for its disparity rather than its concentration of effort. Apart from West Ham, where 5 communists came forward to attack the 16 wards, very few towns saw more than an isolated communist candidate. Such towns as Birmingham and Hull saw only 2 communist challengers; Leeds saw only one. In no major town did communists (or N.U.W.M.) fight even half the seats at stake.

Once again, the election results were so bad that few communist candidates managed more than 5 per cent of votes cast in their wards. The two communists in Coventry amassed just 197 votes between them.[11] Even this was a more notable achievement than in Gateshead, where even a local 'Douglas Credit' nominee polled more votes than the lone communist challenger. Virtually the only moderately good results were in West Ham, where communists polled well in the Tidal Basin and Canning House wards,[12] and occasional northern towns such as Wigan, where a communist took 25 per cent of the vote in Victoria ward, thereby allowing a Conservative to take a normally safe Labour ward. Nor did communist candidates fare well even in areas where unemployment demonstrations or local militancy had been most noticeable. Of the eight contested wards in Birkenhead in 1933, the Communist Party put up candidates in only two. Both were disastrous forays. In Clifton ward, the party polled 2·3 per cent of the votes cast, in Argyle ward only 7 per cent.

It can be argued that, after the disaster of Labour in 1931, potential communist voters were loath to vote communist in Labour areas for fear of letting Conservatives capture the particular seat at stake. If this were the case, however, one would expect communist candidates at least to have done well when they enjoyed straight

K

fights with Labour in very safe working-class strongholds. In such towns as Hull or Burnley, as Table 8.4 demonstrates, even in these circumstances communists fared just as dismally.

TABLE 8.4   COMMUNIST VOTE IN WORKING-CLASS STRONGHOLDS: 1933

ward	Labour vote	comm. vote	% comm.
Hull: West Central	1,996	97	4·6
Hull: East Central	1,979	100	4·8
Burnley: Gannow	1,978	107	5·1
Stockton: Victoria	1,278	79	5·8

Nor could communists take much comfort from the results outside England. Both Scotland and Wales proved bitter disappointments for the communist cause. The most extensive challenge in 1933 was mounted in Glasgow, where the party put forward 15 candidates. Although the party polled moderately well in such working-class strongholds as Cowlairs, Springburn and Gorbals, they failed to take a single seat. Their total poll in Glasgow (of 10,484 votes) was only some 3·4 per cent of the 311,000 votes cast. Their performance compared extremely unfavourably with the newly-founded Scottish Protestant League—whose 71,000 votes (and 4 seats won from the Moderates) was an indication of how well a more popular protest party could poll.

In the large towns elsewhere in Scotland, the communists met with virtually no success. The four communist candidates brought forward in Edinburgh polled only 2,005 votes, out of a total vote in the city of over 60,000.[13] In Dundee, where only two communists were in the field, their best individual result was the 12 per cent obtained in ward six. In the smaller Scottish burghs, most particularly in Kirkcaldy and Falkirk, communist candidates fought almost all the seats at stake, but almost invariably without success, except for the very small burghs such as Lochgelly where personalities probably accounted for such isolated gains as occurred. Perhaps the most galling rout in Scotland was in Greenock, a burgh with a traditionally strong communist vote at past general elections and where Labour had never really emerged as a strong party. In 1933 this changed: Labour gained 4 seats from the Moderates to gain a majority on the council for the first time in its history. The six communist candidates were all humiliated at the polls.

Meanwhile in Wales, although communists polled respectably but without success in such areas as Neath and Llanelli, in Cardiff the party polled as badly as anywhere in England. Only in a very few areas could communists achieve any sort of electoral strength. Most of these were in the industrial valleys, the areas like the Rhondda where mining was solidly entrenched. Indeed, as a national phenomenon, in the midst of the general total failure of communism in Britain, two industries showed some electoral sympathy for the C.P. The first was mining; the second was shipbuilding.

Partly, the explanation of communist support in mining areas was a practical one. The communists gained a considerable following in many of these areas as a consequence of their participation in the miners' fights to maintain or improve conditions in the pits. The Dawdon miners' strike in Seaham, at the end of the 1920s, illustrates the way in which communists could step in and take over the leadership if the unions did not fulfil their role adequately in a particular situation.[14] It was at this time, for example, that miners in many places began to elect communist checkweighmen, a position of considerable responsibility, and hence a sign of complete confidence.[15] This process was reflected at the national level; at the 1936 Labour Party conference, Will Lawther spoke strongly for affiliation with the Communist Party, on the grounds that they had rendered the miners great service.[16]

In addition to the mining valleys of South Wales, and parts of the coalfields of the north-east and Scotland, communist electoral strength could also be detected in certain of the shipyard areas, most particularly in the north-east. Thus in Tynemouth, on the north side of the river Tyne, the communists gained considerably in the first half of the decade. Although the communist vote in Tynemouth was never great enough to return a communist councillor, there were some very close results.

Indeed, Blyth Council for a few years had four communist representatives, all of whom were elected in Croft, a small area of shipyard workers and dockers living in very bad slums by the riverfront. Elsewhere in the north-east, as in the North ward of Jarrow, which had a similar occupational structure, communists also polled well. But these were isolated examples, where communists did well for localised sociological reasons.[17] In general, the stark fact remained that communists had virtually no electoral support.

The Communist Party contested the 1935 General Election on different principles than in 1929 and 1931. The party was dominated by the united front tactics of the anti-fascist era. As a result it withdrew from most contests and urged its members to support the Labour Party.[18] There was no reciprocal gesture from the Labour Party and in the two seats which the communists did contest, East Rhondda and West Fife, they had to face strong Labour opposition. The two candidates, Harry Pollitt and Willie Gallacher, polled well, taking 30·6 per cent and 29·2 per cent of the vote respectively. The latter was sufficient to elect Willie Gallacher as the sole communist M.P. at Westminster. The total vote for the party was 27,117, a creditable showing compared with the total vote of 74,824 for 26 candidates in 1931. Gallacher's success and Pollitt's near miss reflected the traditional strength of the Communist Party in the two areas. Both were mining areas with a strong left-wing tradition.[19] They represented the high-water mark of the party's electoral fortunes in the thirties. They showed that there was significant support for the party in at least a tiny minority of constituencies. More general electoral challenges had proved a failure. Electorally, the party was incapable of fighting the traditional political groupings.

Moreover, in terms of membership the party failed to make a decisive showing either among the employed or the unemployed. Although membership rose in the worst phase of the depression, to 9,000 in January 1932, its main period of growth came with the entry of younger, middle-class recruits in the mid-thirties. Paradoxically the Communist Party achieved its peak membership in the 1930s, not when unemployment was at its worst, but on the eve of the Second World War.[20]

Thus although the Communist Party showed a rapid rise in members in the years 1930–2, it fell back quickly when industry revived. Even at the trough of the depression, its membership represented only a small fraction of those out of work, mainly recruited through the National Unemployed Workers' Movement. While the proportion of unemployed in the party increased from 49 per cent in 1930 to 60 per cent in 1932, the response of the unemployed to the party was extremely varied.[21] The highest membership for the Communist Party was obtained in South Wales and parts of Scotland. Elsewhere, there was little evidence of significant advance and in some industrial areas complete failure. On Tyneside, the Central Executive Committee almost despaired of making a serious impact, commenting that it was 'the weakest and least satisfactory of all Party Districts'. In spite of the high rate of unemployment in the area, the party could claim only 500 members in 1940, while Jarrow, the blackspot of unemployment, had a party membership of seven. Overall, it has been calculated that only 3,140 of the unemployed joined the Communist Party in Britain during the thirties, out of several million who had experienced or been threatened by unemployment.[22]

The industrial wing of the Communist Party fared little better. At the outset of the depression the communists' industrial organisation, the Minority Movement, was urged to set up an independent leadership of the working class, by founding unions to rival the existing trade union movement. The effect was very limited; only two breakaway unions were set up, the United Mineworkers of Scotland, based on the miners of Fifeshire, and the United Clothing Workers in the East End of London. At the end of 1931, the communist membership of the Minority Movement totalled a mere 700. In spite of the industrial conflicts in South Wales and Lancashire in the early 1930s, the Minority Movement failed to capitalise upon the situation. Attempts to found a communist-dominated Seamens' Union went ahead, but had to be called off for lack of support in 1932. By 1933 it was decided to abandon the Minority Movement, which had conspicuously failed to rival the established trade union movement. When the Minority Movement was finally dissolved, there were only 550 party members organised in 82 factory cells.[23]

After 1933 the Communist Party was increasingly dominated by the united front policy. Essentially a result of policy changes in Moscow, the new line abandoned the class against class attacks upon rival left-wing and social democratic organisations and urged co-operation with them to combat the rise of fascism. For the British party it led to attempts to establish formal relations with the organisations which it had rejected and attacked in the years since 1929. None the less, this reversal of policy was put into practice by the party and its satellite organisations. The Minority Movement, for example, even though on the point of expiry, was urged to seek co-operation with the established trade unions. Attacks upon the leaders of the Labour Party were suspended and the party invited the Labour Party Executive and the T.U.C. to consider plans for joint activity.[24] Although these overtures were rejected and the party was unable to allay the suspicions of trade unionists and Labour supporters, the party did begin to find favour with a younger generation of people who were attracted by its stand against fascism. The typical recruit of the mid-1930s tended to be young, middle-class, and attracted by the appeal of the Left. The outbreak of the Spanish Civil War provided the catalyst for many who would in normal circumstances have had little to do with the Communist Party. It was seen to give a lead in the fight against fascism which the other parties failed to provide.[25]

Between 1935 and 1942 Communist Party membership rose from 7,700 to 56,000. The growth of European fascism was undoubtedly one of the major causes of the spurt in membership after 1935, but there may also have been an undercurrent of blackcoated unemployment in the mid-1930s which helped to swell the party's ranks. Many of the new recruits came from the London area. In 1927 only 16·8 per cent of the party's membership came from the metropolis, but by 1942 this had risen to 29 per cent. These included a large number of Jews, brought into politics by the growth of the British fascist movement under Mosley and its activities in the East End. London also contained a large number of middle-class intellectuals who played a prominent part in the idealistic phase of recruitment in the mid-1930s. Even so, it is important not to exaggerate the influence that the party had within these circles. For every person who joined the Communist Party there were dozens who remained apolitical or subscribed to the larger parties. Although membership of the Communist Party became fashionable, it was never sufficiently widespread to affect seriously the fortunes of the major parties.[26]

Thus in the middle and late 1930s the Communist Party was in an ambiguous position. Although it had gained recruits, it was still a minority party. Moreover, the revival of industry was under way and the worst period of unemployment was past. The 'final crisis' had been averted, or at least postponed. On the other hand, the party had benefited from the growing opposition to fascism at home and abroad. Rallies and meetings to oppose the B.U.F. provided a major part of the Communist Party's activities in the latter part of the decade. Left-wing views were fashionable and the party was able to attract the support, if not always the membership, of influential intellectuals and artists. Recruits such as John Strachey and the support of writers such as Auden, Day Lewis and Spender provided the Communist Party with an air of respectability which it had often lacked in the past. Left-wing university organisations were founded. Within a year of its formation in 1931 the Oxford University October Club had 300 members, and the Cambridge Socialist Club 1,000 members by 1938. The Left Book Club provided a sounding-board for left-wing ideas and by 1937 had a membership of 50,000. In addition, the party increased its support in some industrial areas, prompted by the more moderate united front tactics. In some areas, such as South Wales, some of the antagonism between Labour supporters and communists was allayed in the common fight against the threat of fascism and the continuance of unemployment. As a result, communists were sometimes able to become local councillors and trade union officials in these areas. They gave a lead in local agitations, either as trade unionists or organisers of the unemployed, without generating the same hostility which had been evident at the height of the class against class phase.

The case of communist influence in South Wales is particularly interesting. South Wales was one area in which the Communist Party and the N.U.W.M. captured considerable support. Communist candidates in local elections did relatively well and by 1936 there were 17 party members as district and county councillors in the coalfield, 7 of them in Rhondda Urban District. The tenor of political involvement in the South Wales coalfield was revealed with the outbreak of the Spanish Civil War when more than 170 men volunteered for service in the International Brigades; two-thirds of them were miners and three-quarters of them members of the Communist Party.[27] The strength of communism in South Wales was in marked contrast with other areas. It is tempting to see it as a response to the high level of unemployment in the area throughout the thirties. South Wales was a very depressed area; places such as the Rhondda, Aberdare and Merthyr valleys had some of the highest unemployment rates in the country and a third of the working population was unemployed as late as 1936, when much of the rest of the country was beginning to recover. But South Wales was no worse off than many other areas, such as the mining villages of Co. Durham or the Tyneside shipbuilding towns, where there was little overt political response by the unemployed. Moreover, unemployment often had the same effect in South Wales as elsewhere, sapping the vitality of the unemployed rather than goading them into political radicalism. Allen Hutt wrote in 1932 that 'One of the obstacles confronting the revolt of the workers in South Wales is precisely that degradation of which Marx spoke as an accompaniment of the growth of impoverishment under monopoly.' Commenting on the demoralisation and boredom of the miners, he wrote, 'the workers who are suffering in this way are those who were the cream of the working class in South Wales – the most advanced, most militant, most conscious workers'.[28]

But unemployment was not, in itself, the factor which lay behind the growing militancy of South Wales in the 1930s, rather it was a response which drew upon local characteristics and traditions. South Wales had a history of militancy and had formed one of the principal areas from which the early labour movement had drawn its strength. The conflicts over the mining industry in the 1920s had left a legacy of bitterness and almost open class warfare. The Pilgrim Trust investigators who visited South Wales in the mid-1930s remarked upon the atmosphere of bitterness and 'antagonism against the management of the pits'. They concluded that it was a product of the peculiar isolation of the Welsh mining communities: 'They are not part of the world outside but belong to a world of their own, and a measure which has been taken for external reasons and which affects them adversely is in their thinking designed to crush them.' They also remarked upon the susceptibility of South Wales 'to preaching of any kind, political preaching included, and here, if anywhere, a grievance becomes in a moment a battle-cry'.[29] Recent evidence has confirmed that at least in some parts of the coalfield there was a strong political consciousness which had been present for many years. A number of villages were noted for their militancy, such as the 'little Moscows' of Maerdy and Bedlinog.[30] From 1928 to 1933 some twenty Welsh miners went to Russia to receive political education and returned to lead local branches. Thus there was an influential core of activists who provided the lead in many of the demonstrations, strikes and other events in the thirties. The oral history evidence collected in the area has suggested that there was something of a revolutionary syndrome with the same men being involved in strikes, hunger marches, victimisation and the International Brigades.[31]

The growth in strength of the Communist Party came with the revival of the bargaining power of the South Wales Miners' Federation and a measure of economic recovery in the mid-1930s. The 'antagonism' to the mine-owners which the Pilgrim Trust investigators found in the South Wales coalfield was part of the bitter conflict over company unionism which reached a peak in 1935 with a number of disturbances and strikes. Given the general left-wing character of the leadership of the S.W.M.F., Communist Party members were accepted as active participants in the struggle. By 1935 there were over 300 communists in responsible positions in the

S.W.M.F. and they provided the leadership for 'stay-down' strikes. Five communists were elected to the S.W.M.F. leadership and one, Arthur Horner, became President. Thus local communists had more prestige and access to positions of responsibility in the local union hierarchy than in many other areas and Communist Party allegiance was much more usual in South Wales than elsewhere. The party was firmly rooted in many towns and villages by the mid-1930s and in some had supplanted the Labour Party in terms of influence. This acceptance was eased by the more moderate line taken by the Communist Party after a militant phase of the early thirties when it attempted to operate as a disruptive force against the S.W.M.F. and the Labour Party. In South Wales a Joint Council of Action was formed of communists and Labour supporters to sponsor the hunger march of 1936 in defiance of a Labour Party National Executive prohibition on its activities. In addition, many of the unemployed retained their links with the S.W.M.F. by joining its unemployed section, thus allowing them a greater part in local politics and activities. The effect was to create, at least in some parts of South Wales, a much broader backing for militant activity. Thus local traditions of militancy, the close-knit community life of the valleys and the bitter fight against company unionism provided the background for the success of the Communist Party in South Wales and the greater degree of political militancy which could be found there compared with other areas.[32]

Even so it is important not to exaggerate the influence of the Communist Party in South Wales. Significantly, its growth came after the worst of the depression was over. The communists gained support mainly because of their activities as militant unionists and organisers of the unemployed. As a result many of the leading communists of the thirties shed their specifically communist allegiance in favour of other movements after 1939. As the historian of the South Wales miners' involvement in the Spanish Civil War has argued, the losses of activists in the war, the Molotov-Ribbentrop Pact, and the return of a measure of prosperity turned many away from communism and towards trade unionism. Allegiance to the C.P. also tended to be concentrated in particular areas and particular villages. The great majority of Welsh miners continued to support the Labour Party, and even in strong left-wing areas it was not uncommon for men to vote communist in local elections or for colliery lodge branches, while continuing to vote Labour in parliamentary elections. In many parts of South Wales, both off and on the coalfield, the more usual reactions of the unemployed of apathy towards politics were prevalent. Thus communist success in South Wales was a significant variation upon the pattern elsewhere in the country, but was still a minority response to the experience of mass unemployment and the depression.[33]

Why did the communists not have more success in the context of mass unemployment? In part, the answer lies with the constitutional and non-revolutionary traditions of British politics in the years before and after the First World War. The emergence of working-class organisations and the growth of the Labour Party provided a focus for allegiance for a large proportion of the groups who in other countries were the natural constituency of Marxist and communist movements. Britain's victory in the First World War led to a further consolidation of the Labour movement and the real possibility of a Labour government. In addition, communism was an alien philosophy and British intellectuals on the whole remained wedded to the political and constitutional conventions of parliamentary politics. In spite of the defeat suffered by the Labour movement in the General Strike and the disaster of 1931, the majority of Labour supporters showed little disposition to turn to the communists. Its minority status and its unfamiliarity were major disadvantages and it was only with the development of front organisations in the mid-1930s that it was able to expand its membership and draw upon middle-class support for its stand against fascism.

For most of the 1930s, the communists remained a small coterie, influential in one or two areas, but largely outside the mainstream of British politics. Party membership has been characterised as essentially a sub-culture, dependent upon a complex web of determinants. One set of factors decides whether a portion of the population is radically inclined; another its predisposition towards a left-wing group; and a further set determines membership of the Communist Party rather than another group. Thus the support for the Communist Party in parts of South Wales has been explained in terms of 'an unusual combination of causes and determinants'.[34] Depression in the coal industry following a boom in the years immediately after the First World War, traditions of political activism and an intense degree of class-feeling helped to generate a stronger working-class communist group than in other parts of the country. Elsewhere, other allegiances intervened. Religious or political affiliations were stronger. Crucially, the existing political parties do not appear to have been discredited by the depression for more than a minority.

In this context the attitude of the leadership of the official Labour movement played a crucial part in determining whether there was to be a serious swing to the left in British politics during the 1930s. In fact, the most striking feature of the character of the British Labour movement in the thirties was its uncompromising stand against communist influence. The bitter attacks which the communists had made upon the T.U.C. and the Labour Party during the class against class phase had alienated many potential sympathisers within the Labour movement. The polarising tactics of the Communist Party were seen as an attempt to destroy existing Labour Party and trade union influence. Communists were rivals both on the political platform and, with the formation of the Minority Movement, on the shop-floor as well. Although at the local level a degree of co-operation was possible between communists, trade unionists and Labour supporters, at the official level there was an almost inflexible antagonism between the Labour movement and the communists. By 1929 communists were forbidden to attend Labour Party conferences, even as trade union delegates. In October 1934, the T.U.C. put out the Black Circular which forbade trades councils to accept communists as delegates and urged unions to exclude communists from office. As a result, it was only in South Wales and one or two other areas that communists were able to establish a position in the trade unions. In spite of the growing fashion for left-wing views and the development of united front politics in the mid-1930s, the Labour Party refused to consider formal co-operation with the Communist Party. A request for affiliation was rejected in 1936, in spite of the evident, and genuine, desire of the party to join with Labour in the fight against fascism at home and abroad. Thus throughout the 1930s the weight of the official Labour movement was thrown against the communists. Although not adhered to at every level and in every region, it did much to prevent the polarisation of politics which many had expected to occur.[35]

Thus one of the most remarkable features of the political condition of Britain in the thirties was that there was no major leftward swing either on behalf of the unemployed or by workers in employment. The leadership of the Labour Party and the T.U.C. were committed to a moderate line which disavowed any co-operation with the more militant left-wing groupings. In theory this might have left the traditional Labour leaders vulnerable to a swing among the rank and file, but except in a few areas this did not occur. In spite of the setbacks of 1931, the Labour Party managed to keep its constituency organisation intact and begin an electoral recovery. Though the trade unions were hard-pressed by the onset of mass unemployment, reaching their lowest membership in 1933, they still vastly outnumbered any rival organisation of working people. The challenge mounted by the Minority Movement and its breakaway unions was pathetic, achieving a membership of only a few hundred. The doctrines of the Communist Party were alien to the traditions of the British Labour movement and only a small proportion of the working population saw any attraction in joining it against the advice of their traditional leaders.

Henry Pelling has argued that the Communist Party was a 'revolutionary party in a non-revolutionary situation'. Clearly, nothing approaching a revolutionary crisis affected Britain during the thirties. Traditional patterns of political allegiance and conduct remained substantially unaltered in spite of the onset of mass unemployment. Moreover, there was little evidence of a major swing towards the Communist Party even in the worst years of the depression and it is not certain that a more intense or renewed slump would have substantially altered the picture. Traditionally the Communist Party was not regarded by the great majority of the electorate as a realistic contender for their vote. Even the experiences of the depression were not sufficient to persuade more than a small minority to support the party. In that sense the importance of fashionable left-wing sentiments of the middle and late thirties, seen in the new recruits to communism, should not be exaggerated. Communism undoubtedly became more influential in intellectual circles, but it had little appeal for the great mass of the electorate.

IX

The National Unemployed
Workers' Movement

The National Unemployed Workers' Movement or N.U.W.M. was the most important organisation of the unemployed during the depression. It had been founded in 1921 as a militant organisation to campaign on behalf of the unemployed, and from the beginning had strong connections with the Communist Party of Great Britain. Its most important leader and spokesman was Walter Hannington, a young tool-maker and shop steward from London, who was also a founder member of the Communist Party. The origins of the N.U.W.M. lay in the tremendous boost which the Russian Revolution and the First World War gave to left-wing politics in Britain. Both the Communist Party and the N.U.W.M. drew support from the skilled craftsmen who had participated in the Shop Stewards Movement, which had organised strikes and political agitation in the factories of wartime Britain. Many of these activists, including Wal Hannington, were thrown out of work when the post-war boom began to falter in 1920. The result was the formation of the N.U.W.M., and the beginning of a programme of agitation on the issue of unemployment which was to continue throughout the inter-war period.[1]

The first organisations of the unemployed to emerge in the winter of 1920–1 were apolitical groups, usually of ex-servicemen. In autumn 1920, Wal Hannington joined a group in St Pancras and began to agitate for a conference of unemployed organisations in London. After considerable effort on his part, speaking up to five times a day to groups of unemployed workers, the conference met at the end of October 1920. A London Council of the Unemployed resulted, with Wal Hannington as London organiser. Within a month the London Council was meeting twice weekly and had representatives from thirty-one London boroughs. From the outset the organisation took an overtly militant stance. It staged demonstrations outside Poor Law offices and adopted the slogan of 'Work or full maintenance'. The London Council of the Unemployed tried to urge upon the Labour Party and the T.U.C. the need for a twenty-four hour general strike against the government on the issue of unemployment. Though this initiative failed, in the winter of 1920–1 the Council maintained a programme of mass meetings at Labour Exchanges, sit-ins in municipal buildings and street demonstrations, some of which led to clashes with the police. By spring 1921, it was clear that formal co-operation with the Labour Party and the T.U.C. was out of the question for the immediate future and it was decided to create a national organisation of the unemployed. A conference of unemployed organisations was held at the International Socialist Club in Hoxton on 15 April, 1921, attended by fifty delegates from England and Wales. As a result, the N.U.W.M. was formed to co-ordinate organisations of the unemployed in the country. An executive body, the National Administrative Committee, was set up, and at a further meeting at Manchester in November 1921, Wal Hannington was appointed National Organiser. An important infusion of support came at this meeting with the attendance of representatives from Scotland, where the leading organisers were John MacLean and Harry McShane.[2]

In the winter of 1921–2, the N.U.W.M. built up its strength and organisation as the number of unemployed approached $2\frac{1}{4}$ million. As well as campaigning for concessions on relief scales, the N.U.W.M. was active in support of strikes, helping in picket lines and dissuading unemployed workers from acting as blackleg labour. In addition, a fortnightly paper, *Out of Work*, was launched and achieved a circulation of around 60,000 copies. At the local level, branches were open to all unemployed workers for a fee of twopence and a weekly subscription of one penny. The affairs of the local branches were conducted by an elected committee of twelve, with sub-committees for finance, legal affairs, recruitment and other activities. When four or more branches had been established in an area, a district council was formed to co-ordinate policy. Each branch sent delegates and the council held meetings twice a month. In turn, representatives were sent from the district councils to the National Administrative Council, which co-ordinated policy on a national level. Thus the N.U.W.M. created an organisation which was specifically designed to draw the unemployed into militant agitation for relief work, higher benefits, and improved treatment by the authorities.[3]

The early years of the N.U.W.M. illustrated many of the issues which were to affect its position in the years after 1929 and the onset of the worst phase of the depression. Its leadership was clearly communist-dominated and the organisation followed the policies of the British Communist Party and changes in the Moscow line. But it was not simply a communist front organisation, for it possessed some degree of autonomy. This was seen most clearly when clashes occurred between the day-to-day case-work of the N.U.W.M. and the long-term policy objectives of the party. The N.U.W.M. was accused even in the 1920s of losing sight of the strategic objectives of the communist movement because of its absorption with the technical details of unemployment relief and its attempts to obtain improved conditions for the unemployed. It was pledged both to obtain 'Work or full maintenance at Trade-Union rates of wages' and 'to never cease from active strife against this system until capitalism is abolished and our country and all its resources truly belong to the people'. The former proved a much more practical proposition than the latter, and as a result the N.U.W.M. was increasingly drawn during the 1920s into the tactical struggle to obtain better relief scales for the unemployed on both the national and local levels.[4]

At first the movement had some success in keeping its communist affiliations in the background and in its attempts to work in conjunction with the T.U.C. and the Labour Party. Wal Hannington would have preferred to work within the organs of the official Labour movement if he had been able, but he was only allowed to operate on the fringe of official activity by a mixture of his own persistence and the complicity of some Labour supporters. From the beginning, the communist domination of the N.U.W.M. made it highly suspect to the leaders of organised labour. The decisions of the Labour Party in the twenties to refuse affiliation by the Communist Party also sounded the death-knell of co-operation between the N.U.W.M. and the official Labour movement. For a time, between 1923 and 1926, the N.U.W.M. did manage to obtain formal co-operation with the T.U.C., sitting on a Joint Council on Unemployment. But in 1927 the T.U.C. openly condemned the Communist Party of Great Britain and turned its back on the N.U.W.M., declaring itself dissatisfied with the 'bona-fides of the organisation'. A contributory factor had been the T.U.C's intense irritation at the attempt by the

Communist Party to establish rival, communist-run trade unions.[5]

By the late 1920s the relationship of the N.U.W.M. with the Labour movement had reached a low ebb, and after 1929 it was to deteriorate still further. The Communist Party launched a series of attacks upon the Labour Party and the T.U.C., following the class against class policy pronounced by Moscow. The N.U.W.M. followed this line and its links with the Communist Party were strengthened when Wal Hannington was elected on to the Central Committee of the Communist Party in November 1929. Moreover, the N.U.W.M. supported the party during the 1929 election and its leaders stood against prominent Labour politicians. Wal Hannington stood against Margaret Bondfield at Wallsend as one of twenty-five communist candidates. As a result, the N.U.W.M. candidates shared in the electoral failures of the Communist Party and virtually burnt their bridges with the official Labour movement.[6]

In addition, the N.U.W.M. was faced with increasing opposition from the authorities. It was treated by successive Home Secretaries as a potentially subversive organisation. As a result it came under close scrutiny from the Special Branch who placed an informant within the highest counsels of the movement and were well supplied with information about its plans and activities. By the early 1930s this surveillance included both regular and casual informants; the movements of the N.U.W.M.'s leaders were carefully watched and the proceedings of its meetings were recorded by plain-clothes police.[7] Moreover, a section of the conservative press had already come out strongly against the N.U.W.M. for its activities in the 1920s, branding it a subversive organisation. More seriously, however, the labour press had little time for the organisation, refusing to give an unrespectable, communist-led movement its support and publicity.[8]

The N.U.W.M. was therefore in a somewhat unfavourable position to capitalise upon the worsening unemployment situation after 1929. It was being pressed by the Communist Party to build up a mass movement of the unemployed at a time when the Labour Party and the T.U.C. were virulently attacking communist influence in any form. None the less, the pressures from Moscow and the C.P.G.B. were fairly insistent. The Fifth Congress of the Profintern in Moscow in 1930 condemned the faint-heartedness of the N.U.W.M. in not creating a mass following, complaining about the 'opportunistic tendencies' of the movement and its preoccupation with the technicalities of unemployment relief.[9] The N.U.W.M. did its best to respond to the call for more militancy by a new programme of action. At the Seventh National Conference, held at Bradford in February 1931, the Chairman, Sid Elias, called on the movement to 'mobilise the widest possible mass struggle' and to develop the fight against cuts in unemployment relief at both the national and local level. The movement was to 'make an intensive effort' to increase mass agitation among the unemployed through mass meetings, demonstrations and district marches and to make an organised drive for recruiting. Reflecting the strictures of the Moscow directives in 1930, the movement was urged not to allow its case-work to become too dominant. The immediate slogan adopted was 'On to the streets with mass demonstrations'.[10] It was by these standards that the local N.U.W.M. branches were judged by the Executive in London during the months which followed. The branch at Barrhead was rebuked publicly for meeting indoors; it was exhorted to meet on the streets, 'otherwise we are becoming an organised sect of the unemployed instead of a mass movement'.[11]

In order to broaden the basis of the N.U.W.M. still further, the recommendations of Margaret McCarthy, the Secretary of the Burnley Branch, were accepted. She had been to Moscow early in 1931 and had drawn up a report about the obstacles to the unemployed movement in Britain. Her report led to the setting up of unemployed Councils to act as a focus of political action, open to non-members and to the employed.[12] Although they were not especially successful, they represented the desire of the N.U.W.M. to meet the party line even if it meant losing some of its identity as an organisation. Similarly, the N.U.W.M.'s attitude to the General Election of 1931 was defined solely in terms of providing opportunities for recruitment and propaganda. It was not to put forward its own candidates other than in the most exceptional circumstances, for example where there was very strong local support and no Communist Party candidate. Elsewhere it was to demonstrate in support of the Communist Party's nominee and make the most of the propaganda opportunities the election presented.[13]

It was through its activities on behalf of the unemployed that the N.U.W.M. hoped to make the greatest impact. The rise of unemployment to new levels after 1929 provided the opportunity, while the imposition of the economy measures of the National Government, above all the means test, acted as a fresh stimulus to militant activity. In July 1931, the National Administrative Council reported that it was attempting to raise a mass petition against the proposed cuts in unemployment relief. A new slogan was adopted of 'On the streets on August 1st'.[14] This inaugurated a period of frantic activity for the N.U.W.M. leaders as they attempted to implement the class against class policy, organise a campaign of mass demonstrations and raise new recruits. The means test provided the N.U.W.M. with its best propaganda weapon with which to create a mass movement. While the Labour Party and the T.U.C. were only prepared to criticise the harsher aspects of the enforcement of the new regulations, the N.U.W.M. was demanding the abolition of the means test, higher unemployment relief and the provision of large-scale public works. With almost a million people coming within the regulations of the means test by the end of 1931, the movement had a vast reservoir of grievances upon which to draw. It prompted the organisation to undertake its most violent phase of activity in the whole inter-war period and witnessed the peak years of its membership.

In 1929 the N.U.W.M. had only about 10,000 members. By the middle of 1931, this figure had doubled and, by the end of the year, it had reached 37,000 members.[15] The National Administrative Council reported in July 1931 that there were 294 branches, an increase of 50 having occurred in the past three months.[16] The summer report of the N.A.C. spoke of intensive missionary work by the leadership in all the major industrial areas. Wal Hannington was reported to have set up eight new branches in South Wales on one tour.[17] The reports which were sent in by local branches and published in the N.U.W.M.'s monthly bulletin breathed an air of rapid expansion with new branches springing into existence especially in Scotland, Wales, and Lancashire; amongst others, new branches were reported at Leith, Liverpool, Wolverhampton and Wallsend. Existing branches reported greatly increased attendances; the East Fife branch claimed that meetings which had once been attended by forty or fifty people were now attracting over a thousand and it reported that 'new members were flocking in'.[18] Large audiences were reported at Hammersmith — over 1,200 members and 'going up weekly' — and at Merthyr and the Vale of Leven.[19] By January 1932, almost 400 branches were claimed, though this was adjusted to 346 in May.[20] Through the summer of 1932, the N.U.W.M. built up more branches, reaching a total of 386 in September, organised in 32 district councils.[21]

In October 1931 the N.A.C. reported that the movement had been responsible for holding 16 major demonstrations, at which there had been 100 arrests, including the Chairman, Sid Elias, and the

National Organiser, Wal Hannington. Still the Executive was not satisfied, however, and called for more and bigger demonstrations:

> In this situation our immediate and most urgent task is to rouse and rally the whole of the working class to mass and stormy activity against the attacks of the National Government and the employers ... The unemployed, along with the employed workers, by the rapid development of the mass agitation and struggle in every city, town, and village, by drawing scores and hundreds of thousands of workers into daily activity, by every day bringing steadily increasing masses of workers on to the streets in militant demonstrations, by these means CAN THE PROPOSED CUTS BE BEATEN BACK.[22]

Branches were urged to call meetings and demonstrations, to work inside trade unions, and to form all-in fighting committees of both members and non-members. They were called upon to conduct 'day to day mass rallies, steadily mounting in force and intensity, primarily, centrally, and unwaveringly directed to secure the beating back of the proposed cuts in the dole'.[23]

These strident exhortations by the N.U.W.M. leadership were directly related to the demands of Profintern that the N.U.W.M. turn itself into a mass revolutionary party. There was some criticism of the N.U.W.M. at the Twelfth Plenum of the E.C.C.I. in 1932. A general survey of the world-wide class struggle dwelt upon the weaknesses of the British movement:

> What is the weakest part of the fight against unemployment in Britain? It is the fact that, although we have the unemployed organisation of 50,000 paying members, it is largely an organisation of unemployed workers who have been unemployed for many years, and we have failed to draw into the organisation these hundreds of thousands of skilled and semi-skilled workers who have close ties with the trade union branches, who have been unemployed, for the first time in their lives, and are outside the influence and scope of our organisation.
>
> The lessons of last autumn must be learned. When demonstrations at which unemployed and employed workers participated took place we did not draw them in — but we still have good connections with workers inside the factories. This means we lost tremendous opportunities for making a fight against unemployment, not only a fight of the unemployed, but a fight of the whole working class movement, and particularly a fight of

the trade union movement and a presentation of demands for the finding of work. Not only this aspect but every other gives the Party opportunities for bringing out its whole revolutionary lines.[24]

Under this pressure the N.U.W.M. continued its campaign against the economies of the National Government. In London there were violent clashes between the police and the N.U.W.M. when they attempted to hold meetings outside local Labour Exchanges.[25] Demonstrations, meetings, marches and disturbances occurred throughout the spring and summer of 1932. In April, the Chairman of the N.U.W.M., Sid Elias, was called to Moscow in order to 'act as an adviser' in the Anglo-American Section of the Profintern, where he was to demand reports from the N.U.W.M. and urge them on to mount greater and more impressive demonstrations.[26]

At the same time the N.U.W.M. was building up a head of agitation for the autumn. A conference was called by the movement in May to organise opposition to the means test, at which it was decided to organise another national hunger march to present a petition to parliament against the means test. The petition had been in preparation since the previous summer and a drive was now launched to collect a million signatures. A house-to-house canvass was carried out to complete the total and branches were urged by the N.A.C. to give the collection of signatures priority.[27] Almost as a matter of routine, the N.U.W.M. tried to gain access to the T.U.C. Congress at Newcastle in September. As in the previous year, a march was planned to the Congress in support of a letter requesting admission for an N.U.W.M. deputation in order to make a statement 'for united action by employed and unemployed to smash the Means Test'. Although there was support for this from some sections of Congress, Walter Citrine argued against it, protesting that the march of unemployed to Congress was no spontaneous act, but an organised demonstration by the N.U.W.M. as an agent of the Communist Party. Congress upheld the decision of its General Purposes Committee not to receive the marchers on a card vote, by 1,577,000 to 963,000.[28] Meanwhile, the most serious disturbances to date were taking place in other parts of the country. In Birkenhead, there was serious rioting for several days in the middle of September following a march by local unemployed to the offices of the Public Assistance Committee. Several prominent members of the N.U.W.M. and the Communist Party were arrested. A few days later the riots spread to Liverpool where twenty arrests were made. Violence erupted next in Glasgow after a mass demonstration on 30 September. Early in October, rioting spread to Belfast, following a demonstration by unemployed men working on a relief scheme.[29]

During the autumn of 1932, the N.U.W.M. concentrated on the organisation of a national hunger march to London in order to present its million-signature petition against the means test. The demonstrations and clashes which took place as a result of this campaign were the culmination of its most militant phase of activity in the thirties. The authorities prepared thoroughly to receive the eighteen contingents of marchers who were making their way towards London for the opening of the new parliamentary session at the beginning of November. The Labour Party and the T.U.C. condemned the march along with the great majority of the press. The police put on a show of force and after several clashes with the marchers, they were able to prevent the presentation of the petition. Moreover, Wal Hannington and Sid Elias were arrested in the course of the proceedings.[30]

In the following spring, an important policy change overtook the N.U.W.M. with the adoption of the united front line by Moscow. In March 1933 the Communist Party of Great Britain was urged by Comintern to refrain from attacks upon social-democratic organisations and to attempt co-operation. As a result the C.P. made approaches to the executives of the Labour Party, the I.L.P., the T.U.C. and the Co-operative Party, inviting them to consider joint activity. The N.U.W.M. followed this lead, and by May 1933 had made a formal proposal of joint activity to the T.U.C. and the I.L.P.[31]

From 1933 the united front philosophy dominated the tactics of the N.U.W.M. The rise of Hitler and the destruction of the German trade unions and Communist Party reinforced the mood of co-operation with the British socialist and trade union organisations. The difficulty for the N.U.W.M. was that it was still regarded with suspicion by the labour leadership and was therefore beyond the pale of formal co-operation. Only a few months earlier the N.U.W.M. had been openly hostile to the very men from whom they now sought opportunities for joint activity. It was hardly surprising that the T.U.C. rejected firmly the N.U.W.M.'s approaches.[32] On an unofficial level, however, there was some sympathy and support for the organisation from the more militant trade unionists and Labour Party members, especially those from the depressed areas. Many of these people found their loyalty strained by official directives to refrain from demonstrations on behalf of the unemployed. The position of Aneurin Bevan illustrated the problem:

> For Aneurin Bevan, the dilemma was obviously a baffling one. To have allied himself wholeheartedly with the Communist leadership, even if he could surmount his deep-seated antagonism to their methods, would have been to invite political extinction and condemn himself to total ineffectiveness. On the other hand, to have set his face against the whole unauthorised agitation, as advised by the stream of circulars from Transport House, would have been to outrage his own political instincts and to affront and injure the large numbers of militant Socialists who were caught up in Communist-led demonstrations for lack of any other means of expressing their boiling discontents. What he did was to back many of the protest marches in South Wales and elsewhere, to speak frequently on their platforms and to give his name to petitions presented at Downing Street and Westminster; all the while he sought to keep open the channel of protest on the floor of the House of Commons and to make articulate there the furious resentment outside.[33]

The fortunes of the N.U.W.M. arrived at a turning point in 1933. Although the peak of unemployment was reached and the organisation claimed up to 100,000 members, the number of unemployed began to fall by the end of the year and there was evidence of a contraction in the movement.[34] A minor success for the N.U.W.M. was achieved in February 1933 when it was able to take part in a demonstration against unemployment organised by the T.U.C. and the Labour Party. The latter had intended to prevent this and, when requesting permission to hold the demonstration, had assured the police that the N.U.W.M. would be allowed no place in the proceedings.[35] Even more encouraging to its organisers, the N.U.W.M. could now count upon a degree of sympathetic support by a group of trade unionists and Labour politicians who were frustrated by official inaction on the issue of unemployment. When the N.U.W.M. organised a further hunger march in February 1934, they obtained support from many of this group, acting in defiance of official policy, including Nye Bevan and Edith Summerskill. The march took place in spite of opposition from the government, the police, the Labour Party and the T.U.C.[36]

During the opposition to the new Unemployment Insurance legislation of the National Government in 1934–5, the N.U.W.M.

found itself working in informal co-operation with this dissident group. The culmination of the N.U.W.M.'s activity in the mid-1930s was the organisation of another hunger march in November 1936. A reception committee was formed, drawn from the London Labour and Co-operative Parties. The Special Branch reported that the N.U.W.M. was still firmly committed to the united front line. They claimed that it had decided 'to petition all labour, trade union, and co-operation branches and then when the marchers arrived in London, to make the best use of them for communist propaganda purposes'. None the less, the reception committee included Nye Bevan, Ellen Wilkinson and Edith Summerskill.[37]

But in spite of these allies, the N.U.W.M. had as little success with the bulk of the Labour movement through its united front policy as with the class against class movement of the early thirties. The N.U.W.M. had clearly failed by the mid-1930s to become a mass movement which could command the support of the majority of the unemployed. Even when the N.U.W.M., in conjunction with the Communist Party, withdrew candidates from opposition to the Labour Party in the 1935 General Election, in marked contrast to its attitudes in 1929 and 1931, it failed to allay the suspicions of the leaders of organised labour. Although a group of militant socialists drawn from the Socialist League, the I.L.P. and the parliamentary Labour Party were prepared to co-operate with representatives of the Communist Party and the N.U.W.M. in the Unity Campaign, they remained a distinct minority under severe pressure from their party leaders.[38]

The day-to-day work of the N.U.W.M. in the middle and the late 1930s consisted of legal case-work before the Unemployment Assistance Board on behalf of individuals. In 1938 a 'Winter Adjustment Regulation' was passed, authorising special payments to be made during the winter months to the most deserving of the unemployed. The N.U.W.M. made the issue of 'Winter Relief' the focus of its campaigns in the two years before the war. It demanded that all the unemployed should be given the extra allowance and fought a number of individual cases to establish the general principle. It also staged a series of imaginative publicity stunts to win support for the cause. The campaign opened with a 'lie-in' at Oxford Circus by 200 members of the N.U.W.M., chanting 'We want Winter Relief.' Two days later a group of unemployed men sought tea in the Ritz Hotel, only to be forcibly ejected by the police. A petition was presented to the King, appealing for him to intercede with his ministers, 'to ensure that every unemployed family has fire in the grate and a Christmas dinner'. Just before New Year, 1939, a group of men managed to smuggle a 30-foot banner to the top of the Monument in the City of London. When unfurled, it carried the inscription 'For a Happy New Year the Unemployed Must Not Starve in 1939'. On the last day of 1938, the N.U.W.M. carried a coffin in mock funeral procession from Trafalgar Square to St Paul's. On the sides it had written 'He did not get Winter Relief'. Three days later, the coffin was brought to Downing Street. Although it was captured by the police, a new one soon appeared on the streets of the capital. Members of the N.U.W.M. also chained themselves to railings to obtain publicity for the campaign.[39]

By this time, however, the movement was well past the peak of activity and membership which it had achieved in the early 1930s. Its publicity stunts of the late 1930s, although quite successful in terms of the press, had less of an impact than earlier marches and demonstrations.[40] Membership was falling and the gradual reduction of unemployment had taken its toll of active branches in many parts of the country, especially in those areas where the new industries and rearmament were absorbing the skilled workers who had formed an important part of the movement. Thus activity had virtually ceased in south-east Lancashire and the Midlands with the revival of the engineering industry.[41] The N.U.W.M. was now faced with the consequences of its failure to convert an organisation of unemployed workers into one which would remain a focus for activity when people had gone back to work. Many ex-members of the N.U.W.M. simply dropped out of politics once they found a job, while others turned to traditional trade union activity.

The Eleventh National Conference of the N.U.W.M., held in January 1939, reviewed the organisation's achievements in its eighteen years of existence. It concluded:

> The history of the past eighteen years proves conclusively that not a single improvement has been granted by the government authorities without persistent agitations led by our Movement. We can truthfully claim that bad as the conditions of the unemployed still are, they would undoubtedly be much worse had it not been for the existence of the N.U.W.M. ...

But the N.U.W.M. still felt that it had a place: 'If the N.U.W.M. has been vitally necessary in the past, it will certainly remain so in the future as the new industrial slump develops and larger numbers of workers are caught up in the vortex of unemployment.' With these thoughts upon the prospect of a new slump, the N.U.W.M. concentrated upon its campaign for Winter Relief and on broadening its united front appeal. Once again, the conference stressed the need to create links with the T.U.C. and the Labour Party.[42] In a period which had seen the disaffiliation of the Socialist League from the Labour Party and the expulsion of Bevan and Cripps, this aim seemed as remote as ever.

But the N.U.W.M.'s plans were overtaken by the outbreak of the Second World War in September 1939. The absorption of the unemployed into the armed forces and into war-time industry removed the natural constituents of the movement. A special meeting of the National Administrative Council was called shortly after the outbreak of the war at which the decision was taken to wind up the organisation and sell its furniture and effects to pay off outstanding debts. Almost twenty years of campaigning came to an end with the investment of a balance of £25 in non-interest shares in the People's Press Co-operative Society Ltd.[43]

What had the N.U.W.M. achieved in its years of active campaigning? It is important to consider its impact on a number of levels. On the most significant, that of its overall political impact, it must be accounted a failure. In the context of the depression it might have been expected, and clearly was expected by the Communist Party, that the unemployed would prove a fertile field for recruitment into communist activity. If communism was ever to dislodge established political loyalties among the British working classes, it seemed to have a promising opportunity when almost 3 million people were officially registered as unemployed. Moreover, for much of the 1930s, the N.U.W.M. had virtually a clear field in organising the unemployed because of the failures of traditional labour organisations to cope with the situation. Individual unions were, in theory, responsible for their unemployed members, but it was very difficult to retain links with the unemployed. Unions were essentially organisations of men in work, at their plant, factory or other workplace, and they were not adapted either in attitude or organisation to minister to the out of work.[44] An added disincentive was that the financial situation of many unions, including some of the most militant, such as the A.E.U., made it impossible to offer exemption from union dues or make membership available at a concessionary rate.[45] It was hardly surprising that many of the unemployed found union fees a marginal item when living on a subsistence budget. In 1933, when the T.U.C. took steps to provide Unemployed Associations to counter the influence of the N.U.W.M., they were only a very limited success. Two recent historians of the T.U.C. have commented that 'so far as militant action was concerned, they could not compete with the Communist-inspired movement'.[46]

But even with the field clear, the N.U.W.M. failed to become a political organisation which could challenge the major political groupings. In terms of the objectives laid down by its leaders and by communist spokesmen in London and Moscow, the N.U.W.M. failed to become a mass movement, even in the trough of the depression. Wal Hannington expressed his own disappointment in 1936, claiming that 'at no time has the standing membership approached even ten per cent of the unemployed'.[47] Even this was an overestimate, given our knowledge of N.U.W.M. membership figures from its own reports and literature. An analysis of these sources reveals that the most reliable figure for the N.U.W.M.'s peak membership was 50,000 paid-up members. This was achieved in 1932 when the organisation was at its most active. It was this figure which was reported to the Twelfth Plenum of the E.C.C.I. in Moscow in December 1932 by the General Secretary of the British Communist Party, Harry Pollitt.[48] In 1933, unsubstantiated claims were made for a membership of 100,000 people. This latter figure, however, would accommodate the highest estimate of N.U.W.M. membership. The largest number of branches reported was 400 in January 1932. This was later adjusted to 386, the figure which Pollitt reported to Moscow at the end of the year.[49]

In a way, these were impressive enough figures. They represented a greater degree of support than either the Communist Party or the British Union of Fascists could command. Moreover, it could legitimately be argued that the N.U.W.M.'s influence extended beyond its paid-up members. But the peak membership was short-lived and fell off quickly after the worst of the depression was over. By the mid-1930s Hannington was clearly worried that the organisation had failed to attract the majority of the unemployed. Indeed, even its peak membership was unimpressive when compared with the total number of unemployed. The N.U.W.M. remained a minority organisation which drew its support from a restricted group of unemployed workers. Its strongest areas were those with a militant tradition, especially the craft and engineering centres of Scotland, Lancashire, the Midlands and London. Outside these areas, it had a strong following among the South Wales miners, where communist influence was relatively powerful. But just as there was no discernible swing towards extremism in voting figures, so there was no evidence that a majority of the unemployed were prepared to join an extremist organisation of the Left, even one which catered exclusively for their needs.

The N.U.W.M. did, however, have some substantial achievements. The majority of the day-to-day work of the movement consisted of advising the unemployed about the intricacies and technicalities of unemployment relief. There is little doubt that this was the most successful aspect of the N.U.W.M.'s work and owed a great deal to the dedication of Wal Hannington and the legal sections of the N.U.W.M. to the drudgery of this kind of case-work. By the late 1930s, Wal Hannington was one of the most knowledgeable men in the country about the regulations governing unemployment relief. His collection of acts and pamphlets was extensive and testimony to the professionalism with which the work was carried out.[50] The figures speak for themselves. Over 2,000 cases were fought by the N.U.W.M., of which a third were successful. In many parts of the country, unemployed men who had suffered at the hands of Public Assistance Committees or other bodies had reason to thank the N.U.W.M., whatever its motivation. There was no one else to do the work.

The N.U.W.M. could also claim that they had been the only group to campaign actively on behalf of the unemployed in the worst years of the depression. The T.U.C. promoted only the one demonstration, in February 1933, while the Labour Party remained opposed to demonstrations because of the threat to public order. It was the N.U.W.M. which organised every hunger march in the thirties, other than the Jarrow march of 1936. Thus the N.U.W.M. could claim some success in bringing the plight of the unemployed into the limelight, and attempting to keep it there after the worst years had passed. In an age when instant television journalism did not exist and when the documentary movement was only just emerging in film and journalism, there was a real danger that the plight of the depressed areas would be ignored because of the regionalised nature of unemployment. Yet there were limits to the effect which publicity stunts could achieve. Thus a contemporary observer wrote of the Winter Relief campaign:

The demonstrations of early 1939 ... were nothing more than well-organised stunts. Telephone calls to newspapers made well in advance ensured a big press, and although no doubt the demonstrators were out of work, the same faces were to be seen time and again, lying down in the streets or chained to railings, so that taking part in the stunts became for some of them a kind of a job.[51]

Moreover, the N.U.W.M.'s claim that most of the advances secured in the treatment of the unemployed were the result of its agitations was ill-founded. There were the successes in case-work to point to, and some degree of publicity about the problems of the depressed areas. In addition, a number of local demonstrations and marches did have the effect of producing amendments to local allowances.[52] In Scotland, a march of unemployed workers in 1938, organised by the Scottish N.U.W.M., induced the authorities in Edinburgh to improve relief scales.[53] Although such local successes can be attributed to the N.U.W.M., they failed to bring about an end to the means test, the provision of large-scale public works, or a higher rate of unemployment relief. The means test remained in force throughout the 1930s, although in a modified form.[54] Thus on the large-scale issues of unemployed relief, the N.U.W.M. had little impact. The programme it had adopted in the early 1930s remained unfulfilled at the outbreak of war.

Why did the N.U.W.M. fail to have a greater impact? In *Unemployed Struggles*, published in 1936, Wal Hannington gave three reasons for the N.U.W.M.'s limited success. He blamed the representatives of organised labour for failing to co-operate with the movement on behalf of the unemployed, thus critically limiting its influence. He noted the apathy and fatalism which were characteristic of unemployment and tended to inhibit political activity. He also claimed that the unemployed were reluctant to accept unemployment as a permanent condition and therefore regarded joining an organisation for the unemployed as an admission of hopelessness.[55] Indeed, many of these points were confirmed by the reports into conditions in the depressed areas. The Pilgrim Trust found that fatalism was widespread in some of the worst-affected parts of the country, such as the Durham coalfield. Significantly, they did notice more radical tendencies among the unemployed in the east Midlands, in towns such as Leicester, where unemployment was relatively low and the unemployed felt a correspondingly greater sense of grievance. Leicester was the one community in which the Pilgrim Trust investigators found the N.U.W.M. frequently referred to.[56] Elsewhere, the low ebb to which the N.U.W.M. had sunk in many areas was reflected by Orwell's description of one of their socials in Wigan:

> Admission and refreshments (cup of tea and meat pie) 6*d*. About 200 people, preponderantly women, largely members of the Co-op, in one of whose rooms it was held, and I suppose for the most part living directly or indirectly on the dole. Round the back a few aged miners sitting looking on benevolently, a lot of very young girls in front. Some dancing to the concertina (many of the girls confessed they could not dance, which struck me as rather pathetic) and some excruciating singing. I suppose these people represent a fair cross-section of the more revolutionary element in Wigan. If so, God help us. Exactly the same sheeplike crowd — gaping girls and shapeless middle-aged women dozing over their knitting — that you see everywhere else. There is no *turbulence* left in England.[57]

The principal failure of the N.U.W.M. was its inability to break the established leadership of the Labour Party and the T.U.C. in the depressed areas. The hostility and suspicion with which the N.U.W.M. was regarded by these bodies meant that it was fighting an uphill struggle in most areas against entrenched attitudes and influence. The N.U.W.M. was operating throughout the 1930s as a rather suspect organisation, tainted by its association with the Communist Party and denied support from the official Labour movement. As Hannington recognised, the achievements of the N.U.W.M. were severely limited by the opposition of all but a minority of the representatives of organised labour. As a result, in many parts of the country the N.U.W.M., in common with the Communist Party, found itself opposed to the traditional loyalties of the unemployed. In areas such as Lancashire, they suffered from the powerful influence wielded by Roman Catholicism and Non-conformity, both of which were strongly anti-communist.[58]

Thus, in a not unusual configuration of British politics, the N.U.W.M. fought its hardest battles not against the 'class enemies', but against the existing traditions and political groupings of the working classes themselves. Indeed, the communist leadership recognised this as its greatest problem. Harry Pollitt, reporting on the general European situation at the Thirteenth Plenum of the E.C.C.I. in 1933, commented that:

Notwithstanding the fact that the socialist parties and the reformist trade unions in all countries are taking part in the growing political and economic offensive against the working class (the fascization of the state apparatus and the application of fascist methods of violence, the continued sharp reduction of nominal and real wages, the furious increase in the intensification of labour, the cutting down of all forms of unemployment relief and the line taken for the complete abolition of unemployment insurance, compulsory labour, etc.), the Communist Parties and the revolutionary trade unions have not sufficiently liberated the masses of the workers from the influence of the Social-Democratic parties and of the trade union bureaucrats.[59]

The workers, he complained, had failed 'in the mass' to come over to the Communist Parties and unemployed organisations, which were unable to enlist or retain the support of those who took part in demonstrations. Instead, it seemed on the evidence of municipal elections that the 'masses of the workers' were 'throwing themselves into the arms of the social-fascists', that is, the Labour Party.[60]

The leadership of the N.U.W.M. came almost entirely from members of the Communist Party. Its rank and file clearly did not, for the number of Communist Party members in 1932 was only 9,000 compared with the N.U.W.M.'s 50,000.[61] This was recognised by Sir John Gilmour, the Home Secretary, who informed the House of Commons in 1932 that the N.U.W.M. was 'a Communist organisation, but its membership is not entirely confined to communists. There are some quite respectable and decent men who are members of it . . . '[62] The leadership, however, was heavily dominated by party members and it was this which gave the movement its communist bias, in spite of the numerical inferiority of party members in the movement as a whole. Several members moved into N.U.W.M. activity as a natural addition to their membership of the party. Will Paynter was an example: he became a party member before becoming involved in N.U.W.M. activities.[63] The Merseyside organiser of the N.U.W.M. was Joseph Rawlings, a member of the Communist Party since 1920. He had spent some time in Russia in the mid-1920s and then became the local party and N.U.W.M. organiser in 1930.[64] For others, the N.U.W.M. led on to membership of the party; Jack Dash, for example, describes how he was recruited to the N.U.W.M. after attending a meeting outside a London Labour Exchange, and only later joined the C.P.[65]

A marked difference between the history of the N.U.W.M. and the Communist Party was that there was no influx of young intellectuals into the movement towards the end of the 1930s. It was hardly surprising that an organisation primarily directed at unemployed men should remain largely working class. One effect, however, was to deprive the N.U.W.M. of a much-needed infusion of organising talent and the kind of political respectability which might have made it a more effective force. Instead, the organisation remained dependent upon a small group of activists, who consequently became seriously overworked. The burden of political tasks which the Communist Party thrust upon the N.U.W.M. leadership verged upon the insupportable, particularly when so much time was taken up by unemployment insurance case-work. At the same time, there was the movement's literature to be sold, including the *Daily Worker*, which could not at this time be distributed through newsagents. It was significant that the experiment of the monthly bulletin compiled from local branch reports very quickly ran into the difficulty that local branches were not reporting regularly because of the pressure of work.

Another weakness from which the movement suffered was lack of adequate finance. Although there was a great deal of talk about 'red gold' by the Conservative press, there was little evidence that the organisation had access to unlimited funds.[66] Its basic running expenses came from subscriptions, admission fees and the sale of literature. Its newspaper, *Unemployed News*, usually ran at a loss, however, and was a steady drain upon its financial resources. With subscriptions as low as one penny a week, the organisation could count on only £200 a week at the peak of its membership. In addition, it had to pay the living and travel expenses of its permanent staff, rent its premises, and conduct its legal case-work. Although a great deal could be done on unpaid effort, the poverty of the organisation showed in its literature. Far from being glossy, sophisticated propaganda, it usually consisted of duplicated sheets, often virtually illegible through bad copying. Even its annual conference reports were produced in this way. Its output of material revealed not a well-oiled political machine, but a financially hard-pressed, shoe-string organisation. While the Communist Party may well have been able to divert funds to it through the channels of Soviet trade organisations, there was a clear shortage of money for general purposes.[67]

These organisational problems, the small number of permanent activists and its precarious financial position made the movement peculiarly susceptible to disruption by the arrest and imprisonment of its leaders. At one stage in 1933 the majority of the executive of the N.U.W.M. were languishing in prison, to the detriment of the movement's activities in the country as a whole. The police played a cat-and-mouse game with Wal Hannington, who spent a considerable amount of his time either in prison or fighting to stay out of it. By 1932, when Hannington was given 3 months in prison on a charge of attempting to create disaffection among the police and armed forces, he had been arrested five times and served three terms of imprisonment, one of 12 months and two of 1 month.[68] The movement in the regions was subject to the same pressures, for the demonstrations of 1931–2 left behind them a trail of arrests among the provincial leadership. On Merseyside the local N.U.W.M. organisers were arrested and gaoled for their part in the demonstrations at Birkenhead in September 1932, Joseph Rawlings, the Merseyside organiser of the N.U.W.M., receiving two years' hard labour.[69] In the previous year, the Secretary of the Salford N.U.W.M. was arrested for his part in demonstrations at Salford Town Hall and several members of the Salford N.U.W.M. received terms of imprisonment.[70] N.U.W.M. members were usually prosecuted as the 'ringleaders' of any disturbance that occurred. Thus at Birkenhead, while the majority of local men involved in the riots of 1932 received small fines, all the N.U.W.M. members received terms of imprisonment.[71] Given that the N.U.W.M. was dependent upon a fairly small group of activists, these arrests and terms of imprisonment had a disruptive effect upon the movement out of all proportion to the numbers involved or the terms of imprisonment received. After 1933, the N.U.W.M. moderated its policies of mass demonstrations, partly because it fitted in with the new line being promoted by Moscow, but also because the events of 1931–2 had shown the leadership that an open challenge to the forces of law and order was increasingly unproductive.[72]

Moreover, the National Unemployed Workers' Movement displayed some reluctance to play the part chosen for it by the Communist Party. In the critical years between 1929 and 1933, when unemployment was at its worst and the organised labour movement in greatest disarray, the N.U.W.M. was very unwilling to take an overtly revolutionary line. In part, this was necessary discretion if the N.U.W.M. was to survive as a political force. But it went rather deeper than that. The N.U.W.M. leaders were very reluctant revolutionaries. The organisation consistently occupied itself with individual case-work at the expense of its broader political objectives. Wal Hannington himself was deeply involved in the complex issues of unemployment regulations and assistance. More than once, Moscow evinced dissatisfaction with the N.U.W.M.'s preoccupation with the 'tactical' struggle and condemned the 'trade union legalism' of the organisation. On their part, some of the N.U.W.M. leaders, such as Hannington and McShane, were to record their disquiet at the role thrust upon them by the Communist Party in 1931–2, with its demands for bigger and more violent demonstrations, which seemed to promise only an early demise for the movement.

In the worst year of the depression, 1932, the N.U.W.M. responded to a call from Moscow for revolutionary action by drawing up a million-signature petition against the means test. Although some clashes with the police occurred, the N.U.W.M. was essentially defensive in its attitude to political violence. It was highly significant that the N.U.W.M. in the 1930s showed itself to be wedded to a policy of reformism, concentrating its energies on attempts to change the law and improve conditions on behalf of the unemployed. The peculiarities of the British situation, as defined by the Communist Party, extended far beyond the workers themselves, but also into the ranks of the activists. As a result, the attempt which the Communist Party made to channel the resentments of the unemployed into political action was frustrated almost as much by the attitude of the organisation whose responsibility it was to spearhead this work as it was by the reluctance of the unemployed to respond to the appeal of the N.U.W.M. and the Communist Party.

M

X

Hunger Marches and Demonstrations

The hunger marches remain one of the most emotive images of Britain in the 1930s. The most famous of all, the Jarrow march of 1936, has retained its power to symbolise the human consequences of mass unemployment. For some contemporaries the marches were part of an epic and widespread struggle against the policies of successive governments. Wal Hannington wrote:

> The unemployed did not quietly suffer their degradation and poverty. They were hungry; their wives and children were hungry; they marched on the streets in mighty protest demonstrations, and savage battles were fought from day to day in one town after another against the police who were ordered to suppress these militant activities.

And he continued, 'If history is to be truly recorded our future historians must include this feature of the "Hungry Thirties" .'[1] Thus an analysis of the impact of mass unemployment upon British politics and society at this time must attempt to assess the scale and importance of the protests and demonstrations of the unemployed. How widespread was the protest against unemployment? Was it spontaneous? How much of it was communist-inspired?

Protests against unemployment got under way almost as soon as the first effects of depression were felt in the early 1920s. But from the beginning a pattern began to emerge in which the only group prepared to organise demonstrations by the unemployed was the communist-dominated N.U.W.M. In 1922 they mounted a national hunger march to London, in which several contingents of unemployed, totalling about 2,000 people in all, made their way to the capital from the depressed areas. A number of demonstrations were held in the capital and an audience arranged with ministers concerned with the unemployment question. Although these events passed off peacefully, the march caused serious alarm. At one point the police urged shops and offices in central London to barricade their premises in case of disturbances, and the more conservative sections of the press complained bitterly about the inconvenience caused to the normal life of the capital by the presence of the marchers and their sympathisers.[2]

This first large-scale hunger march organised by the N.U.W.M. raised many of the issues which were to dominate its activities in the thirties. Any attempt by an avowedly left-wing organisation to mobilise the unemployed was found to create a tense situation in relation to the authorities. In addition, it influenced the attitudes of the leaders of organised labour towards demonstrations by the unemployed to find the communists taking a leading part in them. Hence, when the N.U.W.M. began to organise renewed marches and demonstrations as unemployment worsened in the late 1920s, it did so without the support of organised labour. In 1927, when the N.U.W.M. organised a march of unemployed Welsh miners to London, it was condemned by the T.U.C. General Council. The General Secretary, Walter Citrine, circulated all trades councils on the proposed route of the march and advised them not to give aid to the marchers. Similarly, the London Trades Council executive campaigned against the march, describing it as 'fostered by the Communist Party for the purpose of augmenting their membership'.[3] In 1929, another march by the N.U.W.M. was met by opposition. In September 1931, the N.U.W.M. led a march of unemployed miners from South Wales to demonstrate at the T.U.C. Congress at Bristol. Walter Citrine was approached by the N.U.W.M. with a request to allow a deputation of marchers into Congress. No reply was received and when the marchers approached the Bristol City boundary, they were met by a cordon of police. After some negotiations between Wal Hannington and the senior police officer, the marchers were allowed into the city centre. However, when the marchers tried to force a way into Congress two days later they were held back by police and stewards. A fight ensued in which the marchers were repulsed from the entrance of the Hall. Other clashes with the police took place at the Horsefair in the centre of the city in which several people were injured and a number arrested.[4]

During the autumn of 1931, the N.U.W.M. built up a programme of marches and demonstrations at Labour Exchanges, Poor Law offices and Town Halls. Persistent demonstrations in London in September led to a number of arrests, but brought no halt to scenes and impromptu meetings in and outside Labour Exchanges in the capital. A large demonstration in Dundee at the end of September led to the banning of all demonstrations and processions in the city. On 1 October there were disturbances outside the Town Hall in Salford, when several hundred men forced their way into the square in front of the building to protest against the cuts in unemployment benefit. Some of them were reported as shouting 'Remember 1914' and the local newspaper recorded the scene:

> For some time there was a pitched battle in the Square. The police officers seemed to be in the centre of a mêlée in which arms and legs were whirling madly about ... The mounted police drew their batons, and, urging their horses forward into the throng, began to drive back the rioters. Many men who were pushed over were trampled on by the crowd before they could get to their feet. Others clung to the police horses until they were shaken off.[5]

The next day, 2,000 demonstrators turned up outside the Town Hall to protest against the arrest of twelve men on the previous day. A week later, 5,000 marchers assembled at Ardwick Green, Manchester, with the intention of marching to the Town Hall and sending a deputation to the city council. When police informed the marchers that they could not use the planned route, they rushed the police cordon. Fighting broke out in which stones and hammerheads were reported to have been thrown, policemen pulled from their horses, and a police baton-charge made. Six people were hurt and thirty-eight arrested. The next day the police put a guard on shops, banks, courts and other public buildings in Manchester and Salford, and Special Constables were mobilised on a large scale for the first time since the General Strike. By the end of 1931 there had been a number of disturbances; over thirty different towns and cities had witnessed clashes between the police and unemployed demonstrators.[6] Disturbances continued into 1932 as the N.U.W.M. kept up a programme of marches and demonstrations against local Public Assistance committees. These were usually aimed at securing relief work, an improvement of relief scales, and the mitigation or abolition of the means test. As a result there were more violent clashes between police and demonstrators. In London, the Chief Commissioner of the Metropolitan Police banned the N.U.W.M. from holding meetings outside local Labour Exchanges. When the N.U.W.M. defied the order, there were frequent disturbances as the police attempted to remove the demonstrators by force. In January 1932, fighting broke out between the police and demonstrators in Keighley and Glasgow; three days later, army reservists were called out to protect the Town Hall at Rochdale against unemployed demonstrators. These disturbances, however, reached their peak in autumn 1932 when severe rioting broke out in London, Belfast and on Merseyside.[7]

The disturbances in Belfast were the first to draw fatal casualties. In the second week of October 1932, 2,000 men working on relief work in the city went on strike to demand an increase in the relief scale they were being paid in lieu of wages. A march was held through the city centre to draw attention to the strike and fighting broke out with the police. There were several baton-charges and shop windows and street-lamps were smashed. On 11 October a further demonstration was planned, but was banned by the police. The organisers, however, went ahead with the march and the police attempted to disperse it with the aid of armoured cars. Widespread fighting spread around the city centre and barricades were built to prevent the entry of the police into the poorer areas where fighting was fiercest.[8] The *News Chronicle* described how 'Charge after charge was made by the police upon the bands of men, but the charges had only a temporary effect.' Even women took part in the terrific onslaught of stones and other missiles, and at times it looked as if the police would be overpowered. With the assistance of the armoured cars the rioters were forced back into the side streets and alleys. This hide-and-seek warfare continued throughout the day, with men and women shouting 'We must have bread'. Eventually the police opened fire, killing one man and seriously wounding several others, one of whom died two days later in hospital.[9]

Forty-eight people were arrested, a curfew imposed, and a military cordon put around the city with police and armoured cars patrolling the city centre. Even after the drafting into the city of seven lorry-loads of Royal Inniskilling Fusiliers armed with machine-guns, the situation was not fully under control. Further disturbances broke out on the following day, resulting in over 100 arrests, and at least another 50 people were injured. In the course of the day the Belfast linen mills went on strike and in the evening the Belfast Trades Council called for a general strike. Further troops from the King's Royal Rifles were drafted in to deal with a situation which threatened to become explosive, particularly as the funeral for the two men killed in the demonstrations was scheduled for the 14th and it was expected that thousands would turn out to join the procession. When the honorary Treasurer of the N.U.W.M., Tom Mann, arrived in the city to attend the funeral, he was arrested by detectives, given a deportation order, detained until the evening and then placed upon the evening boat, only 15 hours after his arrival. In the event, the funeral passed off peacefully; it was attended by several thousand people and guarded by a large turn-out of police, backed up by military reserves. The tense situation which resulted was defused by a concession on the part of the Northern Ireland government, which raised the relief scales for the unemployed.[10]

Yet in many respects the events in Belfast had less impact upon the political scene than the disturbances which took place in Birkenhead and Liverpool during late September 1932. Neither for the first nor last time, the Irish Sea effectively isolated events in Northern Ireland from domestic politics. Attempts in parliament to raise the question of the shootings and the issues out of which they arose were rebuffed with the Home Secretary's appeal to the convention that Westminster should not discuss Northern Irish affairs.[11] But while Ulster was left in political and emotional isolation, events on Merseyside provoked severe disquiet that the N.U.W.M. was realising its intentions to turn the streets of Britain into a battlefield between the unemployed and the police. The first disturbance broke out in Birkenhead, a large and rather depressing port and shipbuilding town on the Mersey estuary, directly opposite Liverpool. The unrest grew out of a march organised in September 1932 to protest against the means test. Deputations demanding higher scales of relief and other concessions for the unemployed made no impact, although marches had been taking place in the town throughout the summer of 1932. In August 1,000 unemployed dockers marched through the streets to protest against the means test. A deputation was sent to the Public Assistance Committee with demands for an increased relief scale for the unemployed. The unions involved went to great pains to emphasise that it was a trade union demonstration and that no communists were allowed to take part. On 7 September, however, when a demonstration of 3,000 unemployed took place in the town, 'The Red Flag' was sung and the crowd was addressed by a Liverpool communist, Leo McGree. In September the local trade union and labour leaders found themselves in an increasingly difficult position, for having opened the season of demonstrations, at least in part because of their frustration with the impasse of local politics, they now found themselves being outflanked by the militants of the C.P. and the N.U.W.M. Under their local leader, Joseph Rawlings, the N.U.W.M. demanded a programme of considerable attractiveness to the local unemployed: an end to the means test, the extension of work schemes, the restoration of the economy cuts in wages and unemployment relief, and a 25 per cent reduction in council rents. The official deputation led by a Labour Alderman and prominent trade unionists asked only for an extension of relief schemes over the winter. The Mayor refused to receive them and would only concede the calling of a special meeting of the Council on the following Tuesday.[12]

On the Tuesday, the unemployed began to assemble at about 3 p.m. in the pouring rain, although the meeting was not to take place until 8 p.m. The crowd waited for five hours only to hear the familiar inconclusive promises from inside the Council Chamber. The crowd grew restive and had to be broken up by baton-charges during which several people were injured. Discontent simmered throughout Wednesday, then on Thursday the town erupted into uproar. The Birkenhead communists organised a march of the unemployed to the P.A.C. offices. It was reported to be over a mile long:

> The procession proceeded in more or less orderly fashion, five and six deep. In the main it was a purposeful gathering, if a motley one. Men in ragged clothes and worn out shoes; men with clothes faded, yet neatly pressed and shoes brightly polished; here and there an upright professional-looking man; men with washed overalls that had not known the grime of the shipyards for months; old men with white hair and bent shoulders; young boys but shortly out of school; each one ready to shout in the chorus of 'Struggle or starve' and 'Down with the Means Test'.[13]

It was estimated that 8,000 men took part, and when they arrived outside the P.A.C. office tension increased. A deputation was sent inside the building and police guarded the doors. The mob surged forward, shouting insults at the police, brandishing poles and chanting 'The Red Flag'. The P.A.C. would only promise to consider the means test at its next meeting on the following Monday. Outside, the crowd was getting out of hand. Leo McGree mounted on a chair and tried to make himself heard. His voice carried above the noise and confusion: 'We must fight to the end, on Monday the Means Test must be a thing of the past in Birkenhead.' The crowd surged away from the building and under its own momentum went to the house of Alderman Baker, Chairman of the P.A.C. As the police had thought the meeting would disperse, they had not provided a guard. When the crowd reached Baker's house, they began to trample over the garden and pelt the outside with stones and dirt. In fact, Baker himself was out, but before this was discovered the police arrived and dispersed the crowd with their batons. A local newspaper recorded that: 'Batons were wielded to good effect by the police; who scattered flying ranks of the mob in all directions, leaving about fifty of them lying screaming and shouting in the road.' But elsewhere in the town, the riots gathered momentum. In the north, a mob collected and smashed the windows of the Co-operative store and started to loot their contents. At the Park, another mob tore up the iron railings and used them as weapons and missiles against the police. The battle went on for several hours in many parts of the town until the early hours of the morning, when some sort of peace was obtained. Thirty-seven demonstrators were treated in hospital. Seven police were also injured, three of them seriously.[14]

All then remained quiet until Friday evening when Joseph Rawlings addressed a crowd outside the P.A.C. offices. He was reported to have said:

> On Monday afternoon all the working classes will have to be in the streets of this town to demonstrate. We don't want 10,000, but 20,000 or 50,000. We will have to be organised into a regiment and we will march as we did in 1914. We will march feeling that we are going to attack and that attack is our best defence.

The police arrived and the meeting dispersed. But when the police tried to follow the crowds into the warren of streets that surrounded the docks they were countered by a sort of guerilla war among the maze of alleys and terraced houses. In the early hours of Saturday morning, Rawlings and six other communist activists were arrested. But on Saturday night the rioting flared up again and went on throughout the night and into Sunday. Sixteen shops were broken into and looted and at one point there was a pitched battle between the police and a mob of 400 rioters armed with iron railings, bricks and bottles. In the narrow streets, women threw household furniture from upstairs windows on to the police, including in one case an iron bedstead. Twenty-seven more arrests were made. The Liverpool police had to be called in on Sunday morning, including a mounted contingent who were brought in by ferry in the early hours. Police reinforcements and the arrest of the communist organisers left the way open for the Labour Party and trades union officials to take control once more. The *Birkenhead News* called on Labour Councillors to restrain the unemployed from further endangering the good name of the town and they, in turn, disowned the disorders which had occurred.[15]

Three days later there were disturbances across the river in Liverpool, following a march through the centre of the city by a large body of unemployed. Further disturbances took place at West Ham, Croydon and North Shields.[16] The clashes on Merseyside and elsewhere led to questions in the House of Commons about police action, but the Home Secretary refused to consent to an inquiry. As a result of further unrest in London, the Home Secretary was forced on 19 October into a defence of his policies and of police action. In reply to a question about the London disturbances Sir John Gilmour commented:

> I want the House to realise that the demonstration yesterday was no spontaneous movement. It is quite clear ... that the National Unemployed Workers' Movement, a Communist organisation, or in the main a Communist organisation, has been the root, and the instigator, of these difficulties.[17]

These remarks were of particular relevance because as he was speaking, the N.U.W.M. was in the midst of the greatest effort of its campaign of 1931–2. Eighteen contingents, making up what the N.U.W.M. called the 'Great National Hunger March against the Means Test', were marching towards London to meet on 27 October. There, with the unemployed of the capital, they were to present a mass petition of a million signatures against the means test and undertake what the *Unemployed Special* described as 'an invasion of Westminster'.[18] The Scottish contingent had already been on the road for three weeks when the Home Secretary spoke in the Commons on the 19th. Other contingents had only just started off. The Norwich constabulary described the orderly departure of the East Anglian marchers on the 16th; the marchers bore a placard of a human skeleton with the words 'Mr Chamberlain says we must cut to the bone.'[19] In all, about 2,000 marchers were involved, mainly drawn from the N.U.W.M. The T.U.C. and the Labour Party naturally opposed the march because of its sponsorship and maintained this opposition on the official level. At the local level, however, the marchers often received sympathetic and active support from local union and Labour branches. The government was highly suspicious of the march; Gilmour referred to the petition as only the 'ostensible object' of the demonstrations in London.[20] The progress of the contingents through England was attended by a certain amount of violence even before the marchers arrived in London. The N.U.W.M. had decided to demand overnight accommodation in the workhouses of the towns through which they passed, but were not prepared to accept the normal 'casual' relief given for vagrants and down-and-outs. There were a number of confrontations and, in some cases, disturbances as a result of these claims and their resistance by the local authorities *en route*. When questioned about the government's attitude to the marchers, the Home Secretary refuted claims that he had given special instructions to the local police forces to deal harshly with them. He made two points: firstly, that he had no direct responsibility for law and order in the localities; secondly, that both he and the Commissioner of Police in London would use every means to avoid clashes, for it 'is not our desire to cause hardship'.[21] In fact, on 29 September the Home Office had advised local police forces and health authorities to maintain strictly the principle of 'casual' relief and advised Chief Officers of Police to make 'all necessary arrangements' to deal with any disturbances that might arise.[22] At Burton-on-Trent on 17 October there was a tense confrontation in the town centre between the women's contingent, supported by local unemployed workers, and the police because of attempts to impose 'casual' regulations upon the marchers, though eventually the marchers were allowed to enter the workhouse on special terms. At Stratford on 20 October the Lancashire contingent was involved in a disturbance with the heavily reinforced local police force in similar circumstances.[23]

The tough official line taken by the Home Secretary was indicative of the seriousness with which the authorities viewed the progress of the march. Indeed, judging from their preparations to receive the marchers in the capital, they were quite seriously alarmed. The police were supplied with information both from local constabularies on the route of march and by informers within the ranks of the N.U.W.M. According to the latter, passed on through the Special Branch, the N.U.W.M. was expecting the demonstrations in London to be the largest ever known.[24] It was stated that the march was to be 'as spectacular as possible' and the marchers would aim to have 'as many clashes with police as can be arranged', using their banners 'in open conflict with the police'.[25] The march organisers were reported to have refused to seek permission for their demonstration and would take 'direct action' to counter any attempts to prevent them reaching the House of Commons. The use of 'methods not previously employed' would be adopted against the police and diversionary demonstrations would be made in the Stock Exchange and outside buildings in the West End. The marchers were said to have plans to use trip wires against the mounted police, and iron bars, which they would conceal up their sleeves, against the police in Hyde Park. Other informers were even more alarmist; there was talk of the police being sympathetic to the marchers and copies of pamphlets and handbills addressed to the police were sent in to Scotland Yard. Other reports suggested the marchers were arming themselves with a variety of weapons, including darts, vitriol, cudgels and firearms.[26] On the basis of this information the authorities prepared for the worst, for though the actual number of marchers was quite small, under 2,000, it was feared that their ranks would be swollen once they reached London by the unemployed of the capital. In addition, the Special Branch had warned that 'the dockers, stevedores, etc.' would take part in the lobby of parliament, 'making their way there by water'.[27] The police were determined to prevent any mass lobby of the House of Commons by enforcing the Seditious Meetings Act of 1817, prohibiting meetings within a mile of Westminster while parliament was in session. Almost 2,000 police were put on duty, including over 100 mounted constables, and 600 special constables were held in reserve.[28]

Apprehensions of violence seemed borne out by the immediate background to the arrival of the marchers. On 24 October there were clashes with the police at County Hall, Westminster, when a deputation of London unemployed organised by the N.U.W.M. presented a series of demands for improved relief scales and work schemes.[29] The next day, a speaker at a meeting in Hackney claimed that riots had forced concessions on relief scales in other parts of the country. Several handbills had been found in London asking the police to display solidarity with the unemployed to defeat cuts in their own pay, but ending with an ominous pledge that: 'If you attack us, we shall know how to defend ourselves, how to fight back'.[30] However, the contingents arrived peacefully in London on the evening of 26 October and were accommodated in a number of institutions and halls in the inner suburbs. On the morning of 27 October the contingents marched to a welcoming rally in Hyde Park, attended by large numbers of police. Shortly after 2 p.m. the marchers and their supporters began to arrive in the park until several thousand people were there. Hannington estimated the crowd at 100,000 but the police report claimed there were only between 10,000 and 25,000. None the less, it was an impressive number. All went well until about 4 p.m., when fighting broke out around the Marble Arch entrance to the park. Hannington blamed the inexperienced special constables for starting the incident, but the police claimed that they had acted to control a group of 500 or more who had broken away from the main body. The exact truth is almost impossible to discern, but the result was a confused mêlée in which both mounted and foot police were called in to disperse the crowds. Several baton-charges were made and twelve people arrested before the fighting died down between 4.30 and 5 p.m. According to police reports, 77 people were injured, 7 of them policemen and the rest demonstrators.[31] Three days later, on Sunday, 30 October, there was a very large demonstration in Trafalgar Square, probably involving more people than the Hyde Park demonstration. Though there was sporadic fighting on the fringe of the crowd, as the police tried to clear roadways on the edge of the square, the meeting proceeded without major interruption.[32]

The main event, to which these demonstrations had only been the preliminary, was the presentation of the N.U.W.M.'s million-signature petition asking for the abolition of the means test and the Anomalies Act, and the restoration of the 10 per cent cut in unemployment benefit. The tactics in regard to presenting the petition were later described by Hannington in the following terms:

> On achieving this target [a million signatures] we had decided
> not to ask a Member of Parliament to present the petition but
> to claim the right for it to be presented by a deputation from
> the Hunger Marchers. We claimed this right under an ancient
> Law entitling Commoners to appear for such purpose at the Bar
> of the House of Commons.[33]

The Special Branch's 'Précis of Further Information re Hunger Marchers' was in no doubt that Tuesday, 1 November, was to be the 'big day', when the N.U.W.M. intended to force their way to the House of Commons and present their petition. As they had been forbidden from petitioning *en masse*, it was expected that this would cause violent clashes with the police and informers forecast 'real bloodshed on that day'. It was reported that the marchers would use diversionary tactics to break through the police cordon around the House, by creating disturbances in restaurants and in the suburbs 'to keep the police on the move'. Reports claimed that seamen and dockers in the East End had been canvassed and asked to attend the demonstration, bringing with them their hooks for handling bales. At least 15,000–20,000 were expected at the demonstration and the Special Branch warned that if the petition was refused or received an unsatisfactory answer 'there will be much window smashing, looting, etc.'[34]

There was serious alarm about what was going to happen and the *Daily Telegraph* was in little doubt about who was to blame:

> How long is London to be subjected to the indignity of having its police forces – regular and special – mobilised to deal with the Communist HANNINGTON and his Marchers, but in reality with HANNINGTON and the revolutionary riff-raff of London? Ninety per cent of the Marchers may well be dupes, pawns in a Communist game directed by the master-intriguers of Moscow ... The abolition of the Means Test is a pretext. The presentation of a Petition is a blind. Hannington, the professional organiser of these marches, is conceited indeed, if he supposes that his communist riff-raff could make a revolution, but that they could do incalculable damage by loot and pillage in an hour or two of mob excitement is undeniable, and that bloodshed would ensue is certain ...[35]

The Times had already made its position clear about the march when, under a headline of 'Liberty or Licence', it asked:

> Is there to be no limit to the right of the workless to hamper the workers? The evil will grow if it is not checked. There are plenty of ways in which legitimate discontent may be rationally expressed. The government must seriously consider whether the spurious importance which these mass marches are bound to be given at home or abroad should not be countered by special restrictive measures.[36]

On the morning of 1 November, *The Times* urged the marchers to go home at their own expense and to stop being 'the dupes of political propagandists who believe in violence as the proper instrument of policy'. The *Manchester Guardian* took a similar line, accusing the Communist Party of 'exploiting the unemployed'.[37]

The N.U.W.M. was not only confronted with a largely hostile press, it had very little support from Labour M.P.s and was completely cut off from official T.U.C. backing. Even the few sympathetic Labour members were finally alienated by the N.U.W.M.'s refusal to present the petition through the normal procedures and insistence on trying to conduct a mass petition of the House of Commons. On the morning of 1 November, the police acted. They raided the headquarters of the N.U.W.M. at Great Russell Street, seized a large number of documents, and arrested Wal Hannington. At Bow Street police court he was charged with 'Attempting to cause disaffection among members of the Metropolitan Police contrary to the Police Act, 1919'. The evidence against him consisted of notes taken by the police of his speech at Trafalgar Square on 30 October when he had urged the police to refuse to act against the hunger marchers. Almost more important than the charge itself, bail was refused and he was taken immediately to Brixton prison.[38] None the less, the march organisers went ahead with the plans for the evening. By the late afternoon demonstrators were moving towards Westminster. But as they reached the vicinity of the House they were met by both mounted and foot police who broke up the large bodies of marchers using the main streets. By about 7 p.m. something like 3,000 demonstrators had arrived in Trafalgar Square via side streets. In the meantime the mass petition, which was the point of all this activity, had been taken by taxi and lodged by the N.U.W.M. leadership in Charing Cross railway station cloakroom so that a deputation could take it to the House of Commons. By now the crowd had gathered around the station entrance and the police had made several baton charges already in an attempt to disperse them. The petition, which was in several large bundles, was being moved out of the station by some of the leaders of the N.U.W.M., including Emrys Llewellyn and Sid Elias, when the Superintendent of 'E' division of the Metropolitan Police approached them and said, 'If you take this petition through the streets with the crowd in their present condition it will be likely to provoke a riot.' The Superintendent later admitted that he did this to gain time until his superiors were aware of what was happening. The Superintendent then directed Emrys Llewellyn to return the petition to the cloakroom, which was done, though 'with some demur'. He reported, however, overhearing some of the committee saying that they could easily bring it out again when the police had gone. This was not to be, for about an hour later the Superintendent entered the cloakroom and took possession of the petition which was immediately taken to Bow Street.[39] With this the focal point of the demonstration, if not of the whole march, had been frustrated. It remained to be seen whether the police's arrest of the petition would create the disturbance which they had sought to avoid in seizing it. Fierce fighting broke out in several different places as news of the arrest of the petition spread.

At 9 p.m. the police called out their reserves to deal with several disturbances, some of them as far from the centre of the city as Shepherd's Bush, where a crowd of 800 was reported to have been dispersed at 11 p.m. A determined attempt to force a way across Westminster Bridge was only prevented with difficulty. At 10 p.m. there was sporadic fighting in Parliament Square, Whitehall, Trafalgar Square, the Strand, Charing Cross Road, Victoria Street, along the Embankment and on Westminster Bridge Road. The area was not entirely quiet until about 1.30 p.m., by which time about 40 people had been arrested and about 50 injured.[40]

Following these events the marchers prepared to leave London on 5 November. The petition was reclaimed by the N.U.W.M. on the 4th and a receipt signed for it by an N.U.W.M. member at Bow Street. The contingents of marchers were escorted to their respective railway stations by the police and left for their destinations without incident. A number of court cases remained to be settled in the aftermath of the demonstrations. The most important was that of Hannington himself. He was tried at Bow Street on 8 November and convicted on the charge of causing disaffection, for which he received 3 months' imprisonment.[41] A number of other offenders were dealt with in the days following the demonstrations. Four men were given 6 months for their part in the Hyde Park disturbances, one 3 months, and two others small fines. In addition five men were given 6 months for their part in the Trafalgar Square disturbances of 1 November.[42] The police had also drawn up charges of conspiracy against three men who were accused of trying to convey to Hyde Park a van loaded with sticks with nails driven through them. The police obviously hoped for a conviction on these men, but were disappointed. The solicitors reported that the men appeared 'before a bench not very happily consisting of Mr Perkins, the chairman, and two other justices with, we believe, strong labour tendencies'. Only one of the men was convicted, but on a lesser charge of vagrancy, for which he received two months' hard labour. The solicitors commented that 'it is at least a very good thing to have obtained a conviction of this man, Quinn, as he is undoubtedly a very hot-headed agitator'.[43]

Growing apprehension among official labour circles that the

N.U.W.M. was dominating the fight against unemployment led the T.U.C. to organise a demonstration in London in February 1933. It was the only large demonstration sanctioned by the official labour movement on the issue of unemployment in the thirties. In contrast to the alarm and fear of disturbances surrounding the N.U.W.M.'s march of the previous autumn, the T.U.C. seemed almost timid in its preparations. In December 1932 the Commissioner for the Metropolitan Police received information that the T.U.C. was planning 'a large, but presumably peaceful demonstration'. In January, the Chief Constable informed the Commissioner that so far the organisers had been very 'tame' and 'anxious to consult the Commissioner as to his wishes re their demonstration'.[44] The T.U.C. were anxious to show that their demonstration would be peaceful; they asked the police whether the women's section of the demonstration would be allowed to carry flags and banners. Permission was granted, and the police also gave permission for news cameras to position themselves in Hyde Park to film the meeting.[45] The chief concern of the police was that the N.U.W.M. might attempt to take part in the demonstration. The Scotland Yard file on the demonstration contained transcripts of interviews between the senior Scotland Yard officials and the official marshals appointed by the National Joint Council, at which the latter confirmed that the N.U.W.M. would not be allowed to take part.[46]

The Special Branch, however, reported to Scotland Yard that the N.U.W.M. were endeavouring to take part and 'turn it into a militant demonstration against the wishes of the T.U.C.' Details were given of how the N.U.W.M. hoped to carry four rostrums to the park – the T.U.C. having refused Hannington permission to speak from one of the official ones – and how various sections of communist movements in London, including the Seamen's Minority Movement and members of the Busmen's Rank and File Movement were to fall in with the main body of the march. It was reported that:

> Wal Hannington has been instructed by the Communist Party to endeavour to get on one of the T.U.C. platforms and speak therefrom. He does not appreciate his selection for this task as, having just come out of prison, he considers that someone else should, to use his own words, 'take a chance of being pinched'. However, as he is 'under a cloud', he is expected to make the attempt. A bodyguard of ten men, under the control

1 General Election poster, 1931

2 Sir Oswald Mosley
inspects Blackshirts, 1936

3 Ramsay MacDonald and the
Cabinet of the National Government, 1931

4   Monseigneur Restaurant, 1931

5   Police break up N.U.W.M. demonstration, 1931

6   The new department stores:
Marks & Spencer, Brixton, 1931

7   The new cinemas: interior of the
New Victoria, London, 1930

8   House to let: suburbia, 1933

9   Ascot fashions, 1935

10   Looking for work

11   Class differences, 1936

12   Setting out on
the Jarrow march, 1936

13   Jarrow marchers arrive in London, 1936

14   Keep fit craze, Hyde Park, May 1935

15   Holidays for the masses in the new prosperity, Brighton, 1937

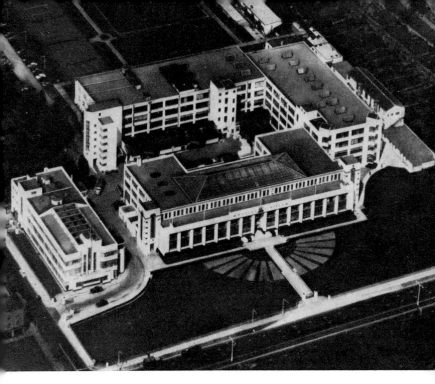

16   New Hoover factory, 1937

17   Traffic jam in Oxford Street, May 1937

18   The Prince of Wales during a visit to the Rhondda Valley, 1932

19   Unemployed: January 1939

of Henry Van Loo, of 30 Church Row, Limehouse East, has been selected to look after Hannington.[47]

The N.U.W.M., however, made it known that they had no intention of disrupting the meeting. Nevertheless, the police had 1,600 men in readiness for any incidents that might occur. In the event, the meeting passed off peacefully. A crowd of 20,000 or more turned up to support the demonstration. Although the N.U.W.M. did manage to set up a platform and pass a series of resolutions against the means test and the economy measures, there were no serious incidents. On 6 February, Walter Citrine thanked the Metropolitan Police for their efforts and help in making the demonstration a success.[48]

The peaceful outcome of this demonstration against unemployment by the T.U.C. was followed by preparations on the part of the N.U.W.M. for another hunger march to London, scheduled to arrive in London on 28 February, 1934. Once again the attitude of the government was that the N.U.W.M. was mounting a march in order to create disturbances. As in 1932, the Ministry of Health and the Home Office worked hand in hand to enforce 'casual' regulations upon the contingents of marchers. The Ministry of Health circulated the General Inspectors of the areas through which the marchers had to pass, referring them to the instructions issued in 1932.[49]

The marchers had various experiences on the route to London. In some places the police seemed determined to enforce the Home Secretary's instructions. At Birmingham the Scottish contingent narrowly avoided confrontation with the police, who entered the workhouse where the marchers were sleeping.[50] The South Wales contingent was led by, among others, Claude Stamfield, an N.U.W.M. organiser, member of the South Wales Miners' Federation Unemployed section, and the I.L.P. He recorded that the marchers were under strict rules to avoid scrounging and drunkenness. He noted down a series of impressions: the reception at Bath, where the official Labour Party ignored them, but where the marchers were fed and looked after by the local rank and file members; the disorganisation at Reading where there was no reception committee and the marchers slept on straw in a cattle market that had been used earlier in the day; the reception at Slough where thousands of Welsh 'immigrants' lined the streets; Windsor, where the castle servants threw money to the marchers; and Eton College where the marchers sang 'The Red Flag' as they passed.[51] Significantly, the marchers were counselled to be disciplined on their entry into the capital. As the eighteen

N

contingents approached London, the Home Secretary warned the House of Commons about the possibility of 'grave disorder and public disturbance which would require Parliament to deal with such demonstrations'. The Attorney-General spoke of the danger of bloodshed arising from the march and the need for the government to take steps to prevent it.[52] The government put in hand extensive preparations and there were even rumours that the police were going to try to stop the marchers reaching London. It was as a result of these threats that the National Council for Civil Liberties was formed, with the support of several prominent Labour Party members, including Clem Attlee and Edith Summerskill. On this occasion the marchers were received in Bermondsey Town Hall by a United Front Congress, which drew support from a wide spectrum of political opinion. Harry McShane and Lewis Jones, the leaders of the Scottish and Welsh contingents respectively, addressed an all-party meeting of 100 M.P.s in the House of Commons. A request was made for a deputation to meet the government, but this was refused, in spite of protests within the House of Commons by a number of left-wing M.P.s. Attlee and the Liberal Leader, Sir Herbert Samuel, spoke in favour of the marchers' deputations being received by the Cabinet. MacDonald protested, asking, 'Has anybody who cares to walk to London the constitutional right to demand to see me, to take up my time, whether I like it or not?' The refusal of the government to receive a deputation of the marchers led to a mass lobby of the House of Commons, to which the police had to be called to evict the marchers from the premises. Eventually after a mass rally in Trafalgar Square the marchers left London by train for their home districts.[53]

Thus after an inauspicious start in which the government had seemed determined to harass and frustrate the march, the N.U.W.M. had achieved considerable success. The aid and support of I.L.P. and Labour Party officials had helped immeasurably to give the marchers respectability and to prevent the government from acting as toughly as it had in 1932. The National Council for Civil Liberties served notice that there were limits to which the government could go in dealing with what it regarded as potentially subversive movements.[54] The N.U.W.M. benefited, too, from playing the public relations game according to the rules. The mass lobby of parliament provided the only violent scenes on the march. The N.U.W.M. spent the rest of their time attempting to persuade M.P.s that their case was a reasonable one and that they had a right to be received either by the Prime Minister or at the Bar of the House of Commons. In contrast to the 1932 march, when they had paid scant attention to building bridges with M.P.s favourable to their cause and positively rejected attempts at mediation on the part of left-wing M.P.s, the N.U.W.M. in 1934 was actively pursuing a united front policy and sought the aid of non-communist groups. The Welsh contingent of marchers, for example, had the support of almost all Labour M.P.s from South Wales and a large number of local union branches and trades councils.[55]

The latter months of 1934 and the first weeks of 1935 were dominated by a vehement agitation against the government's proposals to reorganise the administration of unemployment relief. Up to 1934 this was dispensed via local Poor Law Authorities and Labour Exchanges. The aim of the new regulations was to centralise unemployment relief upon the Unemployment Assistance Board. In itself, this proposal created little stir, for it was widely expected that the levels of unemployment relief would at least be maintained. The second part of the Act, which set relief scales, was scheduled to come into operation on 7 January, 1935. Some disquiet about the new scales began to be shown in the autumn of 1934, when there were widespread demonstrations in Scotland and South Wales. These were led by the N.U.W.M. which attempted, unsuccessfully, to obtain the support of the T.U.C. General Council for the agitation. The announcement of the new relief scales in December, however, transformed the situation, for instead of raising or at least maintaining existing levels of unemployment benefit, many of the unemployed found themselves worse off.[56] When parliament reassembled at the end of January, many M.P.s from the depressed areas were visibly shaken by the degree of animosity which the new scheme had provoked. The government was faced with an unprecedented uproar from M.P.s of all parties. Michael Foot has described it as 'the biggest explosion of popular anger in the whole inter-war period, second only to the General Strike itself'.[57] *The Times* spoke of the 'spirit of 1926' being abroad again.

There were widespread marches and demonstrations in the depressed areas, led, in this instance, by local trade union and Labour Party representatives, often with the support of local religious and professional bodies. On a national level, the T.U.C. acted with caution, fearful lest it become involved in left-wing agitation. Local trades councils were warned not to co-operate with the N.U.W.M. at any stage. The protest movement began to snowball, however, as the genuine outrage at the new proposals swept through the depressed areas in the most impressive display of popular protest to occur in the thirties. On 3 February, the *Manchester Guardian* estimated that in South Wales alone, there were 300,000 people on the street to protest against the new measures.[58] Strikes broke out in the South Wales coalfield and there were disturbances at Merthyr, Abertillery, Nantyglo and Blaina. Other large-scale demonstrations took place in Scotland and Yorkshire.[59] On 5 February, the Minister of Labour, Oliver Stanley, was forced to capitulate and issue a standstill order, which meant that no benefits were to be reduced and any previous reductions refunded.[60] On the following day, the authorities had a sample of what might have occurred had the standstill not been introduced, when a large demonstration in Sheffield led to disturbances in the city centre. There were several casualties and extensive damage. It resulted in the City Council's securing permission from the Ministry of Labour to implement immediate repayment of reductions in unemployment benefit, even before the standstill Act received royal assent on 15 February. A fully revised code of regulations was introduced in July 1936 and was greeted with general approbation.[61] Though the N.U.W.M. had played an active part in the demonstrations against the new regulations, the campaign's effectiveness derived primarily from the broad basis of the opposition to the government. It was essentially a respectable opposition which drew upon the middle ground in the country and parliament. Because moderate opinion was mobilised and violence kept to a minimum, the agitation proved effective.

For the great majority of people the words 'hunger march' and Jarrow are virtually synonymous. The Jarrow march of 1936 remains the most emotive symbol of the thirties, the epitome of the plight of the depressed areas. In many ways this is rather curious. The Jarrow march, or Jarrow 'Crusade' as it became known, was one of the smallest hunger marches to make its way to the capital during the thirties from the depressed areas. The march was organised by the newly elected M.P. for Jarrow, Ellen Wilkinson, and the Mayor and council, in order to draw attention to the dreadful situation in the town since the closure of its largest employer, Palmer's shipyard. Eighty per cent of the workforce was unemployed and had no prospects of improvement without outside help, while the government refused to relocate industry or help the town in any way. Wal Hannington records that he was approached by Ellen Wilkinson for advice about organising a march to petition parliament to reopen the shipyard. According to Hannington, he gave advice on organisation, but also suggested that the Jarrow marchers should join up with the north-east contingent of a march the N.U.W.M. was planning. This was planned to arrive in London at approximately the same time as the Jarrow marchers proposed. Hannington was later informed that the Jarrow march would pursue an independent policy, partly because of the local Labour Party's antagonism towards any involvement in the N.U.W.M., and also because they feared the dilution of their petition in the general aims of the N.U.W.M.'s march.[62]

From early October 1936 Ellen Wilkinson and the march organisers were in contact with the Metropolitan Police, making arrangements for the marchers to present their petition to parliament. The march organisers accepted the stringent conditions laid down by the police for their attendance at the House of Commons to present their petition, namely that they should attend in small groups upon M.P.s who had been named in advance. The march was declared by the organisers to be of a 'non-political' nature, and to show this, two agents, one Labour and one Conservative, were to be employed in advance of the march to make sleeping and feeding arrangements. The Special Branch reported that one known communist was expelled from the march, because of the organisers' insistence that it remain non-political. Because of these favourable reports the Home Office ruled that the marchers would be allowed to have tea in the House of Commons, since 'the marchers show every sign of being orderly, it would be a good way of encouraging and placating them.'[63] The march was not entirely without opposition; the Labour Party Conference at Edinburgh rebuked Ellen Wilkinson for organising the march, on the grounds that hunger marches were associated with communist organisations, such as the N.U.W.M., and their use might lead to disorder and disrepute.[64] On 15 October *The Times* published a statement from the Prime Minister, Stanley Baldwin:

Ministers have had under consideration the fact that a number of marches on London are in progress or in contemplation. In the opinion of His Majesty's Government such marches can do no good to the causes for which they are represented to be undertaken, are liable to cause unnecessary hardship to those taking part in them, and are altogether undesirable in this country, governed by a Parliamentary system, where every adult has a vote and every area has its representative in the House of

Commons to put forward grievances and suggest remedies, processions to London cannot claim to have any constitutional influence on policy. Ministers have, therefore, decided that encouragement cannot be given to such marches whatever their particular purpose, and Ministers cannot consent to receive any deputation of Marchers, although of course, they are always prepared to meet any members of Parliament.[65]

In spite of these discouragements, the preparations for the march went ahead. Funds were raised throughout Tyneside and the march attracted a wide range of support from trade unionists, politicians of all parties, and various churches and voluntary groups. A Crusade Committee bought leather and nails so that the men could repair their own boots. Field kitchens lent by the Boy Scouts were to provide food and the equipment was carried in a second-hand bus. Two hundred men were chosen for their fitness out of a much larger number of volunteers. To a very real extent, the marchers carried the hopes of a whole community with them and their send-off on the 300-mile march was both impressive and moving. On 4 October prayers were said in every church and chapel in Jarrow for the success of the march and a brass band played the marchers to the borough boundary after an inter-denominational service and a blessing by the Suffragan Bishop of Jarrow. The march was to take over a month, but the marchers were generally well received on the route to London. The Special Branch, who kept the march under observation, remarked that 'the demonstrators were warmly welcomed by the inhabitants of the places through which they passed, and no untoward incident calling for police action occurred ... ' In one or two places the marchers met with suspicion, as at York, where they were not allowed into the city and guarded by police when they spent the night. Most striking, however, was the support and help which the marchers received on the route from complete strangers to them and their town. Few, indeed, could remain untouched by the sight of drawn, poorly-fed men, many of whom had not worked for years, marching in disciplined ranks and putting on a show of good spirits however tired and hungry they might feel. Their dignity gave the lie to the more unsympathetic attitudes which often still prevailed about the unemployed.[66]

When the marchers reached London, they turned down the offer of a share in a communist rally in Hyde Park. Instead, they held their own meeting which passed off without incident. It was reported to the police that 'When H.M. the King [Edward VIII] passed through The Mall on the 3rd inst., the Jarrow contingent was placed at a vantage point opposite the Duke of York's steps, and showed their enthusiasm by cheering lustily.'[67] The Jarrow marchers attended the House of Commons, were entertained to tea by sympathetic M.P.s, and taken on a sight-seeing trip down the river. In the words of the Special Branch: 'It was whilst the men were thus engaged that the Jarrow Petition was presented to the House of Commons by Miss Ellen Wilkinson M.P. ... '[68] The petition was presented with these words:

> I beg to ask leave to present to this Honourable House the Petition of the people of Jarrow praying for assistance in the resuscitation of its industry. During the last fifteen years Jarrow has passed through a period of industrial depression without parallel in the town's history. Its shipyard is closed. Its steel-works have been denied the right to reopen. Where formerly 8,000 people, many of them skilled workers, were employed, only 100 men are now employed on a temporary scheme. The town cannot be left derelict, and therefore your petitioners humbly pray that His Majesty's Government and this honourable House, should realise the urgent need that work should be provided for the town without further delay.[69]

Understandably the marchers were disheartened at missing what they had anticipated as the crowning ceremony of the march. Councillor Riley, who had heard the replies of the Prime Minister and Walter Runciman, was reported to have said, 'It means that you have drawn a blank, but they are not going to do this with Jarrow. It does not matter what the consequences are, we are determined. We are not going to suffer this kind of thing'. There was a suggestion of a sit-in strike in the House of Commons until they were given another hearing, but the marchers were 'prevailed upon not to create a scene, and eventually returned to their billets'. On the following day the marchers took a train back to Jarrow. The police report concluded:

> The march throughout the Metropolitan Police District was well organised, and the men well disciplined. The general public were sympathetic and generous, and the demonstration was kept free from political propaganda. During the marchers' stay in London their conduct was exemplary and no incident occurred necessitating police action.[70]

The Jarrow Crusade achieved few tangible results. The government did nothing to revive industry in the town and the marchers even had their unemployment pay stopped while they were on the march because they were deemed to be unavailable for work. They did, however, achieve an immense publicity success. The march, followed by Ellen Wilkinson's book *The Town that was Murdered*, ensured that the memory of the plight of Jarrow would survive long after other, larger hunger marches had been forgotten. In part, the marchers were aided by the leadership of Ellen Wilkinson with her great flair for publicity. The truly desperate situation of the town also attracted genuine sympathy. But the Jarrow marchers also became a folk legend because they obeyed the rules; they conducted their march in co-operation with the authorities and did not seek to challenge them. Above all, they disclaimed any political intentions and clearly rejected communist involvement.

In contrast to the famous Jarrow Crusade, the N.U.W.M.'s march of October to November 1936 received much less publicity and far less sympathy. As in the past, the N.U.W.M. was treated with great suspicion. The authorities were in receipt of detailed information about the movement's plans to mount another march. The Metropolitan Police opened a file on it in July 1936 and was kept informed by the Special Branch throughout September about plans for the march, which was to consist of about 1,400 men and women organised in ten contingents. The authorities learned that it had been decided to petition all labour, trade union, and co-operative societies for help, 'to hide as far as possible in the initial stages the extremist policy of the original organising bodies'. Details were given of the composition of the London reception committee. This included a number of left-wing Labour M.P.s acting in defiance of the official party line on participating in N.U.W.M. demonstrations, including Ellen Wilkinson, Nye Bevan, G.R. Strauss, J. Jagger and Edith Summerskill. It was also reported that the London Labour Party, the London Trades Council, and the London Co-operative party had given official support to the march 'for fear of seeming to leave the unemployed neglected'.[71] Full reports were also given of meetings between the London Reception Committee and the N.U.W.M. organisers.

The contingents from the depressed areas made their way to London without incident. The South Wales contingent under the leadership of Lewis Jones had the official support of the South Wales Miners' Federation for the first time. The spirit with which the march was conducted, at least by this contingent, is recorded in the notes of one of the participants, Eddie Jones, who described the scene as the marchers marched from Newport to Severn Tunnel:

> Merthyr leads and leads well. Monmouth follows. Rests are taken every hour and we partake of a hot meal and cocoa and ham sandwiches and barley water on the route. We have seven stops and cover 20 miles with colours flying very high. The streets are thronged with people awaiting us and a very fine reception committee completes a good day.[72]

Arriving in London, the marchers were received in Hyde Park by a large demonstration, claimed by some papers to be as large as a quarter of a million people. The police estimated that about 12,000 attended.[73] It was an impressive gathering, at which the N.U.W.M. attracted far more support from the Labour Party than ever before. Clem Attlee spoke and shared the platform with Wal Hannington. Nye Bevan claimed that:

> The Hunger Marchers have achieved one thing. They have for the first time in the history of the national Labour Movement achieved a united platform. Communists, I.L.P.-ers, Socialists, members of the Labour Party and Co-operators for the first time have joined hands together, and we are not going to unclasp them. This demonstration proves to the country that Labour needs a united leadership.[74]

But the Special Branch told another story: they reported that Hannington's name was left off the list of speakers chosen by the London Labour Party, because of the refusal of some Labour leaders to speak on the same platform. This was eventually overcome by Hannington's acting as the marchers' spokesman. It was reported that:

> Speeches were moderate in tone and the Communist speakers avoided provocation or extremist remarks. Nevertheless, there was a 'left' undercurrent amongst the audience, who took every opportunity of showing their resentment of the refusal of the Labour Party to accept the repeated demands of the Communist Party of Great Britain for affiliation. Whenever a speaker asked a question such as 'How can we best fight the Means Test', there was an answering shout of 'By a United Front'.[75]

Otherwise the demonstration passed off without incident. It was the last big N.U.W.M. demonstration in London in the thirties, out-doing the 1932 hunger march in terms of the broad basis of support achieved. Yet other than in the *Daily Herald* and the *Daily Worker*, the demonstration achieved far less publicity than the Jarrow march.[76]

Demonstrations by the unemployed tailed off after 1936, though there was a brief revival during the N.U.W.M.'s Winter Relief campaign of 1938–9. But in spite of this chronicle of marches and other demonstrations, the most remarkable feature was the relatively limited character of the protests about mass unemployment. Extra-parliamentary agitation was largely confined to the marches and demonstrations organised by the N.U.W.M. The T.U.C. rally in London in February 1933 and the Jarrow Crusade of 1936 were the only two major examples of protest organised by non-communist bodies. At the local level, some of the demonstrations against the U.A.B. regulations in 1934–5 also involved trade union and Labour Party members. The N.U.W.M.'s demonstrations failed to mobilise more than a small fraction of the total number of unemployed. The hunger marches of 1932, 1934 and 1936 each involved only 1,000–2,000 participants. Although quite large rallies were mounted in London on several occasions, the numbers in-volved fell far short of those claimed by the organisers. The largest meetings on the unemployment issue were those mounted at the conclusion of the N.U.W.M.'s national hunger march in 1932 when 25,000–30,000 people attended rallies at Hyde Park and Trafalgar Square. The peak attendance at any later demonstration was the 12,000 who assembled in London in November 1936 to meet the last of the N.U.W.M.'s national hunger marches. In fact, the great majority of demonstrations against unemployment were smallish affairs and mass rallies were more the exception than the rule.

Moreover, the total amount of disorder which arose out of un-employment was small compared to the expectations of many contemporary observers. If the most militant phase of agitation is examined, between 1929 and 1933, the total number of disturbances totalled about fifty, most of them small-scale affairs of a few scuffles and minor injuries. The most serious disturbances in terms of casualties were the riots in Belfast in October 1932, when two people were killed. On the mainland of Britain there were no fatal casualties arising directly out of demonstrations by the unemployed. During the most serious disturbances in London in October and November 1932, at the conclusion of the N.U.W.M.'s national hunger march of that year, there were only a handful of serious injuries and a number of minor ones. The total cost of the damage was estimated by the police at just over £200, mainly consisting of broken windows, one of which alone had cost £120. This was scarcely violence on a revolutionary scale.[77] Disturbances at Birkenhead in 1932 and in South Wales during 1935 yielded a similar pattern of minor injuries and small-scale damage.

Just as the great majority of demonstrations and protests by the unemployed were organised by the N.U.W.M., so such violence as occurred was largely associated with their marches and demonstrations. On occasions the police were at least partly to blame, reacting over-vigorously or unwisely when dealing with demonstrations, but generally speaking disturbances arose when N.U.W.M. marches or meetings challenged the restrictions placed by the authorities upon routes of march or access to particular buildings or places. Only on a few occasions did the issue of unemployment give rise to larger-scale protests in which there was something approaching popular participation.

The disturbances in Belfast, for example, were the most serious in the British Isles to arise out of unemployment. It is, however, impossible to separate them from the context of violence intrinsic to Northern Irish politics. Belfast had been the scene of sectarian disturbances in 1857, 1864, 1872, 1886, 1893, 1912 and 1920–2. Although the demonstrations by the unemployed displayed little sectarian feeling, once fighting broke out with the police they drew upon a tradition of violent antagonism to authority and perhaps a greater readiness to join in disturbances. Rioting in 1932 moved quickly from the city centre to the working-class areas. The riots then developed a momentum of their own which had little to do with the original grievances of the unemployed. They became anti-police riots, with looting in some of the poorer districts. In turn, the authorities were accustomed to taking a firmer line with disturbances than the police on the mainland of Britain. Not only were batons wielded freely, but the police were also armed and resort to firearms was in itself likely to make any unrest in Northern Ireland more serious than elsewhere. In addition, the paramilitary 'B' Specials were called in and the regular army mobilised with its armoured cars and machine-guns. Only three years after the riots in 1932, renewed sectarian disturbances led to at least 11 deaths and almost 500 people injured in the city.[78]

There were also elements in the situation on Merseyside, and in Birkenhead in particular, which made popular violence on the issue of unemployment rather more likely than in some other communities, including many which suffered from a higher rate of unemployment. A late-Victorian and Edwardian boom town, it grew rapidly from a population of a few hundred in 1851 to 130,000 in 1931. In the late 1920s the *Social Survey of Merseyside* commented that: 'Except for the shopping area and a few older residential districts most of the town proper is made up of dreary streets of seemingly endless working class houses. Variety is afforded by some patches, especially near the docks of really bad slums.' Its rapid growth, large population of immigrant Irish, and restricted range of port and shipbuilding industries had given it a fairly troubled history. The town was no stranger to violence, with both sectarian and labour disturbances before the First World War. In 1916, its police force had to be purged to frustrate the growth of police unionism. Throughout the twenties there were regular sectarian clashes. Two months before the disturbances among the unemployed there were fist-fights between Catholics and Protestants when the latter returned from an Orange outing to Chester.[79]

There is also evidence that Birkenhead was more seriously affected by unemployment than some other communities which had higher percentages out of work. Unemployment in fact never went much beyond a third of the workforce, but the downturn had been especially severe in 1931–2 in the shipbuilding and related industries. The tenor of local politics became highly charged in the spring and summer of 1932 and the Mayor had on more than one occasion to suspend council meetings because of the uproar. Crucially, the town had lost its Labour majority in the local elections of 1931 and the new Conservative council put in hand a number of petty economy measures which raised the temperature of local politics. Unlike many depressed areas, where the Labour Party remained in control of local politics, in Birkenhead a newly elected Conservative majority had to enforce economy measures against the bitter opposition of the ousted Labour group. The local press reflected the passions which were aroused. Under a headline of 'Long Live the Means Test', the *Birkenhead News* claimed that it was a measure 'welcomed by every fair-minded citizen'.[80] Thus N.U.W.M. agitation occurred in a difficult situation where political passions were already running high and where local Labour councillors and trade union officials had already brought people out on to the streets to demonstrate against the Conservative council. This was an unusual turn of events which can only be explained by the nature of local politics. Once it occurred, however, it provided the raw material for the N.U.W.M. to work on. After fighting broke out with the police, a rather similar pattern of events to that in Belfast occurred; there was looting in the poorer districts and the mobs then retreated to the dockside slums. When the police attempted to follow, there was a virtually spontaneous attempt to resist them which owed little to the agitation of the N.U.W.M. and far more to customary antagonism towards the police.

South Wales was an area of persistent disturbances on the unemployment issues and played the most prominent part of all regions in the agitation against the U.A.B. regulations of 1934–5. Such militancy was not surprising given the history of the South Wales coalfield and the relatively high proportion of Communist Party members which it had even before the 1930s. The most militant phase of agitation by the unemployed in South Wales coincided with a general revival of political and industrial activity. Demonstrations against the means test and the U.A.B. regulations occurred against a background of sit-in strikes, picketing, and the fight against company unionism. Unlike the rest of the country, they had the backing of a broad coalition of trade unionists and political activists organised in the South Wales Council of Action. This included trade unionists of all shades of political opinion and created a more widely based militancy than elsewhere. Support for protests by unemployed workers was more whole-hearted in South Wales as a result, and of all the depressed areas it showed the most sustained level of activity. But South Wales was an exceptional case; it had always been a very militant area with a higher degree of political involvement even than other coalfields.[81]

Thus the areas which did show evidence of popular support for demonstrations by the unemployed were affected by rather exceptional factors. Traditions of militancy and violence combined with local circumstances to make some areas more susceptible to disturbances than others. Violence, however, like political extremism was a minority response in the thirties to the impact of mass unemployment. Similarly, marches and demonstrations occupied only a very small proportion of the total number of unemployed. In spite of the publicity given to an event such as the Jarrow march, the general run of unemployed demonstrations were relatively obscure events, involving a restricted group of political activists. The view that hunger marches were a typical response to unemployment was very far from the truth.

What did the hunger marches achieve? Activists such as Wal Hannington believed that they had managed to wring concessions from the government which would not otherwise have been made. There is, however, little evidence that this was the case for, as we have seen earlier, the major initiative in modifying the means test and halting the U.A.B. legislation of 1934–5 came from within the circles of conventional politics. The N.U.W.M. hunger marches might run parallel to agitations by M.P.s and organised labour, but they were certainly not the most effective part of them. The government in 1934–5 was swayed by the protests of M.P.s from the depressed areas, many of them within its own ranks. The threat of renewed disorders in the depressed areas also played a part, but the N.U.W.M.'s experience was that the actual outbreak of disorder was often counter-productive. It tended to alienate moderate opinion, including many of the unemployed themselves. The N.U.W.M. was too closely associated with the Communist Party for the government to take its demonstrations as a genuine expression of protest by the rank and file unemployed. Instead the government sought to prevent any threat to public order and to restrict the impact of unemployed demonstrations. Compared with the success of the broad-based agitation against the U.A.B. legislation and the publicity triumph of the Jarrow marchers, the great majority of demonstrations and hunger marches – those organised by the N.U.W.M. – achieved very little and soon faded into obscurity. Violence was no substitute for influence in the context of British politics in the thirties.

XI

The Fascist Challenge

The history of the fascist movement in Britain has had many interpretations. Some have seen its rise as one of the major threats to the stability of British politics in the 1930s. Thus two recent historians of the decade have written:

> When Sir Oswald Mosley formed his British Union of Fascists in the autumn of 1932 it seemed that many of the ingredients which were shortly to bring Hitler to power existed also in Britain. Here also there was mass unemployment and a paralysing economic depression; here also the middle class was insecure and could be presumed to be searching for a 'saviour' ... [1]

Others have seen the importance of the B.U.F. less in terms of its strength and appeal than in terms of its failure, that 'its presence was marginal to the mainstream of British politics'.[2] More recently Robert Skidelsky has argued in his biography of Mosley that fascism retained a significant following right up to the outbreak of the Second World War, surviving the impact of the Public Order Act of 1936 and the loss of many of its wealthy and influential backers in the mid-1930s. The B.U.F., it has been argued, was reviving in the years before the war and it was only the outbreak of war which prevented it from making further gains.[3]

The British Union of Fascists was formed by Sir Oswald Mosley in October 1932. It was not the first group to adopt the 'fascist' title and the paramilitary character later identified with the B.U.F. The British Fascisti had been founded in May 1923 by Miss R.L. Lintorn-Orman. Later changing their name to the British Fascists, they pursued a programme of patriotism and anti-communism. The organisation's aim was to defend the constitution against attacks from communists and to preserve a disciplined organisation in case of an emergency. In the late 1920s and early 1930s it adopted a more clearly defined programme, with emphasis upon a corporate state, large-scale reforms of the economic and financial structure, and the exclusion of Jews and aliens from public office, the electoral roll and other positions of influence. A considerable amount of attention was given to reforming the trade unions. Strikes were to be declared illegal and compulsory arbitration introduced. Secret ballot was to be introduced instead of card votes, and alliances between trade unions were to be outlawed. In external affairs, Britain was to repudiate treaties which bound her to armed intervention, but use the expanded armed forces to preserve the Empire. It was largely a middle-class movement, deriving its basic appeal from its militant patriotic stance, but with an increasingly fascist emphasis after 1927, when dark uniforms were adopted. By the early 1930s, however, its membership was tiny, probably no more than a few hundred, and was often beset by internal rifts and disagreements about policy.[4] Another right-wing group was the National Fascisti, who seceded from the British Fascists during the 1920s. It had a small membership, mainly concentrated in the London area, and was more self-consciously modelled on Italian lines. In addition, there was the Imperial Fascist League, dominated by Arnold Leese, a veterinary surgeon and ex-member of the British Fascists. The I.F.L. was largely financed by Leese and published a newspaper, *The Fascist*, from 1929. Its membership never reached more than a thousand, but it brought a more strident anti-semitic quality into right-wing politics than had been apparent earlier.[5]

None of these groups had a significant impact upon British politics. They were regarded as crankish movements who caused even the police little anxiety or concern. It was only with the foundation of the B.U.F. by Sir Oswald Mosley that fascism in Britain attained significance. Mosley was born in 1896, the son of wealthy parents and heir to a baronetcy. He was educated at Winchester and Sandhurst, where he showed more aptitude for sport than learning. At the outbreak of the First World War he joined a cavalry regiment, but later moved to the Royal Flying Corps in which he was wounded twice. He entered politics in 1918 as the Conservative member for Harrow, but soon found himself uncomfortable in the party's ranks. In the General Elections of 1922 and 1923, he stood successfully as an Independent Conservative candidate. His break with the Conservatives, however, was only made final when he joined the Labour Party in April 1924. At a by-election in 1926 he was elected Labour member for Smethwick.

Mosley took an early interest in financial and currency questions. He published a pamphlet, *Revolution by Reason*, which advocated nationalisation of the banks and the provision of consumer credits for the unemployed as a mechanism to increase demand and revive the economy. When the pamphlet was published in book form with John Strachey as co-author, he also advocated an economic council to plan and control the financial policy of the country.[6] By 1929 Mosley's attention was increasingly drawn to the problem of unemployment. He recommended the control of credit through the banking system, early pensions and a higher school-leaving age to reduce the labour market, and an emergency programme of public works. When the second Labour Government was formed in 1929, Mosley was appointed Chancellor of the Duchy of Lancaster with a brief to assist the Lord Privy Seal, J. H. Thomas, to develop schemes to reduce unemployment. Thomas, however, failed to pursue a very active policy in the face of the worsening unemployment situation and there were complaints from Mosley and others about his lack of dynamism. In January 1930, Mosley submitted his own set of proposals to the Prime Minister. He advocated an expanded public works programme, including a £100 million road-building scheme. Over £200 million in all was to be spent on various public works: early retirement was to be encouraged and the school-leaving age raised, import controls were to be introduced and a tariff policy pursued, and a central organisation was to aid the rationalisation of industry and provide research and advice. The scheme was given serious consideration, but the cost of the policy and its relative unorthodoxy damned it in the eyes of the Cabinet, especially the Chancellor, Snowden. As a result, it was rejected in May after an adverse report from a Cabinet sub-committee and Mosley resigned from the government.[7]

Mosley persisted with his proposals and took his programme before a meeting of the parliamentary Labour Party, but was defeated by 210 votes to 29. At the Annual Conference at Llandudno in October 1930, Mosley's memorandum was narrowly defeated. Mosley then turned to building up a small group of followers to influence the policy of the government; it included, among others, Nye Bevan, John Strachey and W. J. Brown. All were young, intelligent, and critical of the government's failure to act on the unemployment issue. Up to fifty M.P.s were involved with the Mosley group at one time or another, but few would pledge themselves to sign a public version of his Cabinet memorandum and only

O

seventeen did so when it was released in December. A second version
came out in January under the title *A National Policy*. The latter
document provided for the adaptation of the government to meet
the economic crisis. Prominence was given to an inner Cabinet of
five which was to carry out an emergency programme.[8]

It was widely recognised within political circles, and by Mosley
himself, that this was a programme for a new party as much as for
a pressure group. Although Mosley conceived of his group as a
'centre ginger group', it derived little doctrine from the Labour
Party and his views have been described as essentially a radical
programme, aimed at a reform of institutions rather than the ownership of property. Mosley was clearly in an uncomfortable position,
impatient, ambitious, yet no nearer obtaining his goals than he
had been before his proposals were rejected by the Cabinet. At
this critical point, the patronage of William Morris, later Lord
Nuffield, proved crucial. William Morris had praised Mosley's
December manifesto and in late January presented him with a cheque
for £50,000 in order to form a new party. On 20 February six members of the Mosley group, including Mosley and his wife, decided to
resign from the Labour Party. The New Party was announced on
1 March. Initially the venture generated considerable interest, but
although Mosley had some support from Tory and Liberal circles,
only four M.P.s, including his wife, followed him to form the New
Party. In turn, Mosley and his followers were expelled from the
Labour Party. During 1931 the New Party gradually developed into
a near-fascist party, its evolution largely dictated by Mosley, who
controlled the party and its funds. At the Ashton-under-Lyne by-
election, the New Party put up a candidate to dispute the Labour-
held seat. Mosley campaigned actively with his wife and John
Strachey in favour of their candidate, Allen Young. The Conservatives overturned the Labour majority to win by 1,415. Young made a
respectable showing with 4,472 votes. At the declaration of the
result, Mosley and the New Party members were jeered and booed.
The combination of hostility from Labour supporters and the disappointing result undoubtedly helped to turn Mosley towards a
fascist stance. Mosley took the decision to found a youth movement, which would also provide a corps of stewards to prevent
his meetings being broken up. This led to the resignations
of John Strachey, Allen Young and C. M. Joad, precipitated
by what they saw as the increasingly fascist tendencies of Mosley's
policies.[9]

In the General Election of 1931 the New Party contested only 24 seats, most of them Labour-held seats. It had had little time to build up a national organisation, but it had secured the backing of William Morris for a weekly newspaper, *Action*, the first edition of which was published on 8 October, three weeks before the General Election. In the interim, the political crisis of the Labour Government brought no clear advantage to the New Party. Attempts to negotiate a clear run for New Party candidates against Labour were unsuccessful. Much of the burden of the election campaign was borne by Mosley himself. Some of his meetings were greeted with enthusiasm, but others dissolved into disorder, with Mosley's stewards fighting it out with the opposition. The election results, as we have seen, were a disaster for the New Party. Its total vote was 36,777, less than the communists, and 22 of its candidates lost their deposits. Mosley himself polled 10,534 votes in his wife's former consituency of Stoke-on-Trent. In Ashton-under-Lyne where the New Party had captured over 4,000 votes earlier in the year, its poll dwindled to only 424 votes. Following these shattering blows, the New Party virtually ceased to exist. Its central office was closed down and regional organisation wound up. At the end of December, *Action* ceased to publish. Its circulation had fallen from a peak of 160,000 to 20,000 and it was losing £1,500 a month.[10]

Mosley made a visit to Italy in January 1932 to observe fascism at first hand. He had already shown a distinctive shift towards fascism in his ideas about the New Party's youth movement. He was also under strong pressure from Lord Rothermere to take up these ideas and was assured of the backing of the *Daily Mail* for the enterprise. Mosley was impressed with fascism in its Italian guise, especially by its 'modernity'. But it was not his experiences in Italy which alone converted him to fascism and created the B.U.F. out of the New Party. Skidelsky writes:

> At the core of his rational justification was the notion of the 'crisis'. The liberal economic system was doomed. The existing elites lacked the character and mentality to create a new system in time. Therefore the system would collapse into destitution and disorder. This would give communism its historic opportunity … Since the 'old gangs' could not avert the situation from which communism would benefit, the challenge to communism would have to come from a new movement with an alternative faith and an alternative system capable of winning mass support.

Such movements had already arisen on the Continent. It was necessary to organise a similar movement in England.[11]

But irrational forces moved Mosley at least as much, if not more. Ambition, adventurism, and disgust for the normal procedures of politics combined to lead him into a search for allies in the obscure world of the existing fascist organisations. By the autumn of 1932 he had decided to form a fascist party.

The membership of the existing fascist groups came over to him virtually to a man, although this meant little more than a few hundred members at most, with only a handful of activists. The policy of the B.U.F. was unashamedly modelled on the fascist movements in Italy and Germany. A uniform of a black shirt was to mark out his followers, promote discipline and generate a 'classless brotherhood'. Mosley's views on the role and nature of the new party were expressed in his *The Greater Britain*, published to launch the new movement. In it he wrote:

> Fascism is the greatest constructive and revolutionary creed in the world. It seeks to achieve its aim legally and constitutionally, by methods of law and order; but in objective it is revolutionary or it is nothing. It challenges the existing order and advances the constructive alternative of the Corporate State ... It combines the dynamic urge to change and progress, with the authority, the discipline and the order without which nothing great can be achieved.

He made it clear that the B.U.F. stood by, ready to prevent a communist takeover in the event of a descent into economic and political crisis:

> ... to drift much longer, to muddle through much further, is to run the risk of collapse. In such a situation, new ideas will not come peacefully; they will come violently, as they have come elsewhere. In the final economic crisis to which neglect may lead, argument, reason, persuasion vanish and organised force alone prevails. In such a situation, the eternal protagonists in the history of all modern crises must struggle for the mastery of the State. Either Fascism or Communism emerges victorious; if it be the latter, the story of Britain is told ... In the highly technical struggle for the modern State in crisis, only the technical organisations of Fascism and of Communism have ever prevailed or, in the nature of the case, can prevail. Governments and

Parties which have relied on the normal instruments of government ... have fallen easy and ignoble victims to the forces of
anarchy ... We shall prepare to meet the anarchy of Communism
with the organised force of Fascism ... [12]

Mosley went out of his way, however, to reject the claim that the
fascists would initiate violence. 'Only when we see the feeble sur-
render to menacing problems', he wrote, 'do we feel it necessary to
organise for such a contingency.' He specifically repudiated the
charge that the movement was organised to promote violence.
Rather, he argued, the Blackshirts were organised to defend their
meetings from organised disruption by 'Socialist and Communist
extremists'. He continued:

> When we are confronted by red terror, we are certainly organised
> to meet force by force, and will always do our utmost to smash it.
> We shall continue to exercise the right of free speech, and will
> do our utmost to defend it. Emphatically, this does not mean
> that we seek violence. On the contrary, we seek our aims by
> methods which are both legal and constitutional, and we appeal
> to our country by taking action in time to avert the possibility
> of violence.

The movement, he argued, aimed at 'national reconstruction'. This
would be attained through parliament, though parliamentary power
was not an end in itself. Initially, the movement was to concentrate
upon building up its strength and 'invading every phase of national
life and carrying everywhere the Corporate conception'. But whether
the fascists would come to power through the parliamentary system,
or in the aftermath of a crisis which had passed beyond parliamentary
control depended upon the speed with which the crisis developed and
how rapidly 'the British people accept the necessity for new forms
and for new organisations'. If the crisis were to come before this
awakening, however, 'other and sterner measures must be adopted
for the saving of a state in a situation approaching anarchy'.[13]

The B.U.F. was formally launched on 1 October, 1932. The first
rally was held in Trafalgar Square on the 15th and the movement
began to develop an organisation. A newspaper, the *Blackshirt*,
was started in February 1933 to act as the main propaganda vehicle
for the movement. A number of indoor meetings and parades were
held, some of which began to display the violence which was to be
regarded as an inseparable aspect of the British fascist movement.
There were small-scale disturbances at a fascist meeting in the Free

Trade Hall in Manchester in March, but the B.U.F. was able to escape principal blame as there was clearly a fairly well-organised opposition to the Blackshirts at the meeting. Mosley continued to be a respectable if somewhat ambiguous figure, invited to debates, called on for articles in the press, and receiving publicity through the gossip columns. But as the movement increased in strength, it was the violence to which its meetings gave rise which most frequently attracted publicity. This violence was at least as much the result of antifascist demonstrators interrupting meetings or attacking fascists, but there was also a degree of provocation and ruthlessness in the attitude of Mosley and his defence force. Thus the Home Secretary commented on events in Bristol when a march of fascists had been attacked: 'I think there is no doubt that this disorder was largely due to the adoption of semi-military evolutions by the Fascists, their marching in formation and their general behaviour, which was regarded by the crowd as provocation.'[14]

The number of meetings increased in the autumn and winter of 1933–4. There were disturbances following a rally at Belle Vue in October 1933 and at Oxford two weeks later. Further publicity came with B.U.F. participation in the 'tithe war' in Suffolk, for which nineteen Blackshirts were arrested and bound over. On 22 April Mosley addressed 10,000 people at the Albert Hall. He emphasised the need to come to power peacefully, but condemned the existing system which 'by its whole structure and methods, makes action impossible; more than that, it produces a type of man to whom action and decision are impossible, even if he had the power'. More ominously he argued in a debate with James Maxton that when there emerged 'the organised Communist, the man who knows what he wants; and if and when he ever comes out, we will be there in the streets, with Fascist machine-guns to meet them'.[15] Thus although there was evidence of bias in the allegations against Mosley from some of his opponents, there was also an element in him which relished the combative aspect of politics. Robert Skidelsky has written:

> Mosley was a fighter who attracted fighters to him: had he not been he would not have called himself a fascist. This does not mean that he went around looking for fights. It does mean that avoiding them was not his chief priority. This was reinforced by his contempt for the old gangs and their craven psychology. The fighter took over, the soldier came to the fore.[16]

Although the great majority of B.U.F. meetings were peaceful and well ordered, there was something about their style and *potential* for organised violence which caused serious disquiet among a broad section of opinion. The combined use of mass meetings, uniformed parades, and an impression of overwhelming force at the command of a charismatic leader had no antecedents in British politics. Individual components did, but Mosley's self-conscious adoption of the methodology of Continental fascism generated more suspicion than support. Many felt that the B.U.F. was attempting to bring about the violent crisis from which it hoped to emerge as the country's saviour. But early in 1934 the movement had acquired important support from Lord Rothermere, who swung the *Daily Mail,* the *Evening News,* the *Sunday Dispatch* and the *Sunday Pictorial* behind the fascists. An article, 'Hurrah for the Black-shirts', appeared in the *Daily Mail* on 15 January, 1934. But Rothermere was more of an anti-communist than a fascist. He saw Mosley's movement as providing the leadership which conservative forces required in the face of the Left. As a result he gave prominence to Mosley's views on the need for closer ties with the Empire and for greatly expanded air defences, but played down the 'fascist' label of the movement. None the less, whatever the differences in emphasis between Mosley and Rothermere, the press lord was an important supporter.[17]

It was the Olympia meeting in June 1934 which provided the turning point for the British fascist movement. Until 1934 it was tolerated and received a not unfavourable treatment in the press. There was disquiet expressed in some quarters, including the Home Secretary and the police, about the threat to public order, but the movement had so far appeared as much sinned against as sinning. Rothermere's support was cooling during the spring of 1934, as he became aware of the differences between himself and Mosley, but it was the events at Olympia which drove him and other potential supporters into opposition to the B.U.F. The violence which occurred at the meeting is discussed more fully in the following chapter, but its effects on the B.U.F. are what concern us here. There was considerable furore about the incidents and the fascists were largely blamed for them. Above all, the criticism came not just from the Left, but also from Conservative M.P.s who were horrified by what they had seen. Although there were rival claims, and it was clear that the anti-fascists had deliberately gone out of their way to stage a show of force inside the hall, the balance of evidence was against the B.U.F. The *Daily Telegraph* weighed in by denouncing private armies and organised violence. *The Times* attacked the tactics of the B.U.F. stewards and printed the letter from the three Conservative M.P.s present at the meeting which condemned the 'wholly unnecessary violence inflicted by uniformed Blackshirts on interrupters'. As a recent historian of the B.U.F. has made clear, the Olympia meeting focused attention upon the British fascist movement, brought the government to the brink of legislation, and frightened off more conservative support.[18]

The Olympia meeting left the B.U.F. in a kind of limbo. There was increasing distrust of it from some sections of the press, which the Roehm purge in Germany, three weeks after Olympia, did little to appease. In an open exchange of letters Rothermere disassociated himself from the B.U.F. He claimed that fascism could not hope to succeed in Britain and that he would have nothing to do with a movement which aimed at dictatorship and a corporate state. Lastly, he disagreed with the B.U.F.'s anti-semitism. It was only after the Olympia meeting that this last strand began to become prominent in the B.U.F. Mosley claimed that he was not anti-semitic. Jews were attacked for what they did rather than for being Jews. But such subtle distinctions were lost on many of his followers. Jews had played a prominent part in the anti-fascist demonstrations at Olympia and charges of Jew-baiting by Blackshirts were already beginning to worry the Metropolitan Police and the Home Secretary.[19] Although the B.U.F. failed to develop a racial theory of its own, the 'Jewish conspiracy' fitted well into the atmosphere of persecution and vilification with which fascists emerged from Olympia. Jews were clearly carrying on a policy of opposing Mosley: the behaviour of some of his followers and the similarity of his movement to the one which persecuted the Jews in Europe was too close for comfort. In turn, Mosley blamed Jewish financial pressures for preventing businessmen from showing support and claimed 'Little Jews' were disrupting his meetings. Jewish finance was blamed for the depression and unemployment problem. A programme of 'Britain First' would bar aliens from British jobs and those who proved unwelcome would be deported. At Leicester in April 1935 Mosley declared:

For the first time I openly and publicly challenge the Jewish interest in this country commanding commerce, commanding the press, commanding the cinema, dominating the City of London, killing industry with the sweatshops. These great interests are not intimidating, and will not intimidate, the Fascist movement of the modern age.[20]

But as well as developing a more openly anti-semitic campaign, the B.U.F. also attacked its organisational problems in 1935 with some vigour. All the evidence suggests that membership had slimmed down from a peak in 1934 and Mosley took the opportunity to reorganise the central and local organisation. Inspections of the local branches were carried out and some members dismissed. The military side of the movement was played down and the B.U.F. turned its attention towards becoming more like a political party, organised to take power by conventional means. The National Head-quarters staff was built up to 140 officials, but careful attention was also given to the development of ward and action groups. On the other hand Mosley attacked the social club atmosphere of the move-ment in many localities and developed a more austere approach.[21]

Uniforms and marches, however, continued to play an important part in the drive for members. By 1936, the B.U.F. was concentrating upon the East End of London where its anti-semitic programme was beginning to reap some dividends. The East End contained the largest concentration of Jews in London and they had formed a close-knit community. Competition for jobs and housing, as well as racial prejudice, played a part in providing the fascists with a fertile ground for recruitment. Trade depression in the early 1930s, com-bined with a new flood of Jewish immigrants from Europe, added new strains to the already difficult situation. Fascist branches were set up in Bow in 1934, in Bethnal Green and Shoreditch in 1935, and in Limehouse in 1936. From 1933 the police had been reporting small-scale incidents in the East End of London with fights between Jews and Blackshirts selling newspapers. Marches of small groups of fascists through the East End had already led the police to arrest and prosecute a number of Blackshirts before their main campaign in the East End was mounted in 1936.[22] Complaints about the fascists' behaviour increased during 1935 with stories of fascists terrorising Jews and attacking Jewish property. Complaints about insulting language being used towards Jews led the Home Secretary to issue a stern warning to the Metropolitan Police to act on any incidents which might occur. Few prosecutions resulted, however, as the law stipulated that insulting language could only be an offence if it could be proved that it was used with the intention of causing a breach of the peace.[23]

More serious was the threat of widespread public disorder following Mosley's declaration on 16 July of his intention to fight east
London seats in the L.C.C. elections in March 1937. It led him to
propose a series of marches through the East End of London to
drum up support. A rally in Victoria Park on 7 June was attended by
5,000 people, and nearly 600 police were on duty. The Under-
Secretary of State for Home Affairs claimed that the police attended
over 1,000 meetings in August and September and were having to
draft in large-scale reinforcements. The greatest danger from the
government's point of view was that the fascists would clash with
the anti-fascists. If the two groups met there would undoubtedly be a
riot. Many Fascist meetings and processions had passed off peacefully, including those in the East End, but by the autumn of 1936
it was clear that there was a rising tide of anti-fascist feeling. The
Communist Party was active in anti-fascist movements as a part of
its united front strategy. If they and the social democrats could not
agree about anything else, at least they had a common enemy. As
Robert Skidelsky has perceptively remarked, by the mid-1930s
the fascists and the communists needed each other, for their
mutual vilification gave them a significance which they otherwise
lacked.[24]

Thus when the now renamed British Union planned a march for
Sunday, 4 October, the stage was set for a serious clash. The communists and the I.L.P. were determined to prevent the march by
force, while the Labour Party, the T.U.C. and various Jewish organisations made strenuous efforts to get the march banned or
diverted. Contingents of Blackshirts planned to assemble in Royal
Mint Street near Tower Bridge and then march in four groups to
meetings in Shoreditch, Bow, Limehouse and Bethnal Green. Mosley was to speak at each of the meetings. In spite of appeals and
petitions, arrangements for the march were allowed to go ahead.
Although Labour leaders and newspapers urged anti-fascists to
stay away in case there was disorder, the communists, the N.U.W.M.
and some Jewish organisations decided to prevent the march by
force. Handbills, placards and loud-speaker vans were assembled,
while anti-fascist rallies were planned to take place in Cable Street
in the afternoon and at Shoreditch Town Hall in the evening. By
midday on the 4th, the streets of the East End were filled with
people and between 6,000 and 7,000 police were on duty in the area.
Even before the fascists set off on their march, there were baton-
charges by the police because anti-fascist groups were blocking

traffic and obstructing the police. At Cable Street, a lorry was dragged across the street and overturned. Police both on foot and mounted made repeated charges before they were able to clear the street. When Mosley arrived at Royal Mint Street, his party of 3,000 Blackshirts was faced by a crowd estimated by the police at 100,000 people, later described as the 'largest Anti-Fascist demonstration yet seen in London'. After some fighting between the two groups, the police decided it was time to act. Mosley was requested by Sir Philip Game to call off his march through the East End. He agreed, and led his men westwards along the Embankment where they dispersed without further disturbances.[25]

The 'Battle of Cable Street' and the other disturbances on 4 October led to 88 arrests and 70 people, including police, were treated for injuries received. Of those arrested, 83 were anti-fascists, only one of whom came from outside the London area. The disturbances led directly to the Public Order Act which received the royal assent in December. It gave the police the power to ban processions and prohibited the use of uniforms. It did not, however, stop the B.U.F. from gathering support and holding more rallies and parades in the capital. In the immediate aftermath of these disturbances, Mosley spoke to large and enthusiastic meetings in the East End. The Special Branch recorded that he addressed a meeting of 12,000 people at Victoria Park Square on 11 October, marching later at the head of a procession without serious disorder. The police reported that the Cable Street episode had only been obtained by 'the combined forces of the Communist Party of Great Britain, the Independent Labour Party, sections of Labour and Liberal opinion, as well as Jewish and Gentile religious bodies'.[26] They rejected the idea that the entire population of the East End had risen against Mosley and his followers. They alleged that the main activists in the anti-fascist demonstrations had been communists and one of the leaders in the Cable Street battle was described as 'one of the most violent communists in London'. The police argued that the events at Cable Street and elsewhere on 4 October threw 'out of perspective the events of the month as a whole'. They claimed that far from the anti-fascist forces increasing in strength, the fascists were 'steadily gaining ground' in Stepney, Shoreditch, Bethnal Green, Hackney and Bow.[27] The police believed that the Blackshirts had gained rather than lost since the banning of their march: 'Briefly, a definite pro-fascist feeling has manifested itself throughout the districts mentioned [since the events of 4 October], and the alleged Fascist defeat is in reality a Fascist advance. It is reliably reported that the London membership has increased by 2,000.'[28]

The police continued to monitor support for fascist meetings and demonstrations in London during the winter of 1936-7. It was reported that in November 1936 there were 131 fascist meetings in London with an average attendance of 240 people. Only seven of them led to disorder. By February 1937 there were even more meetings and the police recorded that attendances were up to 1,400. On the other hand the anti-fascist forces were also mobilising under the guidance of the Communist Party, as shown in Table 11.1.

TABLE 11.1   FASCIST AND ANTI-FASCIST MEETINGS IN LONDON:
DECEMBER 1936–FEBRUARY 1937[29]

	fascist	*anti-fascist*
December	61	70
January	103	141
February	222	184

The March 1937 elections for the L.C.C. provided the British Union with a test of its strength. Mosley revised his earlier decision not to contest local elections and devoted the resources of the movement to the campaign. In January it was announced that six candidates would contest three two-member divisions, at Bethnal Green North-East, Shoreditch, and Limehouse. All three were held by Labour. The main focus of the campaign was anti-semitism. Mosley claimed that the 'enemy' was to be attacked where his 'corrupt power' was strongest and Joyce's election address pledged him 'to fight to the end for the people's cause against the tyranny of Jewish power'. Over 150 meetings were called in the election campaign, 57 in Shoreditch alone. Fascist speakers were regularly imported into the area and Mosley spoke several times in each constituency.[30] The results announced on 6 March were a disappointment to the fascists, but did reveal some support in the area, especially in Bethnal Green where the British Union came second. The results are shown in Table 11.2.

The B.U.F. had taken almost a fifth of the vote, but they had also concentrated their resources into the area which was most favourable to them. Many of their younger supporters were doubtless ineligible to vote, but the failure to break the dominance of the Labour

TABLE 11.2   RESULTS IN 3 L.C.C. ELECTIONS: MARCH 1937[31]

Bethnal Green North-East

T. Dawson (Labour)	7,777
Mrs R. S. Keeling (Labour)	7,756
A. Raven Thomson (British Union)	3,028
E. G. Clarke (British Union)	3,022
A. J. Irvine (Liberal)	2,328
H. K. Sadler (Liberal)	2,298

(Labour 59·3 per cent, British Union 23·1 per cent, Liberal 17·6 per cent.)

Stepney (Limehouse)

R. Coppock (Labour)	8,272
Miss H. M. Whately (Labour)	8,042
V. G. Weeple (Municipal Reform)	2,542
G. E. Abrahams (Municipal Reform)	2,431
Mrs A. Brock Griggs (British Union)	2,086
C. Wegg-Prosser (British Union)	2,086

(Labour 64·1 per cent, Municipal Reform 19·5 per cent, British Union 16·4 per cent.)

Shoreditch

Mrs H. Girling (Labour)	11,098
S. W. Jeger (Labour)	11,069
S. L. Price (Municipal Progressive)	3,303
R. S. Falk (Municipal Progressive)	3,217
William Joyce (British Union)	2,564
J. A. Bailey (British Union)	2,492
C. E. Taylor (Independent Labour)	385

(Labour 65·0 per cent, Municipal Progressive 19·1 per cent, British Union 14·8 per cent, Independent Labour 1·1 per cent.)

Party in the East End was a telling blow to the fascists. While Mosley could argue that he had done better than Hitler at a comparable stage in his career, he ignored the argument that Hitler had achieved his result over Germany as a whole and not in his three most favourable constituencies. Significantly, after the L.C.C. elections the National Headquarters made B.U. candidates fight elections from their own expenses and using local personnel. The results, however, were equally disappointing. Sixty-six candidates contested the metropolitan boroughs and provincial towns in November 1937. In the East End the results were a repeat of six months earlier, but in the forty-eight seats contested in London as a whole the B.U. candidates averaged only 560 votes compared with 2,252 for the Labour people. In the provinces they achieved their highest vote in Castle ward in Bridgnorth, Salop, in a straight fight with the Conservatives. In eight provincial contests, the B.U.F. polled under 100 votes, coming bottom of the poll at Edinburgh, Leeds, Sheffield and Southampton. The B.U.F. kept up the electoral struggle in the municipal elections of November 1938, but there was again little comfort for them. Only twenty-three candidates were put forward. In four wards they received over 200 votes, but in ten less than 100. The highest vote was in the Collyhurst ward in Manchester. In all, however, only just over 2,000 people had voted for B.U.F. candidates.[32]

Not only in elections were the fascists finding it difficult to make much headway. The Metropolitan Police reported that the attempts by Sir Oswald Mosley to infuse life into the organisation in spring 1938 had failed to evoke a response outside Bethnal Green. In August the police again reported that the summer campaign waged by Mosley had met with a poor response. Mosley had spoken at 21 meetings in London during July, but apart from a few minor incidents there had been little evidence of either marked enthusiasm or hostility. The police explained the latter by the changed tactics of the Communist Party, which aimed less at open confrontation and instead organised rival meetings. By 1938 the number of anti-fascist meetings had become significantly greater than those of the fascists. The Special Branch reported attending 93 fascist meetings in November and December 1938, but 174 anti-fascist ones. The police also reported that by January 1939 the fascists were holding fewer meetings with smaller attendances, although there was the occasional larger gathering.[33]

The movement was in decline. A ban on processions in the East End, enforced by the Public Order Act in 1937, prevented the B.U.F. from exercising its talents for propaganda in its most favourable area. Instead marches were mounted in other parts of the capital. The ban on uniforms also reduced the appeal of the movement. In addition, the fascists found it difficult to hire halls for their meetings. These restrictions upon its processions and its rallies deprived it of its two principal means of recruitment. Mosley himself turned to a 'Stop the War' campaign in March 1938 but failed to achieve widespread support, although a large and successful rally was held at Earl's Court in July 1939. The B.U.F. was also suffering from internal dissensions and financial difficulties. After the débâcle of the L.C.C. elections in March 1937, Mosley had had to remove all but 30 of his 143 salaried staff. Although most of the people taken off the paid staff were minor officials, two were not. Mosley used the excuse of financial difficulties to purge William Joyce and John Beckett, both of whom were critical of Mosley's tactics and turned to founding a rival organisation, the National Socialist League. A number of other B.U. members, including the editor of *Fascist Quarterly*, left the movement with Beckett and Joyce.[34]

Reports from many parts of the country suggested that by 1939 the B.U. was weakening. But the failure of the peace campaign was soon to be eclipsed by the impact of war. Mosley's pretensions to emulate continental fascism made it difficult for him or his movement to escape the round-up of potentially subversive personnel in the first year of the war. In May 1940, Mosley and other leading members of the movement were detained under the Emergency Powers Defence Regulations and in July these regulations were used to suspend the activities of the British Union and ban its publications for the duration of the war. The fascist challenge from within Britain was driven out of existence as the country wrestled with the consequences of its rise on the Continent of Europe. The government's case against Mosley, however, rested less upon what he had done in the past or any tangible proof of fifth-column activities than upon the role he might play in the event of an invasion.[35]

How significant had the B.U.F. been in terms of numbers and membership? In 1936 the movement claimed 500 branches. Two years earlier, figures of 400 and 370 were claimed, but more detailed counts in the *Blackshirt* revealed a total of only 146 in summer 1934, 34 in the London area and 112 in the rest of the country.[36] Branch numbers reveal little about the total membership and a wide range of figures have been suggested for the number of B.U.F. adherents. The press estimated its membership at between 17,000 and 35,000 in 1934 and 1935. Police reports suggested that the movement's membership had fallen to less than 5,000 in 1937, while on the eve of the war the Home Secretary claimed that the total membership was 9,000. Ex-members of the movement gave widely different claims but the former deputy leader suggested a peak membership of 40,000.[37] The latter figure would encompass the highest estimate of total membership, though, like the N.U.W.M., it was claimed that more people had passed through the movement at various times. The strength of the fascists in different parts of the country is also difficult to estimate with any accuracy. One of the most useful indications of support in 1936 came from the list of 81 constituencies which the B.U.F. proposed to contest in the next General Election. The constituencies were selected because of their support for the movement in the area and the availability of a candidate. Thirty-nine of the constituencies were in London or near to it. Sixteen constituencies were to be contested in Lancashire, 12 in Yorkshire, 6 in the Midlands, and 3 in Wales.[38]

It was undoubtedly in east London that Mosley came nearest to attaining a popular following and attracting a measure of working-class support with the anti-semitic campaign. The local election results showed that the movement had achieved substantial backing, but not enough to destroy the basic voting tendencies of the electorate as a whole. The support for Mosley in the East End, however, can only be explained in terms of popular anti-semitism: the B.U.F. based its appeal upon it and the movement developed almost autonomously under its own leaders.[39] In Lancashire, the B.U.F. developed a following after a large campaign in 1934. In 1935, Mosley spoke at several meetings in the cotton towns and made a point of stressing proposals for protecting the cotton industry. Undoubtedly, the tariff reform campaign and traditions of working-class conservatism helped to give the B.U.F. a stronger appeal there than elsewhere.[40] Yorkshire, too, provided a stronger base than most other areas. It has been claimed that total fascist membership in Yorkshire in 1939 was 5,000, a very large figure which must include a sizeable number of non-active members.[41] Elsewhere, there was support in some rural areas, especially in Suffolk, where the B.U.F. had taken a prominent part in the tithe war.[42] Campaigns were waged in the agricultural counties of southern and south-east England under the patronage of some wealthy agriculturalists. Elsewhere, seaside resorts provided some following, but this support was drifting away by the late thirties.[43]

Who then were the people who joined the B.U.F.? Unfortunately no comprehensive lists of members are available, but it is possible to evaluate the leadership. The overwhelming majority were middle class, but their youth was perhaps the most striking thing they had in common. A sample of 103 of the B.U.F.'s leaders reveals that almost two-thirds were under forty in 1935.[44] The leadership was also relatively well educated and there was a strong military and ex-military influence, represented most notably by Major-General Fuller. Few of the leaders had extensive political experience and Benewick has written that 'there does not seem to have been a mass exodus of activists or loyalists from the traditional parties.' Some lesser officials came over from the Conservatives, but they were a relatively small number.[45]

Colin Cross claimed that the rank and file membership was drawn mainly from lower-middle-class white-collar workers and this was undoubtedly the case outside the East End and some of the northern textile centres.[46] There does seem to have been a younger element in the B.U.F., judging from the replies of local Labour Parties to a questionnaire from headquarters about the level of fascist activities in their area. At Plymouth Sutton it was claimed that three-quarters of the estimated thousand fascists in the area were 'young men and women of independent means'; in Bristol the 'majority of members seem to be young men and women'; at Loughborough 'the appeal has been mainly to youth'; at Newcastle it was described as 'very largely a youth movement'; and at Leeds it was reported that 'most black-shirts are young people'. In addition, there was a strong feminine influence. At Paddington South it was recorded that the Blackshirts 'make a strong appeal to all women', while the report from Stoke claimed that 'loose women appear to be plentiful ... it only wants a red light over the door!'[47]

The reasons why people joined the fascists also received attention from the questionnaire. A variety of reasons were given. At Plymouth it was argued that the strong military presence was responsible for the thousand fascists in the city. The B.U.F. members were described as 'sons and daughters of the military' and 'entirely new to politics'. At Bolton, where there were only sixty-one members, the Labour reply claimed that the fascist menace was deliberately exaggerated by the 'pseudo-Communists' in order to urge the need for a united front. At Harrogate and Loughborough the appeal of the movement was put down to its facilities for sport and socialising. In the former, it was claimed that the B.U.F. confined 'their attention to younger members of the Tory Party, particularly those interested in sports'. At Ashton, anti-semitism was stressed: 'the anti-Jewish stunt is the attraction to local tradesmen, who are feeling the Jewish tradesmen's competition in the town'. In Newcastle, however, the B.U.F. was described as a 'rival Transport Workers' Union' and it was reported that many busmen had joined.[48] Several respondents commented upon the absence of prominent local figures in the B.U.F., though at Liverpool it was reported that one councillor, 'a very irresponsible individual', had left the Tories for the B.U.F.[49]

There was virtually no penetration of the trade union movement and where working-class support was engaged it was on specific local

P

issues. The B.U.F. made a determined bid to win over working-class
support for its anti-semitic and economic programme, but it was
obviously limited in its appeal by the immediacy of the problem in
each area. Its most concerted effort was to win over the lower
middle classes such as shopkeepers, small tradesmen and self-
employed, groups who were supporting fascism throughout Europe.
Robert Skidelsky has shown that by championing the small trader
against the growing power of trusts and monopolies, the B.U.F.
received favourable coverage in a number of trade journals.[50]
Shopkeepers, taxi-drivers, clerical workers and small businessmen
also registered some support for Mosley.[51] In turn, he made specific
appeals to them by opposing big business and offering to restrict
competition when he came to power. It has been argued that the
common feature of these groups, including the young, was their 'high
degree of social and economic marginality'; their attachments to the
major political parties were potentially weaker than other groups and
they provided a potential audience for fascism.[52] But in fact the numbers of them who were prepared to take an active part in the B.U.F.
or to vote for it at local elections appears to have been strictly limited.

Many feared that the unemployed would provide the fascists with
recruits. It was widely believed that it was the unemployed in
Germany who had brought Hitler to power with his promises of
work and the irrational satisfactions of Nazism. However, most of the
recent work on the rise of Hitler has shown that it was less the unemployed than the middle classes who flocked to join the Nazis. In
spite of the depression, the allegiance of German industrial workers
to trade unions and the German equivalent of the Labour Party,
the S.P.D., remained remarkably strong. As a result, the representation of workers in the Nazi Party remained less than that of other
groups.[53] In Britain Mosley and the B.U.F. did attempt to capitalise
upon the frustrations of the unemployed. A campaign in South
Wales was opened in 1935 and Mosley spoke at meetings in several
of the mining towns; branches were opened at Cardiff, Newport and
Swansea. There was, however, little support in the area and the B.U.F.
gained few recruits in the other depressed areas such as Scotland and
the north-east.[54] There was virtually no evidence that unemployment
had generated support for the fascists in Britain to any significant
degree. Just as the majority of the unemployed maintained their
allegiances to the Labour and Conservative Parties in the face of
communist overtures, so they remained largely immune to the appeals
of fascism.[55]

The failure of the B.U.F. to gather more support than it did was testimony to the success of the established parties in maintaining their following. In Germany, it has been shown that the main impact of the depression was not so much to drive the unemployed and working class into the ranks of the Nazi Party, but rather to polarise the middle classes to support a strong party of the right in case of a communist revolution. Thus the success of the Nazi Party lay in its ability to attract conservative middle-class voters, fearful of a left-wing takeover and unsure of their political future. But the British middle classes were largely insulated from this insecurity after 1931, with the return of the National Government with its massive majority, the rout of the Labour Party and the insignificance of the communist threat. There was no obvious reason for large numbers of the electorate to vote fascist in a Britain securely governed by MacDonald and Baldwin who did nothing to perturb the growing prosperity of the middle classes. Some have argued that Britain escaped a larger and more successful fascist movement only because the depression was less severe here than elsewhere. In fact, in the depressed areas the problem of unemployment was at least as severe as in any other part of Europe or the Americas, but there was no evidence of a movement either by the unemployed or the middle classes in these areas towards the B.U.F. The primary reaction of the British electorate in the face of the depression was to vote for traditional parties and a majority voted in a decidedly conservative direction. The National Government provided a bulwark for these people against the communists and in doing so condemned the B.U.F. to a relatively minor role. In Germany the situation had been entirely different: without a strong conservative party to guarantee the security of the middle class which had experienced defeat and humiliation in the war, attempted revolution and the inflation of the early twenties, the Nazis were able to make a successful stand as the party of order. In Britain, that role was fulfilled by the National Government.

Mosley envisaged that he would come to power in the event of a deepening crisis: either the B.U.F. would be swept to parliamentary success or it would take power in the aftermath of a communist insurrection. The B.U.F. was founded, however, at the trough of the depression and was only struggling into life when the depression began to ease. The major period of active campaigning by the fascists was undertaken in the mid-1930s, when prosperity was returning to many parts of the country. As living standards improved and the

unemployment total dropped, Mosley was in an increasingly unfavourable position to capitalise upon frustration and discontent.
He found himself waiting to take power in a crisis which was indefinitely postponed. Moreover, the violence and militancy with
which the movement was associated, whether caused by it or provoked by opponents, meant that the fascists were regarded with deep
suspicion by many sections of opinion. Thus many potential Conservative supporters were alienated by the events at Olympia,
whoever was to blame for them. There were elements in British
political culture which made the use of paramilitary organisations
and the cult of force counter-productive. What has been called the
'civility' of British politics may indeed be a myth, but it is a myth
which played an important part in condemning the B.U.F. to the
political wilderness. Middle opinion in Britain would have little
truck with a movement which seemed to provoke, and possibly
encourage, political violence. Whether true or not, the majority of
British people chose to regard themselves as living in a relatively
well-ordered, gentle society. This widely-shared view of British
society undoubtedly operated against the B.U.F. at several points
in their campaign, such as the withdrawal of Rothermere's support
and the passing of the Public Order Act.

The history of the B.U.F. requires some analysis of its central
figure. It is difficult to conceive of a fascist movement of any significance at all in Britain without Mosley's leadership. He provided it
with drive, intelligence and powerful oratorical skill. But his weaknesses contributed to the failures of the movement. Impulsive,
arrogant and ambitious, he was unable to play the waiting game
which proved so successful to some of the Continental dictators in
their search for power. His action in founding the New Party showed
his failure to appreciate the resilience of British institutions and
political allegiances in the face of the depression. His shift to an
openly fascist stance reaped some dividends but also lost him
valuable support. From the mid-thirties the policies of the B.U.F.
went through an increasingly rapid series of convulsions as Mosley
tried to appeal to a broader section of the electorate. In addition, the
British political system has rarely rewarded men who combine both
high ambition and impatience. Recent history provides many
examples of individuals who have tried to go it alone and failed,
men who achieved little success in the face of a strong party system
and a relatively cautious electorate. Mosley played his hand pre-
maturely and had become an outsider by the end of 1932. Only a

revolution in political behaviour could have brought him to power.

British fascism was almost a non-starter. Anti-semitism had only a minor appeal to the British electorate and the pre-conditions for a breakdown of normal government were absent. British fascism was not only killed by the war, it was weakening both in the provinces and in the capital by the late thirties. Mosley could still command a sizeable audience and retained some popularity as an orator and an unconventional politician, but these attributes were beside the point. Neither through parliamentary means nor through less conventional methods could the fascists achieve success in 1939. Nor at any point had it been very likely that they would.

XII

The Government and Public Order

To many the 1930s appeared a violent decade in which the traditional procedures of parliamentary politics were threatened in one country after another by the challenge of extremist politics. Although the swing towards violence in Britain can be exaggerated, the government was seriously alarmed by the threat to public order offered by organisations such as the N.U.W.M. and the B.U.F. Two major pieces of legislation, the Incitement to Disaffection Act of 1934 and the Public Order Act of 1936, marked attempts by the government to assert its control over the threat from extra-parliamentary movements and preserve its authority in the face of possible civil disorder. Both Acts involved an incursion into individual liberty, but were seen as necessary to contain the challenge presented by hunger marches and fascist meetings. Public order became an issue in the 1930s with accusations from the Left of brutality and discrimination on the part of the police. With the public records now at our disposal it is possible to assess the attitude of the government and its agents towards the various organisations with which it was dealing and the principles which guided its actions during the thirties.

Faced with a renewal of N.U.W.M.-inspired hunger marches, the government's first line of defence was to discourage people from taking part by a number of administrative procedures. These involved co-ordinating the policies of the Home Office and the Ministries of Health and Labour. These tactics had been tried and tested in dealing with the hunger marches of the 1920s.[1] The Ministry of Health sought to enforce 'casual' regulations upon marchers who used workhouses for overnight stops. This meant giving them the same basic diet which was given to vagrants and down-and-outs. The Ministry of Labour was responsible for unemployment insurance and ruled that hunger marchers could not be allowed unemployment relief while on a march because they were unavailable for signing-on at the local Labour Exchange. There could be no question of unemployment pay being forwarded to marchers from their home areas. A memorandum from a ministry official put the position bluntly when he wrote: 'I do not think the department would be justified in incurring expense to enable men to take part in a demonstration which the Government deprecates.'[2] This attitude was maintained throughout the thirties and even applied to the Jarrow marchers. Though the N.U.W.M. marchers were often able to thwart or intimidate local officials into ignoring these instructions, the Home Office and Ministry of Health continued to urge local officials to follow a strict application of casual regulations.

Thus in the build-up to the hunger march of 1932, the Minister of Health reminded local poor law officials that they must enforce casual regulations. The marchers were to be warned that there was no guarantee that their families would be looked after in their absence. The Poor Law authorities were also assured of police assistance in any disturbances that might arise. In turn, the police on the routes of march were ordered to assist the local officials in enforcing these regulations, as well as supplying the government with any useful information regarding the numbers, movements, demeanour and intentions of the marchers.[3] In December 1933 when there was a threat of another hunger march, the standard regulations were invoked. The following January the Ministry of Health informed its inspectors that the marchers had a claim to some relief by law, but that the 'law did not envisage organised bodies going about and therefore the Poor Law Act [of 1930] should be strictly adhered to'. They were informed that:

> Any success achieved by the organisers of the March on the last occasion was due to some extent to weakness displayed by certain local authorities and their officers, who, in their anxiety to avoid possible civil commotion, made concessions by loans of blankets and by issues of rations to the demonstrators and thus conserved for more mischievous purposes funds which had been raised by street collections and otherwise.

He hoped that 'local poor law authorities may be less inclined to weakness of action and their close connection with the police may be of assistance in this regard'.[4] The police were told to keep in close contact with the local authorities in case they were required to enforce the casual regulations upon the marchers. To make the point perfectly clear to Chief Constables, the Home Secretary circulated copies of a statement he had made in the House of Commons and his reply to a question:

It is clear from published statements of the Communist Party that they are the prime instigators of the plans for the march, that it will be under their control and subordinated to their purposes, and that the intention is to represent the march as a 'mass struggle of the unemployed'. I am sure that there will be general agreement that these marches are not in the real interests of the unemployed and that any persons undertaking to furnish means which enable such concerns to take place incur very grave responsibility.

Fed a question by Commander Marsden: 'Is it not a fact that these marchers have never done any good and that they merely bring more distress and trouble to a great number of those who take part in them?' Gilmour replied: 'Yes, Sir, and on that point I hope that Hon. Members on all sides of the house will agree.'[5]

In fact the government was so disturbed by the problem in the aftermath of the 1932 hunger march that a Cabinet committee was set up to look into the legal position of the marches. It consisted of the Home Secretary, the Ministers of Health and Labour, the Secretary of State for Scotland, the Attorney General and the Lord Advocate. At the first meeting, held on 29 November, the Home Secretary declared that it was desirable to review the whole legal position of the marches as it was 'almost certain that the recent communist experiment with the Hunger Marchers would be repeated in the near future by the Trade Unions or similar bodies'. Others argued that it was important to allow discontent a safety valve because of Labour's poor representation in parliament, lest agitation be driven underground. The Home Secretary, however, claimed that during the recent disturbances in London 'the position had become extremely critical' and that in future the 'government ought not to have to wait until matters got to such a dangerous state as to warrant a declaration of emergency'. At the following meeting, on 7 December, the Home Secretary again insisted that he needed strong powers because the leaders of the 1932 march had 'definitely stated it was their intention to provoke street rioting and but for elaborate arrangements made then, there would have been serious disturbances and looting in London'. The real problem, he claimed, was how to disperse the marchers. There was, however, considerable resistance to the idea of the Home Secretary dispensing general jurisdiction over localities in times of peace. The memorandum of the Cabinet committee to the Cabinet concluded that as the law stood, no provisions existed whereby an organised demonstration can be prevented from marching from London or elsewhere, provided it is orderly and well-behaved. Only by invoking the Seditious Meetings Act of 1817, preventing fifty or more people from assembling in any open space within a mile of Westminster, could the police prevent the marchers reaching parliament. Provided the marchers followed a prescribed route and were orderly and well behaved, there was nothing the police could do to interfere. In addition, the committee reported that withholding benefit from the marchers provided no answer in itself and attempts to strengthen the Poor Law regulations would prove difficult to put into practice.[6]

As a result, it concluded that 'recent events ... afford a good opportunity of dealing by new legislation, not merely with the particular problem presented by contingents of marchers concentrating on London, but also with the control of processions in London itself and in other populous centres.' The committee therefore recommended new legislation to make marches illegal when the Home Secretary felt it necessary. A draft Bill was drawn up (23 Geo. 5 Processions, Regulation of) giving the Home Secretary the power to prohibit concentrations of persons outside their areas of normal residence, if he thought disorder was likely to result or abnormal demands would be made on the Poor Law authorities. The Home Secretary would also be empowered to prohibit for a limited period all processions within a particular locality if disorder was likely to result. The penalties were to be a fine of £50 or three months in prison. Though there was favourable comment on the Bill from the Ministry of Health, who thought that it would discourage otherwise peaceful and orderly people from taking part in the marches, and that 'marches would lose much of their effect if decent persons abstained from joining them', the Bill foundered upon the opposition of the Attorney General, Sir Thomas Inskip, who claimed that the powers given to the Home Secretary would be too extensive, and that it was impractical to grant them to local magistrates who were not responsible to parliament. Instead he recommended the use of an Act of Edward III, whereby a court of summary jurisdiction could order someone to enter into a recognizance to keep the peace and to be of good behaviour.[7] The Bill to prohibit marches or processions nearly reached the statute book, for it was drafted and ready to be presented to parliament where the National Government's majority would almost certainly have seen it made law. It highlights the alarm over the hunger marches felt by the government in the years which saw the greatest agitation by the unemployed. It was only the resistance of the lawyers which prevented the Home Secretary from being given the most sweeping powers since the days of Lord Sidmouth and the Six Acts. As a result the government had to rely upon a hotch-potch of legal measures, including laws of Edward III and of 1817. As it happened, the N.U.W.M. threat was abating with the new line from the Communist Party and it was the fascist demonstrations and meetings which were to lead to renewed pressure for changes in the law.

Whatever the legal position of the marchers, however, the government could count upon a largely favourable press in its dealings with the N.U.W.M. It was able to give a lead to public opinion by suggesting that the hunger marches were a major threat to public order. The Home Secretary in 1932 condemned the close connection between the N.U.W.M. and the Communist Party of Great Britain and quoted from an article in the *Daily Worker* which called for 'mass struggle in the streets'.[8] These comments led to shops and offices in central London being barricaded for the arrival of the hunger marchers in October 1932. Two years later the Home Secretary warned that a N.U.W.M. march to London was likely to lead to widespread looting and disorder. Even the apolitical Jarrow Crusaders were met with public criticism from the government for undertaking a march which might be exploited by extremists. Some common features marked the reporting of the N.U.W.M. marches. They usually received little publicity at all in the period of their preparation and journey to London. Once they arrived in the capital, on the other hand, they met an almost blanket condemnation as a threat to public order, verging upon the hysterical in the case of some of the more conservative press. Although it was the largest hunger march mounted in Britain in the early part of the thirties, when the depression was at its height, the N.U.W.M. march of 1932 was not mentioned once in either *The Times* or the *Manchester Guardian* in the week preceding the arrival of its eighteen contingents in London. Once it arrived, the bulk of the press took up an antagonistic stance, so that the only favourable reporting of the march came from the pages of the *Daily Worker*.[9] The B.B.C. quite spontaneously offered to broadcast and dissuade people from attending N.U.W.M. demonstrations if the police 'thought such a course desirable'.[10]

The press was more divided over the demonstration against unemployment organised by the T.U.C. and the Labour Party in February 1933, but even here the threat to public order was turned against the organisers. On the day following the demonstration *The Times* ran an editorial which accused the T.U.C. of rallying its forces 'to make the maximum political capital out of unemployment'. It was accused of assisting the communists who 'really have cause to thank the Labour movement for an excellent opportunity of bringing themselves into public notice in reputable company'.[11] Again in 1934 the bulk of the press took its line from the Home Secretary's warning that a N.U.W.M. march would lead to widespread disorder in London. It remained deeply suspicious of any demonstrations mounted by the N.U.W.M. The 1936 hunger march, which arrived in London about a week after the numerically much smaller Jarrow march, was virtually ignored by the press. The Jarrow marchers received much greater publicity. *The Times*, for example, ran a full column report in which it praised the endurance of the marchers and reported stories of the marchers' blistered feet and fatigue at the end of their 300-mile trek.[12]

In 1937, Ronald Kidd, the Secretary of the National Council for Civil Liberties, claimed that the 'discrediting of the Hunger Marchers was without doubt the deliberate policy of the Government in 1932 and 1934'.[13] Certainly the government was well aware of the need to win the battle for public opinion. The Home Secretary, as he revealed in the Cabinet discussions about the legal position of the marches, was genuinely alarmed by what he saw as a communist-inspired attempt to bring disorder on to the streets. He therefore attempted discreetly to discourage the marches and to minimise their effect. Thus news cameras were not allowed to film the N.U.W.M. demonstration in Hyde Park on 27 October, 1932, and were refused permission on later occasions, though in 1936 the Jarrow marchers were made a significant exception to this ruling.[14] A new dimension was given to the public relations battle, however, by the creation early in 1934 of the Council for Civil Liberties, later the National Council for Civil Liberties, comprising serveral prominent figures, including Clem Attlee, Edith Summerskill, Harold Laski, Kingsley Martin and H. G. Wells.[15] Their aim was summed up in a letter published in the *Manchester Guardian* in the run-up to the

N.U.W.M.'s 1934 march. The letter stated their intention to 'maintain vigilant observation of the proceedings of the next few days'.[16] This was done, it was stated in the letter, because the committee felt that the atmosphere of alarm created by the Home Secretary's warnings to the populace of London and his hints at bloodshed seemed in their view 'unjustified by the facts'.[17]

The formation of the National Council for Civil Liberties was symptomatic of the evolution of public opinion in the thirties on the public order issue. The tough attitude of the police in 1932, the gaoling of Mann and Llewellyn, and the apparent scare-mongering of the Home Secretary had created considerable disquiet even among those who were not intrinsically sympathetic to the N.U.W.M. The Home Secretary's warnings in 1934 that children should be kept off the streets, shop windows barricaded, and the public stay at home were not borne out by the new moderate line of the N.U.W.M. with its emphasis on less militant tactics. Thus by the mid-thirties, the government had to be much more adept in its handling of unemployed demonstrations. Whereas in the early thirties it had been possible for the government to act virtually as it pleased, there was by the mid thirties growing support from the left of the Labour Party for unemployed demonstrations, reflected in a more critical attitude towards the government. In 1936 the Minister of Health Sir Kingsley Wood, suggested that one way of restricting the problem of hunger marches was to encourage 'friendly newspapers' to take a strong line against the marchers.[18] As rallies such as that of 1936 became supported by a wider cross-section of opinion, the government was forced to adopt a more discreet approach. It could still, however, depend upon a largely conservative press to play down any unemployed demonstrations or marches, provided the government did not commit any obvious blunders in handling them. By 1936, the N.U.W.M. was itself much more moderate and the government was able to allow the natural antipathy of the bulk of the press towards communist organisations to achieve its purpose, hence the favourable publicity of the Jarrow marchers compared with the N.U.W.M. marchers of 1936.

It would be wrong, however, to exaggerate the degree of influence of bodies such as the N.C.C.L. The Home Office and the Metropolitan Police had little time for the organisation, regarding it as a biased, left-wing pressure group with no more than nuisance value. As late as 1936, three years after its formation, the organisation was described by the Home Office as being 'a body with close subterranean connections, particularly through its secretary, Mr R. Kidd, with the Communist Party'. It went on to say that: 'Although it has a long nominal roll of distinguished persons as Vice-Presidents and no doubt attracts a considerable body of support for the ideals for which it professes to stand, its *modus operandi* is to vilify the police on all possible occasions.' As a result, the police refused to take the N.C.C.L.'s evidence of police misbehaviour as impartial. None the less, they could not ignore the publicity which N.C.C.L. allegations obtained, especially when backed up by some of its more eminent members. It did have an effect in supplying an ostensibly objective record of police behaviour at demonstrations and meetings, and providing a pressure group which the police could not totally ignore, even if they refused to accept its findings.[19]

The files of the Metropolitan Police show that there was at least one informer in the higher councils of the N.U.W.M. who reported its plans and decisions to the Special Branch. The leaders of the movement, both locally and nationally, were kept under surveillance. During the hunger marches the police maintained a close watch upon any meetings that took place and submitted transcripts to the Special Branch, who passed on relevant information to Scotland Yard. It was on evidence such as this that Wal Hannington was prosecuted after his speech in Trafalgar Square in October 1932, for which he received three months' imprisonment. The police also made use of informants for special occasions.[20] For example, in 1934 the Special Branch reports contained information from a 'reliable agent who has been with the Scottish contingent'. In November 1932 the police used a man to supply information on members of the Manchester contingent who were accused of attempting to convey sticks with nails driven through them to the N.U.W.M. rally in Hyde Park. This is the one occasion on which the identity of an informer is recorded. The person in question was an ex-I.R.A. man from Manchester, recruited as a police informer while he was serving a term of imprisonment for his I.R.A. activities, of whom the police commented, 'after his arrest he was of great assistance to the Police'. In his evidence the informer betrayed a strong religious bias, indeed one of his reasons for giving evidence on some of the Lancashire contingent in the 1932 hunger march was because he regarded them as 'communists and atheists'.[21] In contrast nothing is known about the identity or motives of the informer the police had in the central councils of the N.U.W.M. The probabilities can be narrowed down to members of the National Administrative Council and the London

District Council, but beyond that it is impossible to go. The files which are now open contain a great deal of information on the N.U.W.M. and the plans for the hunger marches, passed on from the Special Branch to Scotland Yard. There is a strong likelihood that other files existed on the N.U.W.M., but these are the only ones which directly related to police work and have therefore come into the open. In this connection it was significant that the Special Branch also made reports upon other organisations which presented some form of threat to public order. Information was also collected on the demonstration organised by the T.U.C. and the Labour Party in February 1933, on the Jarrow march, on the movements of Ronald Kidd, the Secretary of the National Council for Civil Liberties, and on the Left Book Club. The common thread in this police attention was the government's concern to keep an eye upon movements or demonstrations which might create a threat to public order or act illegally.

The full weight of police attention upon the N.U.W.M. was felt in the national hunger march of 1932 when the authorities made careful preparations to deal with the threat of disturbances. Accordingly, the Metropolitan Police had obtained from local constabularies lists of prominent marchers, with details of past criminal or political activities, and in one case photographs to ease recognition. These are some typical entries:

T.W.P. ***, 28 years of age, height 5′6″, brown hair, brown eyes, dark complexion. A single man and dresses respectably. He is a very dangerous agitator and is very defiant when he has come into contact with the Police. He refuses to acknowledge any kind of law and order and has been convicted on several occasions for assaulting the Police.

G.P. ***, Age 45 years, height 5′6″, dark brown hair, grey eyes and sallow complexion. A native of Bristol. A man of most extreme and antagonistic views and is always foremost in getting something for nothing. Always prominent in marshalling processions and is an avowed revolutionary. He is a dangerous man and should be well noted. Previously convicted of riot.

N.R. ***, Age 30 years, height 5′4″, dark hair, pale complexion. Unemployed miner. A native of Ferndale, he is married with two children. He spends most of his time in propaganda for the

Communist Party. He joins in all demonstrations and has no respect for law and order. Has very extreme views and will be to the fore in any attack on the Police. He is in receipt of the dole and special diet from the Parish. Previously convicted of riots.[22]

The police were given information by local constabularies about the progress of the various contingents of marchers and their attitude on the route to London. Thus on 24 October, 1932, the Chief Constable of Oxford reported that the 230 men of the Lancashire contingent had behaved in an orderly manner while in the city, but he believed that they were armed with cudgels which they had concealed during their stay.[23] While the marchers were in London a steady flow of information was maintained to Scotland Yard from the Special Branch and from plain-clothes police attending open meetings. Information was the key to the authorities' battle with the hunger marches, for it enabled them to anticipate and forestall any actions the marchers might take.

In addition, the headquarters of the N.U.W.M. were raided during the 1932 hunger march and a large quantity of documents searched and seized without a warrant, actions for which the N.U.W.M. later received damages and costs against the police.[24] The really crucial impact of the police, however, was the constant toll upon the N.U.W.M.'s national and regional leadership by arrest and prosecution. The timing was usually such as to create maximum disruption to the activities of the N.U.W.M.; thus Hannington was arrested the morning before the presentation of the million-signature petition on 1 November, 1932. In the Birkenhead disturbances of October 1932, the local N.U.W.M. organiser and the rest of the local leadership were rounded up in the early hours of the morning while the riots were in progress in the town. The local organiser, Joseph Rawlings, received 2 years' hard labour. Two other local communists received 3 years' Borstal and two others 9 months in prison. A few days later, the Liverpool N.U.W.M. leader Leo McGree was given 2 years' imprisonment for his part in the disturbances at Liverpool. Similarly, Wal Hannington was given 3 months' imprisonment in November 1932, which took him out of political activity for the winter months of 1932–3. In December 1932, Tom Mann and Emrys Llewellyn, the Secretary of the N.U.W.M., were both gaoled for 2 months on charges of incitement and disturbing the peace. Both were asked to find sureties of £200 and bind themselves to keep the peace. When they refused, they were committed to prison. Sid Elias, the Chairman of the N.U.W.M., was also gaoled for 2 years for sedition.[25]

Thus by 1933, a very heavy toll had been taken of the N.U.W.M. leadership. The imprisonment of Mann, who was seventy-five, and of Llewellyn on fairly slender evidence led to protests not only from the N.U.W.M. and the C.P. but also from the Labour Party Executive, which said that the sentences were examples of 'vindictive treatment meted out to political opponents on account of their pronounced and extreme opinions'. George Lansbury asked questions in the House of Commons and Ramsay MacDonald was moved to inform his Home Secretary that he had received 'some very weighty protests against the prosecution of Tom Mann ... some of my correspondents range from dignitaries of the Church of England to local representatives of law and order, including some of our National Labour and reliable people in the Trade Union Movement'. MacDonald suggested letting them out of prison with a warning, but the Home Secretary stood firm, arguing that: 'Any concession would be regarded as a weakness and would in my considered view encourage the forces of disorder ... ' Llewellyn and Mann served the full term.[26] Following disturbances at Blaina in the South Wales coalfield in 1935, thirty-one men received sentences ranging from 3 months to 15 months' hard labour.[27] The fairly hard clamp-down upon the prime movers in any demonstrations or disturbances had an important impact upon a movement like the N.U.W.M., which depended upon a small core of activists. It also served as a warning that any future demonstrations might suffer the same fate, forcing the N.U.W.M. into a more cautious stance from 1933 onwards. Even if the Moscow line on confrontation with the police had not changed in the course of 1933, there is a strong possibility that the N.U.W.M. would have had to alter its tactics, because of the near-fatal drain upon its key personnel.

In the last resort the conflict between the government and the hunger marchers was fought out on the streets of towns and cities in Britain, including on several occasions the capital itself. Both at the time and subsequently, the police behaviour towards the hunger marchers has aroused controversy. Supporters of the hunger marchers usually blamed the aggressiveness of the police for the outbreak of violence at demonstrations and also blamed them for brutal behaviour towards both the marchers and innocent by-standers. Wal Hannington was in no doubt that the police initiated attacks upon the N.U.W.M. marches and demonstrations in an attempt to suppress them by 'brute force'. After disturbances in Bristol in 1931 he accused the police of 'cowardly and unprovoked' assaults on demonstrators.[28] Will Paynter, another hunger marcher, also left a vivid description of the episode:

> We had not proceeded very far along the street away from the Horsefair when there were shouts and screams. Those of us in the front who ran back to investigate found that the police had broken into the march at several points and were using their batons. A fierce battle developed with the marchers defending themselves as best they could. I went to the help of a lad struggling with two policemen and became involved with several others. I was carried into the police station in time to see the station sergeant delivering a vicious stomach punch to the lad I had tried to help. When the police carrying me released me on the floor I stayed there, for it was inviting injury to stand up. We were searched and put in the cells, but not before we saw a number of others carried in, obviously having been mauled and roughly handled.[29]

Similarly in 1932, Wal Hannington claimed the police in Glasgow on 1 October 'made a savage baton-charge into the crowd, clubbing down unarmed men and women indiscriminately'.[30] At Birkenhead he accused them of conducting a 'police terror' in the working-class districts and blamed the police for the violence which occurred on the national hunger march of 1932 both on the route of the march and when it arrived in London.[31] This was the consistent N.U.W.M. and C.P. view of the violence which accompanied the militant phase of agitation of 1931-2. It received its clearest statement when Allen Hutt maintained in 1933 that the hunger marches had led to a 'process of militarisation' among the police, with ex-army officers occupying the higher posts of the police force, the development of a 'crack corps of mounted special constabulary', and the enrolling of large numbers of special constables. He estimated that between the formation of the National Government and December 1932 there had been over 100 baton-charges on mass demonstrations, over 1,300 arrests, and 421 convictions.[32]

It is easy to dismiss these views as special pleading from committed participants, not only in the events, but in a larger-scale political war against the existing political establishment, of which the police were seen as agents. There were, however, plenty of other

Q

reports of the police's mode of dealing with demonstrations to suggest that at the very least they acted in a fairly tough manner towards N.U.W.M. demonstrations. Reports from newspapers which were by no means inclined to support the movement left vivid descriptions of the way in which police baton-charges were used fairly ruthlessly to disperse assemblies which the police regarded as illegal. For example, the *Bristol Evening Post*, writing of the police action in June 1932 in the city, described how the N.U.W.M. demonstrators marched peacefully through the streets with 'no hint of trouble', then:

> Just what precipitated the trouble is not clear, but suddenly there emerged from side-streets and shop doorways a strong body of police reinforcements with batons drawn. They set about clearing the streets. Men fell right and left under their charge, and women who had got mixed up in the crowd were knocked down by the demonstrators in the wild rush to escape. The cries of men and the terrified shrieking of women added to the tumult. Then came a troop of mounted police charging through Castle Street from the Old Market Street end, scattering the last of the demonstrators. In a few minutes the streets were clear, save for the men who lay with cracked heads, groaning on the pavements and in shop doorways, where they had staggered for refuge.[33]

In almost all the disturbances, the casualties among the demonstrators far outnumbered those among the police. At Birkenhead, 37 people were treated in hospital, including a child of five and a man of seventy. Only 7 police were injured, 3 seriously.[34] At Belfast the casualty list included two fatalities, both of them demonstrators upon whom the police had opened fire.[35] According to the police themselves, the demonstrations in Hyde Park in October 1932 resulted in 77 people being injured, only 9 of them policemen.[36] After the disturbances surrounding the N.U.W.M.'s attempts to present its mass petition on 1 November, the police recorded 44 people injured, 12 of them policemen.[37] In the London disturbances mounted police wielding long batons were used extensively, and the trail of violence and baton-charges throughout the country in 1931–3 aroused disquiet among several members of the parliamentary Labour Party. On 18 October George Lansbury asked the Home Secretary for an inquiry into police behaviour at Birkenhead and followed this up with complaints about the actions of the mounted police during disturbances in London where, he claimed, they had charged from both ends of a street, trapping a number of innocent people. Police actions during the national hunger march of 1932 and later were subject to persistent critical attention from opinion sympathetic to the hunger marchers. The formation of the National Council for Civil Liberties to watch over the conduct of demonstrations was an implied criticism of police conduct by a number of Liberal and Labour figures.[38]

The government did little to conceal the fact that they had acted firmly against N.U.W.M. marches and demonstrations when the need arose. In answer to George Lansbury's questions in the House, the Home Secretary, Sir John Gilmour, admitted that a firm line was being taken because of the nature of the N.U.W.M. and 'the very material connection between those in Moscow and some of this organisation'. He claimed that the disturbances were the result of the refusal of demonstrators to follow routes prescribed for them or to move on when causing an obstruction to traffic. On the question of baton-charges, he did not deny their use, but observed:

> On the other hand, it is worthy of noting that at Birkenhead the technique of street fighting which has been advocated by the Communist International has been considerably developed. For instance, the police found at Birkenhead that trip wires – barbed wire in one case – has been stretched across the road about a foot from the ground, lamps had been extinguished, and manhole covers removed. These examples which I quote are constantly referred to with approval in the Communist Press.

The Home Secretary replied to criticism of the police harming innocent by-standers by saying that people who mingled in crowds of demonstrators had no one to blame but themselves, and could have 'no complaint except against their own folly'.[39] In addition the police reports on their actions in the demonstrations in Hyde Park and around Trafalgar Square during the hunger march of 1932 make it clear that they were acting to disperse any large assembly of men. The laconic statements tell their own story: ' ... more of the disorderly element returned to Trafalgar Square and it became necessary to disperse them ... '; 'Westminster had to be cleared'; 'The West London contingent of about five hundred was broken up by police as it was *about to become disorderly* [authors' italics] in Edgware Road.'[40] The police accounts of incidents in Lambeth on 26 October reported that at Borough Road and London Road 'the crowds were

unruly and were dispersed by force by mounted and foot police,'
while at the junctions of Waterloo, Blackfriars and Westminster
Bridge Roads the crowds, though of similar dimensions, 'were quite
orderly and were dispersed by foot police without any trouble'.[41]
As these statements show, the police did not always require a great
deal of resistance from the demonstrators. Many baton-charges were
aimed at dispersing crowds which the police saw as causing an
obstruction or threatening to cause disorder, though the Home
Secretary claimed that the police had 'used every method in their
power by persuasion and direction' and were forced to act 'by real
opposition'.[42]

It is difficult, and to some extent unrealistic, to attempt to appor-
tion blame for the violence that occurred during the N.U.W.M.
campaign of 1931–2. Both the police and the N.U.W.M. were involved in a wider battle for public opinion in which they presented
only their own side of the case. The actual outbreak of violence was
in almost every instance shrouded in confusion, occupying just that
grey area of evidence in which it is virtually impossible to make firm
judgments. The N.U.W.M. naturally blamed the police for interfering with peaceful demonstrations, though many of the disturbances occurred because N.U.W.M. demonstrators insisted on
holding meetings for marching in defiance of police orders. The justice
of these orders depended on the police perception of the role and
motives of the N.U.W.M. and there is no doubt from the whole
tenor of their internal and public statements that the government
and the police saw the programme of militant campaigning by the
movement as a threat to public order and part of a communist-
inspired attempt to precipitate disorder on the streets. Even if the
intentions of the N.U.W.M. fell short of revolution, the police
could hardly ignore the open exhortations of the movement for
'mass struggle on the streets', 'mass and stormy activity against the
authorities', and the calls for 'day to day mass rallies, steadily
mounting in force and intensity'.[43] On the other hand, the Home
Secretary's implicit acceptance of a tough line against the N.U.W.M.
meant that little quarter was given by the police. It is difficult to
judge events outside London, for the police records for local constabularies are not available, but from the London police records
which are open it is clear that baton-charges were frequent. Though
the Home Secretary complained of 'new tactics' being used by the
demonstrators, it was usually they who came off worst in any clashes
that occurred. The Home Secretary was certainly indulging in a

degree of special pleading himself when the only figures on casualties in a disturbance he quoted gave more injuries to the police than the demonstrators. The London police records show, however, that all major disturbances in London led to greater injuries among the crowds which were dispersed. Unbiased press reports from the provinces yield a similiar conclusion. Police descriptions of the violence, the recurrent disquiet showed by some M.P.s, and the Home Secretary's statements confirm that the police in 1931–2 were taking a tough line against what they saw as a subversive organisation.

The insecurity of the government manifested itself in the Incitement to Disaffection Act of 1934. The 'Sedition Bill', as it was soon called, was presented for its second reading on 16 April and given the royal assent on 16 November. The Act made it an offence for any person to 'maliciously and advisedly' seduce any member of His Majesty's forces from his duty or allegiance. In addition, a person found with documents which could constitute incitement among the armed forces would also be deemed guilty of the offence in certain circumstances. The most controversial provision of the Bill was that which gave a magistrate the power to issue a general search warrant where there were reasonable grounds to suspect an offence. This raised a storm of protest from a wide range of opinion, including the eminent legal historian Sir William Holdsworth. The N.C.C.L. was also active in opposing these provisions and there were a number of mass rallies held against this and other provisions in the Bill. Harold Laski referred to it as the greatest menace to public liberty since 1817, while others preferred analogies to the days of Pitt and Dundas. As a result of these protests, the Bill was modified. A search warrant could only be issued by a High Court judge and in respect of an offence suspected to have been committed within the previous three months. Documents seized had to be listed at the time and only those documents taken which were relevant to an offence under the Act. The latter provision reflected the result of the case brought by the N.U.W.M. against the police for the seizure of documents from their headquarters in 1932. In the case of *Elias* v. *Pasmore*, decided in January 1934, damages were awarded against the police for the seizure of documents which were not used to bring Elias to trial. In order to prevent magistrates exercising partiality, provision was made for all accused to have the option of trial by jury. Although the Act which went on the statute book had been modified, there remained suspicion that the government had equipped itself with further powers to curb political extremism. In fact, the Act was little used, marking more a strengthening of reserve powers than an active instrument of repression.[44]

The rise of the B.U.F. presented both some familiar and some new problems for the government. Like the N.U.W.M., its marches and processions posed a threat of disorder, though violence was usually brought about by clashes between anti-fascist demonstrators and the police. This led to consideration of the need to ban marches and processions in 1934 and 1936. The B.U.F. also raised the question of the attitude of the police towards the conduct of meetings held upon private premises. The right to provide stewards and eject hecklers was well enshrined in law, but difficulties arose when there were complaints of undue violence by fascist stewards at their rallies and meetings — an issue raised in an acute form by the Olympia meeting in June 1934. Lastly, the B.U.F. was a uniformed organisation which made its paramilitary character part of its propaganda and policy. This aspect of the B.U.F.'s activities also raised new and difficult problems for the authorities.

The B.U.F. only became an overt threat to public order towards the end of 1933, when incidents began to occur in the East End of London as a result of members of the B.U.F. marching and selling newspapers in Jewish districts. Although the newspaper vendors were acting within the letter of the law, the police acknowledged that the behaviour of the fascists was deliberately provocative. Mosley on the other hand complained to the police about attacks by Jews upon his newspaper sellers while they were going about their lawful business. His stance was that he did not want to contravene the law, but to establish the right of the B.U.F. to sell its newspapers where it pleased:

> I can assure you that I will do everything in my power to prevent any breach of the peace and to carry out any regulations laid down by the police, but I desire to affirm the right of Englishmen to pursue any legal and peaceful activity in this country without molestation and assault.

The position of the police was illustrated by a fairly typical incident which took place on 7 May, 1933, when a disturbance broke out between a group of Jews and a man selling newspapers. Eight Jews were arrested, as a result of which a crowd assembled and had to be dispersed by the police. Incidents of this kind continued throughout 1933 and into the next year. The police made it a general policy to arrest impartially whoever they felt most responsible for causing the breach of the peace, though they wished to avoid publicity where fascists were arrested for fear of creating more trouble. None the less, several fascists were charged with causing a breach of the peace as a result of minor disturbances in the East End of London in spring 1933.[45]

It was the Olympia meeting of 7 June, 1934, that almost brought matters to a head. The B.U.F. attracted a torrent of unfavourable publicity for the behaviour of its stewards towards interrupters at the meeting. The meeting had received a large build-up both from the B.U.F. and its opponents. There were 12,000 people present, 2,000 of them uniformed Blackshirts, half of whom were acting as stewards. There were many communists who got inside the building as well as large numbers of anti-fascist demonstrators outside. The police had 762 men on duty, a force which was subsequently regarded as barely sufficient to prevent 'a serious disturbance starting, which might have finished in disorder, injuries, and very serious damage to property'.[46] The meeting opened peacefully at 8.40 p.m., but was soon interrupted by shouts and chants from the estimated 500 anti-fascist demonstrators inside the hall. By the time the meeting ended at 10.15 p.m. many of these demonstrators had been roughly handled and thrown out of the meeting. It was the way in which this was done which shocked even spectators who were sympathetic to Mosley and his movement. The use of stewards to eject hecklers was perfectly legal if 'reasonable' force was employed, but as one Conservative M.P. informed the House of Commons: 'I am not against interrupters being ejected at a meeting or for that matter of seeing a man knocked down in a scuffle but when it comes to seeing eight or ten men kicking and beating a man on the ground . . .'[47] The police also gave evidence of the view from outside the hall:

At intervals the door was flung open and one or more persons ejected into the main road. In nearly every case they were bleeding from the head and face and their clothing was badly torn... the situation was at periods a little ugly but in almost all these cases it was through the action of the stewards.

Another wrote:

The ejected persons were either hustled or flung unceremoniously into the street; all appeared to have been badly beaten prior to ejectment, and obviously all resistance had been knocked out of them. They were in a very dishevelled condition, the clothing was almost torn from their backs. The majority were severely bruised about the face and many were bleeding profusely from face and head injuries.[48]

Although the issue was not completely one-sided, the Olympia meeting marked a turning point in public opinion about the B.U.F. The adverse publicity it attracted led the government to consider steps to strengthen its control over meetings and processions.

Even before the Olympia rally, the Home Secretary had begun to pay attention to the need to strengthen the law. In a memorandum submitted to the Cabinet, Sir John Gilmour said that while the B.U.F. professed constitutional methods, there was a danger that it might achieve a position where it would be strong enough to press its claims by force. He proposed a Bill whereby the police would have the power to enter private premises or public meetings if the Chief Constable had reason to believe that violence might occur. To avoid the kind of difficulty presented by hunger marches or fascist parades, the Home Secretary was to have the power to prohibit the concentration of people in any area where they might give rise to disturbances. Chief Constables were also to be given powers to prohibit open-air meetings where they thought a clash of rival factions was likely to occur. After discussion and modification, proposals for strengthening the law were submitted to the Cabinet on 20 July, 1934.[49] The Home Secretary explained that the experience of the Olympia rally suggested that 'unless something is done to check these tendencies, we may expect disorder on an increasingly big scale.' Such a development would, he believed, play into the hands of the fascists. Open-air meetings were to be banned where necessary, local and national marches restricted, and the wearing of political uniforms made illegal. The Bill, however, was not entirely well received. Some arguments used against the proposed Bill of 1932 were raised, for example that the banning of meetings and processions would drive discontent underground. Again, as in 1932, it was felt that too much power was being placed in the hands of the police. The proposals concerning political uniforms raised many questions, not only of defining the law, but of securing a broad basis of support for it both in the Cabinet and in the House of Commons. Gilmour had studied foreign experiments in the area of banning political uniforms, but felt that they gave too much power to the government and would be unacceptable in peace-time. With pressures upon the parliamentary time-table building up, many issues still requiring definition and dissension over other proposals, the Cabinet adopted a wait and see policy.[50]

In the interim, the government tried to avoid violence by other means. The Metropolitan Police prevented a B.U.F. rally at White City on 5 August, 1934, by persuading General Critchley, Chairman of the White City Board, to demand so high a bond upon the safety of the hall that Sir Oswald would have to decline his booking. The police insisted upon the strictly 'confidential' nature of their 'advice' to the owners, but justified themselves on the grounds that they did not want to be in the situation of paying the costs of any disturbances that might occur while they were unable to enter the premises.[51] On other occasions the B.U.F. liaised successfully with the police and carried out their meetings without the violent scenes which had provoked an outcry over Olympia. At a meeting held in the Albert Hall in October 1934 the police placed plain-clothes men inside the hall who were to go outside and inform the uniformed men if there were any serious disturbances. As the police wrote: 'We want to prevent the scenes which took place at the Olympia on 7th June when the Fascists "beat up" people who came to the meeting.' The B.U.F. representative, Mr Francis-Hawkins, assured the police 'that the Fascists were most anxious to conform with the law and would in every way help the police'. The meeting proceeded peacefully and the police reported that the B.U.F. had maintained 'very amicable relations' with them.[52] Although some meetings were prevented by the police when they felt that disorder might take place, most B.U.F. meetings went ahead without overt police intervention. As late as 1936 the Metropolitan Police stated that they were adhering strictly to the principle that they would only attend a B.U.F. meeting if they were required to keep the peace in the event of a disturbance or if they were hired under the normal procedures for any meeting.[53]

During 1936, however, tension between the government and the B.U.F. began to mount. On the one hand the campaign in the East End had provoked the police into providing a much more vigilant watch on anti-Jewish expressions or incidents. On 7 July, 1936, the Home Secretary informed the Metropolitan Police that he wanted anti-Jewish activities dealt with:

I should like to feel assured that not only the senior officials at Scotland Yard and the higher ranks in the police divisions, but each individual police officer who may be called to deal with anti-Jewish incidents is made fully aware that grossly abusive language of the Jews, either individually or as a race, is a serious offence and that there can be no question in this matter of good-humoured toleration of language which in other circumstances might not call for intervention on the part of the police.[54]

This firm statement did not, however, prevent the eruption of small-scale incidents and demands from bodies such as the N.C.C.L., Jewish organisations and a wide section of liberal opinion that the B.U.F. must be prevented from terrorising one section of the community. Moreover, the activities of the B.U.F. were giving rise to a wave of disorders in the country at large during the spring and summer of 1936. There were disturbances at the Carfax Assembly Rooms in Oxford on 25 May; at Hulme, Manchester, on 28 June; at Hull on 12 July; at Bristol in August; and on 27 September at Leeds. Many of these disturbances arose out of clashes between fascists and anti-fascists, or more often between anti-fascist demonstrators and the police. Matters were clearly coming to a head. There were bitter complaints about police behaviour towards demonstrators who had gathered in Thurloe Square on 23 March, 1936, to protest about a B.U.F. meeting in the Albert Hall. The police alleged that they dispersed the crowd because it had become disorderly 'on the fringes'. The Home Secretary resisted demands for an inquiry into the police action and dismissed an inquiry conducted by the N.C.C.L. as 'a singular example of special pleading'.[55] But the concern caused by clashes between the two factions culminated in the Battle of Cable Street on Sunday, 4 October. For the government, these events were the final straw. It seemed that violence was escalating and that further fascist marches could only be avoided by strengthening the powers of the police over paramilitary organisations and their activities.[56]

The Public Order Act therefore came as a reaction to a situation which seemed to be getting out of hand. Laws to regulate processions had been considered in 1932 and to deal with paramilitary uniforms in 1934. Even before the Cable Street incidents, in July 1936 it was reported that the Cabinet was considering a ban on all political uniforms.[57] The pressure for legislation from anti-fascist groups was transformed by the Cable Street affair into legislative proposals. The King's Speech in November announced the introduction of a Bill for strengthening the law on meetings and processions. The Public Order Bill was introduced within a fortnight of the King's Speech and was presented for its third reading by December. The law came into force on 1 January, 1937. The Act created a number of new offences under the law. Its main provision was to prohibit the wearing of uniforms for political purposes in public places or meetings. The definition of a uniform was left to the courts and prosecutions were only to take place with the permission of the Attorney-General. Section 2 also struck at the B.U.F.'s para-military character by making it an offence to organise associations in such a manner as to arouse reasonable apprehension that they were organised 'for the purpose of enabling them to be employed for the use or display of physical force in promoting any political object'. It did, however, permit the use of a 'reasonable number' of stewards on private premises. The Public Order Act also regulated public processions. If a Chief Constable had reasonable grounds for believing a procession would create serious disorder, he could impose conditions upon the organisers to avoid disorder, or with the Home Secretary's approval, ban marches and processions for up to three months. The possession of offensive weapons at public meetings and processions was also prohibited, although the definition of offensive weapons was again left to the courts. It was also made an offence under the Act for any person in any public place or meeting to use threatening, abusive or insulting words or behaviour with an intent to provoke or threaten a breach of the peace.[58]

The passage of the Public Order Act was opposed not only by the B.U.F., but also by left-wingers who believed that some of the proposals could be turned against their activities. Section 3, with its provision to ban processions, could have been used against hunger marches. An article in the *New Statesman* complained that 'Side by side with valuable clauses, the Public Order Bill contains some dangerous provisions'; this section was also opposed by the N.C.C.L. Although there were theoretical dangers in the Act, there was little doubt at the time that the main provisions were aimed specifically at the B.U.F. Its principal clauses struck at its paramilitary and anti-Semitic activities. Above all, it was the use of political uniforms which had aroused provocation not only in the Jewish community but also among the police themselves. During its passage through parliament the provisions of the Bill were modified to take account of the most heated objections. None the less, the speed with which the Bill was dealt with showed that the government had given the issue a degree of priority and were unlikely to go back on any of the major clauses.[59]

But the impact of the Public Order Act should not be exaggerated. It did little to stop the smaller street-corner meetings which were the problem in the East End of London. These continued right up to the outbreak of the war, in spite of prosecutions under other laws. In April 1937 the City Road Police Station reported that the Public Order Act had, for a short time, a quietening effect on the East End, but that anti-Jewish activities had started up again:

> The marchers are often carried away by their anti-Jewish feeling, and acts of damage occur. The unfortunate inhabitants are deprived of sleep, and some of them are more or less terror-stricken, for to the Jewish resident of the East End, the Fascist is a source of grave apprehension. The activity is not all one sided, as the Jewish and Communist element too are active, and their meetings and processions need quite as much policing. It is quite plain that offence breeds reprisal, and the parties are being forced wider apart. Complaints of annoyance, assault and damage come in from both sides.

The police believed that there was 'no immediate prospect of improvement'.[60] In June 1937, the N.C.C.L. claimed that 'serious and well-substantiated allegations were made of organised hooliganism, intimidation and physical assaults by Fascists'. As late as 1939, the Metropolitan Police were recording incidents of Jew-baiting from fascist meetings in the East End, 103 small meetings being attended by the police in November-December 1938 alone.[61]

When the B.U.F. proposed another march through the East End in July 1937, however, it was met by a ban under section 3 of the Public Order Act, forbidding marches of a political character through the area for a period of six weeks. This was partly in response to the demands from local police stations who could not maintain the level of manning required to prevent each fascist meeting from contravening the Public Order Act. One police report put the position bluntly, writing, 'we cannot continue indefinitely sending large numbers of extra police into the East End in order to encourage masses of young people to stage demonstrations which are not peaceful but provocative.'[62] They urged the use of the Public Order Act to ban political processions for three months in the East End. In the event, the six-week prohibition was extended when Mosley showed every intention of staging a march as soon as the ban was lifted. As a result the bans were renewed at three-month intervals and the B.U.F. was prohibited from holding processions through the East End from July 1937 until it was disbanded in 1940. But in 1937 Mosley merely switched his route to Bermondsey and south London where some of the most serious disturbances of the period took place, resulting in 113 arrests and 28 casualties.[63] None the less, selective bans under section 3 continued to be used to defuse potentially dangerous situations, particularly in the London area, although the police allowed marches to take place where they saw little danger of disorder. In addition, the B.U.F. attempted to challenge the ban on political uniforms, but this provision of the Act did put a stop to the use of mass, fully-uniformed demonstrations. Fascist demonstrators had to rely upon a shirt and tie as the most they could allow themselves without risking prosecution. A trickle of prosecutions, similar to those under the section forbidding insulting language, helped to place the police in a more favourable legal position in relation to the B.U.F.[64] The Public Order Act clearly did not end fascist activity in Britain, rather it was a declaration on the part of the authorities that they would tolerate no challenge to their monopoly over the control of force in the state.

It was a common complaint among left-wing circles in the thirties that the police discriminated against them in favour of the fascists. The role of the police in clearing routes for B.U.F. marches and dealing with anti-fascist demonstrators was contrasted with the attitude towards the N.U.W.M. and the hunger marches. Similarly, there was the apparent reluctance of the police to intervene in B.U.F. meetings when hecklers or anti-fascist demonstrators were roughly handled by stewards. For many, such as Orwell, this was a natural alliance between the anti-communist party of order and the authorities, which itself accounted for such discrimination as occurred.[65] On the other hand Skidelsky has argued that this was a piece of 'left-wing mythology', for which there is not 'the slightest evidence'. He argues that the police were not 'pro-fascist or pro-socialist, but pro-police' and that their major concern was to preserve 'public order with the least expenditure of time and manpower'.[66] On balance, the latter view is much nearer the truth than the allegations of the Left. It is plain from the Metropolitan Police records that they were concerned to preserve public order whatever group was causing disruption. The policing of meetings on private premises did create legal problems which were left unresolved even after the Public Order Act. Moreover, the question of uniforms did cause a real antagonism among the police, jealous for their own status and authority. Even on such trivial issues as the arrest of newspaper sellers, the police were frequently urged to seize 'indiscriminately' anybody who seemed to be causing a breach of the peace.[67] By the late 1930s, the B.U.F. was the main threat to public order, occupying police time and manpower much more than the N.U.W.M. It is difficult to see how the Public Order Act could be interpreted as anything other than an anti-fascist measure with its restrictions upon paramilitary organisations. The prosecutions which followed upon the Act were almost entirely confined to the B.U.F. and, in turn, gave rise to allegations of prejudice and discrimination by the fascists themselves.[68]

There must, however, be a degree of qualification to this picture of an unvarying law, wielded by an impartial apparatus of police and Home Office. Whatever the intentions of the government, there is little doubt that the police had a greater initial suspicion of communists than of the B.U.F. There was a degree of discrimination, whether conscious or unconscious, in the attitude of the police towards the fascists. The latter claimed to be a party of order, were disciplined, and usually co-operated fully with the police. In contrast with the N.U.W.M. demonstrations of the early thirties, mounted in spite of rather than in co-operation with the police, the fascists were always careful to clear the ground with the police before making a march or holding a demonstration. They were therefore viewed with less suspicion than the N.U.W.M. Thus although it is true, as Skidelsky has claimed, that the police records contain no favourable remarks about the fascists, it is also true that they contain nothing parallel to the unfavourable comments made about members of the N.U.W.M. From the police's point of view, this may well have been a rational assessment of the situation. The N.U.W.M. and the Communist Party were openly committed to a revolutionary creed and had connections with a foreign power. The B.U.F. could, until the rise of European fascism, be seen as less of a threat. Significantly, it was when this foreign threat became manifest in 1940 that the B.U.F. was disbanded. In some respects, too, the police appeared to be rather more scrupulous about the law when dealing with fascists as opposed to anti-fascists. It was evident that police behaviour at Olympia and Thurloe Square betrayed little sympathy for the opponents of the B.U.F. There was not a single case of the B.U.F. being baton-charged or dispersed by the police, but there were many occasions on which the authorities acted against the

N.U.W.M. or anti-fascists, some at least in dubious circumstances. The Special Branch do not seem to have infiltrated the B.U.F.; whether they found it too difficult, or simply unnecessary, it is impossible to be certain, but the absence of covert surveillance of the B.U.F. by the police is in striking contrast to their practice with the N.U.W.M. Moreover, we should not forget that the police were not a monolithic organisation. High-minded principles of non-discrimination may have been enunciated at the top, but at the local level more basic prejudices could still exist. There were many complaints throughout the late thirties that the police were not acting either very forcefully or sympathetically to suppress anti-Jewish activities in the East End. In spite of these qualifications, however, the police do seem to have reacted less in political terms than in response to the challenge to public order and to their own position as the custodians of law and order. There may well have been a traditional bias against the Left and initially a more sympathetic attitude to the B.U.F., but neither was ultimately allowed to prevent the police from containing the fascist challenge when it became a serious nuisance.

Thus the 1930s saw a two-fold challenge to public order, represented by the organisations of the extreme left and the extreme right. Although some of the difficulties they presented overlapped, in essentials they were quite different. The hunger marches led to a fairly tough line on the part of the authorities, designed to prevent them being used for communist propaganda and recruitment. At one point, they did appear almost as a revolutionary instrument and were dealt with accordingly. From the mid-1930s, however, the problems presented by the B.U.F. were the major preoccupation of the authorities. In response to these threats, some invasion of individual liberty was almost inevitable. In spite of fears to the contrary, however, legislation passed in the thirties was not used in a blatantly repressive way. Both the Public Order Act and the Incitement to Disaffection Act were hedged with qualifications which left as much power as possible in the hands of the courts, rather than in the hands of the executive. What is striking in examining the Cabinet discussions of new legislation is how much regard was given to the sensitivity of parliamentary and public opinion on the issue of individual freedom. Pressure groups such as the N.C.C.L. illustrated just how far the actions of government were increasingly subject to public scrutiny. Though it was not accepted as impartial at the time, the N.C.C.L. was a healthy corrective to any tendency to prejudice on the part of the authorities. Public order had become a public issue to a greater extent than at any time since the First World War. This debate helped to articulate a consensus of opinion about what has been called 'the threshold of violence' permitted in British society. British society proved sufficiently cohesive to produce measures which prevented the initiative being taken from the government by extra-parliamentary groups on either extreme of the political spectrum and a descent into the 'politics of the streets.'

XIII

Left at the Polls: The General Election of 1935 and after

By the autumn of 1935, the National Government had been in office four years. Throughout 1935, especially after the reorganisation of the government in June, there had been rumours of an appeal to the country in the autumn, but the general impression when M.P.s dispersed in the early days of August was that the General Election would not be held until January or February 1936. During August and September, however, events developed rapidly, as on the diplomatic front the tension between Italy and Abyssinia mounted. At home, the annual conference of the Conservative Party was held at Bournemouth early in October, and although Baldwin gave no indication of the date of the General Election it was felt that the appeal would not be long delayed.

On 23 October Baldwin announced that he had asked for a dissolution immediately. Nominations were fixed for Monday, 4 November, and polling for Thursday, 14 November, so that the campaign was confined to the shortest period permitted by law.

Very naturally the National Government's manifesto pointed to its record – economic recovery, the boom in housing – and promised more efforts to assist the distressed areas, extension of old age pensions, and the raising of the school-leaving age to fifteen. Not surprisingly, a chief concern was foreign policy, which was to be a crucial issue of the campaign. The government promised that the League of Nations would remain 'the keystone of British foreign policy' and that Britain would do everything possible to uphold the Covenant and to maintain and increase the efficiency of the League. Baldwin pledged that over Abyssinia there would be no wavering on the policy that had been pursued. At the same time, Baldwin declared that rearmament was necessary to fill in gaps in national defence.

R

The coming of the election found the parties in differing states of readiness. Labour later claimed, partly no doubt to justify its relatively poor performance in the 1935 election, that it had been taken by surprise by the advent of the contest. Such was not the case. At a meeting of the party's N.E.C. as far back as 28 November, 1934, a memorandum from the Research and Publicity Committee warned that an election might take place during the autumn of 1935 and that the party should make preparations based upon that possibility.[1] Certainly, from November 1934 onwards, party organisers were preparing in earnest for a General Election. Henderson was deputed to organise a General Election fund and plans were launched for publicity and literature drives. Despite a perennial lack of finance, particular attention was paid to bringing forward candidates in seats not fought in 1931. In January 1935, the N.E.C. was able to report substantial progress towards the selection of candidates and co-ordination of election preparations. By the spring of 1935, Labour optimism ran high. In mid-April the N.E.C. reported that 'there was a growing confidence on the part of the rank and file.'[2]

To state that Labour was unprepared for an election was simply not true. Labour's total field of candidates, 552 compared to 516 in 1931, reflected the party's renewed strength.[3] Apart from a few very rural English county seats, Labour was challenging virtually every constituency. Thirteen of the party's M.P.s enjoyed an unopposed return. It was ironic, given the depression, that the number of union-sponsored candidates (128) was one of the lowest figures for the interwar period – a reflection of the financial difficulties facing many of them.[4] This overall financial stringency, together with the problem of the breakaway I.L.P. (see pp. 253–4), created clouds on Labour's horizon. But they were but minor irritants compared to the problems besetting the Liberals as the election was announced.

The coming of the 1935 General Election found the Liberal Party disheartened, disorganised and in disarray. Although some wildly optimistic statements from such people as Samuel suggested the party would be able to field 400 candidates in the General Election, those with a knowledge of how far the rot had gone in the constituencies knew that this target was simply wishful thinking.[5] At the end of December 1934, the party had the ludicrously small figure of 60 adopted candidates in the field. Sinclair, in pessimistic mood, doubted if the party could field 100 candidates in a General Election.[6] By early summer the party still only had around 90 adopted candidates and constituency organisation had hardly improved.

With the advent of the election, despite the hopeless financial position of the party, the Liberals managed to field 159 candidates, 41 more than in 1931 but 354 fewer than in 1929. Not a single Liberal enjoyed an unopposed return. Only 10 of the 38 Scottish county seats were fought by Liberals, a mere 6 of the 33 burgh seats. In England, only 71 of the 230 county seats were fought. These were grim figures, reflecting to even the most blind the extent to which the party had collapsed. With Liberal advocacy of Free Trade appearing almost unrealistic in the midst of world recession, and with the Abyssinia crisis forcing the party both to condemn and support the National Government simultaneously, the campaign hardly augured well for Liberals. Gloomy predictions of a Liberal disaster by such figures as Ramsay Muir proved to be only too accurate.

For differing reasons, neither fascists nor communists entered the 1935 election battle – apart from the two special cases of West Fife and Rhondda East. However, there was still a left-wing challenge to Labour in the election in the shape of the I.L.P. Of the I.L.P.'s 17 standard-bearers, the party's best chances were clearly in Glasgow, notably James Maxton at Bridgeton, Rev. Campbell Stephen at Camlachie, John McGovern at Shettleston and George Buchanan at Gorbals. The net result of these various trends in the nominations was a field of 1,348 candidates. The Conservatives brought forward 514, the Liberal Nationals 44 and National Labour a mere 20. Labour fielded 552, the Liberals 159 and the I.L.P. 17.

Compared to the Zinoviev letter of 1924, Lloyd George's challenge in 1929 or the alleged 'scares' of 1931, the campaign in 1935 was relatively uneventful. *The Times* later summed up the 1935 campaign, declaring:[7]

> Though various side-issues were raised the nation as a whole seemed content to vote on the one broad question of whether or not it desired that the National Government should be given a mandate to continue its work, and once the electors had made up their minds on that point there was no great inclination to listen to speeches either approving or condemning the past work of the Government.

Many factors tended to aid Baldwin's campaign in 1935, not the least being the way he had set the tone of the debate. As Mowat has written:

> Baldwin's campaign left the Liberals and Labour party at a disadvantage. He had stolen their clothes, and they could only

protest that he would never wear them: the Conservatives' conversion to the League and the application of sanctions was recent and insincere; it was they who had wrecked the disarmament conference, and their real intention now was to carry out a programme of rearmament.[8]

Labour's line of attack was also directed against the National Government's record on unemployment, depression and the means test. *The Times* believed this last issue had a real impact, declaring that it was one of the few subjects that really generated any heat.

Although *The Times* claimed that foreign affairs had little effect on the campaign, this was perhaps an understatement. Rearmament was certainly stressed in many Conservative speeches, although it was rather played down as the campaign progressed, and much was made of Baldwin's promise to a meeting of the International Peace Society at the Guildhall on 31 October: 'I give you my word that there will be no great armaments.'

In general, however, whether on home affairs or foreign policy, the campaign never came alight to the extent that one would have expected after the greatest depression in British history. Indeed, despite a rough ride for many National Labour candidates, in general the tone of the election campaign had been noticeably quiet. There were a few rowdy meetings, but these were mainly confined to London. *The Times* described North Kensington as the scene of 'the worst displays of rowdyism in London' but there was very little real disturbance. Ramsay MacDonald had the roughest personal time.[9] Overall, however, as *The Times* observed:

On the whole, the campaign was conducted in an orderly manner. There were isolated cases of rowdiness and a certain number of meetings were broken up, but the general report of the party organisers was that the campaign had been one of the most peaceful of modern times.[10]

Certainly, the fall in turn-out tended to confirm this judgment. During the campaign, the government also received a fillip with the results from the municipal elections of November 1935, held within the shadow of the General Election on 14 November. On balance, Labour suffered a net loss of seats. Press Association figures gave Labour 36 gains and 60 losses, the Conservatives 50 gains and 18 losses. This relatively tiny turnover of seats (compared, for example, to the previous years) was none the less much used to bolster the National Government's General Election campaign. Ramsay MacDonald welcomed the results as a 'a pointer to the results of the General Election' while Lord Jessel claimed they were 'a good augury'. On the Labour side, Morrison admitted that the results were 'somewhat unexpected'.

In fact, Labour's setback was exaggerated by the results from the west Midlands. Fifteen of Labour's net loss of 24 seats were concentrated in three west Midland centres.[11] In the 1935 General Election, Birmingham and the Black Country continued this regional trend.

Apart from the west Midlands, Labour's most serious result in 1935 was Leeds, where four Conservative gains gave them control of the council. Despite these reverses, Labour still did extremely well in 1935, with some 167 candidates returned unopposed, and 366 of a field of 898 successful in contested elections.

In this sense, the 1935 municipal elections were a misleading omen for Labour. For the outcome of the General Election was a bitter disappointment for the party. On the night of the poll, the first declared result came from Cheltenham. In a safe Conservative seat, though there was a 10·6 per cent swing to Labour in a straight fight, the Conservative won easily, taking some 70 per cent of the poll. The most significant of the very early results came from Stockton, which Harold Macmillan retained for the government. Again, though Labour had achieved a moderate swing, a far greater swing was going to be needed to win back many industrial seats lost in 1931. Labour's first gain of the evening, at Burnley, followed by an easy victory in Barnsley, were largely offset by highly disappointing results in Salford, where all three divisions were held by the government — whereas in 1929 all three seats had returned Labour members.

The first significant Liberal result was the loss of Dewsbury to Labour, the first of a series of Liberal borough seats to go down to Labour's advance. At the same time, as the evening progressed, the Conservatives were further encouraged by a number of seats, such as Southport and Manchester Withington, returning Conservatives with increased majorities. By late evening, the main trends of the election were clear. Labour was picking up seats, but in nothing like the quantity needed to win the election. Even Clynes's victory in Platting was only by a small majority. Liberals were losing badly — a trend symbolised by the result from Darwen, where Samuel was beaten by 1,157 votes. In particular, Liberal-held industrial seats, such as South Shields and Middlesbrough, were falling fast. Even in these early results, it became clear that the country was not voting uniformly. The failure of Wedgwood Benn to capture Dudley, followed by distinctly low Labour polls in such Birmingham seats as Deritend and Duddeston, were early evidence of a distinct regional pattern in the west Midlands.

The headline of *The Times* on 16 November proclaimed 'A Triumph of Steadiness': and the figures in Table 13·1 bear out that judgment.

TABLE 13.1   RESULTS OF THE 1935 GENERAL ELECTION

party	total votes	% of total
National Government:		
Conservative	10,496,300	47·7
National	86,716	0·4
National Liberal	887,331	4·0
National Labour	339,811	1·6
Total Govt vote	11,810,158	53·7
Opposition:		
Liberal and L. G. Liberal	1,422,116	6·5
Labour	8,325,491	37·8
Communist	27,117	0·1
Others	412,172	1·9
Total Opp. vote	10,186,896	46·3
Total vote cast	21,997,054	100·0

The National Government's losses, though important, were hardly dramatic. The Conservatives suffered only a net loss of 70 seats, and succeeded in recapturing three seats (East Fulham, Swindon and Wavertree) lost to Labour at by-elections. The Liberal Nationals lost 8 seats, all of these to Labour. The National Labour Party suffered heavily. Both Ramsay MacDonald in Seaham and his son Malcolm in Bassetlaw were defeated, the only ministerial casualties in the election. Six National Labour seats were lost to Labour.

In all, 435 National Government candidates were elected; 388 Conservatives, 35 Liberal Nationals, 8 National Labour, and 4 loosely termed as 'National'.

Even Conservative and Liberal National organisers were surprised by the results. 'The prophets were entirely deceived,' observed *The Times* joyfully. It would appear that Lord Hutchison, the head of the Liberal National organisation, had estimated a government majority of 127. Senior Conservative organisers were predicting a 150 majority, allowing for heavy losses in Lancashire which never materialised.

The combined strength of the Opposition numbered 180. Labour secured 154 seats, the Independent Labour Party 4, the Samuelite Liberals 19 together with 1 Communist and 2 Irish Partitionists. After the high hopes of the 1934 period, Labour's net gain of 94 seats came as a bitter disappointment to the party. For though Labour achieved many pleasing results, it was the unevenness of the party's performance that caused most worries. In Scotland, Labour had still only captured 20 of the 71 seats at stake. Wales was rather better, with 18 of the 35 constituencies returning Labour M.P.s. A relatively disappointing area was industrial Lancashire.

While Labour regained three seats in Manchester, in Liverpool the party gained only the Everton division and lost the Wavertree seat won in the February by-election. Salford, as we have seen, failed to return a Labour member for any of its three divisions. The two-membered seats in Lancashire and Cheshire also remained extremely loyal to the National Government, neither Bolton, Oldham, Preston nor Stockport returning a single Labour representative.

Lancashire was not the only industrial area to produce Labour disappointment. In the north-east, such industrial towns as Sunderland, Stockton and the Hartlepools were held for the government, even though the county divisions voted solidly for Labour. Among the other large industrial cities to stay loyal to the National Government were the railway towns. All the most prominent railway centres, including Derby, Swindon, Crewe, Carlisle and York, returned supporters of the government to the new House of Commons. In all, no less than 20 large towns, returning two or more members to parliament, failed to return a solitary Labour representative to Westminster.[12] Not a single Labour M.P. was returned in Birmingham, Cardiff, Newcastle or Leicester. London was the scene of some of Labour's best results. Whether spurred by Morrison's organisation, or encouraged by the L.C.C. victory in 1934, the party went on to gain 17 seats in the General Election—returning 22 Labour members compared to 5 in 1931. The fact remained, however, that in many of the largest boroughs, Labour's representation was still woefully thin.

Nor were the results merely the consequence of the vagaries of the electoral system. In only two of these major provincial boroughs (Stoke 53 per cent and Sheffield 51·5 per cent) had Labour obtained a majority of all votes cast. Only in 8 other cities (Glasgow 43·4 per cent, Liverpool 44·3 per cent, Manchester 42·2 per cent, Leeds 44·5 per cent, Bristol 46·5 per cent, Bradford 43·5 per cent, Hull 46·3 per cent, Cardiff 41 per cent) could Labour poll over 40 per cent of the votes cast. In terms of Labour's share of the total vote, the worst three Labour towns were Portsmouth (29·4 per cent), Birmingham (33·9 per cent) and Edinburgh (34 per cent).

These were figures that gave little consolation to the party. There was, however, one very much happier side of 1935 for Labour. In terms of personalities, the Labour opposition received a much-needed boost. Some 24 former Labour ministers who had gone down to defeat in 1931 were returned. The total included six former Cabinet Ministers: A. V. Alexander (Sheffield, Hillsborough); J. R. Clynes (Manchester, Platting); H. B. Lees-Smith (Keighley); H. Morrison (Hackney, S.); A. Greenwood (Wakefield) and T. Johnston (Stirling and Clackmannan, Western). Among the junior ministers returned were Dalton, Shinwell, Ben Smith and Pethick-Lawrence. The full list was an impressive tally. Despite these successes, several well-known Labour men (including 5 former Cabinet Ministers) had still failed to return to Westminster. Among the ex-ministers who were again rejected were Margaret Bondfield, W. Adamson (who was defeated by the only communist returned to the new House of Commons), Wedgwood Benn, Susan Lawrence, Jack Hayes, and Christopher Addison, whose defeat at Swindon was one of the real surprises. He had regained the seat at a by-election, but W. W. Wakefield fought him again at the General Election and won the seat back for the Conservatives.

The 1935 election virtually marked the end of the road for the National Labour Party. Both Ramsay MacDonald and Malcolm MacDonald, as noted earlier, went down to disastrous defeats. At Seaham, where there was easily the largest turnover of votes in the north-east, MacDonald went under with a 20,498 majority for Emanuel Shinwell. This drastic swing no doubt reflected not only Ramsay MacDonald's diminishing appeal as a consequence of his neglect of the constituency but also the general disillusionment with his politics which now affected most of his former supporters in the Seaham seat.

In Bassetlaw, Malcolm MacDonald's constituency, there was an equally heavy swing of 17·9 per cent against National Labour. This was very near the average figure in the 8 constituencies where there were straight fights between Labour and National Labour in both 1931 and 1935.[13] The swing was most pronounced in London (18·9 per cent), but it was also very high in even the regions of lowest movement, such as the west Midlands.[14] The net result of these heavy Labour swings was the loss of four other seats in addition to Seaham and Bassetlaw.[15] National Labour was now reduced to half its former representation.

The outcome of the election was yet another disaster for the Liberals: the party could retain only half the seats won in the débâcle of 1924. The party, with a mere 21 seats, had been reduced to almost total impotence. It had made only 3 gains from the government.[16] Nine seats were lost to Labour, all, with the exception of Carmarthen, urban seats and mainly concentrated in Yorkshire and the northeast.[17] In addition, the party lost 4 of its traditional strongholds to Conservatives, while the West Leicester seat was won by National Labour.[18]

No significant area returned any number of Liberals: a few agricultural seats, such as Cumberland North, together with isolated urban strongholds such as East Wolverhampton and East Birkenhead were all that the party had left. The Liberals also lost their best men: Herbert Samuel was out at Darwen, Isaac Foot lost Bodmin and Walter Rea was ousted at Dewsbury. Only six Liberals returned had been opposed by both Labour and National Government candidates, three of these in rural Wales.

The party's share of the national vote had fallen to a mere 6·4 per cent, even lower than the 7·2 per cent achieved in 1931. In seats not fought in 1931, where Liberals stood in 1935, on average the party obtained only 13 per cent of votes. Even worse, many of the party's best seats went uncontested in 1935 because of the collapse of local organisation.[19] In the 30 seats contested by all three major parties in 1931 and 1935, the Liberal share of the vote fell by 4 per cent.[20] Whether in terms of votes or seats, whichever way Liberals attempted to analyse the results, there was only gloom to be seen.

On the surface, the Liberal Nationals, with 33 members, appeared to have done well. But their seeming strength was illusory; all were dependent on Conservative votes in their constituencies — indeed, no Liberal National was opposed by a Conservative. Curiously, only in two constituencies, Denbigh and Oldham, were Liberal Nationals opposed even by Liberals. A variety of Liberal National urban seats reverted to Labour, especially in Yorkshire, the north-east and Scotland.[21] Where Liberal Nationals faced straight fights with Labour, the swing was in almost every case greater than in a normal Conservative-Labour contest. In terms of swing, the Liberal Nationals' worst area was London (a 16 per cent swing against them). In Scotland, the swing was also heavy (at 9·3 per cent) whereas in Wales it was kept down to 5·7 per cent.[22]

For the minor parties, the outcome of the election was a mixture of disappointment and isolated successes. Thus, for the communists, as we have seen, Willie Gallacher secured a remarkable personal triumph by winning the Scottish coalfield seat of West Fife, taking 37·4 per cent of the total poll and 13,462 votes. Harry Pollitt took an even higher absolute and percentage vote in East Rhondda, but trailed well behind Labour.[23] For the I.L.P., the results in Glasgow were, by and large, a triumph, but elsewhere the party's fortunes were extremely mixed. Despite the fact that the N.E.C. gave the Glasgow Labour Party additional funds to fight the I.L.P., suitable candidates were almost impossible to obtain. In Gorbals, Bridgeton, Shettleston and Camlachie, the I.L.P. routed the official Labour candidates. The statistics of these I.L.P. victories are set out in Table 13.2.

TABLE 13.2   I.L.P. VICTORIES IN GLASGOW IN THE 1935 GENERAL ELECTION

constituency	candidate	total votes	% of total
Gorbals	G. Buchanan	22,860	75·0
Bridgeton	J. Maxton	17,691	64·9
Shettleston	J. McGovern	18,377	52·8
Camlachie	Rev. C. Stephen	15,070	47·2

Apart from five other constituencies, the I.L.P. lost its deposit everywhere. Outside its entrenched strongholds, the I.L.P. had clearly failed to make any real impression. The poor results even in such parts of Glasgow as the Govan and Tradeston divisions, to-gether with Fenner Brockway's lost deposit in Norwich, were little short of humiliating.

The fate of the I.L.P. was, however, of little consolation to Labour. What, in fact, lay behind Labour's poor performance? A more detailed examination of the swing in 1935 provides at least some of the answers.

On average, in the 230 constituencies in which there was a straight fight between Labour and Conservative in 1931 and 1935, there was an average swing to Labour of approximately 10 per cent. The differences over the whole country were not very noticeable, except that London swung rather more to Labour (a 12 per cent movement) and Wales slightly less so (8 per cent). Otherwise, variations were not very marked.

However, some particular areas and sub-areas showed very marked divergencies from the national pattern. In the case of the major provincial boroughs, these variations of swing were significant.[24] The figures reveal several important trends. In two of these towns, Portsmouth and Plymouth, the rearmament question was clearly a factor keeping the pro-Labour swing at a low ebb. Constituencies with a high percentage of naval or military voters showed swings very much below the average. Thus in Portsmouth North there was only a 1·8 per cent swing to Labour, in the Gillingham division of Rochester only 3·9 per cent and a low swing in Plymouth Sutton. To this list can be added such seats as Dartford (3·7 per cent) or Petersfield, with its large military camp. In addition, a variety of towns dependent on steel and susceptible to rearmament orders also showed low swings (St Helens 6·1 per cent, Warrington 5·5 per cent, Westhoughton 6·9 per cent, Widnes 6·1 per cent).

A far more interesting element to be seen in the swings in large towns concerned the west Midlands. A very distinct regional pattern of low pro-Labour swings could clearly be seen. Thus, in Wolverhampton there was an average swing of only 2·6 per cent to Labour. In the 12 Birmingham divisions (a city in which Labour failed to win a single seat) the average swing was a lowly 5·7 per cent. Even more remarkable was the brewing centre of Burton-on-Trent which registered a mere 0·2 per cent swing to Labour. This working-class town remained solidly Conservative. This trend remained confined very much to the west Midlands. The electoral behaviour of the east Midlands was quite different. Thus Northampton, Nottingham and Leicester, the three largest towns of the east Midlands, swung to Labour by an average 12 per cent, very much in line with the industrial centres of the north.

In addition to the west Midlands, a further disappointment for Labour came in the Newcastle and Gateshead area. In two Newcastle constituencies, in which Labour faced a straight fight with

Conservatives, there were swings of only 6·9 per cent in the North and 7·9 per cent in the West; in the East division, against a Liberal National, there was a swing of only 4·8 per cent, similar to the low swing percentage in Gateshead. These results were doubly disappointing, for Newcastle and Gateshead had been among the worst Labour results in the north-east in 1931.

As a general rule, Labour's recovery was often greatest in 1935 where its vote had slipped most in 1931. Some of the towns with large swings to Labour (such as Leicester) were thus simply redressing the balance. And yet there was a curious paradox of the results in 1935. Labour was doing best in its worst areas. Suburban seats, safe rural Tory fiefs, all showed heavy swings from the National Government. Thus, apart from the special case of Liverpool Wavertree, the next highest swings to Labour were in two of the safest of all Conservative seats, Mitcham (18·8 per cent) and Wallasey (16·5 per cent).[25]

These were not isolated examples, and very large swings also occurred in Richmond (11 per cent), Wimbledon (12·6 per cent), Willesden West (14·7 per cent), Watford (12·9 per cent) and St Albans (10·6 per cent). These were, indeed, somewhat remarkable results. Thus Richmond swung more to Labour than most industrial Manchester seats; Willesden swung more than the Socialist strongholds of working-class Sheffield; while the swing in safe Tory High Wycombe (of 14·3 per cent) was twice that in Jarrow. Even though these statistics can partly be explained by Conservative voters abstaining in very safe seats, and a return of Liberals to the Labour fold, none the less there is still an essential paradox of 1935; Labour did worst in the seats that mattered most. Table 13.3 demonstrates this point.

TABLE 13.3   SWINGS TO LABOUR IN WINNABLE AND HOPELESS SEATS, 1935

Winnable Seat	Swing to Lab.	Hopeless Seat	Swing to Lab.
Newcastle East	4·8	Chichester	8·8
Crewe	6·5	The Wirral	9·0
York	7·9	Isle of Wight	14·0
Salford South	8·6	High Wycombe	14·3

Labour, for whatever reason, must have felt frustrated in 1935. Its best results (constituencies such as Sheffield Central) left it just short of victory); its worst results (as in the west Midlands and Newcastle) were in seats that should have fallen. In the jargon of the 1970s, the National Government marginal seats somehow stayed National. No less than 14 seats (including working-class towns such as Warrington, Barrow-in-Furness, East Leyton, East Ham North and South Cardiff) stayed Conservative by under 600 votes. And yet the Western Isles, a seat not even fought by Labour in 1931, went Labour on this occasion. Luck, which had been with Labour in 1929, was very much on the side of the National Government this time.

Luck, however, is not a satisfactory answer. One explanation lay in Labour's inability to attract the middle ground – in particular, the former Liberal vote which had gone Tory in 1931. A few rural Non-conformist seats showed strong Labour swings in 1935, but by and large the Liberal vote either stayed National or stayed at home.[26] Indeed, in some constituencies in 1935 a continued Liberal collapse to the Conservatives was evident. In such seats as Camborne, Dorset East and Mid-Bedfordshire, the result was a better Conservative performance in 1935 than in 1931.[27]

Labour's inability to attract the Liberal vote in 1935 is perhaps one of the most vital parts of the election result. The shrewder political observers at the time recognised this fact. Trevelyan, certainly, was clear as to the reasons for Labour's defeat. He wrote to a colleague, Arthur Shepherd, on 17 November:

> ... the Liberals as an organisation are gone. Roughly one third voted Labour, two thirds Tory. If it had been the other way round, we should have had 50–100 more seats. All goes much, much slower than we hoped! But if I am right in regarding this as the British form of fascism and that this is the worst reaction we shall have, we are less badly off in the future.

As Trevelyan had observed, Labour had tried to fight the election on Socialism. But, as he sadly wrote: 'The middle class are not ready for it or the black-coated workers. Therefore in Sunderland, Darlington, Leeds, Newcastle, the middle class have won. In the mining areas and proletarian London they did not.'

Trevelyan's comments were basically correct. Labour's working-class support was there, but the middle class had yet to be won. In a few Durham mining seats, Labour had increased its percentage vote beyond its 1929 level. This, however, was not true of other working-class strongholds. As Stannage demonstrates, in the 40 constituencies where there was a straight fight between Labour and Conservative in 1929, 1931 and 1935, there was an overall swing of 5·2 per cent to the Conservatives from 1929 to 1935, a swing caused by direct switching rather than differential turn-out.

Nationally, in the 1935 election, turn-out fell to 71 per cent — a decrease of 5 per cent since 1931 and a lower figure than 1929 or 1924. Wet weather, the small field of Liberal candidates, apathy by Conservatives and indeed apathy by Labour voters who thought their party could not win all helped this fall. Turn-out fell most heavily in Birmingham, Wolverhampton and other parts of the west Midlands. Here, there seems an obvious statistical relationship between apathy and a poor Labour vote. Elsewhere, it is clear that many Liberals stayed at home — most noticeably in the mill towns of the West Riding. The few constituencies in which turn-out increased were almost invariably the result of Liberal (or in a few cases S.N.P.) intervention.[28]

Whatever part turn-out played in the election was of little comfort for the dispirited Labour ranks. In their disappointment, however, Labour tended to miss the significance of several good features of the party's performance. In 1935, Labour had become more of a national party than ever before in its history. Its field of 552 candidates was a record. Its spread of support was far more even. In 1935 there were very few constituencies which were either not contested or in which Labour failed to save its deposit. Of the 81 candidates in all who lost their deposits, only 16 were Labour nominees. Forty were Liberals, 9 were I.L.P.-ers, 16 others were Independents and there was a solitary Conservative.[29]

In English borough seats, Labour's only lost deposits were in middle-class Brighton and in the special case of West Wolverhampton.[30] Apart from the I.L.P. strongholds in working-class Glasgow, only in a very few isolated rural backwaters did Labour candidates forfeit their deposits. It was all evidence of Labour support in constituencies where previously Labour candidatures had been mere propaganda exercises.

In this sense, just as the 1920s had seen an age of realignment in the urban areas, with once-safe Liberal seats going Labour, so in the 1930s this process can be seen, in embryo at least, in the rural areas. A variety of rural and suburban seats showed the movement set out in Table 13.4.

TABLE 13.4 MOVEMENT OF PARTY SUPPORT: 1931–45

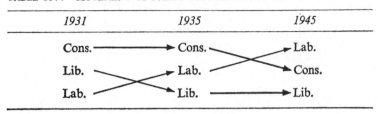

1931	1935	1945
Cons. ⟶	Cons. ⟶	Lab.
Lib. ⟶	Lab. ⟶	Cons.
Lab. ⟶	Lib. ⟶	Lib.

Examples of seats in this category range from Tynemouth in the depressed north-east to Penryn and Falmouth in the south-west. In this sense, in many areas where Labour had been weak in 1929 or 1931, the 1935 results were a marked step forward, even though overshadowed at the time by the party's relative failure nationally.

The verdict of 1935 attracted a variety of explanations. The Conservatives, not surprisingly, stressed that their own record and achievements in office were largely responsible. This was a theme particularly taken up by Stonehaven.[31] Other Conservatives stressed the reassuring role Baldwin had played and argued that Labour's 'wild' policies and campaign, and in particular the proposal to nationalise the banks, had lost votes. Some Conservatives believed the 1935 Budget – and indeed the Jubilee celebrations – had added to the government's prestige.

The explanation that the National Government's record played a large part was shared by some Liberals. The most penetrating Liberal explanation came from Geoffrey Mander, the M.P. for East Wolverhampton. Mander noted that: 'Apart from the failure of the distressed areas, trade *was* better, employment *had* improved . . . the sincerity and broadmindedness of the new leaders was liked and trusted by the British people.'[32]

Labour's own inquest in 1935 was less united on its reasons for lack of success. Both Cripps and Greenwood agreed with Trevelyan that the party had failed to poll the full working-class vote and lamentably failed to win over many Liberals.

But why was this? The right wing of the party attacked the 'silly propaganda' of the Socialist League. Morrison roundly declared that the British people were 'not going to vote in a hurry for a first-class financial crisis'.[33] Morrison shared the general view that the party's base was too narrow to appeal to many Liberals, while even Cole accepted that it had been a grave mistake to campaign with too much emphasis on Socialism.

Virtually all the Labour hierarchy were agreed that lack of leadership had affected the party's performance. Cole declared that the party 'lacked an effective leader more than anything else'. Morrison put the point even more forcefully: '... since 1931 we have not yet evolved a clear leadership ... and the British electorate likes to know the kind of people who are going to govern it.' Certainly, the party lacked anyone equal in electoral appeal and national stature to Baldwin. The se explanations for 1935 rather tended to ignore other shortcomings of the party. Despite much effort, the party's constituency organisation often still left much to be desired. Winnable constituencies lacked even rudimentary offices and organisation.[34] Such cities as Birmingham were hopelessly ill-equipped financially to fight the election – a factor which may help explain the bad Labour result there. The number of full-time agents had declined by 20 per cent compared to 1929 and was even less than in 1924. To make matters worse for Labour, it would appear that shifts in population since the last redistribution also worked in favour of the National Government in areas such as Lancashire. Meanwhile the I.L.P. breakaway from Labour, and the internecine warfare it provoked in such areas as the Clyde, undoubtedly did Labour little good.

All these factors taken together help account for Labour's inability to come remotely near electoral victory in 1935. Fundamental to all this, however, was the fact that very few people saw in Labour a viable alternative to the National Government. This, coupled with Labour's lack of appeal to the mass of moderate ex-Liberal voters, explains the harsh verdict of the electorate.

The verdict of 1935 was never really challenged or disturbed in the last years of the depression. From 1935 to the outbreak of war, in by-elections and in municipal contests, electoral politics maintained a fairly even keel. Although some fascists fought municipal elections (see p. 208), the party did not venture into the parliamentary arena until 1940, when it confirmed itself as the electoral laughing-stock which most people had imagined it to be. Otherwise, two broad trends could be seen. Labour was doing well, but never well enough to secure victory if there had been an immediate General Election. And the Liberals were increasingly becoming an electoral irrelevance.

Between the General Election of 1935 and the outbreak of war in September 1939, the pattern of by-election results was very similar to the results of the 1931–5 period. Labour did well, with many big swings in its favour; but none of the swings was large enough to suggest an overall Labour majority (see Table 13.5). Although Labour gained 13 seats from the government, virtually all had previously been Labour territory.

TABLE 13.5   LABOUR'S BY-ELECTION GAINS, 1935–9

date of by-election	constituency	% swing
18 March, 1936	Dunbartonshire	5·3
6 May, 1936	Peckham	1·5
26 Nov., 1936	Greenock	9·4
29 April, 1937	Wandsworth Central	9·6
13 Oct., 1937	Islington North	7·0
16 Feb., 1938	Ipswich	10·3
6 April, 1938	Fulham West	7·3
5 May, 1938	Lichfield	4·7
7 Nov., 1938	Dartford	4·2
17 May, 1939	Southwark North	7·6
24 May, 1939	Kennington	11·2
1 Aug., 1939	Brecon and Radnor	6·0

Such Labour gains as Wandsworth Central, Ipswich and Kennington (all on swings above 9·5 per cent) were undoubtedly good results. But they were exceptions. The average swing to Labour in the 12 seats it had captured was only 7 per cent. Indeed, after Labour's three victories within four months during the spring of 1938, the tide of Labour's popularity seems definitely to have waned. In a variety of by-elections in late 1938 and early 1939, some very low swings to Labour were recorded.[35] With the exception of an excellent result in Kennington (which showed the highest swing achieved by Labour since the 1935 election) in no seat had Labour achieved a swing of over 6 per cent. Though no doubt the Caerphilly result, with an 8 per cent swing to the Conservatives, was something of a freak, the same could hardly be said of Labour's virtually static share of the vote in Batley and Morley, South Ayrshire and the Aston division of Birmingham. It is a sobering thought, in terms of any 1940 General Election, that in the last three contests before the outbreak of war the average swing to Labour was only 3·7 per cent.

As in the period from 1931 to 1935, the by-elections from 1935 to the outbreak of war gave no encouragement to any of the smaller parties. For differing reasons, no B.U.F. or Communist Party candidates contested any by-elections. A nominee of the British People's

S

Party, H. St J. Philby, fought the Hythe by-election of July 1939, picking up a meagre 576 votes (2·6 per cent of the poll). The few by-elections contested by the S.N.P. also produced only dismal results. In the Dunbartonshire by-election of March 1936, the S.N.P. obtained only 6·2 per cent of the poll, compared to 7·8 per cent at the 1935 General Election and 13·4 per cent in the March 1932 by-election. In June 1937, in a by-election in the safely Conservative Hillhead division of Glasgow, the party managed only 9 per cent. A rather different right-wing candidate fought the Farnham by-election of March 1937; an Independent Conservative, supported by an obscure organisation called the Liberty Restoration League, took 7·5 per cent of the vote in an ultra-safe Conservative stronghold. Another Independent Conservative, with strong support from the east Yorkshire executive of the National Farmers' Union, fought the Holderness by-election of February 1939. Opposing the government's agricultural policy, in a strongly farming constituency he picked up 13·5 per cent of the votes cast.

The two most spectacular examples of Conservative rebels were, of course, to be found in Kinross and West Perthshire, and Cheltenham. Otherwise, both at the time and from historians, most attention centred on the by-elections in Bridgwater and Oxford. In addition to these two well-known contests, another Popular Front candidate, Carritt, fighting the Abbey division of Westminster took 32·6 per cent of the poll.

Labour's by-election performance from 1935 to 1939 was closely mirrored in the municipal election results. In November 1935, as we have seen, Labour slipped slightly from their high-water mark of 1933–4. By November 1936 the tide was flowing much more strongly against them. Labour, having to defend its 1933 gains, suffered a net loss of 81 seats (47 gained, 128 lost) in 1936. Conservatives (and their independent allies) secured a net gain of 81, while the Liberals, even with Labour on the defensive, still suffered a small net loss.

By November 1937, the turnover of seats had settled after the landslide victories of the early 1930s. Indeed, the municipal elections of 1937, which appeared to suggest a slight Labour setback, were in fact distorted by a variety of cross-currents. While the Conservatives secured a net gain of 36 seats (71 gains, 35 losses), Labour had 67 gains and 72 losses. The key here was the Liberals, whose net loss of 28 was almost entirely to Labour. In addition, Labour's performance appeared worse because of a variety of reverses for local reasons in Merseyside.

Very similar national results occurred in November 1938, the last municipal elections before 1945. Labour again lost a little ground to the Conservatives, who secured a net gain of some 20 seats. Once again, Liverpool and parts of Lancashire made Labour's reverse appear worse than it really was. After 1938, Labour slipped back from its position as largest single party in Burnley, Bristol, Hull and Sunderland, but gained a prize with the capture of Gateshead.

If Labour's electoral record after 1935 was relatively unexciting, for the Liberals the period was one of almost unrelieved despair. The results of the 1935 election had been additional proof, not only of the fading popular support for the Liberals, but of the almost total decay into which constituency organisation had fallen. Between 1931 and 1935 such Liberal Associations as had survived until then began to fall apart. The few organisations still active had either defected to the Liberal Nationals or were in a state of suspended animation, waiting for a lead that never came.

The disastrous results of 1935 were followed almost immediately by a by-election humiliation in Ross and Cromarty. In a Highland seat with a strong Liberal tradition, the party could poll only 4 per cent of the votes cast. This shattering result at last prompted the Liberals to attempt to put their house in order. A Liberal Reorganisation Commission (under Lord Meston) was appointed. Despite several important reforms at the top, the Meston report totally failed to revive the party at the grassroots.

There was no obvious sign of a Liberal recovery, either in by-elections or municipal elections. In the first twelve by-elections following the party's disaster in Ross and Cromarty, no Liberal candidates appeared. However, after mid-1937, the by-election scene gradually became a little more cheerful. Liberals did well, although not well enough for victory in the St Ives contest on 30 June, 1937. Two weeks later, in the rural North Dorset division, the party also polled well. But these results were unrepresentative. During 1938, in the eighteen by-elections which occurred that year, only two Liberal candidates appeared. Meanwhile, the depleted ranks of the parliamentary Liberal Party suffered two further defections to the Liberal Nationals.

This breakdown of the party's fighting spirit, at Westminster and in the constituencies, was also reflected in local elections. For after 1935, the visible disintegration of the party at its municipal grassroots continued unabated. This can be seen, both in candidates fielded and seats won, in Table 13.6.

TABLE 13.6   DECLINE OF THE LIBERAL PARTY, 1935–8

	sample	won by Libs.	%
1935	936	94	10·0
1936	1,342	103	7·7
1937	1,084	62	5·7
1938	1,185	85	7·2

In 1931, one in seven council seats had been won by a Liberal. Less than a decade later, this figure had been halved to a mere 7 per cent. In each year, the party suffered a net loss of seats. Nowhere was the decline of the old Liberal Party during the thirties more clearly to be seen than in the radical boroughs of the Midlands. In these Midland towns, Liberal representation had still been healthy in 1930.

By the end of the decade, a transformation had occurred: by 1938, Liberal strength had fallen to 30 out of a total of 240 council seats. Labour had supplanted the Conservatives with the largest aggregate total, having made heavy gains at Coventry (winning control in 1937) and having broken Liberal strength in Leicester, Nottingham and Northampton. Except in Coventry, the Conservatives had also improved their position. The only losers had been the hapless Liberals.

In retrospect, the decade after 1930 had thus seen a continuous and almost uninterrupted Liberal decline in municipal elections. By 1938, except in an occasional stronghold in Yorkshire and Lancashire, the party had almost ceased to be represented on many borough councils; the municipal elections of November 1945, with their sweeping Labour gains, finally ended what remained of the old Liberal Party.

Though the electoral politics of the 1930s showed important changes and realignments, it is paradoxical that in many ways the electoral atmosphere of the decade was so undramatic. In the ballot boxes, at least, there was little evidence that the nation was in the throes of the greatest slump of the century. The slump, far from producing an electoral revolution, failed even to bring to power a Labour Government, though it had destroyed one. The British electoral tradition survived 1931. Maybe the myths of the thirties cast their shadow on voting behaviour after 1945; maybe, also, the thirties saw Labour consolidate its position as the only alternative to the Conservatives. But these were scant comfort for a party in office for only 25 months in the 26 years after 1918.

XIV

The Revolution That Never Was

The onset of mass unemployment seemed to many observers to threaten a period of acute instability in British political life, and even a complete breakdown of the traditional procedures of parliamentary government. The growth of extremist parties, the spread of violent demonstrations, and the helplessness of politicians in the face of the world slump seemed portents of fundamental changes in the character of politics and society. Harold Macmillan, for example, considered that after 1931, 'Something like a revolutionary situation had developed' in Britain.[1] For Stafford Cripps, mass unemployment opened a period in which 'the one thing that is not inevitable now is gradualness'.[2] John Strachey contemplated the need to wield totalitarian power in the event of a breakdown of the political system, while Mosley and the B.U.F. waited for an opportunity to restore order in the event of a communist revolution.[3] For Marxists, the great depression was clearly the 'final crisis' of capitalism. Harry Pollitt wrote in 1933 that 'we are moving to a new round of wars and proletarian revolutions, in which the capitalists and the working class are both striving to find a solution of the crisis, each in their own class interests.'[4]

These apocalyptic prophecies were proved false by events. Britain emerged from the depression with remarkably little change in the nature of her political institutions and the tenor of her public life. Although even modern historians have been tempted to characterise the 1930s as a decade when 'men of moderate political opinions, or of none, began to talk the language of revolutionary violence,' the most significant feature of the decade was the immobility of the great majority of the electorate in the face of the slump.[5] Thus there was no British New Deal, no wholesale rejection of parliamentary democracy, and no mass backing for the parties of the extreme left or right. Attempts to generate extra-parliamentary support by demonstra-

tions and marches were also largely ineffective and even counter-
productive when judged by the performance of the N.U.W.M. and
the B.U.F. Thus we return to the central question of British politics
in the thirties, not why there was so much discontent with the
political system, but why there was so little.

It is often claimed that the depression affected Britain less severely
than other countries. This has been used as an argument for the
failure of Britain to adopt more radical economic policies and for its
ability to survive the challenge of political extremism. Superficially,
this view seems to be borne out by a comparison of the total number
of unemployed in the major industrialised countries during the worst
phase of the depression. Between 1929 and 1932 the total number of
unemployed in the advanced industrial countries rose from around
5 million to almost 25 million.[6] In terms of the absolute number of
unemployed, Britain appears to have escaped relatively lightly
compared with the United States and Germany. The peak year of
unemployment in Britain was 1932, when almost 3 million insured
workers were out of work. In the United States, on the other hand,
there were 16 million people out of work by 1933 and over 6 million
in Germany by 1932. But these are absolute figures and bear no
relation to the size of the workforce in the respective countries. As a
percentage of the total labour force, the British experience of unemployment does not seem to have been very much different from
that of her two major industrial rivals, especially when it is considered
that both the United States and Germany had a high proportion of
their labour force in agriculture, where there was considerable concealed unemployment and under-employment.[7] Britain also had
large groups of workers who were not represented in the official
unemployment figures, so that the peak total number of unemployed
was probably nearer 4 million than 3 million. Thus Britain, Germany
and the United States had roughly comparable rates of unemployment when judged as a percentage of the total labour force. Each
country had three years when more than a fifth of the working
population was out of a job.

Britain had a *different* experience of unemployment from other
countries, but this is not to say that it was any the less painful. The
country had suffered from chronic unemployment in the heavy
industries almost since the end of the First World War and had
failed to share in the industrial boom of the middle and late twenties
to the same extent as her major rivals, Germany and the United
States. After 1929, the problem of unemployment was felt most

heavily in areas which had been grappling with it for almost a decade. Thus unemployment was not a new problem in the depressed areas, but rather an intensification of an existing one. As Goronwy Rees has argued: 'If Britain suffered less than other industrialised countries from the shock of the world economic depression, it was because depression was already a permanent feature of her economy.'[8] Unemployment proved a more persistent problem in Britain during the inter-war period than elsewhere and this conditioned her experience of the great slump after 1929. A corollary of this was that the onset of mass unemployment was less sudden in Britain than in a country such as the United States, which moved rapidly from boom to slump in the space of two years. In Britain, unemployment rose steadily to its peak in 1932–3 from an already high level in 1929. In the United States, unemployment rose within one year, 1931, from four million to ten million. Germany too, experienced a sharper descent into deep depression after the recovery of the late twenties. Thus it could be argued that it was less the absolute level of unemployment which created political upheaval, than the rapidity of its onset.

Britain's experience of unemployment was not necessarily more favourable, however, in spite of its slightly lower percentage of unemployed at the trough of the depression. The structural unemployment which affected Britain's staple industries meant that there was greater build-up in the level of unemployment in Britain's depressed areas than could be found in other countries. Unemployment in Germany, for example, was more evenly spread and the variations between regions and industries were less marked than in Britain. The contrast in Britain between the depressed areas and the more prosperous regions was sharper than in many other countries. Differences in economic structure make it difficult to make direct comparisons between the impact of the depression on the major industrial countries. The United States, Germany and France each retained a large agricultural sector. Germany had almost 40 per cent of its labour force in agriculture and France registered only 347,000 unemployed workers in 1931 because of a relatively small industrial base.[9] Moreover, there was no direct trade-off between political upheaval and the crude rate of unemployment. France suffered severely from political instability in spite of her relatively low rate of unemployment. None the less, it is clear that Britain cannot be regarded as having escaped lightly from the depression. There were aspects of her experience which were worse than that of other countries when measured in terms of regional unemployment rates. As with other countries, however, the worst of the depression was comparatively short-lived. Britain began to experience recovery from 1933–4 and unemployment drifted steadily down from that time. Although there was a slight upturn in unemployment in 1938 and still a million out of work in the first year of the war, mainly concentrated in the depressed areas, the economy began to show signs of growth in several sectors by the mid-1930s. This was clear to most observers; in 1938 G. D. H. Cole pronounced that, 'The "final crisis" is again put off, as it has been put off many times before in the course of the past century.'[10]

Moreover, as we have argued earlier, the slump had more than one face. While large pockets of poverty and hardship remained, not least among the unemployed, the great majority of the population was beginning to feel some significant improvement in living standards by the end of the thirties. By 1939 the average family was better off, healthier, and better housed than it had been in 1929, and had at its command a wider range of amenities and recreation than ever before. For some sections of the middle classes the thirties marked the first taste of affluence, seen in the boom in house ownership, the motoring revolution, the growth of consumer industries, and the development of the service sector of the economy. Even for working-class families standards of comfort improved during the depression. As a recent writer has commented:

> Statistics fail to take full account of the differences made by electricity instead of candles, and gas cookers instead of coal or coke ranges, as standard equipment in working class homes; of improved housing, including indoor water and sanitation; or of radio, the cinema and newspapers within almost everybody's reach.[11]

This improvement in living standards was recognised by social historians, who have noted the rise of the 'blackcoated workers' and the development of the services sector to account for almost half the insured population. Cole and Postgate highlighted the rise of investment in the Building Societies as 'an immensely significant social phenomenon', giving a large section of the middle and working classes a vested interest and sense of ownership which gave British society a fundamental stability.[12] This was the context in which political extremism had to operate, in a period of rising living standards for those in work and recovery in the new industries and revival in the old staples by the mid-1930s.

The major qualification to this picture of the 1930s as an era in which greater economic and social progress was achieved than is often recognised, was the high level of unemployment. It was the problem of the unemployed which gave the period its unique character and provided contemporaries with greatest concern for the stability of the political system. It is therefore upon the reactions of the unemployed themselves that it is necessary to focus if we are to understand the relative stability of Britain in the thirties. The way in which the unemployed perceived their situation is of crucial importance. Both electorally and in terms of allegiance to extremist parties or violent demonstrations, the unemployed showed a remarkable degree of passivity. It is clear from almost every report from the distressed areas that the most common reaction to unemployment was apathy and fatalism. Wal Hannington himself suggested this as one of the primary reasons for the failure of the N.U.W.M.[13] Even in South Wales, probably the most militant area during the thirties, the Carnegie Trust found that in a survey of 1,490 unemployed youths only 20 belonged to any political party, the highest percentage being 3 per cent in the Cardiff area. They reported:

> The overwhelming majority of the men had no political convictions whatsoever. When asked why, they invariably replied, 'What does it matter?' ... It was not so much a 'plague on all your parties' as a 'plague on all your Politics.' It has, perhaps, been assumed too readily by some that because men are unemployed, their natural state of want and discontent must express itself in some revolutionary attitude. It cannot be reiterated too often that unemployment is not an active state; its keynote is boredom—a continuous sense of boredom.[14]

This was also emphasised by George Orwell as the overriding characteristic of the unemployed in Wigan, 'the frightful feeling of impotence and despair which is almost the worst evil of unemployment'; and it was recognised by several left-wing writers other than Wal Hannington.[15] Allen Hutt claimed that 'degradation' and demoralisation had affected even the most militant districts in Britain.[16] Comments from almost every shade of political opinion and from quite impartial investigators confirmed that the overwhelming majority of the unemployed had little interest in political activism. Fatalism, depression and apathy were far commoner among the unemployed than participation in politics. The American, E. W. Bakke, observed of the unemployed in Greenwich, 'the talk of revolution is conspicuous by its absence.'[17]

Bakke was able to evaluate the behaviour of the unemployed in Greenwich during the 1931 General Election. Political meetings, he observed, including those of the communists, concentrated on bread-and-butter issues. The only major manifestation of 'idealism' that he found was in favour of the Conservatives as the 'saviours of the country'. He found that Conservatism made a strong appeal to working men who provided 'some of the most immovable Conservatives' he encountered. On the question of political response to unemployment, he wrote: 'Political action does not rank high among the tactics adopted by the unemployed as a means of solving their problems. In view of the limited part played by politics in the life of the unemployed this is not surprising.' He found that in the field of political activity there was little difference between the employed and unemployed workers. If anything, the unemployed were more fatalistic and difficult to recruit to active politics than those in work.[18] The Pilgrim Trust also concluded from their investigations of the long-unemployed that there was relatively little revolutionary feeling. Rather, they commented upon the absence of a sense of grievance found among groups such as the Durham miners; on the contrary, they were impressed by the 'determination to make the best of things'.[19] Investigations of the psychological response to unemployment suggested that violent feelings and bitterness were intermittent and usually short-lived. Only a minority failed to adjust to unemployment and turned to radical politics rather than settling down to life on the dole.

Depression and unemployment was a familiar condition to thousands of people by the early 1930s. It has been argued convincingly that one reason why the unemployed failed to react was that they could see no appropriate action to take in the face of a crisis which seemed almost beyond human control and for which no-one seemed to have an obvious answer.[20] In conditions where radical voices were suspect and the traditional leaders of organised labour were as helpless in the face of the depression as the National Government, there was little incentive to revolt. This suggests that the perceptions of the unemployed were essentially conditioned by reference to their fellow unemployed and that there was far less ill-feeling and resentment than there would have been if the unemployed had felt themselves to be starving in the midst of plenty. Arguably, by the late 1930s this was what the unemployed were doing, if national comparisons were made. Newspapers of the thirties have a striking air of paradox about them, with pages packed with advertisements for sales and special offers, side by side with accounts of unemployed demonstrations. Allen Hutt drew a sharp comparison in his account of depressed Lancashire, contrasting the poverty of people reduced to putting blank discs in the gas meter, while in Blackpool was being built the biggest and most luxurious hotel in Britain with 2,500 bedrooms (each with telephone and wireless), 3,000 telephones, a ballroom a third of an acre in size, and a garage for 500 cars.[21] Such contrasts were not lost on Orwell, who wrote of the 'queer spectacle of modern electrical science showering miracles upon people with empty bellies'.[22] But by and large the unemployed made their comparisons among themselves, not with the burgeoning affluence of suburban England or the conspicuous consumption of London high society. Orwell too made the comparison between the bitterness and 'dumb amazement' of the unemployed of the 1920s, who felt unemployment as a profound personal disaster, and Wigan in 1936 where he found that the very scale of the depression and its longevity had contributed to a new atttitude:

> In the back streets of Wigan and Barnsley I saw every kind of privation, but I probably saw much less *conscious* misery than I should have seen ten years ago. The people have at any rate grasped that unemployment is a thing they cannot help. It is not only Alf Smith who is out of work now; Bert Jones is out of work as well, and both of them have been 'out' for years. It makes a great difference when things are the same for everybody.[23]

In a way the very concentration of the unemployment problem in the depressed areas had the paradoxical effect of acting as a check upon expressions of violent discontent. Significantly, the Pilgrim Trust investigators found that it was in the more prosperous towns that there was a much greater propensity to join the Unemployed Club and mention the National Unemployed Workers' Movement.[24]

The dole was widely regarded as a palliative to discontent among the unemployed. Writers with experience of conditions before the introduction of unemployment insurance were convinced that it had transformed the situation. One of the earliest reports on unemployment between the wars commented upon the absence of political unrest resulting from unemployment compared with the depressions prior to 1914. This was attributed to 'the success of the relief measures in meeting essential needs for food, and in giving relatively most assistance to the irregularly employed and low-paid workers who can most easily be collected into a mob'.[25] Bakke wrote of his experiences in Greenwich:

> There is evidence that the Scheme [unemployment insurance] has alleviated the worst physical effects of unemployment. It has kept the diet from falling to unhealthy levels; it has kept the workers from falling in arrears on their rent; it has made it unnecessary to dispose of home furnishings to the extent which would have been necessary without it; it has to some extent made it possible for men and women to keep up their associations with their fellows longer; it has kept unrest at a minimum, the political agitation of Communists failing to flourish amongst those secure in the knowledge that the State is assisting them to help themselves.[26]

For Bakke, one of the most vital features of the dole was that it prevented the unemployed becoming a caste apart. He believed that the comparative security provided by the social services had prevented them from becoming more conscious of having interests as unemployed different from workers in general. The dole provided a living, however basic or humiliating its receipt might be. Indeed, as several studies showed, many of the unemployed were better off than they had been on low or irregular earnings. Although the dole was often desperately near the margin of adequacy and sometimes below, it was usually sufficient to keep people from desperation and the political consequences that might have resulted.[27]

The dole also acted indirectly in another way to damp down discontent. For it was upon the administration and levels of relief that discontent tended to focus rather than upon the more fundamental policies of the government, so that the dole acted as a sort of outwork of government policy upon which the organised sections of the unemployed expended most of their efforts. Agitation on behalf of the unemployed in the thirties was directed at the introduction of changes in the administration of unemployment relief, as in the demonstrations against the means test in 1931–2 and against the Unemployment Assistance Board proposals of 1934–5. The former became the focus of the N.U.W.M.'s campaign of hunger marches and demonstrations, while the latter provoked the greatest explosion of popular anger seen in the thirties. Indeed, the embroilment of the

N.U.W.M. in agitation against the means test and in fighting individual cases became so great that it was criticised by Comintern for ignoring the overall objectives of becoming a mass movement and becoming involved in purely tactical battles. In 1934–5 the issue of new relief scales provided for the government an important barometer of the discontent aroused both among the unemployed and, perhaps even more important, among significant sections of public opinion inside and outside Westminster. The government very wisely decided to back down and introduce a standstill order. A more humane approach to the operation of unemployment relief was the only policy many people had to offer. In the absence of a clear alternative to the policy being pursued by the National Government, many members of the Labour Party and the T.U.C. concentrated their political energies upon the issues of unemployment relief, rather than a major restructuring of the National Government's economic priorities.[28]

A further inhibition to widespread protest was the way the dole was administered. In the most critical phase of the depression, the local Public Assistance Committee was the organisation with which the unemployed had most frequently come into contact. It was composed of local councillors and a number of co-opted members. The P.A.C.s were made responsible for administering the means test from 1931.

Thus in most towns unemployment relief was handled by local councillors and community leaders. In Labour-controlled districts, they were often Labour councillors or trade union officials. It was these people who had to operate the means test and assess appropriate levels of relief. If they were too generous, or failed to meet the requirements of Whitehall, they faced being substituted by an official appointed by the government. Most Labour and trade union people involved in administering the means test reasoned that they could at least try to mitigate its operation by staying on. Even left-wing critics were forced to admit that the local P.A.C. official in many areas was frequently a hard-pressed Labour councillor doing his or her best to operate the means test in as humane a way as possible.[29] Thus the traditional leaders of working-class areas were forced to carry out some of the most unpopular aspects of the dole, ensuring a powerful element of social control. There was little point in the rank and file unemployed revolting against their local leaders who were doing as much as they could for them in difficult circumstances.

An additional handicap to the unemployed as a political force was their geographical isolation, hidden away in the closed communities of the Welsh valleys or the pit villages of Co. Durham. Once the trough of the depression was past, after 1933, the problem of long-term heavy unemployment was concentrated, as it had been before 1929, in the regions of the first industrial revolution, the home of Britain's old staple industries, far from the prosperous suburbs and growing industrial estates of the south-east and the Midlands. As J. B. Priestley had found in his *English Journey* in 1934, there were several nations, of which the England of depressed industries and mass unemployment was only one. There were whole communities which had been left virtually untouched by the depression and many for which the years 1930–2 had been only a temporary interruption to steadily rising prosperity. Thus a social survey of Oxford in the late 1930s could dismiss the problem of unemployment as being 'almost negligible'.[30] The unemployed were effectively cut off from the mainstream of public opinion for most of the thirties. The hunger marches were an attempt to break out of this isolation and bring the plight of the depressed areas to the attention of a wider public and of parliament, but initially these attempts were diffused by the widespread suspicion of the motives of the N.U.W.M. as organisers of these demonstrations. Cole and Postgate expressed this isolation when they commented:

> What was the use of rioting in South Wales, or of making orderly demonstrations? Who would take notice of them? And when the unemployed of the distressed districts tried 'hunger marching' on London the leaders of Trade Unionism and of the Labour Party disavowed them, and the police stood ready, at the Government's orders, to prevent them making 'scenes'.[31]

For most of the 1930s unemployment was a regional and provincial problem, which impinged only intermittently upon the general mass of public opinion. This was one reason why the hunger marches had such an impact upon popular consciousness, representing for the inhabitants of more prosperous parts of Britain almost the sole evidence of conditions in the depressed areas. In spite of this, however, the unemployed became a new kind of 'submerged tenth', obvious enough if they were sought out, but more often than not ignored. The depressed English regions were alien enough for many writers, still more so the depressed areas of South Wales, Scotland and Northern Ireland.

It is easy in an age accustomed to instant news coverage and intensive documentary journalism, through the press and television, to assume that the problems of mass unemployment were constantly in the mind of the average Briton in the 1930s, or if not in the mind, at least the staple fare of social comment. But the surprising thing about the 'dole literature' of the middle and late 1930s is that so much of it came out when the worst of the slump was over: Orwell's classic, *The Road to Wigan Pier*, in 1937; Ellen Wilkinson's *The Town that was Murdered* in 1939; The Pilgrim Trust's *Men Without Work* in 1938; and the Carnegie Trust's *Disinherited Youth* in 1943. There were exceptions, but it was the middle and late 1930s which saw the major wave of documentary literature about the condition of Britain, particularly about unemployment. In part this was a response to the prolongation of the slump in the depressed areas, but it also reflected the increasing output of books through book clubs, especially the Left Book Club founded in 1936, and the first paperbacks, produced in 1935, bringing serious social comment to a much wider audience. Linked, however, with the development of the Left Book Club was the rise of unemployment as a political issue by the mid-1930s and the recovery of the fortunes of the Labour Party. A more determined attack, particularly from the Left, upon the survival of unemployment and the condition of the depressed areas began to make itself felt. Even so, it was a relatively muted voice, only one part of an attack which centred increasingly upon appeasement. Thus at the time when unemployment seemed to be becoming a major issue, it was steadily overshadowed by the problems of the rise of fascism.

The failure of extremist movements was one of the most revealing aspects of the thirties and is confirmed by the electoral evidence of the decade. The most remarkable feature of the period was the relative absence of movement by the electorate. The age of mass unemployment had failed to register a decisive impact upon the political structure of the country in terms of allegiance to extremist parties, changed voting patterns, or the development of extra-parliamentary movements. It did leave a legacy of radicalism and alienation in some intellectual circles, but the great majority of the electorate retained their traditional political allegiances. When McKenzie and Silver investigated political attitudes in the post-war period, they were struck by the absence of a 'depression generation'. They concluded that there 'is no evidence that the economic distress of that decade [the 1930s] created a political generation in the working class'.[32]

What many of the more radical voices, especially those of the Left, failed to appreciate was the conservatism of British society. Even in the face of the slump, Britain remained a relatively cohesive and insular society in which there were still a large number of shared assumptions. Class divisions might exist, but were not effectively exploited in the political arena in such a way as to disturb the more fundamental unifying aspects of British society. Orwell referred to this 'emotional unity', commenting that a foreign observer 'sees only the huge inequality of wealth, the unfair electoral system, the governing-class control of the press, the radio and education. But this ignores the considerable agreement that does unfortunately exist between the leaders and the led.'[33]

The survival of popular regard for the monarchy was one aspect of this conservatism. George V was a popular monarch; Muggeridge claimed that he was a figure of 'adulation ... if anything more prevalent among the lower than the upper classes'.[34] Significantly, the Silver Jubilee in 1935 generated widespread enthusiasm. Even more striking was the regard in which Edward VIII was held. His visit to South Wales—just before the abdication crisis broke—and his famous comment that 'something must be done' as he toured a derelict steelworks at Dowlais secured him a place in the affections of large numbers of people, employed and unemployed. In Brynmawr, a chronically depressed mining town, the longest minute in the local council records during the thirties was a discussion of the action they should take for the visit of the King. Eventually a decision was taken to hang a banner over the road inscribed with the words, 'We need your help.' This popular appeal of the 'good Prince' was not dispelled with the abdication. The story of the King's visit, his refusal to stick to the official route and his attempts to meet ordinary people, became a folk legend.[35]

A variety of factors, ideological, organisational and sociological, help explain why the Labour Party was able to weather the depression successfully. As was seen earlier, the party was not broken by the 1931 election; indeed it polled more votes in 1931 than in 1923 when it formed its first administration. Though the Labour Party lost most of its seats and many of its leading figures, it did not lose its rank and file. In a discussion of the political allegiances of the miners in Nantyglo and Blaina, one writer concluded:

> Support for the Labour Party is therefore based mainly on certain concrete advantages obtained in the past and consequent

expectations of more in the future ... and on tradition and the view that the Labour leaders are experienced and know what the people want.[36]

Thus the party was down, but not out. The 1932 municipal elections restored much-needed morale and set the party on the road to recovery.

Although the party lacked finance in the 1930s, it lacked neither candidates nor party workers. Indeed, party organisation flourished both in the constituencies and in the wards. Each municipal contest could be planned in minute detail and carried out by scores of enthusiastic volunteers. Local elections in the thirties provided an important social function as well as a political test. For a few unemployed, canvassing, addressing envelopes and attending to the chores of ward activities acted as a release from the boredom and frustration of unemployment. Perhaps even more important, it brought them into the company of others in a similar plight but fighting the same political battles. Not just election campaigns, but the social meetings of a constituency Labour Party's men's and women's sections provided a social base which helped keep both the party and its rank and file together.

There was a further reason why Labour's supporters remained loyal. For in its personnel and activists, Labour was very close in many areas to the unemployed. In an important study of the northeast, one recent article noted that:

> in South Shields the Labour councillors were predominantly a mixture of miners and shipyard workers, trade unionists known and trusted by their workmates, whereas those councillors who stood as Moderates or Independents were businessmen and other white-collar workers reputedly unsympathetic toward the unemployed.[37]

A further factor would appear to be that, at local level, Labour fought not only on such basic bread-and-butter issues as public health, housing and the means test, but was quick to enact its policies once in control of the council. In Jarrow, where control of the council was secured in 1936, a massive slum clearance programme was immediately put into operation. Similar promises were fulfilled in South Shields after 1937.

In addition, despite the 'betrayal' of such figures as MacDonald and Thomas, by 1931 Labour's traditions in the main industrial

T

areas were sufficiently deep-rooted for the rank and file to stick loyally to the party. A further factor here, most notably in such areas as the north-east, was Labour's deep links with the religious traditions of an area. As a recent study of the Durham coalfield has observed, religious belief may well have helped the parliamentary Labour Party by acting as a strong barrier against the acceptance of militant (and atheistic) communist ideas. To this extent, the strongly entrenched Catholicism of such depressed areas as Jarrow, with its teaching that unemployment was a cross that had to be borne, produced an attitude of passive acquiescence – not radical action. The rabid anti-communism of many local party organisers, together with the party's determinedly hard line on association with extremist groups, in itself helped to cement Labour support; by forcing a choice between membership of the Labour Party and working with the C.P. or one of its so-called 'front organisations', this uncompromising attitude reduced the communists to a minority position. The same basic factors that prevented communists securing Labour's left wing no doubt also affected the I.L.P. As Judith Green has written:

This same attitude prevailed generally in connection with the disaffiliation of the I.L.P., which, while creating many serious personal dilemmas, did not deplete the Labour Party ranks to any great extent. It could be maintained that the I.L.P. affair was not so much 'a split, but a going out'; although the I.L.P. had been very strong in the northern area, by 1931 its influence was dwindling substantially, and there was a vague resentment against its militant parliamentary group as 'splitters' in a situation where it seemed to many of paramount importance to present a united front.[38]

Writing in 1937, G. D. H. Cole recognised that the Labour Party's fortunes rested upon the relationship with trade unionism. Large areas of the country were denied to Labour in the 1935 General Election. In southern England, Labour captured only one seat outside Greater London, in the coalfield area of the Forest of Dean. Cole recognised that many poorer voters still voted Conservative and that many of the voters in the new industrial and suburban areas had failed to come over to Labour. Labour could rely, however, on the trade unionism of the old industrial areas to bring out the Labour vote. These were, in Cole's phrase, 'an unbroken power'. The Labour Party was still in these areas regarded as a trade union party and this gave it its residual strength. Here the Labour Party was, with some qualifications, the working-class party.[39] There were, however, important regional differences. South Wales and parts of Scotland remained more radical in their politics than other industrial areas. Lancashire retained a deviant pattern among the older industrial areas, where the Labour Party only took 28 seats in 1935 against 40 in 1929. The north-east, too, retained distinctive features, with strong Conservative support in many areas, including some of those hardest-hit by unemployment. The Labour Party thus retained a class allegiance, but it was also one conditioned by the regional variations of British politics.

Although the trade unions were faced by a falling membership in the years between 1926 and 1933, the fall was gradual rather than catastrophic. In 1933 the T.U.C. still had 4,392,000 members and during the rest of the decade staged a revival which gave it 6,298,000 in 1939.[40] The early 1930s were clearly difficult years for many unions. Falling membership, weak finances and unemployment produced a period of defensive rather than aggressive policies. Thus the reaction to the onset of mass unemployment from 1929 to 1932 was marked by fewer strikes than the periods of intense militancy after the First World War. Many unions were unable to finance prolonged strike action and only began to regain their strength in the years after 1934. Significantly, the counter-attack on company unionism, new styles of working and pay cuts came with the revival of union membership. The middle and late 1930s saw a rise in the number of stoppages, as shown in Table 14.1.

TABLE 14.1   NUMBER OF STOPPAGES COMMENCING EACH YEAR[41]

year	stoppages	year	stoppages
1929	431	1935	553
1930	422	1936	818
1931	420	1937	1,129
1932	389	1938	875
1933	357	1939	940
1934	471		

The thirties were a period of consolidation for most unions, halting and reversing the decline in their fortunes which the General Strike and the world depression had brought about. Rather than becoming especially militant, the majority of unions concentrated on steady improvements in rates of pay and conditions of work. The large general unions built up membership in a great variety of industries. Although communists were sometimes able to take advantage of the failure of unions to establish themselves in some of the newer industries, such as the car plants of London and the Midlands, or the remoteness of the leadership of the general unions, the leadership of most unions was moderate or right-wing in inclination. Bevin, for example, expelled communist-influenced rank and file leaders of the London busmen from the Transport and General Workers' Union. The General and Municipal Workers also banned communists from election to office in the union. The T.U.C. remained firmly in the control of right-wing unionists who exerted considerable influence over the Labour Party in the years after 1931. Through the National Joint Council, the T.U.C. played a vital part in shaping Labour's foreign and domestic policy.[42]

Thus the decade saw the strengthening of links between the T.U.C. and the Labour Party and their continued command of the allegiance of large sections of the working classes. Indeed, one of the most remarkable features of the decade was the continued loyalty of Labour voters at a time when the party had little hope of parliamentary victory and few new policies to offer to combat unemployment. For a party which could only count upon some of these supporters as relatively recent converts obtained in the years since 1918, this was a considerable feat. But it was the Conservatives who were the most successful political party of the decade, taking a major share of the rapidly dwindling Liberal vote at the polls.[43] Their ability to maintain a stable administration in a period of uncertainty was at once their greatest achievement and their greatest strength. Although its subsequent reputation was to be overshadowed by failures in foreign policy and its inability to produce a solution to unemployment, there were many commentators who were prepared to pay the National Government grudging compliments by the end of the decade. Orwell wrote of it that 'it is almost certain that between 1931 and 1940 the National Government represented the will of the mass of the people'. Nor was this a solitary opinion, for as G. D. H. Cole commented in 1938:

I do not at all like the way Great Britain is governed. But the very slowness of the Labour Party's electoral progress is a sign that, in the matters which most closely touch the everyday lives of the electorate, it is not governed without a good deal of skill. Tory spokesmen are not talking sheer nonsense when

they claim that the National Government has pu
Britain through the greatest depression in history.

There is little evidence that a General Election in 1939 or 1940
would have brought the Labour Party to power. The decisive period
in Labour's road to 1945 lay in the years of the wartime coalition
and the experience of the 'People's War'.[44] There is evidence, however, that apart from the discrediting of the Conservatives as the
party of appeasement as a result of the failures of the early years of
the war, there was an indirect legacy of the 1930s which aided
Labour's rise to power. The findings of the social investigators about
the survival of poverty and other social problems focused attention
upon the way in which many social problems could be alleviated by
planning and greater state intervention. Writers such as Rowntree
pointed the way to improving the social condition of Britain by
ameliorative reform. Child poverty could be cured by family allowances; ill-health by the provision of free school meals and milk;
the problems of the slums by rehousing in new estates. Even without
the issue of unemployment, the social inquiries were diagnosing
social problems and their solutions so precisely that all that was
required was the effort of will on the part of government to put them
into practice. Along with the findings of pressure groups such as
Political and Economic Planning and the Next Five Years group, a
consensus on social questions was emerging during the thirties which
found expression in books such as Harold Macmillan's *The Middle
Way*, published in 1938. Agreement on the need for social reform, a
planned economy and full employment was one of the most significant developments of the decade. Many of the most powerful minds
of the period spent the so-called 'wasted years' producing the blue-
prints for a new era in British social policy.[45]

But the mythology of the 1930s as the 'terrible years' also had
something to contribute. The writings of the most bitter critics
prevented any sense of complacency and added a missionary fervour
which the blander utterances of middle opinion sometimes lacked.
They helped to ensure that no future government would easily
allow unemployment on the scale which had been experienced during
the thirties. The sense of waste and degradation involved in mass
unemployment and depicted in the literature of the day deeply
affected the attitudes of an entire generation. A feeling of 'Never
Again!' conditioned the shaping of wartime and post-war policy. As
a recent historian of the wartime coalition has written: 'The con-

ᴜtion of Britain between the wars, above all the phenomenon of mass unemployment, had profoundly disturbed the public-spirited business or professional person. Economic inefficiency and human deprivation spurred on both the technocrat and the social idealist.'[46]

The 1930s thus had a crucial impact upon the society which emerged from the Second World War. The legacy of bitterness and suffering caused by mass unemployment helped to spur the creation of the Welfare State. For others, however, the 1930s had seen the dawn of affluence which, though interrupted by the austerities of the 1940s was soon to reappear in the post-war world. Both of these forces played a vital part in the peaceful revolution which transformed British society in the middle years of the twentieth century.

Statistical Appendix

TABLE A1   INDEX OF NATIONAL INCOME AT 1900 PRICES (1900 = 100)

	national income	income per head
1925–6	117·9	107·5
1927–9	130·1	117·5
1930–2	129·7	115·8
1933–5	143·1	126·1
1936–8	155·1	134·9

From A. R. Prest, 'National Income of the United Kingdom 1870–1946', *Economic Journal, 1948.*

TABLE A2   STANDARDISED MORTALITY RATIOS PER MILLION
           POPULATION (ALL AGES)

	tuberculosis	typhoid and paratyphoid fevers	influenza
1901–10	649	23,581	254
1911–20	541	8,926	605
1921–30	362	2,729	345
1931–9	245	1,180	222

From A. H. Halsey, *Trends in British Society since 1900* (London, 1972), p.339.

TABLE A3   DEATH RATES PER MILLION POPULATION AT AGES UNDER 15 YEARS

	scarlet fever	diphtheria	whooping cough	measles
1901–10	271	571	815	915
1911–20	123	437	554	838
1921–30	64	298	405	389
1931–9	46	290	197	217

From A. H. Halsey, *op. cit.,* p. 339.

TABLE A4   AVERAGE EARNINGS IN 1931 AND 1935 (SHILLINGS PER WEEK)

	men and boys		women and girls	
	1931	1935	1931	1935
Full-time earnings	57·3	56·6	28·0	27·2
Textiles	48·0	49·2	26·9	27·5
Food, drink, tobacco	57·5	56·6	28·0	26.6
Local government	52·7	52·7	26·2	28·0

From A. L. Bowley, *Wages and Income in the United Kingdom since 1860* (London, 1937).

TABLE A5   MORTALITY BY SOCIAL CLASS: STANDARDISED MORTALITY RATIOS, 1930–2

	married women	single women	all men
All occupied and retired	100	100	100
Class I (Upper and Middle Classes)	81	60	90
Class II (Intermediate)	89	64	94
Class III (Skilled Labour)	99	95	97
Class IV (Intermediate)	103	102	102
Class V (Unskilled Labour)	113	112	111

From A. H. Halsey, *op. cit.,* pp. 341–2.

TABLE A6 INFANT MORTALITY RATE PER 1,000 LEGITIMATE LIVE
BIRTHS

	1928	1929	1930	1931	1932	1933	*average* 1928–33
Wigan	93	129	107	103	91	110	105·5
St Helens	98	114	80	88	89	116	97·5
Brighton	50	54	51	54	41	47	49·5
Oxford	38	64	41	44	61	32	46·7

From C. E. McNally, *Public Ill-Health* (London, 1935), p. 58.

TABLE A7 INFANT MORTALITY RATE BY SOCIAL CLASS OF FATHER
IN ENGLAND AND WALES: RATE PER 1,000 LEGITIMATE
LIVE BIRTHS, 1930–2

Class I (Upper and Middle Classes)	33
Class II (Intermediate)	45
Class III (Skilled Labour)	58
Class IV (Intermediate)	67
Class V (Unskilled Labour)	77

From A. H. Halsey, *op. cit.*, p. 343.

TABLE A8 STANDARDISED MORTALITY RATES FOR MALES BY SOCIAL
CLASS FROM RESPIRATORY T.B. IN ENGLAND AND WALES,
1930–2

Class I (Upper and Middle Classes)	61
Class II (Intermediate)	67
Class III (Skilled Labour)	100
Class IV (Intermediate)	104
Class V (Unskilled Labour)	125

From A. H. Halsey, *op. cit.*, p. 242.

TABLE A9   TOTAL NUMBERS REGISTERED AS UNEMPLOYED – GREAT
BRITAIN, 1929–39 (AVERAGE IN THOUSANDS)

1929	1,216	1935	2,036
1930	1,917	1936	1,755
1931	2,630	1937	1,484
1932	2,745	1938	1,791
1933	2,521	1939	1,514
1934	2,159		

From B. R. Mitchell and P. Deane, *Abstract of British Historical Statistics*
(Cambridge, 1971,) p. 66.

TABLE A10   PERCENTAGE UNEMPLOYMENT IN STAPLE TRADES
COMPARED TO NATIONAL AVERAGES

	1929	1932	1936	1938
Coal	18·2	41·2	25·0	22·0
Cotton	14·5	31·1	15·1	27·7
Shipbuilding	23·2	59·5	30·6	21·4
Iron and Steel	19·9	48·5	29·5	24·8
Average for all industries	9·9	22·9	12·5	13·3

From D. H. Aldcroft, *The Inter-War Economy: Britain, 1919–1939* (2nd edn,
London, 1973), p. 147.

TABLE A11   UNEMPLOYED AS A PERCENTAGE OF INSURED WORKERS
IN REGIONS OF GREAT BRITAIN

	1929	1932	1937
London and S.E. England	5·6	13·7	6·4
S.W. England	8·1	17·1	7·8
Midlands	9·3	20·1	7·2
Northern England	13·5	27·1	13·8
Wales	19·3	36·5	22·3
Scotland	12·1	27·7	15·9
Northern Ireland	15·1	27·2	23·6

From M. P. Fogarty, *Prospects of the Industrial Areas of Great Britain* (London,
1945), p. 5; *Ulster Year Book* (Belfast 1932, 1935, 1938).

TABLE A12   NUMBER OF UNEMPLOYED PER 1,000 WORKERS, SEPTEMBER 1936

	unemployed	unemployed for a year or more	%
Deptford	67	4	6·0
Leicester	74	8	10·8
Liverpool	257	59	23·0
Blackburn	295	112	38·0
Crook	336	188	55·9
Rhondda	445	281	63·1

From the Pilgrim Trust, *Men Without Work* (Cambridge, 1938), p. 46.

TABLE A13   UNEMPLOYMENT IN SUMMER 1936

	unemployment per 1,000 insured workers	% of unemployed out of work for 12 months or more
South-east	62	6
London	76	7
South-west	89	12
Midlands	101	22
North-west	186	23
North-east	212	26
Wales	322	37

From the Pilgrim Trust, *op. cit.*, p. 46.

TABLE A14   MARRIED PERSONS AS A PROPORTION OF TOTAL POPULATION BY AGE AND SEX IN ENGLAND AND WALES NUMBERS PER THOUSAND

	men		women	
	20–4	all ages	20–4	all ages
1901	173	357	272	340
1911	142	372	242	356
1921	177	414	270	383
1931	138	444	257	313
1951	237	523	480	488

From A. H. Halsey, *op. cit.*, p. 43.

TABLE A15   THE LABOUR VOTE IN GLAMORGAN, 1931

	1929 vote	*1931 vote*
Aberavon	22,194	23,029
Caerphilly	21,248	23,061
Gower	20,664	21,963
Llandaff and Barry	21,468	21,767
Neath	29,445	30,873
Ogmore	22,900	23,064
Pontypridd	20,835	21,751
	158,754	165,508

From *Constitutional Year Book, 1932.*

TABLE A16   THE LABOUR VOTE IN DURHAM

	1929	*1931*	*1931 Labour poll as % of 1929 vote*
Barnard Castle	9,281	10,287	110·8
Bishop Auckland	17,838	16,796	94·2
Blaydon	21,221	18,431	86·9
Chester-le-Street	26,975	24,373	90·4
Consett	22,256	19,927	89·6
Durham	18,514	17,136	92·6
Houghton	25,056	22,700	90·6
Jarrow	22,751	18,071	79·4
Seaham	35,615	23,027	64·7
Sedgefield	15,749	15,404	97·8
Spennymoor	20,858	18,072	86·6
	236,114	204,224	86·5

From *Constitutional Year Book, 1932.*

TABLE A17   LABOUR CANDIDATES ELECTED, 1931–2

	1931 candidates	*1931 elected*	*1932 candidates*	*1932 elected*
Birmingham	24	0	26	13
Birkenhead	14	0	13	9
Bradford	22	0	20	11
Derby	12	2	16	9
Liverpool	31	2	32	15
Manchester	21	7	28	16
Reading	11	1	11	7
Salford	14	1	14	8
Sheffield	24	7	20	15
Southampton	13	2	13	9
Stockport	13	0	11	10
Stoke	23	3	27	17
	222	25	231	139

From *Manchester Guardian*, 2 November, 1931, 2 November, 1932.

TABLE A18   CANDIDATES FOR MUNICIPAL ELECTIONS: 1929–35

year	*Con. % of total*	*Lab. % of total*	*Lib. % of total*	*Ind. & others % of total*	*total candidates in sample*
1929	27·5	44·3	12·4	15·8	2,044
1930	30·3	42·5	11·9	15·3	2,022
1931	28·4	43·3	9·4	18·8	1,636
1932	26·8	45·7	9·5	18·0	1,829
1933	24·0	43·1	9·3	23·6	2,942
1934	23·6	43·2	7·8	25·4	2,168
1935	26·5	45·7	7·9	19·8	1,963

From Gillian Peele and Chris Cook, *The Politics of Reappraisal, 1918–1939*, p. 177.

TABLE A19   SEATS WHERE COMMUNISTS OBTAINED OVER 10 PER CENT
OF VOTES CAST IN 1931

constituency	votes cast	% vote
Rhondda East	10,359	31·9
Fife West	6,829	22·1
Greenock	6,440	18·2
Bethnal Green S.W.	2,970	17·4
Rhondda West	4,296	15·7
Aberdeen North	3,980	11·2
Stepney Whitechapel	2,658	11·2

From F. W. S. Craig, *British Parliamentary Election Results* (Glasgow, 1968).

TABLE A20   MEMBERSHIP OF THE BRITISH COMMUNIST PARTY,
1929–39

1929 (December)	3,200	1934 (December)	5,800
1930 (November)	2,555	1935 (July)	7,700
1931 (June)	2,724	1936 (October)	11,500
(November)	6,279	1937 (May)	12,250
1932 (January)	9,000	1938 (September)	15,570
(November)	5,600	1939 (July)	17,756

From K. Newton, *The Sociology of British Communism* (London, 1969), Appendix
1A, p. 159.

TABLE A21   LABOUR REPRESENTATION IN MAJOR BOROUGHS, 1935

London (62 seats)	Cons. 38; L.Nat. 1; Lab. 22; L. 1
Glasgow (15 seats)	Cons. 6; Lab. 5; I.L.P. 4
Birmingham (12 seats)	Cons. 12
Liverpool (11 seats)	Cons. 8; Lab. 3
Manchester (10 seats)	Cons. 6; Lab. 4
Sheffield (7 seats)	Cons. 3; Lab. 4
Leeds (6 seats)	Cons. 3; Nat. Lab. 1; Lab. 2.
Bristol (5 seats)	Cons. 2; Lab. 2; L. 1
Edinburgh (5 seats)	Cons. 4; Lab. 1
Newcastle upon Tyne (4 seats)	Cons. 3; L.Nat. 1.
Bradford (4 seats)	Cons. 2; Lab. 1; L. 1
Hull (4 seats)	Cons. 2; Lab. 2
Nottingham (4 seats)	Cons. 2; Nat. Lab. 1; Lab. 1
West Ham (4 seats)	Lab. 4
Belfast (4 seats)	Cons. 4
Leicester (3 seats)	Cons. 2; Nat. Lab. 1
Plymouth (3 seats)	Cons. 2; L. Nat. 1
Portsmouth (3 seats)	Cons. 3
Salford (3 seats)	Cons. 3
Stoke-on-Trent (3 seats)	Lab. 3
Wolverhampton (3 seats)	Cons. 2; L. 1
Cardiff (3 seats)	Cons. 2; Nat. Lab. 1

From *The Times Guide to the 1935 Election.*

TABLE A22   SWING IN MAJOR CITIES RETURNING 3 OR MORE
MEMBERS EXCLUDING LONDON, 1931–5

town	no. of seats	size of swing to Labour
Portsmouth	3	1·6
Wolverhampton	3	2·6
Edinburgh	5	5·0
Cardiff	3	5·3
Birmingham	12	5·7
Plymouth	3	5·7
Newcastle upon Tyne	4	5·8
Stoke	3	8·3
Nottingham	4	8·9
Glasgow	15	9·2
Leeds	6	10·0
Bristol	5	10·3
Salford	3	10·3
Manchester	10	10·5
Liverpool	11	11·4
Hull	4	11·6
Sheffield	7	12·6
Bradford	4	13·0
Leicester	3	13·5

From F. W. S. Craig, *op. cit.*

TABLE A23   EXAMPLES OF LOW SWING TO LABOUR   MARCH–AUGUST
1939

date	constituency	swing to Labour
9 March, 1939	Batley and Morley	1·8
20 April, 1939	Ayrshire South	0·4
10 May, 1939	Sheffield Hallam	5·6
17 May, 1939	Birmingham Aston	2·6
24 May, 1939	Kennington	11·2
4 July, 1939	Caerphilly	−8·3 (swing to Con.)
25 July, 1939	Monmouth	3·3
27 July, 1939	Colne Valley	4·8
1 August, 1939	Brecon and Radnor	6·0

From Chris Cook and John Ramsden, *By-Elections in British Politics* (London, 1973) pp. 371–2.

TABLE A24   PERCENTAGE OF UNEMPLOYMENT IN BRITAIN, GERMANY
AND THE UNITED STATES, 1929–35

	Britain	*Germany*	*United States*
1929	11·0	14·6*	12·0
1930	14·6	22·7*	14·5
1931	21·5	23·7	19·1
1932	22·5	20·1	23·8
1933	21·3	25·8	24·3
1934	17·7	14·4	20·9
1935	16·4	18·5*	18·5

* Based on insurance statistics rather than trade union figures.
From the Report by the Royal Institute of International Affairs, *Unemployment: An International Problem* (Oxford, 1935).

U

Notes

Unless otherwise stated, all books referred to are published in London.

Chapter I: *Myth and Reality: Britain in the 1930s*

1. A. J. P. Taylor, *English History, 1914–1945* (Oxford, 1965), p. 317.
2. C. L. Mowat, *Britain Between the Wars 1918–1940* (2nd edn, 1968) p. 413.
3. R. Skidelsky, *Politicians and the Slump* (1967). For Taylor's comment see his review in *Observer*, 21 March, 1971.
4. J. B. Priestley, *English Journey* (1934), p. 401.
5. C. L. Mowat, *op. cit.*, p. 463.
6. See especially S. Pollard, *The Development of the British Economy, 1914–1950* (1962), chs iv and v; H. W. Richardson, *Economic Recovery in Britain, 1932–9* (1967); D. H. Aldcroft, *The Inter-War Economy: Britain, 1919–1939* (1970).

Chapter II: *The Dawn of Affluence*

1. See S. Pollard, *The Development of the British Economy, 1914–1950* (1962), chs iv and v; H. W. Richardson, *Economic Recovery in Britain, 1932–9* (1967), D. H. Aldcroft, *The Inter-War Economy: Britain, 1919–1939* (1970), chs 1, 4, 6.
2. For a recent discussion of the performance of the economy, see S. Glynn and J. Oxborrow, *Interwar Britain: A Social and Economic History* (1976), especially chs 1, 3.
3. P. Mathias, *The First Industrial Nation* (1971), p. 431.
4. D. H. Aldcroft, *op. cit.*, ch. 1.
5. See Statistical Appendix, Table A1.
6. D. H. Aldcroft, *op. cit.*, p. 44.
7. *Ibid.*, p. 22; S. Pollard, *op. cit.*, p. 289.

8   S. Pollard, *op. cit.*, pp. 99–101; D. H. Aldcroft, *op. cit.*, pp. 191–6.

9   S. Pollard, *op. cit.*, pp. 101–3; D. H. Aldcroft, pp. 182–7, 201–2.

10 S. Pollard, *op. cit.*, pp. 103–5; D. H. Aldcroft, *op. cit.*, pp. 199–200.

11 S. Pollard, *op. cit.*, pp. 108–9; D. H. Aldcroft, *op. cit.*, pp. 202–6.

12 C. L. Mowat, *Britain Between the Wars 1918–1940* (2nd edn, 1968), pp. 441–5; D. H. Aldcroft, *op. cit.*, pp. 169–74; S. Pollard, *op. cit.*, pp. 114–17.

13 C. L. Mowat, *op. cit.*, pp. 445–6; D. H. Aldcroft, *op. cit.*, pp. 162–9; S. Pollard, *op. cit.*, pp. 117–19.

14 C. L. Mowat, *op. cit.*, pp. 446–8; D. H. Aldcroft, *op. cit.*, pp. 150–5; S. Pollard, *op. cit.*, pp. 110–14.

15 *Ibid.*, pp. 120–3; D. H. Aldcroft, *op. cit.*, pp. 155–60.

16 S. Pollard, *op. cit.*, pp. 123–4; D. H. Aldcroft, *op. cit.*, pp. 160–2.

17 C. L. Mowat, *op. cit.*, pp. 225–8; N. Branson and M. Heinemann, *Britain in the Nineteen Thirties* (1971), p. 68; S. Pollard, *op. cit.*, pp. 125–31.

18 M. Jones, *Life on the Dole* (1972), p. 56.

19 S. Pollard, *op. cit.*, p. 133; D. H. Aldcroft, *op. cit.*, pp. 93–5.

20 S. Glynn and J. Oxborrow, *op. cit.*, pp. 111–14; S. Pollard, *op. cit.*, pp. 161–74.

21 *Ibid.*, p. 164.

22 D. H. Aldcroft, *op. cit.*, p. 233; G. Rees, *St Michael: A History of Marks and Spencer* (1969), pp. 82, 125.

23 See also S. Pollard, *op. cit.*, pp. 175–80; *JS 100: The Story of Sainsbury's* (1969), especially pp. 40–52.

24 S. Pollard, *op. cit.*, p. 176.

25 *Ibid.*; C. L. Mowat, *op. cit.*, pp. 499–500.

26 See D. H. Aldcroft, *op. cit.*, pp. 230–42; S. Pollard, *op. cit.*, pp. 287–9.

27 See Statistical Appendix, Table A1.

28 See S. Pollard, *op. cit.*, pp. 289–96; D. H. Aldcroft, *op. cit.*, ch. 10.

29 See N. Branson and M. Heinemann, *op. cit.*, pp. 139–47; D. H. Aldcroft, *op. cit.*, pp. 353–62.

30 *Ibid.*, pp. 356–8.

31 *Ibid.*, p. 367.

32 S. Pollard, *op. cit.*, p. 293.

33 D. H. Aldcroft, *op. cit.*, pp. 367–8.

34 *Ibid.*

35 *Ibid.*, p. 241. See also G. D. H. Cole and R. Postgate, *The Common People, 1746–1946* (4th edn, 1971), p. 638.

36 See G. D. H. and M. I. Cole, *The Condition of Britain* (1937), pp. 26–9; S. Pollard, *op. cit.*, pp. 285–6; C. L. Mowat, *op. cit.*, pp. 517–21.

37 N. Branson and M. Heinemann, *op. cit.*, pp. 162–6; S. Glynn and J. Oxborrow, *op. cit.*, pp. 189–202.

38 C. L. Mowat, *op. cit.*, p. 514.

39 A. H. Halsey (ed.), *Trends in British Society since 1900* (1972), p. 338.

40 See Statistical Appendix, Table A2.

41 See Statistical Appendix, Table A3.

42 A. M. Carr-Saunders and D. Caradog Jones, *A Survey of the Social Structure of England and Wales* (Oxford, 1937), p. 214.

43 H. Llewellyn Smith (ed.), *The New Survey of London Life and Labour* (1934), vol. i., pp. 200, 204.

44 J. Boyd Orr, *Food, Health and Income* (1936), Table II, p. 18.

45 *Ibid.*, p. 50.

46 C. L. Mowat, *op. cit.*, pp. 508–9.

47 *Ibid.*, pp. 507–11.

48 E. D. Simon and J. Inman, *The Rebuilding of Manchester* (1935).

49 B. S. Rowntree, *Poverty and Progress* (1941), pp. 232–4.

50 E. D. Simon and J. Inman, *op. cit.*, p. 81.

51 See N. Branson and M. Heinemann, *op. cit.*, pp. 184–7; S. Glynn and J. Oxborrow, *op. cit.*, pp. 234–40.

52 See D. H. Aldcroft, *op. cit.*, pp. 214–22; C. L. Mowat , *op. cit.*, pp. 232–3.

53 *Ibid.*, pp. 231–2, for developments in the 1920s; N. Branson and M. Heinemann, *op. cit.*, pp. 238–43.

54 D. H. Aldcroft, *op. cit.*, p. 239; J. A. R. Pimlott, *The English-man's Holiday* (1947), pp. 215–21.

55 A. Prochaska, *London in the Thirties* (1973), p. 22.

56 J. Hilton, *Rich Man, Poor Man* (1944), p. 120.

57 C. L. Mowat, *op. cit.*, pp. 248–50, 500.

58 See D. Fraser, *The Evolution of the Welfare State* (1973), ch. 8; S. Glynn and J. Oxborrow, *op. cit.*, ch. 9; D. H. Aldcroft, *op. cit.*, pp. 369–74.

59 M. Muggeridge, *The Thirties* (2nd edn, 1971), p. 255.

60 See P. Addison, *The Road to 1945* (1975), pp. 35–44; also A. Marwick, *Britain in the Century of Total War* (2nd edn, 1970), pp. 242–9.

Chapter III: The Hungry Thirties
1 British Medical Association, *Inquiry into Minimum Weekly Expenditure* (1933). See also R. F. George, 'A New Calculation of the Poverty Line', *Journal of the Royal Statistical Society*, 100 (1937).
2 B. S. Rowntree, *Poverty and Progress*, (1941), pp. 103–4.
3 *Ibid.*, pp. 96–102, 156–9.
4 H. Llewellyn Smith (ed.), *The New Survey of London Life and Labour* (1934), vol. iii, pp. 6–8, 124–5.
5 H. Tout, *The Standard of Living in Bristol* (Bristol, 1938), pp. 25–36.
6 B. S. Rowntree, *op. cit.*, pp. 104–5.
7 *Ibid.*, pp. 125–6.
8 H. Llewellyn Smith (ed.), *op. cit.*, vol. iii, p. 88.
9 B. S. Rowntree, *op. cit.*, pp. 116–17.
10 H. Tout, *op. cit.*, pp. 44–6.
11 Survey Committee of Barnett House, *A Survey of the Social Services in the Oxford Area* (Oxford, 1938), p. 97.
12 H. Tout, *op. cit.*, pp. 36–40.
13 B. S. Rowntree, *op. cit.*, pp. 156–7.
14 The *Listener*, 26 October, 1961.
15 H. Llewellyn Smith (ed.), *op. cit.*, vol. iii, pp. 188–9, 194–5, 204–7.
16 B. S. Rowntree, *op. cit.*, pp. 72–3.
17 F. Brockway, *Hungry England* (1932), pp. 205–6.
18 Survey Committee of Barnett House, *op. cit.*; see also B. S. Rowntree, *op. cit.*, p. 80.
19 *Ibid.*, p. 53; see also evidence in G. D. H. and M. I. Cole, *The Condition of Britain* (1937), pp. 248–52.
20 Quoted in N. Branson and M. Heinemann, *Britain in the Nineteen Thirties* (1971), p. 100.
21 *Ibid.*, p. 101.
22 F. Brockway, *op. cit.*, pp. 29–33.
23 See Statistical Appendix, Table A4.
24 B. S. Rowntree, *The Human Needs of Labour* (2nd edn, 1937), pp. 124–7.
25 J. Boyd Orr, *Food, Health and Income* (1936), pp. 55–6.

26 G. C. M. M'Gonigle and J. Kirby, *Poverty and Public Health* (1937), pp. 130 ff.

27 *Ibid.*, p. 53.

28 G. D. H. and M. I. Cole, *op. cit.*, pp. 128–30.

29 See Statistical Appendix, Table A5.

30 See G. D. H. and M. I. Cole, *op. cit.*, pp. 94–5; C. L. Mowat, *Britain Between the Wars, 1918–1940* (2nd edn, 1968), pp. 513–14.

31 Infant mortality is here considered as the number of children under one year dying per thousand live births.

32 See G. D. H. and M. I. Cole, *op. cit.*, pp. 92–4; C. L. Mowat, *op. cit.*, pp. 514–16.

33 *Ibid.*; R. M. Titmuss, *Birth, Poverty and Wealth* (1943), p. 73.

34 See Statistical Appendix, Table A6.

35 Quoted in C. E. McNally, *Public Ill-Health* (1935), pp. 58–61.

36 A. Hutt, *The Condition of the Working Class* (1933), pp. 83–5.

37 R. M. Titmuss, *op. cit.*, pp. 32–3.

38 B. S. Rowntree, *Human Needs*, p. 297.

39 See Statistical Appendix, Table A7.

40 *Registrar General's Statistical Review of England and Wales, 1937*, pp. 152–3; see also G. D. H. and M. I. Cole, *op. cit.*, pp. 92–9.

41 C. L. Mowat, *op. cit.*, p. 516.

42 G. D. H. and M. I. Cole, *op. cit.*, p. 99.

43 A. Hutt, *op. cit.*, pp. 82–3.

44 G. D. H. and M. I. Cole., *op. cit.*, p. 92.

45 R. M. Titmuss, *op. cit.*, p. 43.

46 D. M. Goodfellow, *Tyneside: The Social Facts* (Newcastle, 1942), pp. 52–3.

47 G. C. M. M'Gonigle and J. Kirby, *op. cit.*, pp. 39–40, 53–7.

48 See D. Fraser, *The Evolution of the Welfare State* (1973), pp. 193–6.

49 J. Boyd Orr, *op. cit.*, pp. 4–7.

50 G. C. M. M'Gonigle and J. Kirby, *op. cit.*, pp. 63–6.

51 J. Boyd Orr, *op. cit.*

52 *Registrar General's Statistical Review of England and Wales, 1937*, p. 94.

53 See Statistical Appendix, Table A8.

54 G. D. H. and M. I. Cole, *op. cit.*, pp. 105–6; C. E. McNally, *op. cit.*, pp. 174–5.

55 D. M. Goodfellow, *op. cit.*, p. 27.

56 *Ibid.*, pp. 22–3

57 C. E. McNally, *op. cit.*, pp. 174–5.
58 For a contemporary survey, see G. D. H. and M. I. Cole, *op. cit.*, pp. 81–6.
59 H. Barnes, *The Slum: Its Story and Evolution* (1931), pp. 306–7; see also G. D. H. and M. I. Cole, *op. cit.*, pp. 156–66, and H. Marshall and A. Trevelyan, *Slum* (1933), pp. 118–20.
60 D. Caradog Jones (ed.), *The Social Survey of Merseyside* (Liverpool, 1934), vol. i, pp. 264–6.
61 *Ibid.*
62 H. Marshall and A. Trevelyan, *op. cit.*, pp. 38–41.
63 E. D. Simon, *How to Abolish the Slums* (1929), pp. 1–2.
64 A. Hutt, *op. cit.*, pp. 10–11, 35–6.
65 E. D. Simon and J. Inman, *The Rebuilding of Manchester* (1935), pp. 60–1.
66 *Ibid.*
67 F. Brockway, *op. cit.*, pp. 73, 84–5.
68 H. Quigley and I. Goldie, *Housing and Slum Clearance in London* (1934), pp. 142–3.
69 *Ibid.*
70 G. D. H. and M. I. Cole, *op. cit.*, p. 173.
71 *Ibid.*, pp. 180–6; See also B. S. Rowntree, *op. cit.*, pp. 232–4, and E. D. Simon, *op. cit.*, pp. 99–101.
72 G. D. H. and M. I. Cole, *op. cit.*, pp. 79–80, 437.
73 H. Llewellyn Smith (ed.), *op. cit.*, vol. iii, pp. 204–7.
74 B. S. Rowntree, *op. cit.*, p. 99.
75 J. Boyd Orr, *op. cit.*, p. 50.
76 A. Briggs, *Social Thought and Social Action: A Study of the Work of Seebohm Rowntree* (1961), p. 292.

Chapter IV: The Problem of Unemployment

1 See Statistical Appendix, Table A9.
2 See S. Pollard, *The Development of the British Economy, 1914–1950* (1962), pp. 110–25; D. H. Aldcroft, *The Inter-War Economy: Britain, 1919–1939* (1970), ch. 5; C. L. Mowat, *Britain Between the Wars 1918–1940* (2nd edn, 1968), ch. 5.
3 D. H. Aldcroft, *op. cit.*, pp. 162–3.
4 C. L. Mowat, *op. cit.*, pp. 273–4.
5 Pilgrim Trust, *Men Without Work* (Cambridge, 1938), p.6.
6 C. L. Mowat, *op. cit.*, pp. 275–83.
7 See Statistical Appendix, Table A10.

8   See Statistical Appendix, Table A11.

9   See W. H. Beveridge, 'An Analysis of Unemployment, II', *Economica* 4 (1937).

10 *Second Industrial Survey of South Wales* (Cardiff, 1937), pp. 27, 38, 41–2, 60–5, 70–1.

11 *Ministry of Labour, Report for the Year 1934* (Cmd. 4861: 1935), pp. 17, 18, 44.

12 See Statistical Appendix, Table A13.

13 Pilgrim Trust, *op. cit.*, pp. 9–10.

14 *Ibid.*, p. 15.

15 See Statistical Appendix, Table A12.

16 Pilgrim Trust, *op. cit.*, pp. 6–46.

17 J. Jewkes and A. Winterbottom, *Juvenile Unemployment* (1933), p. 31.

18 J. Gollan, *Youth in British Industry* (1937), p. 157.

19 Save the Children Fund, *Unemployment and the Child* (1933), p. 74; see also A. J. Lush, *The Young Adult* (Cardiff, 1941), p. 26, and *Social Survey of Merseyside*, vol. iii, p. 208.

20 The Carnegie Trust, *Disinherited Youth* (Edinburgh, 1943), p. 14.

21 F. Brockway, *Hungry England* (1932), pp. 142–6.

22 Findings quoted by J. Gollan, *op. cit.*, pp. 25–6.

23 G. D. H. and M. I. Cole, *The Condition of Britain* (1937), pp. 223–8.

24 *Ibid.*

25 See R. Skidelsky, *Politicians and the Slump* (2nd edn, 1970); A. J. P. Taylor, *English History 1914–1945* (Oxford, 1965), chs 8 and 9; R. Bassett, *1931: Political Crisis* (1958); C. L. Mowat, *op. cit.*, ch. 7.

26 R. Skidelsky, *op. cit.*, pp. 422–34.

27 See R. McKibbin, 'The Economic Policy of the Second Labour Government, 1929–1931', *Past and Present*, 68 (1975).

28 *Ibid.*

29 *Ibid.*; see also D. H. Aldcroft, *op. cit.*, pp. 314–22.

30 A. Marwick, 'Middle Opinion in the Thirties: Planning, Progress and Political Agreement', *English Historical Review*, 79 (1964).

31 D. H. Aldcroft, *op. cit.*, pp. 312–14; R. Skidelsky, *op. cit.*, pp. 302–5; B. B. Gilbert, *British Social Policy 1914–1939* (1973), pp. 193–4.

32 Public Record Office, CAB 27/490: Report of Unemployment Committee, 1932, and Cabinet Minutes, pp. 1–12.

33 Ministry of Labour, Reports of Investigations into the Industrial Conditions in Certain Depressed Areas (Cmd. 4728: 1934).

34 W. Hannington, *The Problem of the Distressed Areas* (1937), pp. 25–8.

35 *Ibid.*, p. 28.

36 *Report of Commissioner for Special Areas of England and Wales*, 1936.

37 D. H. Aldcroft *op. cit.*, p. 103; S. Pollard, *op. cit.*, pp. 132–3.

38 W. H. Beveridge, *Full Employment in a Free Society* (1944) pp. 63–5.

39 W. Hannington, *op. cit.*, pp. 116–17.

40 CAB 27/490: Report of Unemployment Committee, 1932, p. 4.

41 W. Hannington, *op. cit.*, pp. 115–67; see also the comments recorded in J. Gollan *op. cit.*, pp. 170–2.

42 For unemployment benefit in the thirties, see B. B. Gilbert, *op. cit.*, pp. 162–94; D. Fraser, *The Evolution of the British Welfare State* (2nd edn, 1975), pp. 172–83; M. Bruce, *The Coming of the Welfare State* (4th edn, 1974), pp. 262–74.

43 See R. McKibbin, *op. cit.*; B. B. Gilbert, *op. cit.*, pp. 162–75.

44 N. Branson and M. Heinemann, *Britain in the Nineteen Thirties* (1971), pp. 20–9; M. Bruce, *op. cit.*, pp. 267–70; B. B. Gilbert, *op. cit.*, pp. 176–8.

45 G. D. H. and M. I. Cole, *op. cit.*, pp. 213–16.

46 M. Bruce, *op. cit.*, p. 268.

47 Quoted by W. Hannington, *op. cit.*, p. 48.

48 See N. Branson and M. Heinemann, *op. cit.*, pp. 27–8; *Birkenhead News*, January 1932.

49 M. Bruce, *op. cit.*, pp. 270–4; B. B. Gilbert, *op. cit.*, pp. 175–92.

50 CAB 27/490 Cabinet Minutes, p. 9.

51 For the Social Service Movement, see Pilgrim Trust, *op. cit.*, part 5, and The National Council of Social Service, *Unemployment and Community Service* (1936).

52 A. Hutt, *The Condition of the Working Class in Britain* (1933), pp. 44–5; for other hostile criticism, see W. Hannington, *op. cit.*, ch. 10.

Chapter V: The Impact of Unemployment

1 W. H. Beveridge, *Unemployment: A Problem of Industry* (1909).

2 *The Third Winter of Unemployment* (1922).

3 R. C. Davison, *The Unemployed* (1929).

4 Even the surveys carried out in 1932 under the auspices of the Board of Trade were primarily industrial in their concern.

5 E. W. Bakke, *The Unemployed Man* (1933).

6 Pilgrim Trust, *Men Without Work* (Cambridge, 1938), pp. 1–5.

7 Carnegie Trust, *Disinherited Youth* (Edinburgh, 1943).

8 See especially A. J. Lush, *The Young Adult* (Cardiff, 1941), and the relevant sections of the *Social Survey of Merseyside* (Liverpool, 1934).

9 Most famous, perhaps, was W. Greenwood, *Love on the Dole* (1933); but see also E. Wilkinson, *The Town that was Murdered* (1939); H. Jennings, *Brynmawr* (1934); J. Hilton, *Rich Man, Poor Man* (1944).

10 For A. Hutt's political career, see H. Pelling, *The British Communist Party* (1958), pp. 89–90, 139, 187n.

11 Published respectively in 1937, 1945 and 1937.

12 Preface to G. A. W. Tomlinson, *Coal Miner* (1937), pp. 10–11.

13 Pilgrim Trust, *op. cit.*, pp. 164–71; A. J. Lush, *op. cit.*, p. 28; Carnegie Trust, *op. cit.*, pp. 44–5.

14 *Ibid.*, p. 52.

15 M. Cohen, *I Was One of the Unemployed* (1945), pp. 11–12.

16 B. S. Rowntree, *Poverty and Progress* (1941), pp. 114–17.

17 H. Tout, *The Standard of Living in Bristol* (Bristol, 1938), pp. 44–6.

18 Pilgrim Trust, *op. cit.*, p. 109.

19 *Ibid.*, p. 110.

20 *Ibid.*, pp. 110–11,

21 *Ibid.*, pp. 111–12.

22 According to the Pilgrim Trust, 'The households of the "Means Test" cases ... were relatively speaking well situated', *ibid.*, p. 110.

23 F. Brockway, *Hungry England* (1932), pp. 75–7, 205–6.

24 Quoted in G. C. M. M'Gonigle and J. Kirby, *Poverty and Public Health* (1937), pp. 190–1.

25 C. E. McNally, *Public Ill-Health* (1935), p. 160.

26 N. Branson and M. Heinemann, *Britain in the Nineteen Thirties* (1971), p. 204.

27 See G. D. H. and M. I. Cole, *The Condition of Britain* (1937), p. 95.

28 *Ibid.*, p. 99.

29 *Ibid.*, pp. 99–100.

30 *Ibid.*, pp. 94–9.

31 Pilgrim Trust, *op. cit.*, p. 140. See also the Report by the Royal Institute of International Affairs, *Unemployment: An International Problem* (Oxford, 1935), p. 19, which recorded that 'the quite reasonable idea that unemployment, by reducing the standard of living, must increase the mortality rate does not in reality, fit in with the facts'. They claimed that improved health services and falling food prices had prevented a rise in mortality in the major European towns affected by unemployment.

32 Pilgrim Trust, *op. cit.*, p. 140.

33 See G. D. H. Cole and M. I. Cole, *op. cit.*, pp. 105–6, and D. M. Goodfellow, *Tyneside: The Social Facts* (Newcastle, 1942), p. 20.

34 D. M. Goodfellow, *op. cit.*, pp. 22–3.

35 Pilgrim Trust, *op. cit.*, pp. 136–8.

36 H. L. Beales and R. S. Lambert, *Memoirs of the Unemployed* (1934), Appendix B, pp. 271–5.

37 M. Cohen, *op. cit.*, p. 159.

38 There is a considerable literature about the place of suicide as an index of social dislocation. For some of the issues see J. D. Douglas, *The Social Meanings of Suicide* (Princeton, 1967).

39 Pilgrim Trust, *op. cit.*, pp. 136–8; H. L. Beales and R. S. Lambert, *op. cit.*, p. 275.

40 See F. Brockway, *op. cit.*, p. 171.

41 See *Birkenhead News*, 23 Jan., 10 Feb., 13 Feb., 13 April, 23 Oct. and 29 Oct., 1932.

42 F. Brockway, *op. cit.*, pp. 171–9.

43 Quoted from *Hansard*, 27 Nov., 1934, in J. Gollan, *Youth in British Industry* (1937), p. 190.

44 Pilgrim Trust, *op. cit.*, pp. 45–6, 105.

45 A. M. Cameron, *Civilisation and the Unemployed* (1943), pp. 22–3.

46 See Carnegie Trust, *op. cit.*, pp. 58–60.

47 Pilgrim Trust, *op. cit.*, pp. 138–41.

48 H. Jennings, *op. cit.*, p. 139.

49   See P. Eisenberg and P. F. Lazarsfield, 'The Psychological Effects of Unemployment', *Psychological Bulletin* (1938), pp. 358–90.

50   G. D. H. and M. I. Cole, *op. cit.*, pp. 187–90.

51   J. B. Priestley, *English Journey* (1934), pp. 341–2.

52   A. M. Cameron, *op. cit.*, pp. 24–32.

53   Pilgrim Trust, *op. cit.*, p. 145.

54   *Ibid.*, pp. 178–9.

55   J. Jewkes and A. Winterbottom, *Juvenile Unemployment* (1933), pp. 14–16.

56   Carnegie Trust, *op, cit.*, pp. 66–8.

57   Pilgrim Trust, *op. cit.*, pp. 175–6.

58   G. Meara, *Juvenile Unemployment in South Wales* (Cardiff, 1936), pp. 11–12.

59   See H. Mannheim, *op. cit.*, pp. 126–52.

60   Public Record Office, H.O.45/19066: Juvenile Delinquency. Summary of investigation by A. M. Carr-Saunders, p. 1. See the file of newspaper clippings in H. O. 45/17928. Juvenile offences as a whole rose from 11,137 in 1930 to 28,875 in 1938.

61   *Birkenhead News*, 17 Feb., 1932.

62   H. Mannheim, *op. cit.*, pp. 132–52.

63   *Ibid.*, pp. 132–4; see also J. H. Bagot, *Juvenile Delinquency* (1941), p. 55.

64   H.O. 45/19066: Juvenile Delinquency, *op. cit.*, pp. 3–4; H.O. 45/19065: conclusions, p. 5.

65   Pilgrim Trust, *op. cit.*, pp. 143–200.

66   *Ibid.*, pp. 144–9.

67   *Ibid.*, pp. 158–63.

68   *Ibid.*

69   *Ibid.*, p. 81.

70   See W. G. Runciman, *Relative Deprivation and Social Justice* (1966), pp. 60–4.

71   Pilgrim Trust, *op. cit.*, p. 75.

72   J. B. Priestley, *op. cit.*, p. 281.

73   G. Orwell, *The Road to Wigan Pier* (2nd edn, 1969), p. 80.

74   See Carnegie Trust, *op. cit.*, pp. 6–8.

75   G. Orwell, *op. cit.*, p. 86.

76   J. B. Priestley, *op. cit.*, p. 314.

77   E. W. Bakke, *op. cit.*, pp. 178, 183, 263.

78   G. Orwell, *op. cit.*, p. 78.

79   See marriage rates in A. H. Halsey (ed.), *Trends in British Society since 1900* (1972), pp. 43–5.

80 E. W. Bakke, *op. cit.*, p. 263.
81 Carnegie Trust, *op. cit.*, p. 54.
82 B. S. Rowntree, *op. cit.*, pp. 368–71, 470; W. Meakin (ed.), *The Social and Economic Aspects of the Drink Problem* (1931), p. 156.
83 H. Mannheim, *op. cit.*, pp. 167–9.
84 See B. S. Rowntree, *op. cit.*, pp. 368–71; E. W. Bakke, *op. cit.*, p. 263.
85 B. S. Rowntree, *op. cit.*, p. 399.
86 E. W. Bakke, *op. cit.*, p. 263.
87 Pilgrim Trust, *op. cit.*, pp. 124–7.
88 G. Orwell, *op. cit.*, p. 78.

Chapter VI: Labour and the Working Class: The General Election of 1931

1 C. L. Mowat, *Britain Between The Wars* (1955), p. 356.
2 See Chris Cook, 'Liberals, Labour and Local Elections' in Gillian Peele and Chris Cook (eds), *The Politics of Reappraisal 1918–1939* (1975), p. 169.
3 *The Times Guide to the 1931 Election* (1931).
4 See C. L. Mowat, *op. cit.*, pp. 410–11.
5 See Michael Kinnear, *The British Voter* (1968), p. 52.
6 See F. W. S. Craig, *British Parliamentary Election Statistics* (Glasgow, 1968), p. 49.
7 Figures quoted in Tom Stannage, 'The British General Election of 1935', unpublished Ph.D. thesis, Cambridge University, 1972. This is by far the best study of this election and is a model of an election analysis.
8 See Chris Cook, *A Short History of the Liberal Party* (1976), p. 116.
9 The lost deposits in the 1931 election were: New Party 22 (out of 24); Labour 16, Liberals 30, I.L.P. 8, Conservatives 1, Others 16.
10 The figures were: Conservatives 19, 918 (45·6 per cent), Labour 13,264 (30·3 per cent), New Party 10,534 (24 per cent).
11 See Statistical Appendix, Table A15,
12 See Statistical Appendix, Table A16.
13 Statistics derived from Michael Kinnear, *op. cit.*, p. 50.
14 *Ibid.*
15 See R. Bassett, *1931: Political Crisis* (1958).

16 See Judith Green, 'Some Aspects of politics in the North East during the Depression', unpublished dissertation essay, St Hugh's College, Oxford University, 1971.
17 *Ibid.*

Chapter VII: Politics and the People, 1931–5
1 See Minutes, Labour Party N.E.C.
2 *Ibid.*
3 See Chris Cook and John Ramsden, *By-Elections in British Politics* (1973), pp. 366–9.
4 Minutes, N.E.C.
5 The Wakefield result was: Labour 13,586; Conservative 13,242.
6 See Statistical Appendix, Table A17.
7 For Labour's earlier strength in the 1920s in Birmingham, see Chris Cook, *The Age of Alignment* (1975), pp. 54–5.
8 For Wolverhampton politics during this period, see G. W. Jones, *Borough Politics, A History of Wolverhampton Borough Council* (1969), *passim.*
9 See Statistical Appendix, Table A18.
10 See Gillian Peele and Chris Cook (eds), *The Politics of Reappraisal 1918–1939* (1975), p. 170.
11 See *Birmingham Post*, 2 Nov., 1934; *Manchester Guardian*, 2 Nov., 1934.
12 See Chris Cook and John Ramsden, *op. cit.*, p. 115.
13 *Oxford Times*, 8 Nov., 1933.

Chapter VIII: The Communist Party
1 H. Pelling, *The British Communist Party* (1958), p. 67.
2 The total communist vote in 1924 was 55,346; in 1929, 50, 634.
3 See Statistical Appendix, Table A19.
4 Michael Kinnear, *The British Voter* (1968), p. 62.
5 *Daily Worker*, 5 Nov., 1931.
6 See, for example, J. T. Murphy's denunciation: Murphy to Politburo, 8 May, 1932, quoted in H. Pelling, *op. cit.*, p. 68.
7 *Ibid.*, p. 67.
8 *Ilford Recorder*, 6 April, 1933.
9 *Tottenham Herald*, 7 April, 1933.
10 In Shipley, the communist candidate in the West Ward achieved

a mere 2·8 per cent of the vote; see *Yorkshire Observer*, 3 April, 1933.

11 *Birmingham Post*, 2 Nov., 1933.

12 In the five wards fought by Communist candidates in West Ham, the total votes cast were: Labour 8,001; Communist 2,526; Municipal Reform 1,101; I.L.P. 135.

13 The best communist result was in Portobello ward. In a straight fight a Communist polled 1,057 votes against the 4,664 polled by the Moderate.

14 See *Daily Herald*, 2 Nov., 1934.

15 See, for example, H. Pelling, *op. cit.*, p. 85, for the communist revival in the South Wales coalfield.

16 *Report of the 36th Annual Conference of the Labour Party*, p. 210.

17 In Blyth and Tynemouth, C.P. members first stood as N.U.W.M. candidates, only later changing to an explicitly communist ticket.

18 H. Pelling, *op. cit.,* pp. 87–8.

19 K. Newton, *The Sociology of British Communism* (1969), pp. 172–4.

20 See Statistical Appendix, Table A20.

21 K. Newton, *op. cit.*, p. 34.

22 *Ibid.*

23 See H. Pelling, *op. cit.*, pp. 56–72; see R. Martin, *Communism and the British Trade Unions, 1924–33* (Oxford, 1969).

24 H. Pelling, *op. cit.*, pp. 69–72.

25 *Ibid.*, pp. 73–108; K. Newton, *op. cit.*, pp. 68–70.

26 See *ibid.*, pp. 176–7.

27 H. Francis, 'Welsh Miners and the Spanish Civil War', *Journal of Contemporary History*, vol. 5, no. 3 (1970), p. 182.

28 *Ibid.*; see also D. Smith, 'The struggle against Company Unionism in the South Wales Coalfield, 1926–39', *Welsh History Review*, vol. 6, no. 4 (1973). For Hutt's comment, see A. Hutt, *The Condition of the Working Class in Britain* (1933), pp. 44–5.

29 Pilgrim Trust, *Men Without Work* (Cambridge, 1938), pp. 68–9.

30 South Wales Miners' Library, Swansea: Final Report on the South Wales Coalfield History Project, July 1974, pp. 139–40.

31 *Ibid.*, pp. 134–5; H. Francis, *op. cit.*, p. 179.

32 See D. Smith, *op. cit.*, pp. 362–70, and H. Francis, *op. cit.*, pp. 179–80.

33 *Ibid.*, p. 189; for voting allegiances see Final Report of South Wales Coalfield History Project, *op. cit.*, pp. 139–40.
34 K. Newton, *op. cit.*, p. 137.
35 See H. Pelling, *op. cit.*, pp. 84, 105.

Chapter IX: The National Unemployed Workers' Movement
 1 For the early years of the N.U.W.M. see W. Hannington, *Never on Our Knees* (1967), pp. 78–102. On the Shop Stewards' Movement, see B. Pribicevic, *The Shop Stewards' Movement and Social Control, 1910–1922* (Oxford, 1959). For the early Communist Party, see H. Pelling, *The British Communist Party* (1958), ch. 1, and L. J. MacFarlane, *The British Communist Party* (1966).
 2 W. Hannington, *op. cit.*, p. 118.
 3 *Ibid.* For an excellent study of the N.U.W.M. and one of its strongest areas see R. H. C. Hayburn, 'The Responses to Unemployment in the 1930s with particular reference to South-East Lancashire', unpublished Ph.D. thesis, Hull University, 1970.
 4 For 'The Unemployed Workers' Charter', see W. Hannington, *op. cit.*, pp. 178–9.
 5 H. Pelling, *op. cit.*, pp. 63–4.
 6 *Ibid.*
 7 See R. Hayburn, 'The Police and the Hunger Marchers', *International Review of Social History* (1973), and J. Stevenson, 'The Politics of Violence' in Gillian Peele and Chris Cook (eds), *The Politics of Reappraisal 1918–1939* (1975).
 8 For press and Labour Party reactions to the hunger marchers of 1927, see W. Hannington, *op. cit.*, pp. 205–6, 226–8.
 9 H. Pelling, *op. cit.*, p. 64.
10 Marx Memorial Library: Agenda and resolutions of the Seventh National Conference of the National Unemployed Workers' Movement, p. 5.
11 Marx Memorial Library: Report on meeting of National Administrative Council, 3–4 Dec., 1932.
12 Marx Memorial Library: Agenda and resolutions of … Seventh National Congress, pp. 4–5.
13 *Ibid.*, Draft resolution six.
14 Marx Memorial Library: Report on Meeting of National Administrative Council, 11–12 July, 1931.

x

15 See H. Pelling, *op. cit.*, p. 65.
16 Marx Memorial Library: Report of Meeting of National Administrative Council, 11–12 July, 1931.
17 *Ibid.*
18 See the N.U.W.M. monthly bulletins for Feb., April–May, June, Aug.–Sept. and Oct.–Nov., 1931.
19 *Ibid.*
20 N.U.W.M. monthly bulletin, Jan. 1932; Report of N.A.C. meeting, 7–8 May, 1932.
21 Report of the N.A.C. meetings, 17–18 Sept., 1932.
22 Report of the N.A.C. meeting, 3–4 Oct., 1931.
23 *Ibid.*
24 *E.C.C.I., Twelfth Plenum Report* (Moscow, 1932), p. 59.
25 W. Hannington, *Unemployed Struggles, 1919–1936* (1936), pp. 230–43.
26 *Ibid.*; H. Pelling, *op, cit.*, p. 65.
27 Marx Memorial Library: Report of N.A.C. meeting, 11–12 July, 1931; Report of N.A.C. meeting, 17–18 Sept., 1932.
28 W. Hannington, *Never on Our Knees*, p. 251.
29 See Chapter X, pp. 169–70.
30 *Ibid.*
31 Marx Memorial Library: Report of N.A.C. meeting, 27–28 May, 1933.
32 H. Pelling, *op. cit.*, pp. 73–6.
33 M. Foot, *Aneurin Bevan* (1962) vol. i, p. 159.
34 See N.U.W.M. monthly bulletin for Feb.–March 1933.
35 See Chapter X, pp. 179–81.
36 *Ibid.*, pp. 181–2.
37 Public Record Office, Mepol 2/3053: Précis of Special Branch information, 8 Nov., 1936, item 22A.
38 See M. Foot, *op. cit.*, chs 8 and 9; H. Pelling, *A Short History of the Labour Party* (2nd edn, 1965), pp. 83–5.
39 W. Hannington, *Never on Our Knees*, pp. 324–8.
40 See, for example, the comments of J. Symons, *The Thirties: A Dream Resolved* (2nd edn, 1960), pp. 146–7.
41 See R. H. C. Hayburn, 'The Responses to Unemployment … ' pp. 534–6.
42 Marx Memorial Library: Draft resolution of the Eleventh National Conference of the National Unemployed Workers' Movement, 28 Jan., 1939.
43 W. Hannington, *Never on Our Knees*, p. 329.

44 Many unions were very slow to organise unemployed sections, even those used to unemployment in the twenties. See, for example, the case of the South Wales Miners' Federation, in D. Smith, 'The Struggle against Company Unionism in the South Wales Coalfield, 1926–39', *Welsh History Review*, vol. 6, no. 4 (1973), pp. 362–8.

45 See J. B. Jeffreys, *The Story of the Engineers, 1800–1945* (New York, reprint edn, 1970), pp. 239–40.

46 J. Lovell and B. C. Roberts, *A Short History of the T.U.C.* (1968), p. 129.

47 W. Hannington, *Unemployed Struggles*, p. 323.

48 E.C.C.I., *Twelfth Plenum Report*, p. 58.

49 *Ibid.*

50 Held at the Marx Memorial Library.

51 J. Symons, *op. cit.*, p. 146.

52 See Chapter X. The scales at Birkenhead were raised after the disturbances of 1932; see *Birkenhead News*, 21 Sept., 1932.

53 See H. McShane, *Three Days that Shook Edinburgh* (Glasgow, 1938).

54 See Chapter IV.

55 W. Hannington, *Unemployed Struggles*, p. 323.

56 Pilgrim Trust, *Men Without Work* (Cambridge, 1938), pp. 55–6.

57 S. Orwell and G. Angus (eds), *The Collected Essays, Journalism, and Letters of George Orwell* (1971), pp. 206–7.

58 H. Pelling, *British Communist Party*, p. 85.

59 E.C.C.I., *Thirteenth Plenum Report* (Moscow, 1933), p. 14.

60 *Ibid.*, pp. 14–15, 63.

61 For Communist Party membership, see Statistical Appendix, Table A20.

62 *Hansard*, fifth series, cclxix (1932), pp. 274–5.

63 W. Paynter, *My Generation* (1972), pp. 34, 84–5.

64 Details from the *Birkenhead News*, 29 Oct., 1932.

65 J. Dash, *Good Morning Brothers!* (1969), pp. 24–6, 38.

66 See 'Russian Banks and Communist Funds', Parliamentary Papers, 1928, xii, 275–332; for press allegations, see W. Hannington, *Never on Our Knees*, p. 273.

67 For the financial arrangements of the Communist Party, see H. Pelling, *British Communist Party*, pp. 43–4.

68 Arrested in 1922, 1925, 1926, 1929, 1931, 1932; sentenced 1922, 1925, 1931, 1932; fined 1929.

69 *Birkenhead News*, 29 Oct., 1932.

70   *Manchester Evening News*, 1 and 2 Oct., 1931.
71   See *Birkenhead News*, 17 Sept., 29 Oct., 1932.
72   See J. Stevenson, 'The Politics of Violence'.

Chapter X: Hunger Marches and Demonstrations
 1   W. Hannington, *Never on Our Knees* (1967), p. 246.
 2   *Ibid*; see M. Turnbull, 'The Attitude of Government and Administration towards the "Hunger Marches" of the 1920s and 1930s', *Journal of Social Policy*, vol. 2 (1973).
 3   W. Hannington, *Unemployed Struggles, 1919–1936* (1936), pp. 204–5.
 4   *Ibid*., pp. 234–7; W. Paynter, *My Generation* (1972), pp. 85–7.
 5   *Manchester Evening News*, 1 Oct., 1931.
 6   *Manchester Evening News*, 2, 7, 8 Oct., 1931.
 7   W. Hannington, *Unemployed Struggles*, pp. 230–43.
 8   See J. J. Campbell, 'Between the Wars', in J. C. Beckett and R. E. Glasscock (eds), *Belfast: The Origin and Growth of an Industrial City* (1967), p. 151.
 9   W. Hannington, *Unemployed Struggles*, p. 255.
10   *Ibid*., pp. 255–7; J. J. Campbell, *op. cit.*
11   *Hansard*, fifth series, cclxix (1932), p. 4.
12   See *Birkenhead News*, 2, 9 Jan., 24 Feb., 2, 9 April, 20 Aug., 1932.
13   *Birkenhead News*, 17 Sept., 1932.
14   *Ibid.*
15   *Ibid*., 21 Sept., 1932.
16   W. Hannington, *Unemployed Struggles*, p. 254.
17   *Hansard*, fifth series, cclxix (1932), pp. 274–5.
18   *Unemployed Special*, Sept. 1932; W. Hannington, *Unemployed Struggles*, pp. 230–42.
19   Public Record Office, Mepol 2/3064: information from Norwich Constabulary, item 25N.
20   *Hansard*, fifth series, cclxix (1932), pp. 277.
21   *Ibid*., 279–80.
22   Home Office Papers, series 158, vol. 28, p. 167.
23   W. Hannington, *Unemployed Struggles*, pp. 243–68.
24   Mepol 2/3064: information concerning hunger marchers, 21–6 Oct., 1932, items 20D, 22J, 25R.
25   Mepol 2/3064: Information concerning demonstrations on 18, 27 and 30 Oct., item 20A.

26 *Ibid*: Mepol 2/3064: information concerning hunger marchers, 21–6 Oct., 1932, items 20D, 22J, 25RI.

27 *Ibid*., item 20A.

28 Mepol 2/3065: report on police preparations, items 6N, 6P.

29 W. Hannington, *Unemployed Struggles*, pp. 245–7.

30 Mepol 2/3064: report on hunger marchers, 31 Oct., 1932, items 27B, 21F.

31 W. Hannington, *Unemployed Struggles*, pp. 245–7; Mepol 2/3065: report on Hyde Park demonstrations, item 3C; *The Times*, 28 Oct., 1932.

32 W. Hannington, *Unemployed Struggles*, pp. 250–1; *The Times*, 31 Oct., 1932.

33 W. Hannington, *Never on Our Knees*, p. 267.

34 Mepol 2/3064; report on hunger marchers, item 26A.

35 *Daily Telegraph*, 1 Nov., 1932.

36 *The Times*, 28 Oct., 1932.

37 *Manchester Guardian*, 1 Nov., 1932.

38 W. Hannington, *Never on Our Knees*, pp. 269–70.

39 *Ibid*., pp. 270–2; Mepol 2/3066: report on events of 1 Nov., 1932, items 6A and 6B.

40 *Ibid*.

41 W. Hannington, *Never on Our Knees*, pp. 273–7.

42 Mepol 2/3065: item 7B; Mepol 2/3066: item 5R.

43 Mepol 2/3067: items 2A, 5B, 5C, 5D, 7A, 7B.

44 Mepol 2/3050: Report on Trades Union Congress General Council Demonstration in Hyde Park, Lacock to Commissioner, 21 Dec., 1932; Lacock to Commissioner, 19 Jan., 1933.

45 *Ibid*., Lacock to Commissioner, 19 Jan., 1933.

46 Mepol 2/3050.

47 Mepol 2/3050: items 43L, 43M.

48 Mepol 2/3050: Citrine to Commissioner, 6 Feb., 1933.

49 H.O. 158/29, p. 29: M.O.H. to General Inspectors, 22 Jan., 1934.

50 W. Hannington, *Never on Our Knees*, p. 293.

51 Claude Stamfield MSS: diary of 1934 hunger march, Swansea University Library.

52 W. Hannington, *Never on Our Knees*, p. 293.

53 *Ibid*., pp. 294–303.

54 For the formation of the National Council for Civil Liberties, see P. Cockburn, *The Years of The Week* (1968), pp. 113–14.

55 See Claude Stamfield MSS, *op. cit.*; H. Francis, 'Welsh Miners

and the Spanish Civil War', *Journal of Contemporary History*, vol. 5, no. 3 (1970), p. 180.

56 See B. B. Gilbert, *British Social Policy, 1914–1939* (2nd edn, 1973), pp. 182–92.

57 M. Foot, *Aneurin Bevan* (1962), vol. i, pp. 201–2.

58 W. Hannington, *Never on Our Knees*, p. 309.

59 H. Francis, *op. cit.*, p. 178; H. Branson and M. Heinemann, *Britain in the Nineteen Thirties* (1971), pp. 24–6.

60 B. B. Gilbert, *op. cit.*, p. 185.

61 W. Hannington, *Never on Our Knees*, pp. 309–11.

62 *Ibid.*, pp. 214–15.

63 Mepol 2/3097: Special Branch report on the Jarrow march, 6 Nov., 1936, item 28A.

64 Report of the 36th Annual Conference of the Labour Party, p. 230.

65 *The Times*, 15 Oct., 1936.

66 J. Symons, *The Thirties: A Dream Resolved* (2nd edn, 1960), pp. 58–61; E. Wilkinson, *The Town that was Murdered* (1939).

67 Mepol 2/3097: Special Branch report on the Jarrow march, 6 Nov., 1936, item 28A.

68 *Ibid.*

69 *Ibid.*

70 *Ibid.*

71 Mepol 2/3053: Special Branch précis of information, 8 Nov., 1936, item 22A.

72 Eddie Jones MSS, Swansea University Library, diary of 1936 hunger march.

73 Mepol 2/3053: Special Branch information on hunger marchers, 9 Nov., 1936, item 16A. The attendance figure is much lower than usually cited by people using Hannington's estimates.

74 M. Foot, *op. cit.*, pp. 238–9.

75 Mepol 2/3053: Report on demonstration on 8 Nov., 1936, item 22A.

76 See J. Stevenson, 'The Politics of Violence', in Gillian Peele and Chris Cook (eds), *The Politics of Reappraisal 1918–1939*, (1975), pp. 162–4.

77 Mepol 2/3065: return of damage occasioned during hunger march demonstrations Oct.–Nov. 1932, item 6S.

78 See J. J. Campbell, *op. cit.*; A. Hazlet, *The 'B' Specials* (1932), pp. 130–1.

79 D. Caradog Jones, *Social Survey of Merseyside* (Liverpool,

1934), vol. i, p. 57; W. R. S. McIntyre, *Birkenhead Yesterday and Today* (Birkenhead, 1948); *Birkenhead News*, 13 July, 1932.

80 *Birkenhead News*, 9 Jan., 1932.
81 See H. Francis, *op. cit.*

Chapter XI: The Fascist Challenge

1 N. Branson and M. Heinemann, *Britain in the Nineteen Thirties* (1971), p. 281.
2 R. Benewick, 'The Threshold of Violence', in R. Benewick and T. Smith (eds), *Direct Action and Democratic Politics* (1972), p. 51.
3 R. Skidelsky, *Oswald Mosley* (1975), pp. 332–3.
4 R. Benewick, *The Fascist Movement in Britain* (2nd edn, 1972), pp. 27–36.
5 *Ibid.*, pp. 36–8.
6 See O. Mosley, *Revolution by Reason* (Birmingham, 1925), and O. Mosley and J. Strachey, *Revolution by Reason* (1925); R. Skidelsky, *op. cit.*, pp. 129–55.
7 For the fullest discussion of Mosley's economic ideas and his relation to the second Labour Government, see R. Skidelsky, *op. cit.*, pp. 178–220; see also W. F. Mandle, 'Sir Oswald Mosley's Resignation from the Labour Government', *Historical Studies (Australia and New Zealand)* (1961).
8 See J. Strachey, 'The Mosley Manifesto: Why we have issued it', *Spectator*, 13 Dec., 1930.
9 R. Skidelsky, *op. cit.*, pp. 247–63; W. F. Mandle, 'The New Party', *Historical Studies (Australia and New Zealand)* (1966).
10 R. Benewick, *The Fascist Movement*, pp. 75–83; W. F. Mandle, 'The New Party'.
11 R. Skidelsky, *op. cit.*, pp. 288–9.
12 O. Mosley, *The Greater Britain* (1932), pp. 15–16, 149–60.
13 *Ibid.*
14 *Hansard*, fifth series, cclxxxviii (1934), pp. 14–15, quoted in R. Benewick, *The Fascist Movement*, p. 93.
15 The debate took place at the Friends' Meeting House, Euston Road, on 24 February, 1933, under the chairmanship of Lloyd George. Mosley's exact words were the subject of a libel action against the Daily News Ltd in 1938. This is the version from Mosley's secretary's short-hand notes produced at the trial: see R. Benewick, *The Fascist Movement*, p. 141.

16 R. Skidelsky, *op. cit.*, p. 358.
17 R. Benewick, *The Fascist Movement*, pp. 98–9.
18 R. Skidelsky, *op. cit.*, pp. 377–8; *The Times*, 2 June, 1934.
19 See Mepol 2/3069: Report on disturbances between B.U.F. and Jews, 7 March, 1933.
20 *Manchester Guardian*, 15 April, 1935, quoted R. Benewick, *The Fascist Movement*, p. 156; see also R. Skidelsky, *op. cit.*, pp. 379–92.
21 C. Cross, *The Fascists in Britain* (1961), p. 137; R. Skidelsky, *op. cit.*, pp. 323–4.
22 See Mepol 2/3069: Report on prosecutions of B.U.F. members for causing a breach of the peace, 16 May, 1933, item 5A.
23 Mepol 2/3043: Home Secretary to Commissioner of Metropolitan Police, 22 July, 1936, item 1A. For the legal issues, see D. Williams, *Keeping the Peace* (1967), pp. 153–69.
24 R. Skidelsky, *op. cit.*, p. 359.
25 *Ibid.*, pp. 393–410; R. Benewick, *The Fascist Movement*, pp. 217–32.
26 Mepol 2/3043: Report on events of October 1936, item 21B.
27 *Ibid.*
28 *Ibid.*
29 Mepol 2/3043: Report on fascist and anti-fascist activities, items 26A, 376.
30 R. Benewick, *The Fascist Movement*, p. 281.
31 *Ibid.*, pp. 281–2.
32 *Ibid.*, pp. 282–5.
33 Mepol 2/3043: Reports on activities of the B.U.F., 2 April and 9 Aug., 1938; 3 Jan., 1939.
34 R. Benewick, *The Fascist Movement*, p. 272.
35 See R. Skidelsky, *op. cit.*, pp. 447–53.
36 R. Benewick, *The Fascist Movement*, p. 110.
37 *Ibid.*; R. Skidelsky, *op. cit.*, p. 331.
38 R. Benewick, *The Fascist Movement*, p. 111.
39 See W. F. Mandle, *Antisemitism and the British Union of Fascists* (1968). For the local leaders, see R. Skidelsky, *op. cit.*, pp. 396–7.
40 For H. Pelling's comment that 'if any totalitarian creed stood a chance of adoption by the Lancashire workers, it was likely to be fascism', see H. Pelling, *The British Communist Party* (1958), p. 85.
41 See R. Skidelsky, *op. cit.*, pp. 325–6.

42 *Ibid.*, p. 326.
43 Probably in part the result of the strength of military and ex-military supporters; see R. Benewick, *op. cit.*, pp. 122–3.
44 W. F. Mandle, 'The Leadership of the British Union of Fascists', *The Australian Journal of Politics and History* (1966), pp. 360–83; see also C. Cross, *op. cit.*, pp. 179–80.
45 R. Benewick, *The Fascist Movement*, p. 124.
46 C. Cross, 'Britain's Racialists' *New Society*, 3 June, 1965; C. Cross, *The Fascists in Britain*, pp. 149–50.
47 Labour Party Records, Return of questionnaire on fascist activities.
48 *Ibid.* A National Socialist Busmen's Group was formed in July 1937, competing with the communist-led Busmen's Rank and File Movement for support among dissident members of the T.G.W.U.
49 *Ibid.*
50 R. Skidelsky, *op. cit.*, pp. 327–8.
51 *Ibid.*, pp. 328–9.
52 R. Benewick, *The Fascist Movement*, p. 129.
53 D. Schoenbaum, *Hitler's Social Revolution* (1967), ch. 1; see also W. S. Allen, *The Nazi Seizure of Power* (1965).
54 For the campaign in South Wales, see R. Skidelsky, *op. cit.*, p. 326.
55 K. Newton, *The Sociology of British Communism* (1959), pp. 34–39.

Chapter XII: The Government and Public Order

1 See M. Turnbull, 'The Attitude of Government and Administration towards the "Hunger Marches" of the 1920s and 1930s', *Journal of Social Policy*, vol. 2 (1973), pp. 131–6.
2 Public Record Office, Pensions and National Insurance records, series 7, vol. 67.
3 H.O. 158/28, p. 167a: Home Secretary to Chief Constables, 29 Sept., 1932; PIN 7/126 pt. III.
4 H.O. 158/28, p. 470: Memorandum of Home Secretary to General Inspectors of Health, 9 Dec., 1933; H.O. 158/29, p. 27: Circulars to Chief Constables and General Inspectors, 22 Jan., 1934.
5 *Ibid.* The Home Secretary's statement was made in the House on 21 Dec., 1933.

6 See CAB 23/73, p. 26: Cabinet Minutes, 23 Nov., 1932, and CAB 27/497: Proceedings of Cabinet Committees, 28 Nov., 7, 21 Dec., 1932.

7 *Ibid.*

8 See *Hansard*, fifth series, cclxix (1932), pp. 274–5.

9 See J. Stevenson, 'The Politics of Violence', in Gillian Peele and Chris Cook (eds), *The Politics of Reappraisal 1918–1939* (1975), pp. 154–5.

10 Mepol 2/3064: item 27A.

11 *The Times*, 6 Feb., 1933.

12 *Ibid.*, 2 Nov., 1936.

13 *Civil Liberty*, no. 2 (1937).

14 J. Stevenson, *op. cit.*, pp. 153, 163.

15 See N. Branson and M. Heinemann, *Britain in the Nineteen Thirties* (1971), pp. 286–7.

16 W. Hannington, *Never on Our Knees* (1967), pp. 294–5.

17 *Ibid.*

18 Quoted M. Turnbull, *op. cit.*, p. 141.

19 Mepol 2/3112: Summary of material regarding 'Jew Baiting' in East London, 7 Jun., 1937.

20 W. Hannington, *op. cit.*, pp. 269–70; see R. Hayburn, 'The Police and the Hunger Marchers', *International Review of Social History* (1973).

21 Mepol 2/3067: items 2A, 5B, 5C, 5D, 7A, 7B. For the agent in the Scottish contingent, see Mepol 2/3071: Information on the National Hunger March, 1934, quoted in R. Hayburn, *op. cit.*, pp. 638–9.

22 Mepol 2/3064: Lists of prominent hunger marchers supplied by Glamorgan and Norwich constabularies, items 25K, 25N. Names and addresses have been withheld.

23 Mepol 2/3064: report of Chief Constable of Oxford, 24 Oct., 1932, item 25K.

24 W. Hannington, *op. cit.*, pp. 269–70, 278–9; Mepol 2/3067: Report on police raid, 2 Nov., 1932, item 5K.

25 See M. Turnbull, *op. cit.*, pp. 139–40; R. Hayburn, *op. cit.*, p. 635, n.2.

26 *Ibid.*

27 D. Smith, 'The Struggle against Company Unionism in the South Wales Coalfield, 1926–39', *Welsh History Review*, vol. 6 (1973), p. 370.

28 W. Hannington, *op. cit.*, p. 236.

29   W. Paynter, *My Generation* (1972), p. 86.

30   W. Hannington, *op. cit.,* p. 239.

31   *Ibid.,* pp. 252–3, 263–6.

32   A. Hutt, *The Condition of the Working Class in Britain* (1933), pp. 243–4.

33   *Bristol Evening Post,* 10 June, 1932, quoted in A. Hutt, *op. cit.,* p. 244.

34   *Birkenhead News,* 17 Sept., 1932.

35   A. Hazlet, *The 'B' Specials* (1972), pp. 130–1.

36   Mepol 2/3065: report on demonstration in Hyde Park, item 3C.

37   Mepol 2/3066: reports on disturbances on 1 Nov., 1932, items 6A and 6B.

38   *Hansard,* fifth series, cclxix (1932), pp. 264–74.

39   *Ibid.,* pp. 274–80.

40   Mepol 2/3066: reports on disturbances on 1 Nov., 1932, items 6A and 6B.

41   Mepol 2/3064: report of disturbances on 26 Oct., 1932, item 26f.

42   *Hansard,* fifth series cclxix (1932), pp. 278–9.

43   Marx Memorial Library, Report on the Seventh National Conference of the N.U.W.M., 21–23 Feb., 1931, draft resolution number three; Report of National Administrative Council Meeting 3–4 Oct., 1931.

44   See D. Williams, *Keeping the Peace* (1967), pp. 187–91.

45   Mepol 3069: reports on disturbances between B.U.F. and Jews, 7 March, 11, 16 May, 11 Oct., 1933, items 9A, 9B, 5A, 28A.

46   Mepol 2/4319: Reports on Olympia Meeting, 7 June, 1934, item 40c.

47   The debate took place on 14 June, see *Hansard,* fifth series, cclxxx (1934), p. 2004. A number of speakers did defend the B.U.F.; see R. Skidelsky, *Oswald Mosley* (1975), pp. 371–2; see also R. Benewick, *The Fascist Movement in Britain* (2nd edn, 1972), pp. 171–2.

48   Mepol 2/4319: Reports on Olympia Meeting, 7 June, 1934, item 40C; 8 June, 1934, item 39c.

49   CAB 24/249: Cabinet Paper 144, 23 May, 1934; CAB 24/250.

50   C.P. 189, 11 July and 13 July, 1934. See also R. Benewick, 'The Threshold of violence', in R. Benewick and T. Smith (eds), *Direct Action and Democratic Politics* (1972), pp. 55–6.

51   Mepol 2/3073: Correspondence re White City Demonstration, 5 Aug., 1934.

52 Mepol 2/3077: Arrangement concerning Albert Hall Meeting, 28 Oct., 1934.

53 Mepol 2/3083: 7 Oct., 1936.

54 Mepol 2/3043: Home Secretary's memorandum on 'Jew-baiting', 22 July, 1936, item 1A.

55 Mepol 3089: Report on Fascist meeting at Albert Hall and complaint about police action at Thurloe Street, March 1936. See also R. Benewick, *The Fascist Movement*, pp. 203–9.

56 See, for example, Mepol 3043, items 5C and 4A, where the police argued that it would be a 'good thing' if they were seen to be doing something to curb B.U.F. activities, 3 Aug., 1936.

57 See R. Skidelsky, *op. cit.*, pp. 415–17; R. Benewick, 'The Threshold of Violence', pp. 58–9.

58 D. Williams, *op. cit.*, pp. 56–61, 132–8, 155–62; R. Benewick, *The Fascist Movement*, pp. 235–44.

59 D. Williams, *op. cit.*, p. 57; R. Skidelsky, *op. cit.*, pp. 417–21.

60 Mepol 2/3110: Report on political marches in East London, 24 April, 1937.

61 Mepol 2/3112: Summary of incidents of 'Jew-baiting' in East London, 7 June, 1937; Mepol 2/3043: Report of meetings attended by Special Branch, 3 Jan., 1939, item 133A.

62 Mepol 2/3110: Report on political marches in East London, 24 April, 1937.

63 R. Benewick, *The Fascist Movement*, pp. 248–51; Mepol 2/3043: Report of B.U.F. march in South East London, item 75A.

64 See Mepol 2/3043: Reports on B.U.F. activities, 3 Jan., 1939, item 133A.

65 See G. Orwell, 'England Your England', in *Inside the Whale and other Essays* (1962), pp. 81–2.

66 R. Skidelsky, *op. cit.*, p. 420.

67 See, for example, Mepol 2/3069: Report on disturbances between B.U.F. and Jews, 11 Oct., 1933.

68 R. Benewick, *The Fascist Movement*, pp. 247–8.

Chapter XIII: Left at the Polls: The General Election of 1935 and after

1 Labour Party N.E.C. Minutes, 28 Nov., 1934.

2 *Ibid.*, April 1935.

3 Figures from F. W. S. Craig, *British Parliamentary Election Statistics* (Glasgow, 1938).

4 Labour's average expenditure per candidate in 1935 was £365, compared to £777 for each Conservative.

5 See Chris Cook, *A Short History of the Liberal Party* (1976), p. 121.

6 *Ibid.*, p. 122.

7 *The Times Guide to the 1935 Election* (1935).

8 C. L. Mowat, *Britain Between the Wars 1918–1940* (2nd edn, 1968).

9 MacDonald was defending his Seaham constituency against Shinwell.

10 *The Times Guide to the 1935 Election.*

11 See Gillian Peele and Chris Cook (eds), *The Politics of Reappraisal 1918–1939* (1975), p. 170.

12 See Statistical Appendix, Table A21.

13 Much the most detailed analysis of swing in 1935 can be found in Tom Stannage, 'The British General Election of 1935', unpublished Ph.D. thesis, Cambridge University, 1972.

14 See, for example, the Lichfield and Tamworth constituency.

15 These National Labour losses were heaviest in the coalmining and industrial seats won in 1931. The losses included Finsbury, Ilkeston, Seaham, Bassetlaw, the Forest of Dean and Tottenham South.

16 These three gains were Cumberland North, Barnstaple and Berwick-on-Tweed.

17 The Liberal losses here included most of their remaining industrial strongholds: Dewsbury, Middlesbrough East, South Shields, Bishop Auckland, Colne Valley, Wrexham, Whitechapel and Carmarthen.

18 Chris Cook, *A Short History of the Liberal Party*, p. 122.

19 For example, many of the middle-class seats in which Liberals were to do so well in the post-war period.

20 Trevor Wilson, *The Downfall of the Liberal Party* (1966), p. 200.

21 Among seats lost were the last industrial strongholds in London and the north-east, including Barnsley, Consett, Durham, Burslem, Dunfermline and Shoreditch.

22 Statistics derived from Stannage, *op. cit.*

23 The result in East Rhondda was: Labour 22,088 (61·8 per cent), Communist 13,655 (38·2 per cent).

24 See Statistical Appendix, Table A22.

25 Mitcham had a 26,824 Conservative majority in 1931; Wallasey had a massive 32,449 majority.

26 For examples of swings to Labour in Non-conformist areas, see the Louth and Horncastle Divisions of Lincolnshire.
27 The Conservative share of the vote was *up* 4·9 per cent in Camborne, 9 per cent in East Dorset and 3 per cent in Mid-Bedfordshire.
28 The turn-out statistics are fully discussed in Stannage, *op. cit.*
29 The solitary Conservative was C. R. M. F. Cruttwell in Oxford University.
30 In Wolverhampton, the local Labour Party had split. Brown, the former M.P., had fought the 1931 election as Independent Labour. In 1935 he again fought as Independent Labour. See G. W. Jones, *Borough Politics, A History of Wolverhampton Borough Council* (1969), p. 60.
31 For Stonehaven's comments, see Stannage, *op. cit.*
32 See *Liberal Magazine*, October 1935.
33 See Stannage, *op. cit.*
34 Stannage cites the example of Rushcliffe.
35 See Statistical Appendix, Table A23.

Chapter XIV: The Revolution That Never Was
1 H. Macmillan, *Winds of Change* (1966), p. 288.
2 *Report of the 31st Annual Conference of the Labour Party*, p. 205.
3 See J. Strachey, *The Coming Struggle for Power* (1932).
4 Introduction by H. Pollitt to A. Hutt, *The Condition of the Working Class in Britain* (1933), p. xv.
5 A. Marwick, *Britain in the Age of Total War* (1970), p. 226.
6 G. Rees, *The Great Slump* (1970), p. 85.
7 See Statistical Appendix, Table A24.
8 G. Rees, *op. cit.*, p. 40.
9 *Unemployment: An International Problem* (1935), p. 71; G. Rees, *op. cit.*, p. 115.
10 G. D. H. Cole, *Economic Prospects: 1938 and After* (1938), p. 14.
11 S. Pollard, *The Development of the British Economy, 1914–1950* (1962), p. 293.
12 G. D. H. Cole and R. Postgate, *The Common People, 1746-1946* (6th edn, 1971), pp. 638–9.
13 W. Hannington, *Unemployed Struggles, 1919–36* (1936), p. 323.
14 Carnegie Trust, *Disinherited Youth* (Edinburgh, 1943), pp. 78–9.
15 G. Orwell, *The Road to Wigan Pier* (2nd edn, 1969), p. 77.
16 A. Hutt, *op. cit.*, pp. 44–5.

17 E. W. Bakke, *The Unemployed Man* (1933), pp. 60–1.

18 *Ibid.*, pp. 228–36.

19 Pilgrim Trust, *Men Without Work* (Cambridge, 1938), pp. 74–6.

20 W. G. Runciman, *Relative Deprivation and Social Justice* (1966), pp. 61–2.

21 A. Hutt, *op. cit.*, p. 69.

22 G. Orwell, *op. cit.*, p. 80.

23 *Ibid.*, pp. 76–8.

24 Pilgrim Trust, *op. cit.*, pp. 55–6.

25 *The Third Winter of Unemployment* (1922), pp. 74–5.

26 E. W. Bakke, *op. cit.*, p. 251.

27 *Ibid.*; A. J. P. Taylor has also emphasised this point, see A. J. P. Taylor, *English History, 1914–1945* (Oxford, 1965), p. 149.

28 See H. Pelling, *A Short History of the Labour Party* (2nd edn, 1965), pp. 75–84.

29 See F. Brockway's interview with a woman P.A.C. member at Great Harwood in Lancashire, in *Hungry England* (1932).

30 Survey Committee of Barnett House, *A Survey of the Social Services in the Oxford Area* (Oxford, 1938), p. 97.

31 G. D. H. Cole and R. Postgate, *op. cit.*, pp. 627–8.

32 R. McKenzie and A. Silver, *Angels in Marble* (1968), p. 90.

33 G. Orwell, 'England Your England', in *Inside the Whale and Other Essays* (1968), p. 76.

34 M. Muggeridge, *The Thirties* (2nd end, 1971), p. 268.

35 *A Town on the Dole* (Abertillery, 1936), p. 1.

36 P. Massey, 'Portrait of a Mining Town', in *Fact* (November 1937), pp. 41–2.

37 Quoted in Judith Green, 'Some Aspects of Politics in the North East during the Depression', unpublished dissertation essay, Oxford University, 1971. In the smaller industrial villages, such as Seaton Delaval, the contrast was even more stark; in 1931, the six councillors, out of a total of thirteen, who opposed the Labour majority were colliery officials, including the mine manager and cashier.

38 *Ibid.*

39 G. D. H. and M. I. Cole, *The Condition of Britain* (1937), pp. 416–17.

40 See B. R. Mitchell and P. Deane, *Abstract of British Historical Statistics* (Cambridge, 1971), p. 68.

41 *Ibid.*, p. 71.

42 See H. Pelling, *op. cit.*, ch. 5.
43 See G. D. H. and M. I. Cole, *op. cit.*, pp. 411–18.
44 *Ibid.*, p. 421; see also P. Addison, *The Road to 1945* (1975), pp. 49–52.
45 *Ibid.*, pp. 35–51.
46 *Ibid.*, p. 183.

Bibliographical Note

No writer on the years between the wars can fail to acknowledge a great debt to C. L. Mowat's *Britain Between the Wars, 1918–1940* (London, 2nd edn, 1968) which still provides the best standard history of the period. A. J. P. Taylor's stimulating *English History, 1914–1945* (Oxford, 1965) and A. Marwick, *Britain in the Century of Total War* (London, 1968), also contain many valuable insights. N. Branson and M. Heinemann, *Britain in the Nineteen Thirties* (London, 1971), is sometimes useful, but is too committed to the mythology of the 1930s for general reliability. G. Rees, *The Great Slump* (London 1970), provides a readable account of the world-wide effects of the Great Crash with some suggestive comments on the British experience. M. Muggeridge, *The Thirties* (London, 2nd edn, 1971), and J. Symons, *The Thirties* (London, 1960), are both interesting accounts of the decade from contemporaries.

On economic affairs there are a number of excellent works: S. Pollard, *The Development of the British Economy, 1914-1950* (London, 1962), and D. H. Aldcroft, *The Inter-War Economy: Britain, 1919–1939* (London, 1970), are both indispensable. More specialist studies can be followed up in the comprehensive bibliography in Aldcroft. A critical study of the more extravagant claims of Britain's economic performance in these years is B. W. E. Alford, *Depression and Recovery? British Economic Growth, 1918–1939* (London, 1972). S. Glynn and J. Oxborrow, *Interwar Britain: A Social and Economic History* (London, 1976), is also useful.

There is a large literature on social developments. Many of the works on specific issues have already been mentioned in the text. G. D. H. and M. I. Cole, *The Condition of Britain* (London, 1937), and A. M. Carr-Saunders and D. Caradog Jones, *A Survey of the Social Structure of England and Wales* (Oxford, 2nd edn, 1937), provide essential starting points. Of the works dealing with living

Y

standards, B. S. Rowntree, *Poverty and Progress* (London, 1941), and H. Tout, *The Standard of Living in Bristol* (Bristol, 1938), are particularly valuable. H. Llewellyn Smith (ed.), *The New Survey of London Life and Labour* (London, 1934), is a mine of information on social conditions in the capital. On health, J. Boyd Orr, *Food, Health and Income* (London, 1936), and B. S. Rowntree, *The Human Needs of Labour* (London, 2nd edn, 1937) are important contributions. Among the most influential writers on malnutrition were G. C. M. M'Gonigle and J. Kirby, *Poverty and Public Health* (London, 1937), and C. E. McNally, *Public Ill-Health* (London, 1935).

For studies of unemployment see the Pilgrim Trust, *Men Without Work* (Cambridge, 1938), and the Carnegie Trust, *Disinherited Youth* (Edinburgh, 1943). These remain the definitive works, dealing respectively with the long-term unemployed and unemployed youth. E. W. Bakke, *The Unemployed Man* (London, 1933), paved the way for many later inquiries with its study of unemployment in Greenwich. H. L. Beales and R. S. Lambert, *Memoirs of the Unemployed* (London, 1934), provides some important first-hand accounts of the experience of unemployment. The great classic of the semi-documentary literature on unemployment is G. Orwell, *The Road to Wigan Pier* (London, 1937). Equally well known is E. Wilkinson, *The Town that was Murdered* (London, 1939). Of the other literature W. Hannington, *The Problem of the Distressed Areas* (London, 1937), and A. Hutt, *The Condition of the Working Class in Britain* (London, 1933), are both valuable, though written from a politically committed point of view. W. Greenwood's novel, *Love on the Dole* (London, 1933), remains one of the most perceptive accounts of the human consequences of unemployment. Of recent unpublished works on the effects of unemployment, two important contributions are R. H. C. Hayburn, 'The Responses to Unemployment in the 1930s with particular reference to South-East Lancashire', Ph. D. thesis, Hull University (1970) and B. J. Elliott, 'The Social and Economic Effects of Unemployment on the Coal and Metal Industries of the Sheffield Region, 1918–35', M. A., Sheffield University (1969).

For social policies and welfare provisions in this period, see the appropriate chapters in M. Bruce, *The Coming of the Welfare State* (London 4th edn, 1968), and D. Fraser, *The Evolution of the British Welfare State* (London, 1973). B. B. Gilbert, *British Social Policy 1914–1939* (London, 1970), has a good discussion of the evolution of welfare provisions in the inter-war period and their political implications.

For general social conditions in the 1930s, J. B. Priestley, *English Journey* (London, 1934), and Fenner Brockway, *Hungry England* (London, 1932), are both useful. For statistics on social conditions, A. H. Halsey (ed.), *Trends in British Society since 1900* (London, 1972), is indispensable, while J. Stevenson (ed.), *Social Conditions in Britain between the Wars* (London, 1977), has extracts from many of the social inquiries of the period.

On political affairs there are a very large number of published works. Inevitably, however, there has been a tendency for historians to concentrate on such themes as foreign affairs and appeasement rather than on party politics at home. As a consequence, despite a host of biographies and autobiographies, there are serious gaps in the history of the 1930s. There is, for example, no detailed study of the National Government; nor is there a definitive history of the Conservative Party. There is no published full-length study of the 1931 election.

These gaps have to some extent been covered by more specialist studies. For the 1929–31 period, see R. Skidelsky, *Politicians and the Slump* (London, 1967), and R. Bassett, *1931: Political Crisis* (London, 1958). There is some analysis of the 1931 election in M. Kinnear, *The British Voter: An Atlas and Survey* (London, 1968). *The Times Guide to the 1931 Election* is indispensable, as is F. W. S. Craig, *British Parliamentary Election Results* (London, 1968). For electoral developments at local level in the 1930s, see C. Cook, 'Liberals, Labour and Local Elections', in G. Peele and C. Cook (eds), *The Politics of Reappraisal 1918–1939* (London, 1975). For by-elections, see C. Cook and J. Ramsden, *By-Elections in British Politics* (London, 1973). The background for the Labour Party can be found in H. Pelling, *A Short History of the Labour Party* (London, 1965). The companion volume for the Liberals is C. Cook, *A Short History of the Liberal Party* (London, 1976). An excellent but as yet unpublished study of the 1935 election is Tom Stannage, 'The British General Election of 1935', Ph.D. thesis, Cambridge University, 1972. The perspective of political developments in the decade is well captured in P. Addison, *The Road to 1945* (London, 1975).

For the extremist movements of the thirties, see H. Pelling, *The British Communist Party* (London, 1958), and R. Martin, *Communism and the British Trade Unions 1924–33* (Oxford, 1969). K. Newton, *The Sociology of British Communism* (London, 1969), is an interesting attempt to establish the basis of communist support in modern Britain and contains much valuable information. There is no full-length study of the National Unemployed Workers' Movement and the major printed sources remain W. Hannington, *Unemployed Struggles, 1919–1936* (London, 1936), and *Never on Our Knees* (London, 1967).

The British Union of Fascists has been examined by R. Benewick, *The Fascist Movement in Britain* (London 2nd edn, 1972), and C. Cross, *The Fascists in Britain* (London 1961). Both are valuable as general accounts of the fascist movement in Britain. R. Skidelsky, *Oswald Mosley* (London, 1975), is the best available study of the central personality of British fascism, marred by being too sympathetic towards its subject. Mosley's own works, especially *The Greater Britain* (London, 1932) and *My Life* (London, 1968), are essential for an understanding of the direction of Mosley's thought.

On the specific question of the political reactions to unemployment, see the general works on unemployment cited above. W. G. Runciman, *Relative Deprivation and Social Justice* (London, 1966), has some valuable material on the response to economic adversity during the depression. For the question of political violence see J. Stevenson, 'The Politics of Violence', in G. Peele and C. Cook (eds), *The Politics of Reappraisal, 1918–1939* (London, 1975).

Index

Warrington, low Labour swing
in 1935, 255

Watford, high Labour swing in
1935, 256

Wednesbury, Labour by-election
victory (1932), 116

Weeple, V. G., 209

Wegg-Pearson, C., 209

Wells, H. G., 223

Welwyn Garden City, 22

Wembley Stadium, Festival of
Youth, 26

West Cumberland, unemployment, 56, 64

West Ham: communist vote
(1933 local elections), 133;
disturbances (1932), 173;
I.L.P. in, 124, 125; and means
test, 70; Upton by-election
Labour victory (1934), 118

West Hartlepool, unemployment
and 1931 Labour vote, 109
(Table 6.4)

West Midlands: Labour weakness
in, 120; low Labour swing in
1935, 255, 257; municipal
elections (1935), 249

West Renfrewshire, and 1931
Election, 106

Western Isles, and 1935 Election,
257

Westhoughton, low Labour
swing in 1935, 255

Westminster (Abbey division)
by-election (1939), 262

Weston-super-Mare: by-election
(1934), 118, 122; Liberal
by-election disaster (1934), 122

Whately, Miss H. M., 209

Whitechapel: by-election (1930),
95, 129; communist vote in
(1931), 131

white-collar employment, 16

Widnes, low Labour swing in
1935, 255

widows, and poverty, 37

Wigan, 89, 93, 161, 271;
communist vote (1933 local
elections), 133; death rate,

40; municipal elections (1934),
121

Wilkinson, Ellen, 155, 185, 186,
187, 188, 275

Willesden West, high Labour
swing in 1935, 256

Wimbledon: high Labour swing
in 1935, 256; 1931 Election,
112 (Table 6.5)

Windsor, hunger marchers at,
181

'Winter Relief' campaign, 155–6,
157, 159

Wirral, Labour swing in 1935,
256

Wolverhampton: Labour
weakness in, 120; low Labour
swing in 1935, 255;
N.U.W.M. in, 150

Wolverhampton East, and 1935
Election, 253

Wolverhampton West, and 1935
Election, 258

Women's League of Health and
Beauty, 26

Wood, Sir Kingsley, 224

Wood Green, 1931 swing to
Conservatives, 111

Woodburn, Arthur, 119

woollen industry, 13

Woolwich East by-election
(1931), 96

Woolworth's, 15

working classes: communism
and, 130, 132–6 and Table 8.4,
137, 142, 161–2; Conservative
swing in 1935, 257–8, 259;
diet, 40; and fascism, 212,
213–14; and Labour, 94, 104,
107–11, 117; living conditions,
18–19, 21–3, 33–4, 268;
poverty, 33–4, 37–8, 40

Workington, steelworks, 12

Wythenshawe Garden Suburb,
22

York: child poverty, 36; elderly
poverty, 36; housing, 22;
infant mortality, 42; Labour